Ultimate Guide to CGRC Certification

---

*Prepare for CGRC with
domain insights and test strategies*

Arun Kumar Chaudhary

bpb

www.bpbonline.com

First Edition 2025

Copyright © BPB Publications, India

ISBN: 978-93-65894-851

To View Complete
BPB Publications Catalogue
Scan the QR Code:

www.bpbonline.com

Dedicated to

My mom, wife, and daughter

About the Author

Arun Kumar Chaudhary is a highly accomplished and seasoned professional with over 14 years of experience in information security, risk management, and compliance. He holds a master's degree in communication engineering (EEE) from Nanyang Technological University (NTU) and a diploma in cyber law from the Asian School of Cyber Laws. He has extensive expertise in cybersecurity, cloud security, application security, data security, data privacy, risk, and governance. He has actively contributed to ISACA by writing exam questions and remains an engaged member of ISS2 and ISACA. Arun is a prominent speaker at leading cybersecurity conferences and has a proven track record in developing security policies, procedures, and providing internal staff training.

Arun is passionate about improving cybersecurity practices and educating others through his writing and consulting work. He is committed to helping organizations navigate the ever-evolving landscape of information security and privacy. His strong academic background, coupled with his passion for teaching, allows him to effectively engage with students and facilitate their understanding.

He has the following certifications: CISSP, CCSP, CRISC, CISA, CISM, CDPSE, CEH, COBIT 2019, CPFA, LA ISO 27001, LA ISO 42001, CGDPR, ITIL.

About the Reviewers

❖ **Deepu Thomas** is an information security professional with 20 years of experience, spanning roles as a practitioner, consultant, and trainer. He has worked with organizations across industries, helping them enhance their security posture and achieve compliance with industry standards.

As an experienced instructor, Deepu delivers certification training for globally recognized bodies such as ISC2 and ISACA, with a focus on information security management. He is passionate about empowering learners, ensuring they gain both knowledge and practical insights to excel in their careers.

Deepu currently serves as a corporate trainer at Koenig Solutions Pvt. Ltd.

❖ **Sandeep Sehgal** is a seasoned professional with over 18 years of experience in cybersecurity training, governance, risk, and compliance. He has led numerous awareness programs and policy initiatives to strengthen organizational security postures. His expertise extends to cloud security, where he has worked extensively on implementing secure architectures and mitigating risks across platforms. Recently, Sandeep has been at the forefront of AI compliance and process automation, helping businesses align with emerging regulatory standards. He is a certified cybersecurity professional and holds a master's degree in computer science. Sandeep combines technical expertise with strategic vision to drive secure digital transformation and foster a culture of security and innovation.

❖ **Saurabh Garg** is a passionate cybersecurity practitioner with extensive experience across security domains, including **Governance, Risk, and Compliance (GRC)**, cloud security, data protection, and infrastructure security. As a seasoned security architect, he specialises in designing robust security controls and solutions for multinational enterprises.

Holding industry-leading certifications such as CGRC, CISSP, CCSP, CIPP/E, CISM, CISA and ISO 27001, Saurabh brings deep expertise in helping organisations assess and enhance their IT security posture. In addition to his architecture skills, he has worked as a security presales and transformation consultant with leading **global system integrators** (**GSIs**), enabling businesses to strengthen their cybersecurity strategies effectively.

Acknowledgement

First and foremost, I would like to express my sincere thanks to all those who contributed to the completion of this book. I would like to extend my heartfelt gratitude to my family and friends for their continuous support and encouragement throughout this journey. Their dedication, expertise, and commitment were instrumental and have been a constant source of motivation.

I would also like to extend my appreciation to my mentors and colleagues who provided insight and feedback in polishing the content and enhancing the quality of this book. I would like to express special thanks to my lovely wife **Priya** and my little daughter **Alaya**, who are an integral part of my life and have inspired me to complete this book.

Furthermore, I am extremely grateful to BPB Publications for their guidance and expertise in achieving the completion of this book. Their support and assistance were invaluable in navigating the complexities and overcoming the challenges of the publishing process.

I would also like to acknowledge the support of technical reviewers and editors who provided constructive feedback and contributed to the refinement of this manuscript. Their insights and suggestions have significantly improved the quality of the book. Last but not least, I want to express my thanks to the readers who have shown interest in my book. Your support and encouragement have been deeply appreciated.

Thank you to everyone who participated in making this book a reality.

Preface

In today's fast-paced and ever-changing business environment, the landscape of regulatory compliance is continuously evolving. This is mostly influenced by advancements in technology, global economic changes, and the increasing complexity of business operations. As a result, the need for effective governance, risk management, and compliance practices has become more significant. This book discusses the major areas of GRC, seeking to navigate today's business challenges with clarity and confidence.

This book aims to provide a comprehensive knowledge of GRC principles, which offers an understanding of how organizations can govern risk, ensure compliance, and establish good governance frameworks. It contains immense knowledge and real-world examples to navigate the challenges and opportunities within the GRC domain and will help beginners and experienced professionals to gain knowledge and bring their capabilities to the next level.

It comprises 21 insightful chapters with a wide range of topics essential for understanding the complexities of GRC. This book starts with the introduction of security principles, governance structure and compliance standards providing a solid foundation of basics. From there, we explore the system categorization, control selections, control assessments and enhancing security controls to understand in-depth.

Through practical examples, comprehensive explanations, and a structured approach, this book aims to equip readers with a solid understanding of GRC. The purpose is to adequately prepare you to get certified in GRC. This book serves as a reliable reference for aspiring risk professionals and leaders to expand their knowledge in risk management and industry best practices. Professionals will gain considerable insights into the principles of privacy framework, risk assessment, risk management, and risk treatment.

Chapter 1: Introduction to Security and Privacy Principles - This chapter describes the fundamentals of security principles, including confidentiality, integrity and availability. It provide key security concepts like identification, authentication and authorization essential to drive the security, risk and compliance program. This chapter focuses on data lifecycles, security policy, security principles and roles and responsibilities.

Chapter 2: Governance Structure and Policy - This chapter outlines the organizational framework, including committees and reporting lines, that supports effective oversight and management. Clearly defined roles and responsibilities specify the duties and accountabilities of individuals and groups, delineating who is responsible for governance, decision-making, and adherence to policies. This chapter also focuses on NIST and the governance framework.

Chapter 3: Risk Assessment and Compliance Standards - This chapter highlights risk analysis to identify and assess potential risk, evaluate their likelihood and impact to prioritize risk effectively. This chapter also defines the requirements and guidelines that organizations must follow to ensure adherence to regulatory and industry-specific requirements.

Chapter 4: Introduction to System Scope - This chapter describes the system purpose and functionality that outlines the primary reason or need for the system. This chapter also specify the limits of the system, identifying what is within its scope and what is external. This chapter also outlines the information types and system boundaries, defining stakeholders and system requirements based on the scope identified.

Chapter 5: System Categorization and Control - This chapter outlines the applicable baseline and inherited controls along with comprehensive understanding of the system's environment. This chapter outlines FIPS 199 and 200 to help organizations determine security controls based on data types and impact levels. This chapter also assesses the effects that changes or events might have on the system's performance, security, and compliance. This chapter also focuses on data privacy standards and personal information.

Chapter 6: Introduction to Control Selection and Approval - This chapter describes the various control framework, including CIS Benchmark, Singapore PDPA and AICPA. It defines security controls based on their purpose and function, such as preventive, detective, and corrective controls, to systematically address different aspects of risk management. This chapter also focuses on privacy assessment to analyze privacy risks.

Chapter 7: Evaluating and Selecting Controls - This chapter outlines the details about customizing security controls to fit the specific needs and risks of an organization, adapting generic controls to align with the particular context. This chapter also define alternative measure implemented when standard controls cannot be applied. This chapter also describes assurance, trustworthiness and focus on creating overlays and system of record notice.

Chapter 8: Enhancing Security Controls - This chapter determine appropriate control enhancements (e.g., security practices, overlays, mitigating controls) and explain metrics used to monitor and evaluate risk levels and performance. This chapter outlines the audit strategies to comply with regulations and overall effectiveness of controls. This chapter also covers the vulnerability management and performance monitoring.

Chapter 9: Introduction to Implementing Controls - This chapter identifies control types (e.g., management, technical, common, operational control) and control implementation aligned with organizational expectations and compliance. **plan of action and milestones (POA&M)** defines the plan of action and outlines the specific actions required to address issues, assigns responsibilities, and tracks progress. This chapter also focuses on configuration identification to provide insight into the management of configurations.

Chapter 10: Deploying Security and Privacy Controls - This chapter outlines the control implementation consistent with compliance requirements and identifies the compensating controls. It also covers configuration management to track changes effectively and privacy control guidelines to safeguard personal information and ensuring compliance with privacy laws and regulations.

Chapter 11: Documenting Security Controls - This chapter provides a detailed overview of risk governance to ensure risks are continuously assessed and addressed, and outlines risk register details to track and manage identified risks. This includes residual security risk or planned implementations documentation (e.g., POA&M, risk register).

Chapter 12: Introduction to Control Assessment and Audit - This chapter outlines the assessment objectives, scope, resources, schedule and deliverables. This chapter also covers the techniques and procedures used to carry out an assessment, including interviews, surveys, document reviews. This chapter includes stakeholder roles and responsibilities along with detailed audit scope identified and how evidence can be gathered as per standard.

Chapter 13: Conducting Assessment and Audit - This chapter describes the evaluation of security and privacy controls to determine the effectiveness of controls, ensuring compliance with policies and regulations. It also covers the method used to conduct audits, including the processes, tools, and techniques employed to review compliance. This chapter helps to verify and validate the evidence as part of the audit process.

Chapter 14: Developing Report and Risk Response - This chapter covers the identified risk and risk response (e.g., avoid, accept, share, mitigate, transfer) based on identified vulnerabilities. It highlights the risk management strategy to summarize the risk mitigation plan and register the residual risk based on the risk appetite. This chapter also covers non-compliant findings with newly applied corrective actions reassessed and validated.

Chapter 15: Introduction to System Compliance - This chapter describes how an organization adheres to regulatory requirements, standards, and internal policies. This chapter also outlines the security and privacy documents required to support a compliance decision by the appropriate party (e.g., authorizing official, third-party assessment organizations) compiled, reviewed, and submitted. This chapter also includes disaster recovery plans, backup strategies, and continuity measures to minimize downtime and data loss.

Chapter 16: Determining System Risk Posture - This chapter outlines system risk acceptance criteria, residual risk criteria, and stakeholder concurrence for risk treatments. It covers the overview of an organization's risk landscape, including the identification and assessment of various risks, and the potential impact. The chapter includes test cases, resources required, and criteria for success to ensure the system meets its requirements and operates as intended.

Chapter 17: Documenting System Compliance - This chapter describes the system authorization documentation that provides reliable evidence of the system's security controls. This also includes the formal notification process and documentation related to the findings of an audit conducted on a system. This chapter also covers the training activities, including details on the training programs, participants, completion dates, and effectiveness evaluations. We focus on configuration management minimize security risks.

Chapter 18: Introduction to Compliance Maintenance - This chapter covers the change management process, including planning, approving, implementing, and reviewing changes to minimize the impact on organizational risk, operations, and compliance requirements. It describes the importance of acceptance testing as per the stakeholder's requirements. This chapter also covers the incident response to identify the incident, containing its impact, eradicating the cause, recovering affected systems, and learning from the event to improve future responses.

Chapter 19: Monitoring Compliance - This chapter covers the compliance measurement process for ongoing compliance activities review with stakeholders, as well as system and assets monitoring (e.g., physical and logical assets, personnel, change control). We outline the routine updates, patches, repairs, and performance monitoring to address issues, improve functionality, and ensure that the system continues to meet operational and security requirements. This chapter also focuses on key compliance standards to manage risk and establish organizational governance.

Chapter 20: Optimizing Risk and Compliance - This chapter covers continuous monitoring, testing, and documentation updates (e.g., service level agreements, third-party contracts, policies, procedures). It also focuses on configuration scanning to identify and manage vulnerabilities. This chapter describes the modified monitoring strategies based on updates to legal, regulatory, supplier, security, and privacy requirements.

Chapter 21: Practice Tests - This chapter covers 2 practice tests to evaluate the readiness and preparation for the CGRC exam. There are 50 questions in each practice test covering all the topics, core concepts and knowledge.

Coloured Images

Please follow the link to download the
Coloured Images of the book:

https://rebrand.ly/4vqpnk2

We have code bundles from our rich catalogue of books and videos available at **https://github.com/bpbpublications**. Check them out!

Errata

We take immense pride in our work at BPB Publications and follow best practices to ensure the accuracy of our content to provide with an indulging reading experience to our subscribers. Our readers are our mirrors, and we use their inputs to reflect and improve upon human errors, if any, that may have occurred during the publishing processes involved. To let us maintain the quality and help us reach out to any readers who might be having difficulties due to any unforeseen errors, please write to us at :

errata@bpbonline.com

Your support, suggestions and feedbacks are highly appreciated by the BPB Publications' Family.

Did you know that BPB offers eBook versions of every book published, with PDF and ePub files available? You can upgrade to the eBook version at www.bpbonline. com and as a print book customer, you are entitled to a discount on the eBook copy. Get in touch with us at :

business@bpbonline.com for more details.

At **www.bpbonline.com**, you can also read a collection of free technical articles, sign up for a range of free newsletters, and receive exclusive discounts and offers on BPB books and eBooks.

Piracy

If you come across any illegal copies of our works in any form on the internet, we would be grateful if you would provide us with the location address or website name. Please contact us at **business@bpbonline.com** with a link to the material.

If you are interested in becoming an author

If there is a topic that you have expertise in, and you are interested in either writing or contributing to a book, please visit **www.bpbonline.com**. We have worked with thousands of developers and tech professionals, just like you, to help them share their insights with the global tech community. You can make a general application, apply for a specific hot topic that we are recruiting an author for, or submit your own idea.

Reviews

Please leave a review. Once you have read and used this book, why not leave a review on the site that you purchased it from? Potential readers can then see and use your unbiased opinion to make purchase decisions. We at BPB can understand what you think about our products, and our authors can see your feedback on their book. Thank you!

For more information about BPB, please visit **www.bpbonline.com**.

Join our book's Discord space

Join the book's Discord Workspace for Latest updates, Offers, Tech happenings around the world, New Release and Sessions with the Authors:

https://discord.bpbonline.com

Table of Contents

CHAPTER 1

Introduction to Security and Privacy Principles

Introduction

This chapter provides an overview of essential security concepts needed for understanding how to protect information within an organization. This chapter begins by explaining key security principles, such as **confidentiality, integrity, and availability (CIA)**, and how these principles guide the development and maintenance of secure systems. This chapter also addresses the importance of data classification and the data lifecycle, which helps in identifying and managing critical assets.

In addition to security principles, the chapter covers the **system development lifecycle (SDLC)**, detailing how to manage security from both data and system perspectives. It includes discussions on security roles and responsibilities, as well as creating a system threat model. It concludes with a focus on data privacy principles and core components. This chapter also includes practical examples and keynotes to help with understanding and exams.

Structure

The chapter covers the following topics:

- Security principles
- Fundamental security concept

- System development lifecycle
- Data classification and data lifecycle
- Security standards and procedures
- Security roles and responsibilities
- Threat modeling
- Data privacy

Objectives

By the end of this chapter, you will understand the core concept of security. You will be familiar with the security terms and terminology used in an organization. You will gain the key learnings on security principles, security roles and responsibilities, security policies, threat models, and data privacy. You will learn about the data classification and full lifecycleof data.

Security principles

CIA are the core elements of security principles to ensure that the information systems and data are protected from various threats. Together, these security principles help create a robust security framework that protects the data from unauthorized access, ensures its accuracy, and keeps it accessible to those who need it. These security principles are also called the CIA triad, needed for a secure environment. Let us understand the security principle in detail. *Figure 1.1* shows how data is protected with CIA:

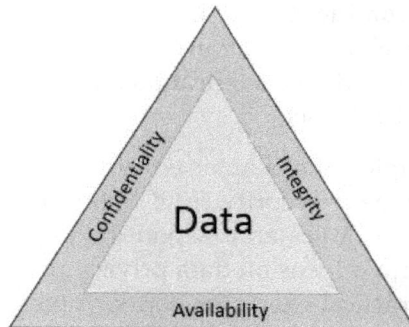

Figure 1.1: CIA triad

Confidentiality

Confidentiality means to protect the system or data from any unauthorized access. The users can intentionally or unintentionally disclose sensitive data if the right security measures are not in place. There are multiple security measures that can be implemented to ensure the confidentiality of data; however, it is crucial to classify data properly. The security measures can include encryption at rest and in motion, **role-based access control (RBAC)**, and data classification.

The following provides a list of some controls and how they map to the components of the confidentiality:

- **Encryption of data at rest**: This ensures that stored data is protected from unauthorized access by making it unreadable unless decrypted by authorized users.

- **Encryption of data in transit**: This secures data being transmitted over networks, preventing interception or eavesdropping by encrypting the data during transfer.

- **Encryption of data in use**: This protects data while it is being processed in memory or during active operations, ensuring confidentiality even when the data is not stored or in transit.

- **Access control**: Access control limits access to sensitive data based on user roles and permissions, ensuring only authorized users can access or modify confidential information.

Integrity

Integrity means to protect the system or data from any unauthorized modification. The users can modify the data, resulting in corrupt or non-reliable data if the right security measures are not in place. The data can be corrupted by running malicious codes in the system, inserting incorrect values in the application, deleting configuration files, etc. The security measures can include strict access control, hashing, validating application inputs and intrusion detection.

The following provides a list of some controls and how they map to the components of the integrity:

- **Hashing**: Hashing ensures data integrity by generating a unique hash value for data. Any alteration in the data will change the hash, allowing detection of unauthorized changes.

- **Digital signing**: Digital signature verifies the authenticity and integrity of software or documents by signing them with a private key.

- **Configuration management**: This maintains consistent and authorized configurations for systems and software. It ensures that any changes to the configuration are tracked and authorized.

- **Change control**: Change control manages and tracks changes to systems, applications, and data. It ensures changes are reviewed, tested, and documented to prevent unauthorized modifications.

Availability

Availability means to keep the system up and keep data available in a timely manner to authorized users. Users can sometimes face disruption to the system or connectivity loss if there is no redundancy to the system or network. The disruptions can occur in various ways, like natural disasters, network outages, connectivity loss, application failure, etc. Security measures can include preventing **denial of service** (**DoS**) attacks, redundancy for critical systems, and maintenance of backup systems.

The following provides a list of some controls and how they map to the components of the availability:

- **Clustering**: Clustering ensures system availability by grouping multiple servers to work together. If one server fails, another takes over and minimize downtime.

- **Load balancing**: Load balancers distribute network traffic across multiple servers, preventing any single server from becoming overwhelmed and improving availability by ensuring even workload distribution.

- **Data backups**: Regular backups ensure that data can be restored in the event of system failure or data loss, ensuring continued availability and quick recovery.

- **Failover configurations**: Failover configurations automatically switch to a backup system or component when a failure is detected, maintaining system uptime and availability without manual intervention.

- **Rollback functions**: Rollback allows systems to revert to a previous stable state after an error or failure, minimizing downtime and ensuring continued availability.

Practical illustration

Let us take an example of a health application. You have installed a health application with credentials and you are the authorized user. The hospital uploaded your health records into the application for you to access the information anytime. You do not want anyone to access your health records and hence the application will encrypt your data to prevent it from unauthorized access. This is an example of confidentiality.

You will notice that the application uses digital signatures to verify that the health records have not been modified while sending you in the application. You want to make sure that no one has changed any content of your health records and that the data is accurate. This is an example of integrity.

Let us continue with the same application. You want to have continuous access to the health records available in the application. At the backend, the application maintains multiple servers and data backups to ensure that the application is up always. This is an example of availability.

Fundamental security concept

Authentication, authorization, and accounting (**AAA**) services. This includes implementing authentication protocols, managing user permissions, and tracking activities for compliance and security.

Authentication

Authentication is the initial step in the security process where a user or system proves their identity before gaining access to resources or services. Most of the time, you use a password or a **personal identification number** (**PIN**) to log into any applications or access any system. Authentication can be much more effective with the combinations of various methods, like password and code, sent on registered mobile phone, password and fingerprint, etc. When two or more methods are combined, it is called **multi-factor authentication** (**MFA**) or **two-factor authentication** (**2FA**).

Key aspects of authentication

There are four common methods of authentication: Knowledge, possession, biometrics, and location, explained in the following table:

Method of authentication	Description
Something you know	This is knowledge-based, something you remember or have noted down somewhere. The examples are passwords, PINs, answer to security questions, etc.
Something you have	This is possession-based, something that you hold physically. The examples are smart cards, hardware tokens, **one-time password** (**OTP**) received in mobile phone, etc.
Something you are	This is biometric-based, something that represents the unique characteristic of yourself. The examples are fingerprints, iris scan, etc.
Somewhere you are	This is location-based, something that identifies the user's geographic locations. The examples are IP address, geofencing, etc.

Table 1.1: Authentication methods

There are three main authentication protocols to govern the authentication process explained in the following table:

Authentication protocols	Protocol type	Description
OAuth	Token-based authorization protocol	OAuth is a protocol that allows one application to securely access another application's resources without sharing your password. It is commonly used when you want a third-party application to interact with your data on a different service.
OpenID	Identity verification protocol like **single sign-on (SSO)**	OpenID is a protocol that allows you to use one login credential of application like *Facebook* or *Google* account to sign in to different websites or applications. This helps to access multiple services without maintaining separate password for each application. OpenID provides SSO and identity verification.
Kerberos	Network authentication protocol	Kerberos is a protocol that allows you to securely log into services and applications in a computer network. This protocol ensures that both the user and the service can trust each other's identity.

Table 1.2: Authentication protocols

Authorization

Authorization is the next process after authentication to determine what actions a user or system can perform on specific resources within a system. This process mainly takes care of permissions based on different roles assigned to different users. For example, a user with the developer role will have full access, and a user with the auditor role will have read access only.

Key aspects of authorization

Some key aspects of authorization is as follows:

- **Access control**: Access control specifies who can access data or resources and what action users can perform, such as read, write, modify, delete etc.

- **Roles or permissions**: Every user has different permissions to the data or services based on the roles assigned to the user. For example, a user might have read-only permission to a document, while another user might have edit permissions.

- **Policies**: Authorization policies are crucial to define the rules and conditions under which user access is granted or denied. The policies can be based on factors, like user roles, attributes, etc.

System development lifecycle

The SDLC is a structured and well-established approach to develop and manage information systems. The lifecycle consists of various aspects of the system or product, from planning, deploying, and managing an information system. There are seven phases in SDLC, as shown in *Figure 1.2*:

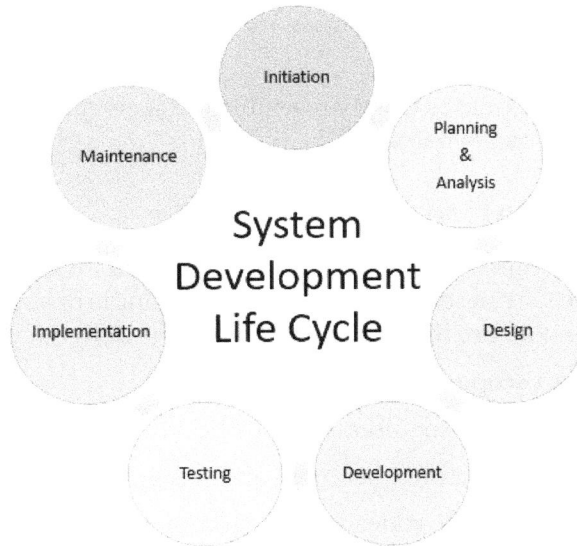

Figure 1.2: SDLC phases

Following is a brief explanation of each phase for your understanding:

- **Initiation**: Initiation is the first phase of SDLC that focuses on defining the project's scope, objectives, and feasibility by identifying stakeholders and gathering high-level requirements.

- **Planning and analysis**: Planning and analysis is the second phase of SDLC that focuses on the purpose of the system and understanding the business requirements and system needs.

- **Design**: Design is the third phase of SDLC that focus on the blueprint of the system based on the requirements. This phase defines the detailed system architecture, including design specifications, user interface and data structure.

- **Development**: Development is the fourth phase of SDLC that focuses on developing system components. This phase elaborates on writing software codes and integrating various modules as per the blueprint and design specifications.

- **Testing**: Testing is the fifth phase of SDLC that focuses on various types of tests to ensure the system is free from any defects. This phase covers different types of testing including functional testing, interface testing, integration testing, **user acceptance testing (UAT)** and system testing.

- **Implementation**: Implementation is the sixth phase of SDLC that focus on the actual deployment of system developed after testing phase. This phase covers the installation and configuration of system to bring system live for respective users.

- **Maintenance**: Maintenance is the seventh and final phase of SDLC that focuses on the operations aspect. This phase includes system monitoring, updating the system, addressing issues, etc.

The software development phases closely resemble the seven phases of the SDLC, though there are some variations in the names of the phases.

Practical illustration

Since you have gone through the seven phases of SDLC, you must be wondering what the actual deliverables for each phase are. You can take an example of application development whereby, at each phase, you are required to provide some deliverables:

- **Initiation**: Project scope and feasibility.
- **Planning and analysis**: Requirement specification document and purpose.
- **Design**: System architecture document and design document.
- **Development**: Executable codes and integration document.
- **Testing**: Test plan and test cases.
- **Implementation**: Implementation document and user guide.
- **Maintenance**: Support document and maintenance report.

Data classification and data lifecycle

Data classification and data lifecycleare two important aspects of managing data effectively and securely. Implementing a data classification process allows organizations to apply the right security measures based on data sensitivity and ensure compliance with regulations. On the other hand, understanding the data lifecycleenables organizations to establish effective data governance and security measures at every stage of their data's lifespan.

Data classification

Data classification is the process of categorizing data into different levels based on the sensitivity, value, and importance of data to the organization. The same data can be of different levels to different organizations based on their industry type and security policies. Data classification helps organizations to implement adequate security controls and procedures to safeguard data in storage as well as during data handling.

Data classification levels

Depending on the type of organizations (government or non-government), the data classification level varies. The following figure explains the data classification levels for both type of organizations:

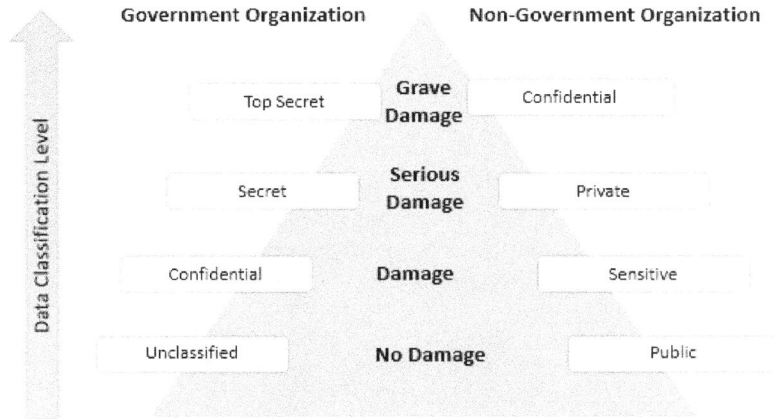

Figure 1.3: *Data classification levels*

Following are the details of data classification levels for a government organization:

- **Unclassified**: Unclassified data means any data that has not been classified as confidential, secret, or top secret. The unclassified data does not contain any sensitive data, and disclosure will not cause any damage to the organization.

- **Confidential**: Confidential data means any data that has confidential information and unauthorized disclosure will cause damage to the organization. For example, employee personal data, administrative documents, etc.

- **Secret**: Secret label means any data that has sensitive information and unauthorized disclosure will cause serious damage to the organization. For example, the national defence plan, undercover operations, etc.

- **Top secret**: Top secret label means any data that has restricted information and unauthorized disclosure will cause grave damage to the organization. For example, nuclear weapon information, tactical plans, etc.

Similarly, following are the details of data classification for non-government organizations:

- **Public**: Public data means any data that can be shared to anyone. The example includes advertising data.

- **Sensitive**: Sensitive data means any data that is not as highly classified as confidential or private data. The examples include internal communications or project plans.

- **Private**: Private data means any data that is personal or sensitive but not as critical as confidential data. The examples include employee records, customer data, and personal contact details.

- **Confidential**: Confidential data means any data that is sensitive within an organization, and unauthorized access will cause serious damage. The examples include employee data, business information data, etc.

Data classification process

The data classification process starts with identifying the data that needs to be categorized. Once the data is identified, establish a criteria for the classification label based on the sensitivity or nature of the data. Once the data is categorized, it is labeled as internal, confidential, or restricted based on the organization's policy. Following this, the necessary security controls are implemented to protect the data. The following figure shows the data classification process:

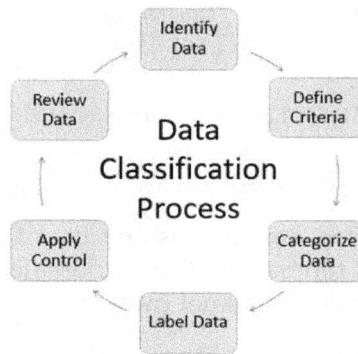

Figure 1.4: Data classification process

Some security control examples are encryption, RBAC, etc. Finally, data classification is reviewed at a regular time period to ensure the relevance of data classification.

Data lifecycle

The data lifecycle is very similar to the SDLC with some differences due to the way data is handled and managed throughout the lifecycle. For example, a system developed through the SDLC will manage and process data according to the data lifecycle stages.

The key phases of data lifecycle are:

- **Planning**: Planning is the first phase before creation or acquisition of data. This phase is important for identifying the value and sensitivity of data.

- **Designing**: Designing is the next phase to identify the data structure, storage system. The structured format is designed for future use.

- **Creating or acquiring**: Create or acquire is the phase where the data is actually created or transferred from other systems.

- **Operating or monitoring**: Operation is the next phase, where the activity of data is monitored, and the data is processed, used, and shared.

- **Archiving**: Following operations, archiving is the phase where inactive or less frequently used data is moved to long-term storage due to historical, compliance, or legal requirements.

- **Disposal**: Disposal is the last phase of the data lifecycle, during which the data is permanently removed from the system if it is no longer in use.

Data states

There are three states of data namely, data at rest, data in motion, and data in use. The knowledge of data states is crucial for identifying and implementing the right security measures.

Data at rest

Data at rest means that the data is static and is stored in some storage without being read or written. Some examples are backups stored in storage, files kept in folder or cloud, etc.

Security considerations

The data at rest can be protected by implementing various security solutions. The most effective solution is encryption and access control. Encryption helps to protect the data at rest even if the storage device is lost or compromised. The strict access control strengthens and control the access to the system where data is stored. Some organization also use data masking solution to obfuscate the sensitive data during storage.

Encryption methodologies

Following are the common encryption methods for data at rest.

- **Advanced Encryption Standard (AES)**: AES-256 is widely used for encrypting data at rest due to its high security and efficiency. Data is encrypted using a symmetric key, meaning the same key is used to encrypt and decrypt the data.

- **Transparent Data Encryption (TDE)**: TDE is used for encrypting databases at rest, particularly in systems like *Microsoft SQL Server* and *Oracle databases*. The encryption occurs at the file-system level and is transparent to users and applications.

- **Full Disk Encryption (FDE)**: Tools like BitLocker (Windows) or **Linux Unified Key Setup** (LUKS) (Linux) encrypt the entire disk to ensure that all data stored on it is encrypted.

Data in motion

Data in motion means that the data is moving across network, between the systems and is not static. The examples are API calls, data transfer between client and server, internet communication, etc.

Security considerations

The data in motion can be protected by implementing various security solutions. Encryption protocols, secure authentication, and authorization are the most effective solutions for data in motion. When you do web browsing, you might have noticed that **Hypertext Transfer Protocol Secure (HTTPS)** uses **Transport Layer Security (TLS)/ Secure Sockets Layer (SSL)** to secure web traffic between browsers and web servers. TLS/SSL is critical for securing data in motion by encrypting the data, authenticating, and ensuring data integrity. Secure protocols like HTTPS and network security solutions, like firewalls, intrusion detection systems, etc., can add layers of security for data in motion.

Encryption methodologies

Following are the common encryption methods for data in transit:

- **TLS**: TLS 1.3 is the most commonly used protocols for encrypting data in motion, especially for web traffic (HTTPS). TLS uses asymmetric encryption (public/ private key pairs) during the handshake to establish a secure symmetric encryption key for the session.

- **Internet Protocol Security (IPsec)**: IPsec is used for securing network communication by encrypting data at the IP layer. It is commonly used in **virtual private networks (VPNs)**.

- **VPN**: VPN encrypts the data traffic between the user's device and the VPN server using protocols like IPsec or OpenVPN.

- **Secure Shell (SSH)**: SSH is used for secure remote access and data transfer (e.g., **Secure Copy Protocol (SCP)**or **Secure File Transfer Protocol (SFTP)**. It employs asymmetric encryption for authentication and symmetric encryption for session data.

Data in use

Data in use means that the data is actually being processed and analyzed by users or systems. Some examples are data processed in data analytics tools, data managed in applications, etc.

Security considerations

The data in use can be protected by implementing various security solutions. The most common solution is data masking and session management. Session management ensures the secure handling of data while processing and data masking techniques make the data unreadable while in use. Some organizations also use memory encryption and strict access control to protect the data in use. As you know, access control can be effective by implementing RBAC and least privilege. In-memory encryption, as the name implies, the encryption is done at memory level while data is in use or processed.

Encryption methodologies

Following are the common encryption methods for data in use.

- **Trusted execution environments (TEEs)**: TEEs, like *Intel Software Guard Extensions* (*SGX*) or *TrustZone*, provide a secure environment where data can be processed while remaining encrypted in memory.

- **Homomorphic encryption**: Homomorphic encryption allows data to be processed and analyzed while still encrypted. This is useful in scenarios where sensitive data needs to be processed without revealing the actual data (e.g., privacy-preserving computations in cloud environments).

- **Application-level encryption (ALE)**: Some applications may implement their own encryption mechanisms to secure data in use. For example, when data is being processed for sensitive transactions, the application may encrypt the data in memory before performing operations on it.

Security standards and procedures

Every organization has critical data and there is a need to protect the information and systems that store and process the information. This is usually achieved through structured framework by implementing security policies, standards, guidelines and procedures. You might have come across these terms often and they seem somewhat similar, but these terms are not interchangeable. The following diagram shows the relationships of security policy components:

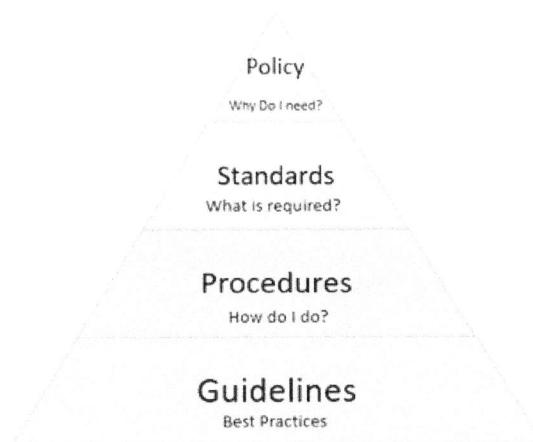

Policy
Why Do I need?

Standards
What is required?

Procedures
How do I do?

Guidelines
Best Practices

Figure 1.5: CIA organization policy relationship

Let us look at them in detail:

- **Policy**: An information security policy is a high-level document that defines the scope of security and establishes security principles required by the organization. Policies reflect an organization's goals, objectives, and culture and are intended for broad audiences. The policies are mandatory in every organization, and are applied to everyone, including employees and contractors. The policy is approved by the senior management or the board and drives standards, procedures, and guidelines. Some examples are information security policy, data privacy policy, etc.

- **Standards**: Standards are mandatory criteria or rules that support the security policy to ensure consistency and compliance. Standards can be directed to a broad audience or limited to specific groups or individuals. They define the minimum acceptable level of performance or quality. Standards define the benchmark for performance and compulsory requirements for the use of hardware, software, technology, and security controls. Some examples are password standards, data encryption standards, etc.

- **Procedures**: Procedure are detailed, step-by-step describing the exact actions required to implement policies and standards. A procedure can be applied to the entire system or on single product and can be performed by IT professionals, security personnel, and other staff members dealing with specific tasks. Some examples are incident response policy, backup policy, etc.

- **Guidelines**: Guidelines are best practice documents or recommendations that provide operational guide on how to achieve compliance. Guidelines are more flexible than policy, standards and procedures to help individuals and organizations achieve complex tasks by suggestions based on industry best practices. Some examples are email usage guideline, data handling guidelines, etc.

Practical illustration

In the previous section, we explored the definitions of security policy, standards, procedures, and guidelines. Now, let us examine a practical scenario for each term using passwords as our example:

- **Password policy**: Password policy dictates that all the passwords must be at least 8 characters long and must include alphanumeric, and special characters, and need to be changed every 90 days.

- **Password standard**: Password standard describes that all the passwords must have a minimum of 8 characters and include at least one uppercase letter, one lowercase letter, one number, and one special character. Passwords cannot be reused within the last seven password changes.

- **Password procedure**: Password procedure provides the step-by-step details. To change your password, log into the company's password management system, select change password, enter your old password, and create a new password that meets the complexity requirements. Follow the on-screen prompts to complete the change.

- **Password guidelines**: Password guidelines recommend industry best practices. Use a passphrase made up of random words or a combination of unrelated words to create a strong password. Avoid using easily guessable information such as birthdays or common words.

Security roles and responsibilities

Security roles and responsibilities outline the roles of any individual or group involved in security-related work to ensure the effective management and protection of information assets. Each security role is crucial to manage data securely and creating a robust security posture to ensure compliance with policies and regulations. The roles include, creating security strategies, implementing and maintaining security measures, responding to incidents, managing third-party vendors, etc. The following roles are very common in most of the organizations.

Chief information security officer

A **chief information security officer** (**CISO**) is a senior-level executive who oversees an organization's information security program that protects an organization's data and system. The key responsibilities of a CISO roles are:

- To provide guidance on security programs and strategies within an organization.
- To ensure that security programs are aligned with the organization's objective and security policy.
- To oversee the response to major security incidents and data breaches.
- To provide leadership and direction to the security team and oversee risk program.

Security manager

The security manager oversees the day-to-day security operations, manages security personnel, and ensures compliance with standards and regulations. The key responsibilities of security managers are:

- To develop and implement effective security strategies and solutions to protect the organization against threats or security risks.
- To implement security policies and procedures as directed by CISO or security leaders.

- To lead the incident investigation and provide reports on incidents and security risks.

- To oversee the implementation of security solutions, like **web application firewall (WAF)**, end point protection, monitoring solutions, etc.

Risk and compliance officer

The risk and compliance officer's role is crucial in ensuring that a company adheres to all legal obligations, rules, and regulations The key responsibilities of a risk and compliance officer are:

- To provide compliance advisory to business units and business functions.

- To provide support to senior compliance officers in organizing, designing, and delivery of compliance training.

- To develop internal company policies and report to management concerning the organization's compliance with laws and regulations.

- To coordinate with internal and external audits related to security and privacy.

Security architect

The security architect's role is to design and develop robust security architecture. The key responsibilities of security architects are:

- To understand the security requirements from relevant stakeholders, like security professional, developers, business analyst, etc.

- To design and create detailed security architecture and solutions, including logical and physical.

- To develop security best practices and design mitigation strategies for the risks identified.

Security engineer

A security engineer implements various technologies and processes to prevent, detect, and manage cyber threats. The key responsibilities of security engineers are:

- To implement, configure, troubleshoot, and maintain the security infrastructure of the organization.

- To maintain and monitor security systems for threats and vulnerabilities and setup preventive measures.

- To identify current and emerging technology issues including security trends, vulnerabilities and threats.

Security auditor

A security auditor reviews and verifies that the security policy is properly implemented and there are sufficient security solutions. The key responsibilities of an auditor are:

- To assess and evaluate the organization's data security controls, processes, and systems.

- To conduct compliance evaluations and perform complete checks to ensure that the organization remains compliant with regulatory standards.

- To review internal security controls and test the strength of these controls to minimize the likelihood of unauthorized access.

- To perform risk assessments, review security policies and procedures, and conduct in-depth examinations of the organization's technical infrastructure, systems, and networks.

- To provide detailed audit reports, communicate findings to management, and work with stakeholders to implement corrective actions and enhance security posture.

End user

The end users are all employees and any users who has the access to the secured system. The key responsibilities of end users are:

- To understand and adhere to security policies and procedures and operate within the security parameters.

- To report any security incident and suspicious activities, like phishing email, malware attack, DoS, etc. to IT security team.

- To participate in all security awareness training to understand and maintain the security landscape.

There are various other roles like **data privacy officer/data protection officer** (**DPO**), security analyst, security operations, data owner, data custodian, etc. depending on the business functions and organization policy.

Threat modeling

In today's world, most IT systems are vulnerable to various threats. These threats can originate from outside or within the organization. Threat modeling is a way for an organization to tackle threats or vulnerabilities and can be applied to a wide range of things, including software, applications, systems, networks, and business processes. Threat modeling is the structured and repeatable security process to identify, categorize, evaluate and address the potential security threats in an organization. Some organizations consider threat modeling as a risk identification technique that inspects attack vectors, threat agents and vulnerabilities.

Types of threat modeling

There are various types of threat modeling available that can vary based on the following three characteristics:

- The logical entity to be modeled (data, software, system, etc.).

- The phase of the system lifecycle (threat modeling at the initial stage, product ready stage, etc.).

- The goal of threat modeling (reduce software vulnerabilities, improve overall system security, protect particular types of data, etc.).

Practical illustration

Let us walk us through the common form of threat modeling used in various organizations:

- **Software threat modeling**: Software threat modeling is performed during software design to reduce software vulnerabilities.

- **System threat modeling**: System threat modeling is performed to improve the overall security of operational systems.

- **Data threat modeling:** Data threat modeling is a particular type of system threat modeling focused on protecting particular types of data within systems.

Threat modeling process

There are several different threat modeling frameworks and methodologies. However, the key steps are similar in most of these processes. The following figure shows the five critical steps for threat modelling:

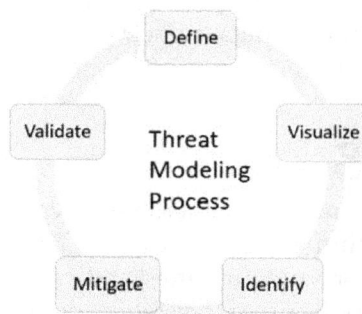

Figure 1.6: Threat modeling steps

The five steps for threat modeling are:

- **Define (What we want to achieve)**: The first step of the threat modeling process is to define and describe the security requirements. For example, the scope can be system, application, network, infrastructure etc.

- **Visualize (What to build)**: Once the objectives are defined, the next step is to visualize the model by creating the application diagram. The visualization can be built by data flow diagrams or process flow diagrams to capture all the components.

- **Identify (What can go wrong)**: After visualization, the next action is to identify the actual threats. The number of threats can be huge associated with each asset and its operation. Additionally, the threats or vulnerabilities are assessed to determine the level of risk each threat poses and are prioritized.

- **Mitigate (What to do if something goes wrong)**: Based on the prioritization, the mitigation plan is created and implemented to reduce the risk to acceptable level.

- **Validate (What we achieved)**: Validate is the final step of threat modeling process whereby all the threats are examined if the threats are mitigated.

Threat modeling framework

As you know, threat modeling identifies potential threats and attack vectors for systems or applications. A framework is a structured approach to improve the organization's threat-handling process. There are various threat modeling methodologies and frameworks developed based on asset-centric, attacker-centric, and software-centric approaches. An attack-centric approach focuses on the types of possible attacks, and an asset-centric approach focuses on the assets that need to be protected. A software-centric focuses on the system design, data flows between various layers, and how it is configured. Following is some of the most common threats modeling framework.

STRIDE

STRIDE is the popular threat modeling framework developed by Microsoft to identify threats and vulnerabilities during the design process of an application or system. STRIDE is an acronym and each of these letters are associated with different type of threats. S refer to *spoofing*, T refer to *tampering*, R refer to *repudiation*, I refer to *information disclosure*, D refer to *DoS* and E refers to *elevation of privilege*. Let us understand each of these threats in simple terms:

- **Spoofing**: Spoofing is a threat with the objective of gaining unauthorized access to the target system by fake identity.

- **Tampering**: Tampering means unauthorized changes to system or data at rest, data in motion and data in use.

- **Repudiation**: Repudiation is a threat whereby a user denies the action performed by him/her in the system or application.

- **Information disclosure**: Information disclosure is a threat whereby sensitive or confidential data is disclosed to unauthorized personnel or system.

- **DoS**: A DoS threat is initiated by overloading unwanted traffic in the server or system. The actual services may be impacted in terms of latency or there may be interruptions to the services.

- **Elevation of privilege**: Elevation of privilege is a threat whereby the least privilege account is transformed into high privilege account.

PASTA

Process for Attack Simulation and Threat Analysis (PASTA) and is a risk-based threat modeling framework. PASTA is a seven step methodology that looks at security from the attacker's point of view. It combines risk and impact analysis to create a clear picture of potential risks to a business. The following figure represents the seven steps of PASTA:

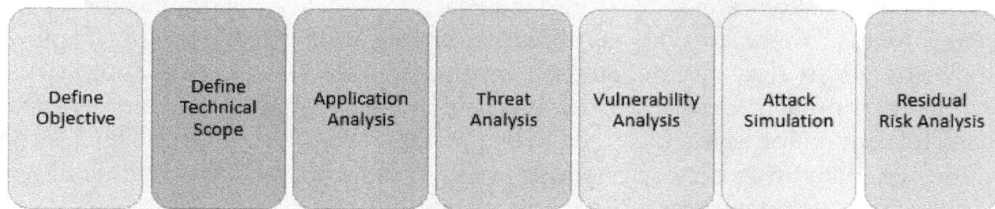

Figure 1.7: Seven steps of PASTA

The seven steps are clearly elaborated. The very first step is to identify the critical assets and define a clear objective. The next step is to determine system architecture and components as part of the technical scope. The third step is to break down the application into various modules to identify the threats. The next step is to determine the potential threats and attack vectors. The fifth step is to perform a vulnerability assessment to identify the weaknesses for threats to exploit. The next step is to perform the attack simulation in a test environment by exploiting the threats identified. The final step is to implement the mitigations for risk assessed and document the residual risk.

MITRE ATT&CK

MITRE Adversarial Tactics, Techniques, and Common Knowledge (MITRE ATT&CK). The MITRE ATT&CK framework is the updated knowledge base to provide a model for cyberattack behaviors. It framework can simulate cyberattacks and also recommend cyber defense. MITRE ATT&CK framework can help organization to create effective security controls, to manage incident response and to configure system securely.

The MITRE ATT&CK matrix has 14 tactics (objectives) namely reconnaissance, resource development, initial access, execution, persistence, privilege escalation, defense evasion, credential access, discovery, lateral movement, collection, command and control, Exfiltration, and impact. Each of these tactics has several techniques and sub techniques.

There are four main steps in MITRE ATT&CK framework, as shown in the following figure:

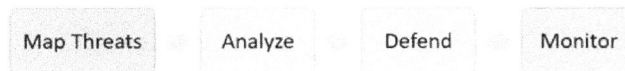

Figure 1.8: Four steps of MITRE ATT&CK

Let us look at each step briefly:

1. **Map threats**: This is the first step is identifying threats alignment with MITRE ATT&CK tactics and techniques.

2. **Analyze**: This step evaluates the mapped techniques that can be used to exploit against the organization.

3. **Defend**: This step implements the necessary security controls to defend the attack against mapped techniques.

4. **Monitor**: This is final step that continuously monitors the risk of compromise related to MITRE ATT&CK techniques.

OCTAVE

Operationally Critical Threat, Asset, and Vulnerability Evaluation (OCTAVE) methodology. OCTAVE focuses on evaluating risks from an operational perspective rather than technological risks. OCTAVE encourages a culture of security awareness and proactive risk management within the organization.

There are mainly five steps in OCTAVE to support operational risks, as shown in the following *Figure 1.9*:

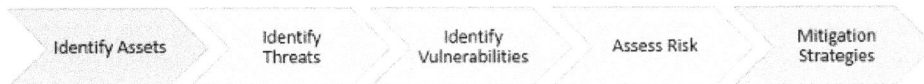

Figure 1.9: Five steps of OCTAVE

Let us look at the steps in detail:

1. **Identify assets**: This is the first step to list and categorize all critical assets within the organization.

2. **Identify threats**: This step identifies all the potential threats that could impact the listed assets.

3. **Identify vulnerabilities**: This step is the essential to determine the vulnerabilities that could be exploited by threats.

4. **Assess risks**: This step assesses risks by determining the likelihood and impact of threats exploiting vulnerabilities.

5. **Develop mitigation strategies**: This is the final step to develop mitigation strategies to address the identified risks.

NIST

The NIST framework is developed by The *National Institute of Standards and Technology* to help organizations identify, analyze, and manage security threats. NIST offers a threat modeling methodology that focuses on data security by providing guidelines and best practices.

The threat modeling approach presented in the *NIST 800-154* publication has the following four steps:

- Identify and characterize the system and data of interest.
- Identify and select the attack vectors to be included in the model.
- Characterize the security controls for mitigating the attack vectors.
- Analyze the threat model.

Data privacy

In simple terms data privacy refers to the proper handling of personal data or **personally identifiable information** (**PII**) data such as names, addresses, social security numbers and credit card numbers, etc. Data privacy is not limited to personal data but also includes sensitive data, financial data, **personal health information** (**PHI**), intellectual property data, etc. within an organization.

Data privacy or information privacy is focused on how data should be collected, stored, managed, shared, archived and deleted. Data privacy complies with data privacy laws, such as *General Data Protection Regulation* (*GDPR*) and *Health Insurance Portability and Accountability Act* (*HIPAA*). Data privacy deals with purpose of data collection, processing, privacy preferences of individual and data governance.

Data privacy is actually a part of data protection that covers the secure handling of data in compliance with data protection regulations. The following figure explains the component of data protection and some examples to correlate the difference between data security and data privacy (often individuals get confused with both these terms):

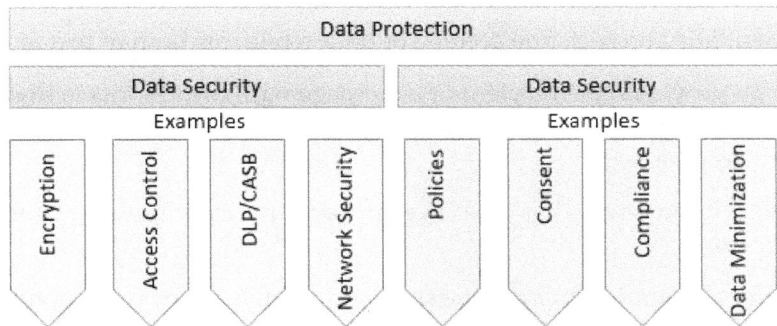

Figure 1.10: Data protection

Data privacy is generally composed of the following six elements:

- **Consent**: Consent refers to acquiring permission from an individual before collecting, using and sharing personal data.

- **Data security**: Data security refers to protecting data from unauthorized access, malicious attack, theft, breaches, etc. by implementing security controls, like firewall, access control, encryption etc.

- **Transparency**: Transparency means that the individual should be informed about each action, how the data is collected, processed and shared.

- **Data minimization**: Data minimization refers to the principle of collecting the minimum data required for a specific purpose and retaining it for duration it is needed.

- **Right of individuals**: Right of individual means individual has rights to access, modify, delete and restrict use of their personal data.

- **Compliance**: Compliance ensures that an organizations follows legal requirements, implements best practices, and are held accountable for their data handling practices.

Conclusion

In this chapter, we discussed key security principles and how to use them to keep data safe in an organization. We explored the SDLC, which shows how to manage data from start to finish. We also focused on threat modeling which provides useful frameworks for handling the data lifecycle. Finally, we covered the basics of data privacy principles.

In the next chapter, we will learn about governance structure, NIST framework and governance policies.

Key terms

- Confidentiality protects the secrecy of data while it is both at rest and in transit.

- Integrity provides the recipient of a message with the assurance that data was not altered (intentionally or unintentionally) between the time it was created and the time it was accessed.

- Availability ensures that the system or applications are running without interruptions.

- Data lifecycle management is the strategic practice of applying policies, processes, and technologies to effectively manage data throughout its life-time from creation to deletion.

- AAA is a security framework for controlling and tracking user access within a system or network.

- **STRIDE**: Useful for evaluating security at various levels, such as network, application, system.

- **PASTA**: Useful for simulating and analyzing attack scenarios.

- **OCTAVE**: Useful for assessing risks from an operational perspective.

- **MITRE**: Useful for understanding adversary behaviour of threats.

Join our book's Discord space

Join the book's Discord Workspace for Latest updates, Offers, Tech happenings around the world, New Release and Sessions with the Authors:

https://discord.bpbonline.com

CHAPTER 2
Governance Structure and Policy

Introduction

This chapter introduces the concept of organizational governance and explains how setting goals and objectives supports effective governance. It starts by outlining the key principle of governance: Establishing top-level objectives and policies. This foundation ensures that the organization's strategy, policies, and resources align with its goals and values. The chapter also explores the governance structure, detailing the roles and responsibilities necessary for effective governance. It highlights how these roles contribute to ensuring that the organization's strategies and resources are properly aligned with its overarching goals and values.

In addition to governance principles and strategies, the chapter discusses the importance of organizational culture, policies, and standards in managing operations effectively. Finally, it provides an overview of various governance frameworks, including **control objectives for information and related technology** (**COBIT**), *International Organization for Standardization (ISO)*/IEC 27000, **Information Technology Infrastructure Library** (**ITIL**), and **Capability Maturity Model Integration** (**CMMI**), demonstrating how these frameworks can be used to enhance governance practices within an organization.

Structure

The chapter covers the following main topics:

- Principle of governance
- Governance structure
- System authorization roles
- Governance culture
- Governance policies and standards
- Governance framework

Objectives

By the end of this chapter, you will have a solid grasp of core governance principles, organizational structure, and culture. You will be familiar with the roles and responsibilities of various stakeholders within the organization and will understand how different governance frameworks can support the organization's objectives and operations.

Principle of governance

Governance starts with the establishment of top-level objectives and policies that are translated into more actions, processes, and procedures across each department in the organization. Every organization has top-level management, including the board of directors, chief executive officers, top-level governing body, etc. to establish the objective of an organization. Governance drives the objective of an organization and comprises of both internal and external governance. External governance can be in the form of laws, regulations, industry standards, and other sources of requirements from the outside. Internal governance refers to the structures and processes within the organization itself that support external governance. For example, if there is a compliance requirement to protect sensitive data using specific controls, then policies and procedures must support those requirements. Let me briefly discuss the ISO standards that support the governance principle.

International organization for standardization

ISO is an independent and internationally recognized standard that provide guidelines to help organizations in improving their processes, products, and services globally. There are various series of ISO standards that ensure quality, safety, efficiency, information security, and interoperability across various industries and sectors. They are as follows:

- **ISO 9000 series**: ISO 9000 standards focus on quality management and provide the framework to ensure the organization's products and services meet the regulatory requirements.

- **ISO 14000 series**: ISO 14000 standards focus on environment management and provide a framework to guide organizations in minimizing environmental impact as per regulations.

- **ISO 27000 series**: ISO 27000 standards focus on information security management and provide guidance to manage and protect information security in an organization. This standard is very common and covers areas, such as risk management, data protection, and security controls to ensure that sensitive information is safe from any threats.

- **ISO 37000 series**: ISO 37000 standards focus on ethical governance practice and provide guidance for governing bodies to clearly define their purpose and values.

- **ISO 45000 series**: ISO 45000 standards focus on occupational health and safety management and provide guidance on managing workplace health and safety risks, prevent work-related injuries and illnesses.

Let us understand the ISO 37000 standard in detail to understand the governance standard.

ISO/IEC 37000

ISO 37000 provides guidance for governing bodies to clearly define their purpose and values, align their strategies with these goals, and ensure they create value for all stakeholders to achieve their objectives effectively. ISO 37000 includes the following:

- **ISO 37001**: The ISO 37001 standard focuses on anti-bribery management systems and provides guidance on implementing, maintaining, reviewing, and improving an anti-bribery management system within an organization.

- **ISO 37002**: The ISO 37002 focuses on whistleblowing management systems and provide guidance on implementing, maintaining, reviewing, and improving a whistleblowing management system within an organization.

- **ISO 37003**: The ISO 37003 focuses on the management of legal risk associated with bribery and provides guidance on how organizations can identify, assess, and manage legal risks associated with bribery.

- **ISO 37004**: ISO 37004 focuses on monitoring the implementation of an anti-bribery management system and provides guidance on how organizations can monitor and measure the effectiveness of their anti-bribery management system.

The following figure explains the 11 topics about governance principle:

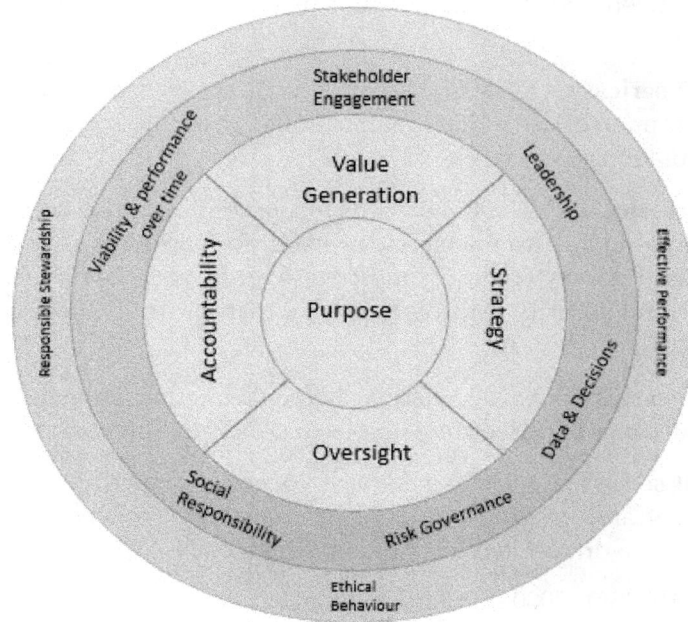

Figure 2.1: *Organization governance overview*

ISO 37000 is a purpose-centric guidance that helps boards or leaders to take better governance decisions. The guidance explains what good governance looks like across the following 11 topics:

- **Purpose**: The reason for existence from all perspectives.
- **Value model**: Components needed to create and generate value to achieve the purpose.
- **Strategy**: Plans and actions to align with the value generation model.
- **Oversight**: Monitoring performance to ensure the organization meets its goals.
- **Accountability**: Holding people responsible as per the governing body's authority.
- **Stakeholder engagement**: Interacting with stakeholders and meeting their expectations.
- **Leadership**: Leading ethically and effectively.
- **Data and decisions**: Using data to inform decision-making.
- **Risk governance**: Managing uncertainty to support the organization's purpose and goals.
- **Social responsibility**: Making transparent decisions that meet societal expectations.

- **Viability and performance over time**: Staying sustainable and effective for both current and future generations.

Note: Core principles of good corporate governance to outperform other organizations are fairness, accountability, responsibility, disclosure, and transparency.

Governance structure

Every organization has their own way for managing business. Most organizations are setup by function, which means the organization has different departments, each handling specific tasks to help achieve the company's goals. For example, an organization focused on developing applications might have separate departments for infrastructure engineering, application development, quality testing, marketing, risk and compliance, etc.

The governance structure ensures that strategy, policies, and resources are aligned with the goals and values of the organization. The governance structure usually includes the board of directors, who set the organization's goal and supervises management, and executive leaders, like the **chief executive officer** (**CEO**), **chief information security officer** (**CISO**), and **chief technology officer** (**CTO**), who carry out these goals and run daily operations. Some organizations have a special committee for different tasks, like managing risk, auditing, and handling compliance.

Security is considered the utmost priority for all organizations and all members of governance structure, including employees, play a crucial role in managing risk. Each level in an organizational hierarchy is directly or indirectly linked to each other, and the risk involved in any department will affect the overall risk of the organization. Let me take an example as shown in the following figure to explain the governance structure:

Figure 2.2: *Governance structure*

Roles and responsibilities

Organizations can establish a robust governance structure by clearly defining the roles and responsibilities that promotes accountability, transparency, and effective decision-making. Following are the key roles and responsibilities associated with governance structure.

Board of directors

The board of directors is mainly a group of individuals that comprises of the of CEO, **chief financial officer (CFO)**, CTO, executives, and independent directors elected by shareholders. Board of directors is the highest governing body in an organization that oversee the business strategy and making decisions.

Their responsibilities are as follows:

- To set long-term goals and make sure that the organization is working towards its vision and goal, as per legal requirements.

- To establish a governance framework and a compliance framework to ensure that the organization meets its legal obligations.

- To establish policies and ensure compliance with laws, regulations, and ethical standards.

- To ensure that the company's organizational structure and capabilities are appropriate for implementing the chosen strategies.

- To provide a strategy for a sound Risk Management Framework to effectively monitor and manage risks within an organization.

Committees

In most of the organization. There are mainly four executive committees governed by the board of directors:

- **Risk committee**: The risk committee focuses on managing the risk program in an organization. Following are their responsibilities:

    o To assist the board of directors in overseeing the management's responsibility of implementing an effective Risk Management Framework .

    o To ensure that the Risk Management Framework is designed to identify, assess, and manage organization risk with appropriate controls or safeguards.

    o To review and approve the risk policies, risk assessment and risk analysis.

- **Audit committee**: The audit committee has a critical role in overseeing financial reports, the organization's internal controls, and compliance with laws and regulations. The following are their responsibilities:

- o   To review major accounting and reporting issues, as well as recent updates in rules and regulations, and to understand how these might affect the financial statements.

- o   To oversee the audit results with both management and external auditors, including important issues that need to be shared with them, according to auditing standards.

- o   To assist in managing controls related to financial reporting, information technology security, and operational matters.

- o   To provide a whistleblower program for employees to report unethical behavior or financial irregularities and to ensure the concerns are investigated.

- **Finance committee**: The finance committee overseas the financial health of an organization and monitors the financial statement to ensure accuracy and compliance. Some of the responsibilities are as follows:

- o   To review and approve the organization's capital plan and budget.

- o   To ensure if the organization has enough capital and how it can be increased over the period of time.

- o   To develop and review financial policies and procedures to evaluate financial performance and ensure effective management.

- o   To provide guidance on long-term financial planning, including investment strategies and spending on major capital projects.

- **Nominations committee**: The nomination committee refers to a group of board members who are responsible for the corporate governance of an organization. Some of their responsibilities are:

- o   To oversee the selection and appointment of individuals to the organization's board, senior executive and key leadership positions.

- o   To review the board's skills each year to ensure they help the company meet its goals and align with its strategy.

- o   To understand the company's long-term strategy clearly and make board recruitment decisions based on the company's needs for both the near and distant future.

- o   To access the framework for board performance and recommend improvements to governance practices.

Executive management

Executive management consists of the top leaders in an organization who handle daily operations and carry out the strategies decided by the board of directors. The executive management team usually consists of the CEO, CFO, **chief operating officer** (**COO**) or any respective functional leaders. Some of the responsibilities of executive managements are as follows:

- To enhance the leadership and management systems within the company.

- To promote guidance systems for staff, track the performance and satisfaction of managers, and handle other related tasks.

- To manage multiple ongoing projects, oversee people, address issues, handle meetings, meet deadlines, and prepare presentations simultaneously.

- To drive business growth by making sure all team members are focused on the same goals and promoting collaboration.

- To enhance strong communication skills to clearly convey objectives, ensuring everyone understands their role and feels ready to contribute to the organization's success.

Effective teamwork between team members and between the executive manager and other department heads is key to ensuring productivity and efficiency. Some key executive management roles are given in the following table:

Role	Responsibilities
CEO	Leads the organization, makes major decisions
CFO	Manages financial planning, reporting, and risk
COO	Oversees daily operations and ensures business continuity
CTO	Leads technology strategy and oversees the IT department
CMO	Manages marketing strategies and activities

Table 2.1: Executive members role

Some CEO responsibilities:

- To set the organization's strategy with input from senior executives and the board.

- To define top-level business goals with the board and senior managers, like the company VP. To ensure that the strategy is implemented effectively, and targets are met.

- To delegate key tasks to senior executives in charge of different departments and ensure they reach their goals.

Some CFO responsibilities:

- To oversee the creation of financial reports for shareholders, investors, government, and the public.

- To manage cash flow to maintain enough liquidity and forecast future cash flow.

- To lead the finance department and work with the commercial team to ensure the business achieves a good **return on investment** (**ROI**).

Some COO responsibilities:

- To oversee the daily operations of all departments and ensure departmental and business goals are met.

- To evaluate the organization's performance and report metrics back to the CEO.

- To manage relationships with partners and vendors and collaborate with the CEO to set company strategy and goals.

Some CTO responsibilities:

- To define and implement the organization's technical vision and stay updated on technology trends.

- To lead and manage the technology team, including software developers, engineers, data scientists, and other IT professionals.

- To design the organization's technical systems and infrastructure to ensure they are scalable, secure, and reliable.

- To lead research and development, try out new technologies, and encourage creativity within the tech team.

Some CMO responsibilities:

- To increase brand awareness and make sure the brand's internal identity matches public perception.

- To set and manage the marketing and sales budget and monitor their performance.

- To understand customer interactions with the brand and strengthen its market position.

- To lead customer service and relationship management and oversee product development and new initiatives.

Department managers

Department managers lead teams focused on specific areas, like sales or marketing. Successful department managers need key skills such as strong communication, problem-solving, teamwork, organization, and employee management. They typically work in an office environment where they oversee teams and handle daily operations.

Their responsibilities are as follows:

- To guide employees and handle responsibilities like setting strategic goals and ensuring that projects succeed.

- To oversee the daily activities in their division, set goals for the department, manage the budget, and ensure that employees work productively and efficiently.

- To liaise with upper management, like company executives, to create project funding plans and budgets.

- To monitor, evaluate, and oversee employees to make sure they complete their tasks according to company standards.

- To conduct regular performance evaluations to review employee progress and assist in improving their skills.

- To communicate the job expectations to employees to ensure quality and delegating tasks based on experience and job roles.

System authorization roles

Every organization will have different hierarchy for governance based on the nature of the business. The system authorization program is driven by perspective and needs within an organization. For the program to work effectively, it is important to clearly define and document everyone's roles and responsibilities to prevent confusion and ensure all areas are covered. Following is the standard hierarchy for most of the organization:

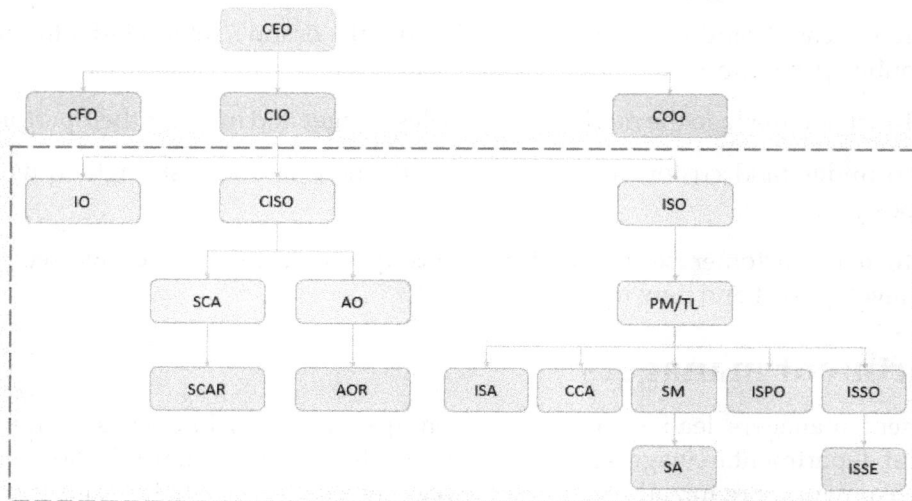

Figure 2.3: Organization roles

Here is the detail of each role highlighted in red dotted box:

Role	Responsibilities
Information owner (IO)	Safeguard data within an organization and manage risks associated with the data throughout its lifecycle.
Chief information security officer (CISO)	Oversee organization's security strategy and risk management.
Information security officer (ISO)	Oversee the overall management and security of an information system, setting security policies and managing risk.
Security control assessor (SCA)	Evaluate and assess the effectiveness of implemented security controls.
Authorizing official (AO)	Grant formal authorization for a system to operate based on a security risk assessment and compliance requirement.
Security control assessor representative (SCAR)	Assist the SCA by supporting security assessment, gathering and reviewing evidence.
Authorizing official representative (AOR)	Assists the AO by providing recommendations, supporting documentation, and security assessments.
Project manager/team lead (PM/TL)	Oversee the successful completion of projects, lead the team, coordinate tasks and addresses any risks.
Information security architect (ISA)	Design and implement information security architecture aligned with the strategic and business objectives.
Common control provider (CCA)	Implement and maintain security controls shared across multiple systems or organizational units.
Information system security officer (ISSO)	Manage and secure all security aspects of the system.
Information system security engineer (ISSE)	Assess security risks, recommend and integrate security controls.
System manager (SM)	Oversee the day-to-day operations, management, and maintenance of an information system.
Information system privacy officer (ISPO)	Assess privacy risks and oversee the implementation of privacy policies and controls.
System administrator (SA)	Maintain organization's IT systems, monitor system performance and troubleshoot issues.

Table 2.2: System authorization roles

Governance culture

Organizational culture, or company culture, is the set of shared values, attitudes, and practices that make up a company's personality. It greatly affects how satisfied employees are with their work. During organizational change, culture can either help or hinder the process. A culture that values collaboration and flexibility will adapt well, while a rigid culture might find lot of difficulty. Leaders need to understand organization's culture when managing change.

Leaders play a crucial role in shaping organizational behavior through their interactions with each other and the wider team. Their actions and attitudes define the standard for how employees are expected to behave. Ideally, these behavioral norms should reflect the organization's stated values and mission. However, there can often be a disconnect between the stated culture and the actual culture, which is observed through day-to-day practices and behaviors. This gap between the stated and actual culture reveals the organization's true cultural landscape.

Organizational culture is always evolving, influenced by the times as well as the actions of leaders and staff. As conditions change and new challenges arise, the culture adjusts accordingly. This dynamic nature of culture is crucial in risk management. It affects how an organization perceives and responds to potential threats. A culture that embraces adaptability and proactive problem-solving will handle risks more effectively than one that is rigid and resistant to change.

There are mainly four types of company culture:

- **Type one**: Clan culture

  Clan culture emphasizes on teamwork and collaboration across teams, with a flat organizational structure. Clan culture provides friendly working environment and managers often act as mentors rather than providing orders.

- **Type two**: Adhocracy culture

  Adhocracy culture encourages people to share ideas and supports taking risks. This leads to significant innovation, learning, and growth for both employees and the organization.

- **Type three**: Market culture

  Market culture emphasizes on financial success and meeting goals. focuses on how each employee contributes to generating revenue. Every employee has a specific role in achieving these goals and it can be high-pressure environment but also rewarding.

- **Type four**: Hierarchy culture

  Hierarchy culture focuses on clear career paths and well-defined managerial processes. This is a controlled culture and most activities follow established procedures, with less emphasis on innovation and creative thinking.

Governance policies and standards

Good governance should provide a basic set of policies that guide how work should be done effectively and efficiently within an organization. Every organization will have different set of policies and procedures depending on the type of business functions. The board of directors along with senior executive drive the security policies and procedures. These policies and procedures need to be applied across the entire organization to ensure that security works effectively at every level.

Governance policies in simple terms are formal rules and guidelines enabled by board of directors to effectively lead and govern its operations. The board sets clear policies to guide how both individual members and the whole group should act to promote good governance. These policies outline how the board should make decisions, guide management including its goals, responsibilities, and how it should be held accountable. There are various policies focused on specific area like ethical behavior, laws and regulations, risk management, accountability, etc. Some examples for a few specific policies are as follows:

- **Risk management**: The risk management policies cover the various steps of risk management that includes guidance on risk identification, risk assessment and risk management process.

- **Ethical behavior**: The governance policies cover the standards for ethical behavior that covers conflict of interests as well as confidentiality and integrity to ensure ethical conduct.

- **Laws and regulations**: The governance policies adhere to regulations and legal requirement to ensure the organization comply with regulatory issues and industry standards.

Governance standards are specific criteria or benchmarks that guide how policies should be implemented and maintained. They help ensure that governance practices are consistent, effective, and aligned with best practices.

Governance framework

IT governance solutions are essential for organizations to manage and control their IT resources efficiently. It provides a structured approach to ensure that IT investments align with business objectives and deliver value. By implementing IT governance frameworks, organizations can establish clear guidelines for IT decision-making, prioritize projects based on strategic goals, and ensure that IT operations are both cost-effective and secure. These solutions help in managing risks, complying with regulations, and optimizing the use of technology to support overall business strategy.

There are various popular IT governance frameworks like COBIT, ITIL, and ISO/IEC 38500 etc. that provide organized methods for managing IT services and resources. These frameworks provide clear guidelines on defining roles, setting performance goals, and improving processes over time. Let us look at some frameworks in detail.

Control objectives for information and related technology

COBIT is an IT management framework developed by the **Information Systems Audit and Control Association (ISACA)** to help businesses develop, organize, and implement strategies around information technology management and governance. The COBIT framework is designed to align IT management with business goals. It outlines a set of general processes for managing IT, detailing each process with its inputs, outputs, key activities, objectives, performance measures, and a basic maturity model. This structure helps organizations ensure their IT supports business needs effectively and allows for continuous improvement.

COBIT governance system components

Each organization needs to create, customize, and maintain a governance system with various components in order to meet governance and management goals. The governance system interaction enables the holistic approach in an organization. Governance system components include processes, organizational structures, policies, information, culture, skills, IT services and infrastructure, etc. as shown in the following figure:

Figure 2.4: COBIT governance system

The COBIT governance system provides a framework for managing and overseeing IT in organizations:

- **Processes**: The process is created to manage IT effectively and align IT objectives with business objectives. Processes are organized practices and activities designed to achieve goals and produce results that support IT objectives.

- **Organizational structures**: Organizational structures define the roles and responsibilities and support key decision-making capabilities in an organization.

- **Principles, policies and procedures**: Principles, policies and procedures are the important aspect to ensure consistent and effective operations within an organization.

- **Information**: Information is everywhere in an organization, including all the data it produces and uses. COBIT focuses on the information needed for the governance system to work effectively.

- **Culture, ethics and behavior**: Culture, ethics, and behavior are often overlooked but are crucial for successful governance and management.

- **People, skills and competencies**: People, skills, and competencies are essential for making good decisions, performing tasks, taking corrective actions, and completing tasks successfully to support organization goals.

- **Services, infrastructure, and application**: Services, infrastructure, and applications are essential components of IT systems and includes infrastructure, technology, and applications that provide the organization governance system.

Principles of COBIT framework

COBIT 2019 has six principles essential for the effective management and governance of the enterprise. They are shown in the following figure:

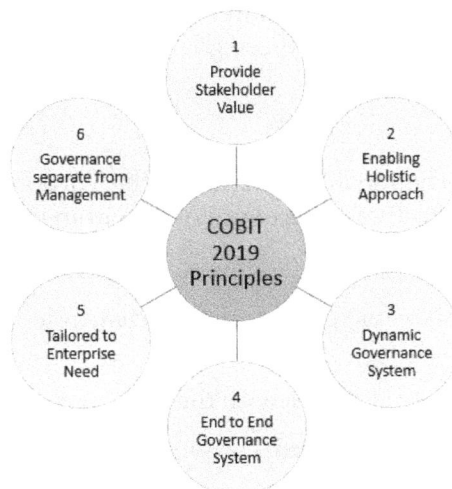

Figure 2.5: COBIT 2019 principles

Let us go through the following six principles in detail:

- **Principle one**: Provide stakeholder value. The first principle states that COBIT framework enables to meet all the needs and requirements of your stakeholders by offering them appropriate values. Good governance and management are crucial to deliver the business value to the stakeholders. This means balancing benefits, risks, and resources, and having a clear strategy to achieve this value.

- **Principle two**: Enabling holistic approach. The second principle encourages a comprehensive approach by considering all aspects of IT and business processes, which means your entire organization must work as a single unit.

- **Principle three**: Dynamic governance system. The third principle insists that a governance system should be flexible. When changes are made, like updates in strategy or technology, their impact on the governance system needs to be reviewed. This helps keep the system effective and ready for the future.

- **Principle four**: End-to-end governance system. The fourth principle enables to focus on an entire organization. This principle ensures that IT is fully integrated with business processes, so all aspects of IT contribute to organizational objectives. It should cover every technology and information process used to achieve the organization's goals, no matter where it is located.

- **Principle five**: Tailored to enterprise needs. The fifth principle is focused on the tailored approach. A governance system should be customized to fit the specific needs of the organization. This involves adjusting and prioritizing its components based on key design factors relevant to the enterprise.

- **Principle six**: Governance separate from management. The sixth and final principle focuses on separating governance and management due to different objectives. Governance sets the goals and ensures they are met, while management handles the day-to-day work to achieve those goals.

ISO/IEC 38500

ISO/IEC 38500 is the international standard for the corporate governance of IT and provides guidance for the effective governance of IT within organizations.

ISO/IEC 38500 standard is based on the following six principles:

- **Responsibility**: This principle establishes clear roles and responsibilities for IT governance.

- **Strategy**: This principle aligns IT with the organization's strategic objectives.

- **Acquisition**: This principle ensures acquisitions for valid reasons.

- **Performance**: This principle ensures the necessary level of performance by measuring and monitoring the performance of IT systems and processes.

- **Conformance**: This principle ensures that IT practices conform with laws and regulations.

- **Human behavior**: This principle ensures respect for humans and manages the human aspects of IT governance.

ISO/IEC 38500 provides guidelines for overseeing and making decisions about an organization's IT and communication services. It helps ensure that IT is managed effectively and supports the organization's goals.

ISO/IEC 27000

The ISO/IEC 27000 standards, also known as the **information security management system (ISMS)** standards, are a set of standards for managing information security. ISO/IEC 27000 is similar to other management standards, such as those for quality or environmental protection. It covers a wide range of topics, including security, privacy, and IT, making it useful for organizations of all sizes. ISO/IEC 27001 outlines the overall framework for an ISMS, while ISO/IEC 27002 offers detailed guidelines on specific controls and objectives. The controls presented within the document act as a guide for those who are responsible for initiating, implementing, or maintaining an ISMS.

The ISO 27000 series include several standards, each with a different focus on ISMS. They are divided into the following three categories:

- **Requirements**: Standards that specify what needs to be done.

- **General guidelines**: Standards offering broad guidance on best practices.

- **Sector-specific guidelines**: Standards tailored to specific industries.

The following six key standards in the ISO 27000 series play a major role in managing ISMS:

- **ISO/IEC 27001**: Defines the requirements for setting up and maintaining an ISMS, including necessary controls.

- **ISO/IEC 27002**: Offers the guidelines on implementing information security controls based on ISO/IEC 27001.

- **ISO/IEC 27003**: Provides guidance on understanding and applying ISO/IEC 27001.

- **ISO/IEC 27004**: Provides guidelines on how to monitor and evaluate the effectiveness of an ISMS.

- **ISO/IEC 27005**: Offers guidance for assessing and managing information security risks.

- **ISO/IEC 27006**: Outlines requirements for certification bodies that audit and certify ISMSs.

ISO/IEC 27001:2022

The ISO 27001:2022 Annex A controls have been updated to address current security challenges. While the main ISMS processes remain the same, the Annex A controls have been revised to better handle modern risks. The updates cover the following four areas:

- **Organizational**: 37 controls

  Organizational controls include rules and measures that guide an organization's overall approach to data protection, and this covers policies, procedures, and structures, etc.

- **People**: 8 controls

  The people control helps businesses to manage how staff handle data and interact with each other. The people control includes managing secure hiring, personnel security, and providing training and awareness.

- **Physical**: 14 controls

  The physical control safeguards and protects physical assets. The physical control includes access control systems, guest procedures, proper disposal of assets, storage rules, clear desk policies etc. to keep confidential information secure.

- **Technological**: 34 controls

  The technological control sets rules for a secure IT system. It covers authentication methods, system settings, backup strategies, information logging, etc.

Information Technology Infrastructure Library

ITIL, is a detailed framework designed to help organizations manage their IT services efficiently. It offers a structured approach to IT service management by providing guidelines, best practices, and processes. These tools ensure that IT services are aligned with the organization's business needs and goals, leading to improved service quality and better overall performance.

ITIL has seven guiding principles, as described:

- **Focus on value**: The first ITIL principle focuses on delivering value to customers. IT services should be seen as tools to achieve customer results, not just technical solutions.

- **Collaborate and promote visibility**: This ITIL principle focuses on collaboration as successful IT service management. ITIL promotes open communication and teamwork and encourages transparency and shared responsibility to make better decisions.

- **Optimize and automate**: This principle encourages ongoing improvements and automation. The repetitive tasks can be automated to streamline processes and deliver value-added service.

- **Start where you are**: This principle encourages organizations to review their current state and improve their existing processes and practices.

- **Progress iteratively with feedback**: This principle is focused on continuous improvement. This means organizations should regularly plan, implement, and review their processes and services to keep making them better.

- **Keep it simple and practical**: This ITIL principle focus on simplicity and avoiding any complexity. It focuses on solutions that are straightforward, effective, and aligned with business goals.

- **Think and work holistically**: This principle promotes a holistic approach, guiding organizations to consider the entire service lifecycle and all aspects of service delivery. ITIL offers practical advice on managing and improving IT services, including the roles and responsibilities required to support and operate them.

Information Technology Infrastructure Library service lifecycle stage

The ITIL framework mainly contains five stages, as mentioned in the *Figure 2.5*. Every stage relates to each other, and the stages are in continuous cycle starting with service strategy, as shown in the following figure:

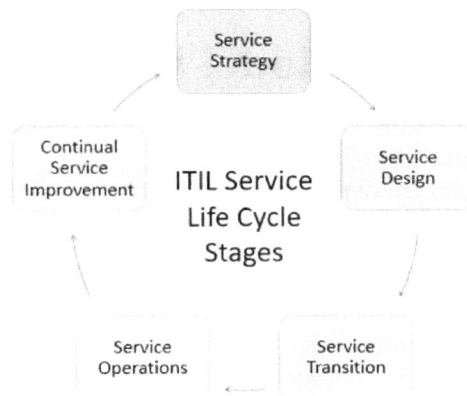

Figure 2.6: *ITIL Service lifecycle stage*

Let us look at the stages in detail:

- **Service strategy**: Service strategy ensures that IT actions match business needs. IT organizations do this by planning how to best serve customers and working with the business to identify necessary IT services and capabilities.

- **Service design**: Service design stage is followed by the service strategy stage once the IT decides on the services to develop. In this stage, new IT services are created, and existing ones are improved to add more value to the business.

- **Service transition**: After designing a service, it needs to be built and added to the IT infrastructure. The service transition phase manages how new services are created and deployed to avoid disrupting existing ones.

- **Service operation**: Service operation ensures that IT services run smoothly and efficiently for customers. This stage involves handling daily tasks, user requests, fixing issues, and managing infrastructure.

- **Continual service improvement (CSI)**: CSI is the final stage in which IT services are monitored and reviewed for improvements. A CSI manager may suggest and track changes to see how they affect efficiency and costs.

Practical illustration

Each stage has various process areas. Examples of a few processes are:

- **Service strategy**: Demand management, service portfolio management.
- **Service design**: Capacity management, service level management.
- **Service transition**: Change management, configuration management.
- **Service operation**: Incident management, problem management.
- **CSI**: Seven step improvement.

Capability Maturity Model Integration

CMMI is a framework that helps organizations improve processes across various areas, such as software development, project management, and service delivery. It is designed to help improve performance, increase efficiency and achieve higher-quality outcomes.

CMMI has five maturity levels that help organizations improve their processes progressively. Maturity levels range from one to five, with level five being the highest and the target that organizations aim to achieve. CMMI Level 0 indicates that an organization has an no adequate or incomplete process for managing its projects. Following are the CMMI levels that establish the current maturity status of an organization and outline how it can progress:

- **Level 0—incomplete**: At this stage, the goal may not have been established and work may not have been completed.

- **Level 1—initial**: This is the initial stage where the processes are seen as unpredictable and poorly controlled. The environment may not be stable that could lead to increased risk and inefficiency.

- **Level 2—managed**: This is the second stage where the processes are characterized by projects and are frequently reactive. The projects are planned and controlled at this level but still have lots of issues.

- **Level 3—defined**: This is the third stage where the processes are well-characterized and well-understood. The organization is more proactive than reactive, and the organization wide standards provide guidance.

- **Level 4—quantitatively managed**: This is the fourth stage where the processes are measured and controlled. The organization is utilizing quantitative data to implement predictable processes that meet organizational goals and is ahead of risks, with more data-driven insight.

- **Level 5—optimizing**: This is final stage where the processes are stable and flexible. The organizational focus is on continued improvement and responding to changes in an efficient manner.

When organizations reach Levels four and five, they are highly mature, constantly evolving and adapting to meet stakeholder and customer needs.

Cybersecurity Maturity Model Certification

The *Department of Defense (DoD)* created the **Cybersecurity Maturity Model Certification** (**CMMC**) to improve the enforcement of existing cybersecurity rules, especially for protecting **federal contract information** (**FCI**) and **Controlled Unclassified Information** (**CUI**). While CMMC does not add new security requirements, it requires stricter enforcement.

Under the previous system, defense contractors could self-assess their compliance. With CMMC, most contractors must now undergo independent assessments by **certified third-party organizations** (**C3PAOs**) to confirm compliance. The CMMC has three levels of compliance, determined by the type of information the organization handles. To work on defense contracts, organizations must comply with the CMMC level specified in the contract and undergo the appropriate assessments.

CMMC 2.0 simplified the framework to three levels, as shown in the following figure:

Figure 2.7: CMMC levels

Here is the detail of each level:

- Level 1 applies to organizations handling FCI only. Organizations at this level must perform annual self-assessments to verify compliance.

- Level 2 applies to organizations that handle CUI. Compliance at this level involves meeting the 110 security controls specified in NIST SP 800-171. Most organizations at this level will need to undergo third-party assessments every three years.

- Level 3 applies to organizations working with CUI and facing **advanced persistent threats (APTs)**, state-sponsored attacks targeting critical defense programs. To achieve Level 3, organizations must comply with both the 110 NIST SP 800-171 security controls and an additional 24 enhanced security controls from NIST SP 800-172.

Factor Analysis of Information Risk

Factor Analysis of Information Risk (**FAIR**) is a governance model that helps organizations understand, analyze, and quantify information risk. The framework helps organizations to identify potential risks and assess their impact by evaluating factors such as likelihood and potential harm. FAIR is the only international standard for measuring information and operational risk in financial terms. It offers a model for analyzing and quantifying cyber and operational risks, unlike frameworks that use qualitative charts or numerical scales. FAIR helps build a strong approach to managing information risk.

Steps for Factor Analysis of Information Risk assessment

Perform the following steps to use the FAIR assessment effectively and reduce the risk of breaches and penalties:

- **Organize system**: This is the first step to identifying and listing your system components, including data, vendors, suppliers, access points, and any third-party involvement.

- **Identify potential threats**: The second step identify various risks, such as data breaches, unauthorized access, and exposed information.

- **Organize risks and consequences**: Once the risks are identified, this step classifies risks as high, medium, or low.

- **Evaluate controls**: The fourth step that assess the effectiveness of your security measures, like authentication and administrative controls.

- **Calculate impact**: This is the final step that determines the potential impact of each risk and threat.

Factor Analysis of Information Risk model

FAIR risk assessment focuses on the likelihood of events rather than just their possibility. It prioritizes evaluating how probable a risk is rather than simply considering if it might occur:

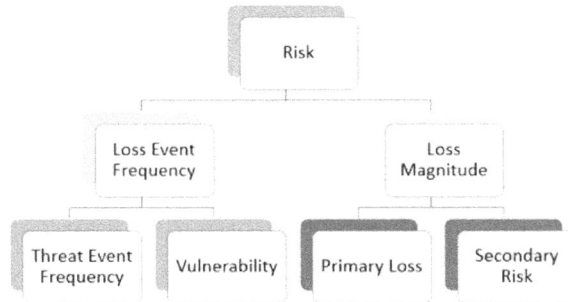

Figure 2.8: *FAIR risk model*

Conclusion

In this chapter, we covered governance principles, organizational structure, and culture, which helped align an organization's activities with its strategic goals and regulatory requirements. We explored how clearly defined roles and responsibilities improve communication and enhance the overall efficiency. We also discussed the governance framework, which offers the structure and guidelines needed to ensure the organization operates effectively, meets its goals and manages risks well.

In the next chapter, we will delve into risk assessment methodologies, compliance standards, and the NIST risk framework.

Key terms

- **ISO 27001**: Focuses on information security controls to protect people, processes, and technology through three main principles known as the CIA triad.

- **ITIL:** Focus on service management and delivery, and ITIL is operational.

- **COBIT**: Focus on management and governance of information technology business process.

- **CMMI and ISO 9001**: Focus on enhancing the quality, efficiency, and effectiveness of organizations, but they take different approaches to achieve this goal.

- A governance framework, or governance structure, is a comprehensive system of rules, procedures, and responsibilities that guides how an organization operates and interacts with its stakeholders.

Join our book's Discord space

Join the book's Discord Workspace for Latest updates, Offers, Tech happenings around the world, New Release and Sessions with the Authors:

https://discord.bpbonline.com

CHAPTER 3
Risk Assessment and Compliance Standards

Introduction

This chapter introduces the concept of risk governance and the methodologies used for risk assessment to protect an organization from cyberattacks and other hazards. It begins by defining the organization's risk appetite and tolerance, which outline the levels of risk the organization is willing to accept and manage. It also provides guidance on setting up a risk framework, including the establishment of a risk committee and the use of effective methods for assessing and analyzing risks, such as evaluating potential threats and their impacts.

The chapter differentiates between qualitative and quantitative risk analysis and details the four steps of the risk assessment process aimed at minimizing the impact of risks on business operations. It focuses on the *National Institute of Standards and Technology* (*NIST*) **Risk Management Framework** (**RMF**), explaining its seven steps for effective risk management, and includes information on *NIST Special Publication (SP) 800-53* for assessing security and privacy controls, as well as setting baseline controls.

Additionally, the chapter provides an overview of various compliance standards, including *Payment Card Industry Data Security Standard* (*PCI DSS*), *General Data Protection Regulation* (*GDPR*), and *Health Insurance Portability and Accountability Act* (*HIPAA*). It highlights how aligning these compliance requirements with organizational objectives helps in accurately identifying and managing potential risks.

Structure

The chapter covers the following topics:

- Risk governance
- Risk analysis
- Risk management process
- Risk assessment
- Risk assessment matrix
- NIST Risk Management Framework
- NIST guidance on preparing risk management
- NIST Special Publication 800-53
- Compliance standard

Objectives

By the end of this chapter, you will have a solid understanding of risk governance, risk strategies, and risk analysis. You will learn about risk assessment methods and risk management processes in detail. You will also become familiar with international standards like the NIST RMF and NIST SP 800-53, as well as various compliance standards such as PCI DSS, ISO 27000, HIPPA, etc.

Risk governance

As you have observed in the previous chapter, governance sets the rules for an organization, covering legal, ethical, and professional standards. Risk governance specifically focuses on the rules for managing risks related to both business operations and IT systems. Risk governance is established by executive management and sets the framework for how an organization approaches risk. Risk governance begins with defining the organization's risk appetite and tolerance, which outline the levels of risk the organization is willing to accept and manage. This is complemented by a risk strategy that provides a roadmap for identifying, assessing, and addressing risks.

In addition to these foundational elements, risk governance involves implementing various policies that support effective risk management. This includes adopting specific methodologies for risk assessment and analysis to evaluate potential threats and their impacts. Organizations also need to establish procedures for risk treatment and response, determining how to mitigate or handle risks when they arise. Continuous risk monitoring processes are crucial for tracking and reviewing risks over time to ensure that the management strategies remain effective and relevant.

Risk governance is a framework with processes, structures, and practices to ensure risks are managed well and support the organization's goals. The key components of risk governance are shown in the following figure:

Figure 3.1: *Components of risk governance*

Let us go through these components in detail:

- **Risk identification**: The first and most important step in managing risks is identifying potential risks. These risks can include financial challenges, operational hurdles, strategic uncertainties, or compliance issues. Organizations need to thoroughly examine their operations to recognize and understand these risks.

  Risk identification involves understanding both internal factors, like weaknesses within the organization, and external factors, such as market changes, that could pose threats or offer opportunities. Organizations use various tools and techniques to uncover potential vulnerabilities. By being proactive at identifying risks, organizations can better prepare to address and overcome them effectively.

- **Risk assessment**: Risk assessment is a key process where identified risks are carefully evaluated using methods like risk matrices and heat maps. By examining factors, such as potential impact and likelihood, organizations can prioritize which risks to address first. This helps them focus their resources on managing the most significant threats.

  A thorough risk assessment gives organizations a clear understanding of their risks, enabling them to make informed decisions and take proactive steps to reduce potential harm. This process helps organizations protect their interests and maintain a secure environment amid changing conditions.

- **Rist mitigation**: Risk mitigation sometimes can be referred as **risk management**. Although risk management has broader aspect that includes creating strategies to reduce, transfer, or accept risk. Risk mitigation and response are key parts of managing risks effectively. Strategies to handle risks, include avoiding them completely, reducing their likelihood or impact, sharing the risks with others, or accepting them as part of doing business.

  Organizations often use these strategies to manage risks successfully. By selecting and applying the right approach, organization can lessen the negative impact of risks and protect their interests.

- **Risk monitoring**: Risk monitoring is essential for effective risk management. This involves continuously monitoring potential risks and new threats. Regular monitoring helps detect any emerging risk quickly that allow organization to take necessary action. Risk monitoring also involves regularly conducting audits and assessments to keep up with any changes in the risk environment.

  Risk reporting is equally important, as it provides stakeholders with timely and accurate information about the organization's risks. This ensures that decision-makers have the right information and insights to make informed decisions and take proactive steps.

- **Risk communication**: Effective communication is vital in risk management. Organizations should setup clear communication channels to share information with employees, management, and external stakeholders. It keeps everyone informed about the risks and the steps being taken to handle them. Regular updates ensure transparency and accountability in managing risks.

  For example, a program manager might hold regular meetings with the team to review risks and mitigation plans. Open communication helps to engage various stakeholders and gather useful insights from various viewpoints. This proactive approach not only helps in the early detection of risks but also ensures that the organization can address them before they escalate.

- **Risk culture**: Risk culture refers to the shared values and behaviors that guide how an organization handles risk. Building a risk-aware culture is key to successful risk management. This means creating an environment where employees are encouraged to actively identify and report risks. It ensures that everyone in the organization understands the importance of addressing risks.

  To promote a positive risk culture, organizations should set clear expectations, offer training and support, and recognize and reward employees who engage in effective risk management. When risk management is seen as a shared responsibility, everyone in the organization becomes more vigilant and engaged in spotting potential issues. Encouraging open communication about risks helps employees feel comfortable reporting potential problems without fear.

- **Risk governance structure**: The effective risk governance framework establishes clear roles and responsibilities for risk management. This typically involves setting up a dedicated risk committee or designating specific risk management roles to senior executives.

  A risk committee oversees the organization's risk management strategy, ensuring that risks are identified, assessed, and addressed appropriately. Senior executives play a key role in integrating risk management into the organization's overall strategy and making high-level decisions on risk-related issues. By defining these roles clearly, organizations can ensure that risk management is systematic and aligned with their goals.

Risk analysis

There are various kinds of risks related to digital assets, systems, and data; organizations must address these risks. Risk management always starts from for upper management, who are responsible for initiating and supporting risk analysis by defining its scope and purpose. The security professional handles the actual risk analysis to support the organization's risk management. Since it is impossible to eliminate all risks from IT systems, upper management must decide which risks are acceptable and which are not. This involves detailed assessments of assets and risks to make the right decisions about risk acceptance.

There are two main approaches to assess the risk in an organization, namely quantitative and qualitative risk analysis. Choosing between these methods depends on factors, such as the organization's objectives, available resources, and risk tolerance. Often, combining both approaches offers a comprehensive view of IT risks, enabling more effective management and decision-making.

Quantitative risk analysis

Quantitative risk assessment involves numerical data and statistical methods to measure risks precisely. This method of risk analysis provides clear, numerical results and generates reports with specific dollar amounts for risk levels, potential losses, countermeasure costs, and safeguard values. This approach is straightforward, especially for those familiar with spreadsheets and budgets, as it assigns a monetary value to each asset and threat.

This approach provides concrete figures on potential impacts and probabilities which makes it useful for scenarios requiring detailed analysis, such as financial forecasting or evaluating system vulnerabilities based on data.

Key elements of quantitative analysis

Quantitative analysis has mainly six elements, as shown in the following figure:

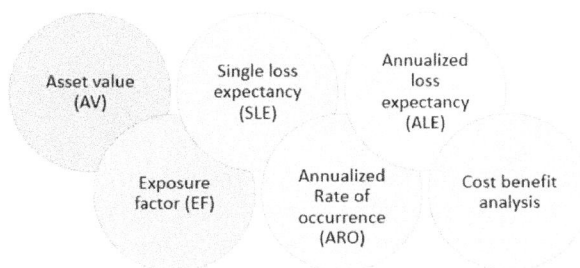

Figure 3.2: Elements of quantitative analysis

Let us learn about the elements:

- **Asset value (AV)**: The dollar value assigned to an asset is known as **AV**.

- **Exposure factor (EF)**: The EF is the percentage of loss an organization would face if a particular asset is affected by a risk.

- **Single loss expectancy (SLE)**: The EF helps calculate the SLE. The SLE is the cost of a single instance where a specific risk harms an asset:

$$SLE = AV \ x \ EF$$

- **Annualized rate of occurrence (ARO)**: The ARO is the expected number of times a specific threat or risk will happen in a year.

- **Annualized loss expectancy (ALE)**: The ALE is the total estimated cost of a specific threat occurring each year for a particular asset:

$$ALE = SLE \ x \ ARO$$

- **Cost benefit analysis**: To determine if a safeguard is worth to implement, calculate its cost, and compare it to the benefits it provides. This helps ensure that the safeguard improves security without being too expensive:

ALE before safeguard – ALE after implementing the safeguard – annual cost of safeguard (ACS) = value of the safeguard to the company

Some steps to calculate quantitative analysis are as follows:

1. List all assets of an organization and assign a value to each known as **AV**.
2. Identify all possible threats for each asset and calculate the EF and SLE for each threat.
3. Assess how likely each threat is to occur within a year, known as **ARO**.
4. Calculate the overall potential loss for each threat, called the **ALE**.
5. Research countermeasures for each threat and determine how they impact ARO and ALE.
6. Conduct a cost/benefit analysis of each countermeasure and choose the best option for managing each threat.

Qualitative risk analysis

Qualitative risk assessment relies on descriptive and subjective evaluations. It focuses on the nature and characteristics of risks, using expert opinions and risk matrices to categorize and understand risks in broader terms. Instead of assigning specific dollar amounts to potential losses, it ranks threats on a scale to evaluate their risks, costs, and impacts. This approach is valuable when numerical data is limited or when a strategic perspective is needed.

Qualitative risk analysis relies on the risk manager's perception and understanding of the severity and likelihood of risks. The goal is to identify and prioritize risks that need more attention, based on their potential impact and probability.

When performing qualitative risk analysis, you can use the following techniques to assess the likelihood and impact of risks:

- **Brainstorming**: Generating ideas about potential risks.
- **Interviewing**: Asking experts about possible risks.
- **Delphi technique**: Gathering opinions from a group of experts.
- **Historical data**: Looking at past risk information.
- **SWOT analysis**: Identifying **strengths, weaknesses, opportunities, and threats (SWOT)**.
- **Risk rating scales**: Using scales to evaluate the severity of risks.
- **Project scope statement**: Defining the project's goals and boundaries.
- **Risk management plan**: Outlining how risks will be managed.
- **Risk register**: Documenting identified risks and their details.
- **Organizational process assets**: Using existing tools and processes for risk management.

Comparison of quantitative and qualitative

Choosing the right method depends on the organization's culture and the specific risks and assets. Often, multiple methods are used together, and their results are compared in the final risk analysis report for upper management.

The following table shows some differences between quantitative and qualitative approaches:

Parameter	Quantitative analysis	Qualitative analysis
Concept	Objective approach and deals with numbers	Subjective approach and deals with descriptions
Value measurement	Data can be measured	Data can be observed but not measured
Complexity	More complex and more time consuming	Less complex and less time consuming
Data	Relies on historical data, financial metrics, and mathematical models	Relies expert opinions, stakeholder input, and descriptive information
Who can perform	Performed by technical or security staff.	Performed by non-security staff

Table 3.1: Quantitative vs qualitative

Risk management process

A risk management strategy is crucial for guiding an organization's approach to managing risks. It helps shape key aspects of the risk management process, including the selection and assessment of security controls, contingency planning, and system authorization decisions. By defining how risks should be managed, the strategy ensures that security measures are appropriate and effective.

Additionally, a well-defined risk management strategy informs both investment and operational decisions. It provides a framework for prioritizing resources and making informed choices about where to allocate funds and efforts. This strategic approach helps organizations balance risk and opportunity, ultimately supporting better decision-making and long-term stability. The following figure shows the risk management process steps:

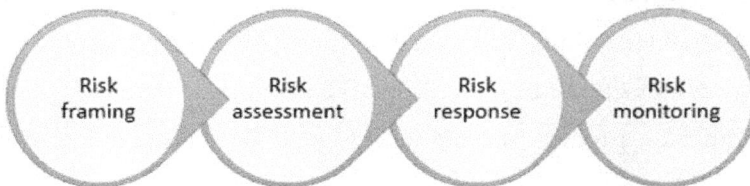

Figure 3.3: Risk management process

Let us look at the steps in detail:

1. **Risk framing**: Risk framing is a crucial initial step in risk management that helps define the context in which risks are assessed and managed. It involves outlining several key elements, including:

    a. Risk assumptions to describe some threats.

    b. Risk constraints, such as legal, regulatory, and contractual requirements.

    Additionally, risk framing addresses the organization's risk tolerance, which determines how much risk it is willing to accept. It considers organizational priorities and trade-offs, helping to align risk management with the overall goals of the organization. This process may also involve detailing the tools and techniques used to provide a comprehensive framework for addressing and mitigating risks effectively.

2. **Risk assessment**: Risk assessment is a critical process that involves identifying potential risks, evaluating the likelihood of their occurrence, and understanding the potential impact they may have on the business. It also includes determining the costs associated with implementing strategies to mitigate, reduce, or eliminate these risks.

3. **Risk response**: Effective risk response requires a clear understanding of the risk's nature, potential impact, and the organization's capacity to manage it. There are usually four ways to provide risk response:

    a. **Risk avoidance**: Risk avoidance is the strategy used to completely eliminate exposure to a risk. For example, you might decide not to collect sensitive customer data to avoid the risks of protecting that information.

    b. **Risk acceptance**: Risk acceptance means choosing not to take any action to address a risk, even though it involves accepting the potential vulnerability. Unlike risk avoidance, which eliminates the risk, risk acceptance involves tolerating the risk as it is.

    c. **Risk mitigation**: Risk mitigation is a common approach to handling risks. It involves reducing the chance or impact of a risk by implementing controls or countermeasures.

    d. **Risk transference**: Risk transference involves shifting the risk to another party, often through a contract and ongoing fees. Unlike risk mitigation, which reduces the risk itself, risk transference moves the responsibility and liability for the risk to someone else.

4. **Risk monitoring**: Finally, it is important for an organization to continuously monitor risks and the actions taken. This ensures that the organization handles risks effectively and a risk register helps keep track of these risks and responses over time.

Risk assessment

Risk assessment is the process of identifying potential hazards in an organization that could harm the ability to operate effectively. Risk assessment helps to uncover the inherent risks and encourage the development of processes and controls to minimize the impact of risk on business operations.

By identifying potential hazards, risk assessments are essential for ensuring the health and safety of employees and customers. For example, recognizing specific risks can help an organization implement appropriate controls and measures to effectively address and manage those risks.

It is nearly impossible to effectively safeguard the organization from hazards or cyberattacks without conducting a risk assessment. A NIST risk assessment plays a crucial role in identifying and addressing cyber risks. Four key steps to conduct a risk assessment according to NIST guidelines, are shown in following figure:

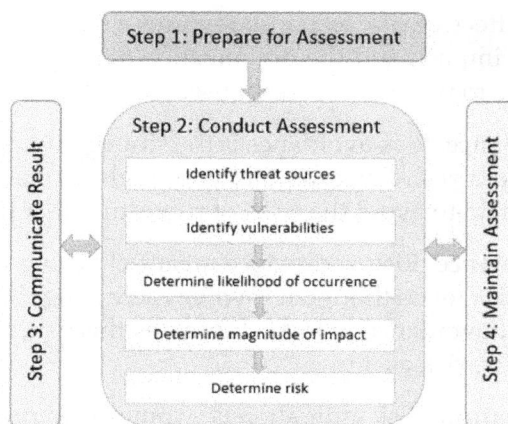

Figure 3.4: NIST risk assessment

Let us look at the four steps of risk assessment in detail:

1. **Prepare for the risk assessment**: Preparing for the risk assessment is the initial and crucial step in the process. This stage involves gathering background information and setting the context for the risk assessment. Proper preparation creates a solid foundation for accurate risk analysis, allowing you to effectively determine the severity of risks and prioritize them appropriately.

    The following are the key tasks in preparing for the risk assessment:

    a. Identify the purpose and clearly define the goals of the risk assessment.

    b. Determine the scope by outlining the boundaries of the assessment, including which assets, processes, etc. Will be evaluated.

    c. Identify any assumptions you are making and constraints you may face that could affect the risk assessment process.

    d. Determine what information sources will be used for the assessment, such as historical data, expert opinions, etc.

    e. Decide on the methods and models you will use to assess and evaluate risks.

2. **Conduct the risk assessment**: Every organization need strong security measures to protect the assets. The organization must conduct risk assessment to build an effective solution. This step is crucial to identify the vulnerable areas within an organization and to develop strategies to address these risks.

    The risk assessment process begins with collecting detailed information about the organization's current IT security setup. This includes data on systems, networks, as well as organization existing policies and procedures. With this information, you can then identify the potential threats that might exploit any weaknesses in the system.

The following are the key tasks in conducting the risk assessment:

Identify the potential sources of threats that could impact the organization. There are many possible security threats, so it is crucial to be aware of as many as you can to protect your organization effectively.

    a.   Determine what kinds of threat events these sources might cause. To protect yourself from threats, you first need to know what those threats are.

    b.   Find vulnerabilities within your organization that could be exploited. These vulnerabilities will help to identify the right measures.

    c.   Determine how likely it is that these threats will occur. This step considers all the factors to assess the likelihood of events.

    d.   Evaluate the potential impact of these threats. This step helps organization to evaluate the risks based on how much impact they could have on the organization.

3.   **Communicate the results**: The third step in the risk assessment process involves sharing the results and information about identified risks. This step is crucial for ensuring that all decision-makers in the organization have the risk-related information necessary to make informed decisions. By communicating these findings clearly, organizations ensure that everyone involved is aware of potential risks and can take appropriate actions to address them. This shared understanding supports better decision-making and enhances the organization's overall risk management efforts.

Following are the key tasks in communicating the results of risk assessment:

    a.   Create detailed and clear reports that outlines the findings of the risk assessment. This includes identified risks, their potential impacts, and recommended mitigation strategies.

    b.   Arrange meetings or presentations to discuss the risk assessment results with key stakeholders.

    c.   Provide clear, actionable recommendations based on the risk assessment, so that decision-makers know how to address and mitigate the identified risks.

    d.   Keep records of the communication process, including reports, meeting minutes, and follow-up actions. This ensures accountability and helps track the progress of risk mitigation efforts.

4.   **Maintain the risk assessment**: The final step in the risk assessment process is to keep the assessment ongoing and up-to-date. This involves regularly updating the assessment to reflect any changes in the organization's risk landscape. By maintaining the risk assessment, you ensure that the information used for risk-based decision-making remains relevant and accurate.

Risk assessment always needs to be evolved as the organization's environment, technology, and threat landscape changes. Regular updates help in identifying new risks and adjusting strategies to address emerging threats. Keeping the assessment up-to-date ensures that decision-makers always have the most current information to make informed choices and effectively manage risks.

The following are the key tasks in maintaining the risk assessment:

a. Regularly monitor risk factors identified in assessments and track how they change over time.

b. Update the risk assessment to reflect new monitoring activities and any changes in the risk environment.

c. Periodically review the risk assessment process and criteria to ensure they remain relevant and accurate.

d. Keep detailed records of updates and modifications to the risk assessment, including reasons for changes and their impact.

e. Schedule periodic reviews to assess the overall effectiveness of the risk assessment and make necessary adjustments.

Real-world examples

Some real-world examples are as follows:

- On Friday, July 19 2024, over 8.5 million computers were affected in what is considered one of the worst cyber incidents ever. The security company *CrowdStrike* released a Windows update with a defect that caused widespread problems.

- In April and May 2024, *Ticketmaster* data breach revealed millions of customers' personal and financial details. Cybercriminals accessed Ticketmaster's database to steal sensitive information like names, email addresses, phone numbers, and payment data.

Risk assessment matrix

Risk assessment matrices are widely used tools for visualizing and evaluating risks. Typically, these matrices are presented as charts or tables that identify risks based on their likelihood and severity. By intersecting these two factors on the matrix, organizations can measure the overall risk level.

The risk assessment matrix helps in identifying which risks are most critical and require immediate attention by showing risk priority. This visual representation makes it easier to prioritize risk management efforts and allocate resources effectively. The following table shows an example of risk matrix; however, it may change from organization to organization:

		Severity				
		Negligible	Minor	Moderate	Major	Severe
Likelihood	Very likely	Medium	High	Critical	Critical	Critical
	Likely	Medium	High	High	Critical	Critical
	Possible	Low	Medium	High	High	Critical
	Unlikely	Low	Medium	Medium	High	High
	Very unlikely	Low	Low	Low	Medium	Medium

Table 3.2: Risk assessment matrix

The risk matrix table helps to identify the risk level. The matrix is usually a grid with vertical axis representing the likelihood (or probability) of a risk occurring, and the horizontal axis representing the impact (or severity) of the risk if it does occur. Using the matrix helps organizations to prioritize risks by showing which ones are most critical. This way, resources can be managed more effectively, focusing on the most important risks first.

NIST Risk Management Framework

NIST in its partnership with the *Department of Defense (DoD)*, developed a RMF to improve information security and strengthen risk management processes. NIST SV 800-37 Revision 2 describes the RMF and provides guidelines for applying the RMF to information systems and organizations. The RMF provides a disciplined, structured, and flexible process for managing security and privacy risk. The RMF provides a flexible seven step process that integrates cybersecurity, privacy, and supply chain risk management throughout the **system development lifecycle (SDLC)**. This framework is aligned with NIST standards and guidelines, helping organizations meet the requirements of the *Federal Information Security Modernization Act (FISMA)*. It covers aspects, such as control selection, implementation, assessment, and continuous monitoring.

The RMF was initially designed for federal agencies. However, it is now widely adopted by state, local agencies, and private sector organizations for its comprehensive approach to risk management.

The NIST RMF consists of seven stages, as shown in *Figure 3.5*:

Figure 3.5: NIST RMF

The seven steps can be detailed as follows:

1. **Prepare**: The first and crucial step in RMF is to prepare. To prepare the organization for managing security and privacy risks, it is required to establish a clear risk management strategy aligned with organizational goals and regulations.

    The main outcomes of this step are as follows.

    a. To identify key risk management roles.

    b. To establish the organization's risk management strategy.

    c. To determine the organization risk tolerance.

2. **Categorize**: The second step in RMF is to categorize. It is essential to understand the information and the potential negative impact on the **confidentiality, integrity, and availability (CIA)** of systems. The important step is to classify and label the information processed, stored, and shared based on the impact analysis in the organization.

    By understanding the impacts, organizations can prioritize risk management tasks and develop strategies to protect against threats that could weaken system security and information integrity. This approach helps in improving the effective risk management procedures and the organization can respond proactively to potential vulnerabilities.

    The main outcomes of this step are:

    a. To identify and document the system characteristics.

    b. To classify the information based on organization policy.

    c. To authorize official reviews and approves categorization decision.

3. **Select**: The third step is to select the baseline security controls. This involves selecting standard security measures that provide a foundational level of protection. This step also helps to assess and identify any additional security adjustments for the organization's specific risks. Furthermore, this step revises the baseline security controls and helps maintain robust security in line with the organization requirements and risk profile.

   The main outcomes of this step are:

   a. To select baselines and perform customization as per organization need.

   b. To select controls based on standard categorization as common, hybrid, or system-specific.

   c. To establish a system-level continuous monitoring technique.

   d. To plan for security and privacy, based on selected design and strategy.

4. **Implement**: The fourth step is to implement the selected security and privacy controls as outlined in the organization's strategy. The best approach is to begin by integrating these controls into your systems and processes to ensure they effectively protect against identified risks. This includes configuring technical safeguards, updating policies, and training staff on new procedures. By managing control implementation with organization security and privacy strategies, you ensure that your defenses are both effective and adaptive.

   The main outcomes of this step are:

   a. To implement the controls outlined in the security and privacy plans.

   b. To ensure that security and privacy policies are up-to-date and aligned with risk management objectives.

   c. To provide a foundation for continuous monitoring and adjustment to adapt to new threats.

   d. To meet regulatory and standards requirements.

5. **Assess**: The fifth step is to assess the implemented controls effectiveness and measuring the quality. The best approach is to start reviewing the controls to ensure they are configured as designed and integrated properly into the system and organizational processes. Additionally, check for any deviations from the planned implementation and address them promptly. After reviewing controls, assess the quality of the controls by testing their performance in real-world scenarios. This includes examining how well they detect and respond to threats and whether they effectively mitigate identified risks.

   The main outcomes of this step are:

   a. To assess security controls and whether they have been implemented as intended and are functioning correctly.

    b. To verify if the control evaluations are carried out according to the assessment schemes.

    c. To evaluate the performance of security controls and provide insights into the effectiveness in mitigating risks.

    d. To provide critical information for making informed decisions about risk management strategies and resource allocation.

6. **Authorize**: The sixth step in RMF is to authorize. Top management plays a crucial role in approving the secured system based on the organization's risk appetite. Management evaluates the system's effectiveness in managing risks while considering its potential operational impact.

   Based on this assessment, management decides whether to authorize the system for operation or to make necessary adjustments to address any remaining risks. This decision ensures that the system aligns with the organization's risk tolerance and regulatory requirements, maintaining a balance between operational needs and risk management.

   The main outcomes of this step are:

       a. To receive approval from top management to operate and meet the organization's risk tolerance and regulatory requirements.

       b. To establish a foundation for ongoing monitoring and review.

       c. To ensure that the system's operation aligns with the organization's risk appetite and strategic objectives.

7. **Monitor**: The final step in RMF is to monitor the effectiveness of security controls. This involves continuously tracking the performance of the controls and making necessary adjustments based on the findings. This step also includes documenting any changes made to systems or operations, based an analysis of their impact. The next crucial task in this step is to report the findings and adjustments to the management for their support.

   The main outcomes of this step are:

       a. To track system and operational environment using a continuous monitoring technique.

       b. To examine the output from ongoing monitoring efforts.

       c. To report findings, security posture to the management.

RMF alignment with SDLC

The RMF emphasizes risk management by promoting the development of security and privacy capabilities into information systems throughout the SDLC. RMF 2.0 is the first NIST publication to include full integration of privacy risk management into the existing information security risk management processes. SDLC is crucial in RMF because it provides a structured approach to design, develop and maintain secure information systems. By following SDLC, organizations can ensure that the systems are secure, compliant with regulations, and meet stakeholder requirements. SDLC also ensures that security controls are properly tested and effective. The following table shows the RMF steps mapped with SDLC:

New SDLC phases	RMF 2.0 stages
Initiation	Prepare, categorize
Development / acquisition	Select, implement, assess
Implementation / assessment	Implement, authorize, assess
Operations / maintenance	Monitor
Disposal	NA

Table 3.3: RMF alignment with SDLC

The SDLC phases align with the seven stages of RMF as follows: The initiation phase of SDLC corresponds to the prepare and categorize steps of RMF. The development/acquisition phase aligns with the select, implement, and assess steps. The implementation/assessment phase maps to the implement, authorize, and assess steps of RMF. Finally, the operations/maintenance phase corresponds to the monitor step of RMF.

NIST guidance on preparing risk management

The first step in the RMF is prepare. The purpose of the prepare step is to carry out essential activities at the organization, mission and business process, and information system-levels of the organization. This step help to prepare the organization to manage its security and privacy risks using the RMF. The following figure shows the first step of NIST RMF:

Figure 3.6: NIST RMF

Preparation can achieve effective, efficient, and cost-effective execution of risk management processes. The following figure shows the task associated with preparation step:

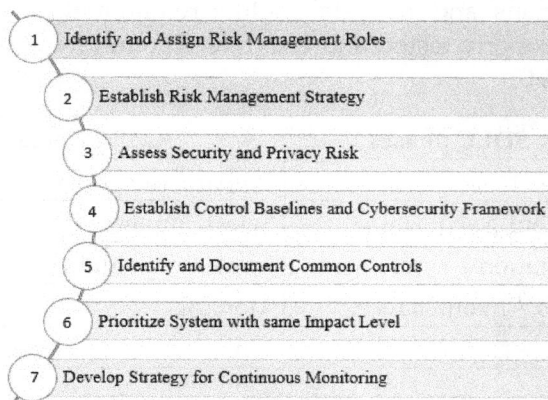

1	Identify and Assign Risk Management Roles
2	Establish Risk Management Strategy
3	Assess Security and Privacy Risk
4	Establish Control Baselines and Cybersecurity Framework
5	Identify and Document Common Controls
6	Prioritize System with same Impact Level
7	Develop Strategy for Continuous Monitoring

Figure 3.7: RMF preparation tasks

Here are the details of the preparation task at the organization level:

- **Task 1**: Identify and assign risk management roles:

  The roles and responsibilities in risk management processes may involve both internal and external personnel and vary based on the organization's structure. While the core functions remain the same, roles can differ, with some individuals taking on multiple roles. It is important to avoid conflicts of interest, such as ensuring authorizing officials may not act as system owners. Combining security and privacy roles requires careful consideration due to different expertise and potential conflicting priorities. The following table shows the roles to identify and assign risk management:

Primary responsibility	Supporting roles	SDLC phase	References
Head of agency, chief information officer, senior agency official for privacy	Authorizing official or authorizing official designated representative, senior accountable official for risk management or risk executive, senior agency information security officer	Initiation	NIST SP 800-160 v1; SP 800-181; NIST CSF

Table 3.4: Roles to identify and assess risk

- **Task 2**: Establish risk management strategy:

  The risk management strategy outlines how risks are assessed, addressed, and monitored, including separate plans for security, privacy, and supply chain risks. Risk tolerance is the level of risk an organization is willing to accept when managing the entire risk management process. It affects decisions made by senior leaders and sets limits on those decisions. It guides decision-making by defining priorities, acceptable risks, and trade-offs. The strategy ensures consistent risk evaluation across the organization and includes methods for ongoing monitoring and response. The following table shows the roles to establish risk management strategy:

Primary responsibility	Supporting roles	SDLC phase	References
Head of agency	Senior accountable official for risk management or risk executive, chief information officer, senior agency information security officer, senior agency official for privacy	Initiation	NIST SP 800-30; SP 800-39; SP 800-160 v1; SP 800-161; NIST CSF

Table 3.5: Roles to establish risk strategy

- **Task 3**: Assess security and privacy risk:

  Organizational-level risk assessment combines system-level risk assessments, continuous monitoring, and strategic risk considerations. It evaluates the overall risk from the operation of information systems, their connections with other systems, and the use of external providers. The assessment may include factors like system segregation, varying environments, and supply chain risks. These results help organizations to establish a cybersecurity framework profile and manage risks effectively across different systems and operations. The following table shows the roles to assess security and privacy risk:

Primary responsibility	Supporting roles	SDLC phase	References
senior accountable official for risk management or risk executive, senior agency information security officer, senior agency official for privacy	Chief information officer, mission or business owner, authorizing official or authorizing official designated representative	Initiation	NIST SP 800-30; SP 800-39; SP 800-161

Table 3.6: Roles to assess security and privacy risk

- **Task 4**: Establish control baselines and cybersecurity framework:

  To address specific organizational needs, tailored control baselines can be developed to reduce risk and meet business or mission requirements. These baselines consist of customized controls and guidance derived from established frameworks like SP 800-53B. Tailored baselines allow organizations to add, remove, or adjust controls to suit their requirements while ensuring adequate protection. Tailored baselines may be developed for specific environments, such as cloud systems, industrial control systems, or privacy concerns. Additionally, organizations may create cybersecurity framework profiles to align cybersecurity outcomes with their mission, business needs, and resources. The following table shows the roles to establish control baselines and cybersecurity framework.

Primary responsibility	Supporting roles	SDLC phase	References
Mission or business owner, senior accountable official for risk management or risk executive	Chief information officer, authorizing official or authorizing official designated representative, senior agency information security officer, senior agency official for privacy	Initiation	NIST SP 800-53; SP 800-53B; SP 800-160 v1; NIST CSF

Table 3.7: Roles to establish control baseline

- **Task 5**: Identify and document common controls:

  Common controls are security measures that multiple systems within an organization can inherit, such as physical security, monitoring, and personnel security. These controls are managed by designated providers, who are responsible for implementing, assessing, and monitoring them. System owners do not need to assess or document these controls. Risk assessments ensure the controls meet security and privacy requirements. Providers must document and report on the controls, and authorization officials accept the risks when these controls are inherited by systems. The following table shows the roles to identify and document common controls:

Primary responsibility	Supporting roles	SDLC phase	References
Senior agency information security officer, senior agency official for privacy	Mission or business owner, senior accountable official for risk management or risk executive, chief information officer; authorizing official or authorizing official designated representative, common control provider, system owner	Initiation	NIST SP 800-53

Table 3.8: Roles to identify and document common control

- **Task 6**: Prioritize system with same impact level:

  Organizations can prioritize systems within each impact level to make better risk-based decisions. For example, moderate-impact systems can be split into subcategories like low-moderate, moderate-moderate, and high-moderate, with higher priority given to the more impactful ones. This helps in selecting the right controls and tailoring baselines to address risks. It also highlights critical systems for business operations. Cybersecurity framework profiles can assist in aligning systems with mission objectives for more effective prioritization. The following table shows the roles to prioritize the system with the same impact level:

Primary responsibility	supporting roles	SDLC phase	References
Senior accountable official for risk management or risk executive	Senior agency information security officer, senior agency official for privacy, mission or business owner, system owner; chief information officer, authorizing official or authorizing official designated representative	Initiation	NIST SP 800-30; SP 800-39; SP 800-59; SP 800-60 v1; SP 800-60 v2; SP 800-160 v1; NIST CSF; FIPS 199; FIPS 200

Table 3.9: Roles to prioritize system

- **Task 7**: Develop strategy for continuous monitoring:

  Continuous monitoring is essential for evaluating an organization's security and privacy and the effectiveness of its controls. It helps track risks, including supply chain risks, and supports ongoing system authorization. The strategy defines monitoring frequencies, assessment methods, and reporting, using automation for more frequent control checks. Key officials collaborate to set criteria for efficient, real-time risk management. The senior accountable official approves the strategy. The following table shows the roles to develop strategy for continuous monitoring:

Primary responsibility	Supporting roles	SDLC phase	References
Senior accountable official for risk management or risk executive	Chief information officer, senior agency information security officer, senior agency official for privacy, mission or business owner, system owner; authorizing official or authorizing official designated representative	Initiation	NIST SP 800-30; SP 800-39; SP 800-53; SP 800-53A; SP 800-137; SP 800-161; NIST CSF

Table 3.10: Roles to develop continuous monitoring strategy

NIST Special Publication 800-53

NIST SP 800-53 is an information security standard that outlines privacy and security controls for information systems. Initially NIST SP 800-53 was designed for *U.S. federal agencies*, however, now it has become a general standard for broader use since its fifth revision. NIST SP 800-53 is published by the NIST, that helps organizations comply with the FISMA and manage cost-effective security programs.

Two related documents, 800-53A, and 800-53B offer additional guidance and baseline standards based on 800-53:

- NIST SP 800-53A provides procedures for assessing the security and privacy controls used in Federal Information Systems and organizations.

- NIST SP 800-53B provides baseline security and privacy controls for information systems and organizations.

Revision 5 of NIST SP 800-53A was released on January 2022 with an outcome-based approach. NIST SP 80-53A reorganizes security and privacy controls to focus on achieving specific outcomes, rather than just following a set of steps.

Process of NIST SP 800-53

This section outlines the process for assessing security and privacy controls within organizational systems and their operational environments. It begins with the preparatory activities conducted by organizations and assessors to get ready for control assessments. This includes developing detailed security and privacy assessment plans.

The process then involves carrying out the control assessments, followed by the analysis, documentation, and reporting of the results. Finally, it covers the post-assessment phase, which includes analyzing the report findings and undertaking follow-up activities to address any identified issues. This comprehensive approach ensures that security and privacy controls are effectively evaluated and continuously improved. The following figure shows the four steps of conducting security and privacy control assessment:

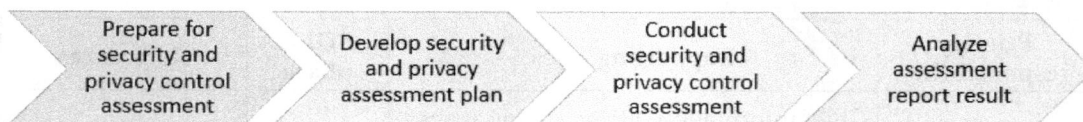

| Prepare for security and privacy control assessment | Develop security and privacy assessment plan | Conduct security and privacy control assessment | Analyze assessment report result |

Figure 3.8: NIST SP 800-53 process

Compliance standard

Government and financial compliance requirements vary widely, serving as minimal baselines that organizations must meet. However, these requirements can be interpreted and applied differently depending on an organization's specific business goals. To ensure effective risk management, it is crucial to align compliance requirements with the organization's objectives and identify potential risks accurately.

For instance, a company might implement a policy that mandates logging for all servers containing customer **personally identifiable information** (**PII**) and requires passwords to be at least ten characters long. This policy helps the organization comply with various regulations by addressing both security and data protection standards. Mapping compliance requirements to business goals ensures that the organization not only meets legal obligations but also effectively manages risks associated with its operations.

Following are a few common standards that organizations often follow to meet the needs of their global customers across various industries.

System and Organization Controls

System and Organizations Controls (SOC) reports, established by the *American Institute of Certified Public Accountants (AICPA)*, assess an organization's cybersecurity practices. SOC-certified organizations undergo regular audits of their IT controls, policies, and procedures. There are mainly three types of SOC audit reports designed to achieve different goals or to address different audiences:

- SOC 1 focuses on controls that impact customers' financial reporting, like payroll management, and ensures controls to protect financial data. For example, if a company handles payment data for a healthcare provider, a SOC 1 audit ensures that financial information is properly protected.

- SOC 2 assesses a service provider's controls based on **Trust Services Criteria (TSCs)** like security, confidentiality, availability, integrity, and privacy. The security TSC is mandatory, while the others are optional. SOC 2 audits are commonly used by tech service companies, like cloud providers.

- SOC 3 offers the same information as SOC 2 but in a more general, high-level format. SOC 3 is for the public, while SOC 2 is more detailed and usually provided to clients and stakeholders. For example, a cloud service provider like AWS may display a SOC 3 badge publicly but provide an SOC 2 report to customers upon request.

In addition to SOC 1, SOC 2, and SOC 3 compliance, there are type 1 and type 2 reports. SOC 1 and SOC 2 usually have type 1 and type 2 reports, while SOC 3 has only type 2 reports. The following list provides more details on SOC reports:

- **Type 1**: Type 1 reports assess design and implementation of controls based on policies, processes, and procedures at a specific point in time.

- **Type 2**: Type 2 reports go further by evaluating both the design and implementation of controls, as well as their operating effectiveness over a period of time, usually 6-12 months.

General Data Protection Regulation

The GDPR is an EU compliance standard designed to safeguard the privacy of European citizens' personal data. Personal data refers to any information that can directly or indirectly identify a living person, including basic details like names, phone numbers, and addresses, as well as more complex data such as interests, past purchases, health information, and online behavior.

Processing data includes all activities related to data management, such as collecting, organizing, using, storing, sharing, disclosing, and deleting information. Every organization that processes personal data, which encompasses nearly all entities with employees and customers, must comply with GDPR requirements. In summary, the GDPR mandates that personal data is managed in a way that ensures privacy and integrity, protecting individuals' rights and data security.

Health Insurance Portability and Accountability Act

The HIPAA of 1996 is a federal law designed to establish national standards for safeguarding sensitive **protected health information (PHI)**. The primary goal of HIPAA is to prevent the unauthorized disclosure of this information without the patient's consent or knowledge.

To enforce HIPAA's requirements, the *U.S. Department of Health and Human Services (HHS)* introduced the *HIPAA Privacy Rule*, which sets guidelines for handling and protecting personal health information.

Additionally, the *HIPAA Security Rule* specifically addresses the protection of electronic health information covered by the HIPAA Privacy Rule. It sets standards for securing electronic health records, ensuring that sensitive data is protected from breaches and unauthorized access. Together, these rules help maintain patient privacy and data security across the healthcare industry.

California Consumer Privacy Act

The *California Consumer Privacy Act (CCPA)* is a state law that enhances privacy rights and consumer protection for California residents. The CCPA was started in 2018 and it gives residents more control over their personal data, including the right to know what information is collected, access it, and request its deletion.

The CCPA requires businesses that handle personal data to be transparent about their data practices, offer consumers the option to opt out of data sales and implement safeguards to protect the data. It applies to businesses that meet certain thresholds, such as having substantial revenue or processing significant amounts of consumer information. In summary, the CCPA aims to strengthen privacy protections and give individuals more control over their personal information.

Payment Card Industry Data Security Standard

The PCI DSS was established in 2004 by major credit card companies, including *Visa, MasterCard, Discover, JCB,* and *American Express*. Managed by the *Payment Card Industry Security Standards Council (PCI SSC)*, PCI DSS sets security standards designed to protect credit and debit card transactions from data theft and fraud.

Any organization that processes credit or debit card transactions must meet PCI DSS requirements. Achieving PCI certification is widely regarded as the best practice for securing sensitive payment data, helping businesses build trust with their customers and maintain secure transactions. The PCI DSS covers four main areas namely, protecting cardholder data, implementing access control measures, securing network systems, and ensuring encrypted data transmission.

International Organization for Standardization 27001

As we have discussed earlier, *ISO 27001* is an international standard for information security management. It provides a comprehensive framework for protecting various types of information, including employee data, financial records, and intellectual property. The standard is designed to help organizations of all sizes and industries manage their information securely and cost-effectively.

ISO 27001 focuses on safeguarding the CIA of information within an organization. It involves identifying potential risks to the information and establishing measures to prevent those risks from occurring. The *ISO 27001:2022* revision has Annex A, which lists 93 controls organized into four sections.

FedRAMP

Federal Risk and Authorization Management Program (*FedRAMP*) is a *U.S. government* wide initiative that ensures cloud services used by federal agencies meet strict security standards. FedRAMP is a cybersecurity risk management program that governs the acquisition and use of cloud services by U.S. federal agencies. Only FedRAMP-approved SaaS, IaaS, and PaaS companies and cloud service providers are eligible to work with these agencies. It helps protect government data and streamlines the process for agencies to adopt cloud services. The program aligns with cloud computing guidelines in NIST SP 800-53, which standardize security requirements for cloud services in line with OMB Circular A-130, FISMA, the FedRAMP authorization act, and FedRAMP policy.

The authorization process is a key step in getting FedRAMP approval. After a **cloud service provider** (**CSP**) completes their documentation and prepares their system, they submit their **system security plan** (**SSP**) to the agency sponsor or **Joint Authorization Board** (**JAB**). The SSP details how the CSP follows security controls based on NIST 800-53 Revision 5, with possible additional agency-specific requirements. Once submitted, the agency sponsor or JAB reviews the SSP and performs an initial assessment, which may include interviews and document reviews, to ensure compliance with FedRAMP standards.

FISMA

The FISMA defines a framework of guidelines and security standards to protect government information and operations. FISMA applies to all federal agencies and contractors that focus on managing cybersecurity risks and ensuring best practices. FISMA requires federal agencies to implement IT security programs to protect IT systems and networks. FISMA also designates the NIST to create cybersecurity standards, like NIST SB 800-171, which provides guidelines for protecting **Controlled Unclassified Information (CUI)** on non-federal systems. FISMA assigns responsibilities to different agencies to secure federal data. It requires program officials and agency heads to conduct annual reviews of information security programs to keep risks at acceptable levels in a cost-effective and efficient way.

Conclusion

In this chapter, we covered risk governance and the risk management process. This chapter also detailed the risk assessment methodologies and strategies to minimize the impact of risk on business operations. Additionally, this chapter also highlighted the real-world case studies and international standard risk framework which helped organizations to ensure effective risk management.

In the next chapter, we will delve into system scope, system interfaces, system boundary and categorization of information system to illustrate how these requirements contribute to the effective development of the system.

Key terms

- **Qualitative use case**: Ideal for evaluating risks when there is not much numerical data available or when you need a broad, strategic perspective on potential risks.

- **Quantitative use case**: Ideal for situations where exact measurements are essential, like financial forecasting or detailed project risk assessments.

- The GDPR applies to all personal data of individuals within its scope, while HIPAA is more specific, covering only PHI.

- Organizations that handle credit card information on behalf of merchants, even if they are not merchants themselves, must also comply with PCI DSS.

- FISMA aimed to establish a baseline level of IT security standards for both federal agencies and government contractors

- NIST 800-53 applies to a wide range of Federal Information Systems, while FedRAMP specifically targets CSPs working with government agencies.

CHAPTER 4

Introduction to System Scope

Introduction

This chapter introduces the system definition and its scope, providing a comprehensive framework for understanding what the system is intended to achieve and the boundaries within which it will be developed and implemented. It begins by detailing the stakeholder and system requirements to understand the different components necessary for system integration. By understanding the needs and expectations of stakeholders and the specific requirements of the system, you can ensure that the system is developed to meet its objectives while addressing potential risks and security concerns. By defining the system objectives, this chapter aims to optimize resource utilization, manage risks effectively, and ensure that the system fulfils its intended purpose.

Additionally, the chapter addresses information tier levels, which are essential for organizing data systematically to enhance overall system performance. It also covers data classification, providing insights into the value of data across different categories and how to manage and protect it effectively. Lastly, the chapter outlines the types of systems, tailored to meet operational and security needs, taking into account the complexity involved. This structured approach ensures that all aspects of the system are addressed comprehensively and coherently.

Structure

The chapter covers the following main topics:

- Information security and privacy
- Stakeholder and system requirements
- System documentation
- Categorization of information system
- Data classification
- System boundary

Objectives

By the end of this chapter, you will have a comprehensive understanding of system scope and components, which are crucial for implementing necessary security controls to manage operational risks effectively. You will learn how to define and manage system interfaces and boundaries to ensure a seamless integration, uphold security, and maintain smooth system operation. Additionally, the chapter will cover the three tiers of information levels used in organizations, providing insights into how these tiers can be utilized to manage information risks effectively. This knowledge will equip you with the tools to design and maintain robust systems that balance functionality, security, and risk management.

Information security and privacy

Information is a crucial asset that must be safeguarded against evolving and complex security threats. Collecting user data is a common practice for most websites and applications, offering valuable insights to enhance user experiences and inform decision-making. This data can be used to personalize content, guide product development, and identify issues in current systems, providing organizations with a competitive advantage and optimizing resource use.

However, collecting and storing user information comes with important considerations. Privacy, security, ethical, and legal issues must be carefully managed to protect data and fulfil responsibilities to users. Mishandling these aspects can lead to significant financial losses, reputational damage, and legal consequences.

To address these challenges, an effective security strategy must start with a clear understanding of the associated risks. It involves evaluating how various tools and techniques can be deployed to secure information. By assessing these risks and implementing a range of protective measures, organizations can better defend against potential breaches and ensure the privacy of sensitive data.

Risk management strategy

Executing the **Risk Management Framework** (**RMF**) requires strong collaboration between information security programs and privacy programs. The security and privacy programs have distinct objectives, their goals often overlap and complement each other, like:

- Information security programs focus on protecting information and systems from unauthorized access, use, or modification to ensure **confidentiality, integrity, and availability** (**CIA**).

- Privacy programs focus on managing risks related to **personally identifiable information** (**PII**) and ensuring compliance with privacy laws.

When implementing the RMF, organizations must carefully coordinate their information security and privacy efforts. This involves aligning the objectives of both programs to ensure that each step of the RMF addresses both security and privacy concerns. By encouraging collaboration between information security and privacy programs, organizations can enhance their ability to protect sensitive data, ensure regulatory compliance, and effectively manage risks related to personal information. This integrated approach helps safeguard data and meet both security and privacy objectives more efficiently.

System definition

Boundaries, in the context of an information system, delineate the system's extent and scope, providing a clear framework for understanding what is included and how it interacts with other elements. This involves specifying the following two key aspects:

- **System components**: System components must be clearly identified. This includes all hardware, such as servers, workstations, and networking devices, as well as software applications and tools that make up the system. It also contains data elements, including databases and data storage solutions, and network elements like routers and switches. By cataloguing these components, organizations can ensure a comprehensive understanding of what constitutes the system and manage it effectively.

- **System interfaces**: System interfaces need to be defined. This involves outlining how the system connects and interacts with other systems. Internally, this means detailing interactions with other systems, within the organization, such as integration with **enterprise resource planning** (**ERP**) systems or internal databases. Externally, it involves specifying how the system interfaces with third-party systems, which could include external databases, partner networks, or cloud services.

Together, defining system components and interfaces establishes the boundaries of an information system, providing a structured approach to managing its scope and ensuring all interactions are well understood and controlled.

System scope

The scope of a system contains both its physical and logical boundaries, defining the extent and limitations of the system's operations and interactions:

Physical boundaries refer to the actual locations where system components are situated. This includes data centers, office locations, and any other physical environments where hardware, such as servers, workstations, and network devices are deployed. Identifying these physical boundaries helps in understanding the geographical and infrastructural context of the system, facilitating effective management, maintenance, and security of the physical assets.

Logical boundaries on the other hand, refer to the virtual aspects of the system. This includes network segments that delineate the system's operational environment within a larger network, as well as software applications and data repositories that the system utilizes. Logical boundaries define how the system is segmented within the network, which applications it uses, and where its data is stored and processed. Understanding these boundaries is crucial for managing data flows, ensuring integration with other systems, and maintaining security protocols.

Together, the physical and logical boundaries provide a comprehensive view of the system's scope, enabling effective planning, implementation, and management of the system's resources and interactions.

System qualifier

The system qualifier comprises of the essential characteristics and attributes that establish the boundaries and context of a system. It plays a crucial role in identifying the nature of the system, its limitations, and the environment in which it operates. Understanding these qualifiers is vital for effective system design and implementation.

There are mainly three aspects of system qualifier:

- **Type of system**: The type of system can range from software applications to hardware devices and network systems, each with distinct functionalities and purposes. The knowledge of type of system helps stakeholders to align their expectations and resources accordingly.

- **Operational environment**: This refers to the specific conditions under which the system operates, such as whether it functions within a secure network, a cloud environment, or on local infrastructure. The operational environment significantly influences the system's performance, security, and usability.

- **Stakeholder requirements**: This involves recognizing the users and stakeholders along with understanding their needs and expectations from the system. By addressing these requirements, organizations can design systems that not only fulfil functional objectives but also enhance user satisfaction and engagement.

Data and system sensitivity

The sensitivity of a system is fundamentally determined by the data it processes. If the data is removed, the system itself is no longer considered sensitive, even if it remains valuable due to the cost of replacement. The true sensitivity of a system arises from the data it handles, whether it is being processed, stored, or transmitted.

To assess the overall sensitivity of a system, you can aggregate the sensitivity levels of the data based on key security objectives like CIA. *Federal Information Processing Standard (FIPS) 199* uses this approach, defining the high-water mark as the highest sensitivity level of the data handled. This method helps categorize the system by considering the worst-case potential impact, ensuring that the security measures are robust enough to address the most critical data vulnerabilities.

Sensitivity assessment process: To determine the sensitivity of data is most effectively achieved by evaluating it against the three core security pillars: CIA. The sensitivity assessment involves determining how each security objective applies to the data and then ranking its sensitivity according to established standards. For each security pillar, you assess how crucial it is to protect the data from unauthorized access (confidentiality), ensure its accuracy and trustworthiness (integrity), and guarantee its availability when needed (availability).

By evaluating data through these lenses, you not only establish its sensitivity in each individual area, but also derive an overall sensitivity ranking based on the combined impact of all three areas. The relative importance of CIA will vary depending on the nature of the system and the specific data it processes. This approach helps in creating a comprehensive understanding of data sensitivity and guides appropriate protective measures accordingly. We have already discussed CIA in *Chapter 1, Introduction to Security and Privacy Principles*.

Stakeholder and system requirements

Stakeholder and system requirements play a crucial role in the development and management of information systems. *National Institute of Standards and Technology (NIST)* offers detailed guidelines to help organizations identify, analyze, and document these requirements comprehensively. This structured approach ensures that the end systems align with the needs and expectations of all relevant stakeholders while functioning effectively within their operational context.

By following stakeholder and system requirements, organizations can effectively bridge the gap between user needs and system capabilities, leading to the successful implementation and management of information systems. The following figure shows the relationship between stakeholder and system requirements:

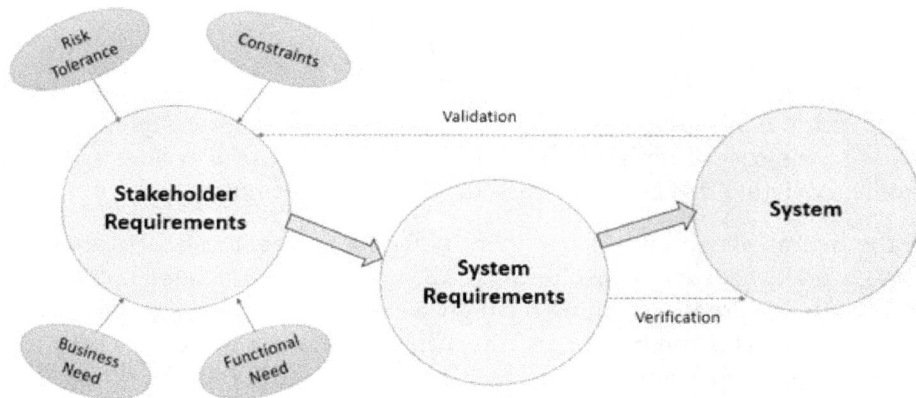

Figure 4.1: Stakeholder and system requirements

Stakeholder requirements

Stakeholder requirements represent the needs and expectations of individuals or groups who have a vested interest in the system, such as end-users, customers, and regulatory bodies. NIST emphasizes the importance of engaging stakeholders early and thoroughly to gather accurate and relevant input. This process involves using various methods like interviews and workshops to capture their needs and expectations, which are then meticulously documented.

The key aspects of stakeholder requirements are:

- Identify all relevant stakeholders, such as end-users, customers, regulatory bodies, and decision-makers. Understand their roles and what they expect from the system.

- Collect requirements using methods, like interviews, surveys, and focus groups. This helps ensure that the system design meets stakeholder needs.

- Clearly record the requirements in an organized way, detailing what stakeholders need and any constraints or limitations they have.

System requirements

System requirements, derived from stakeholder needs, define the specific functionalities, performance attributes, and constraints of the system. NIST guidelines, particularly those found in publications like NIST SP 800-53, outline how to specify these requirements in detail, ensuring that both functional aspects (what the system must do) and non-functional aspects (how well it must perform) are addressed. This ensures that the system not only meets stakeholder expectations but also adheres to security, performance, and regulatory standards.

The key aspects of system requirements are:

- **Functional requirements**: Describe what the system should do, including its specific functions and features, like data processing, user access controls, and communication protocols.

- **Non-functional requirements**: Define how the system should perform, focusing on attributes like performance, security, reliability, and usability.

- **Constraints**: Note any limitations or restrictions on the system, such as regulatory requirements, technology limits, or budget restrictions.

Stakeholder and system integration

Integrating stakeholder and system requirements is key to ensuring that the system meets all requirements and works well. NIST highlights the following structured approach for this:

- **Requirement analysis**: Requirement analysis involves examining the needs of stakeholders to determine how these needs translate into specific functions and features for the system. This process ensures that the system will address the key requirements and solve the problems identified by stakeholders.

- **Requirement specification**: Requirement specification follows where detailed system requirements are created. This includes outlining both the specific functions the system must perform and the performance attributes it must meet. The goal is to ensure these specifications align closely with stakeholder needs, covering what the system should do and how it should operate.

- **Validation and verification**: Validation and verification are ongoing processes that involve regularly checking to ensure that the system requirements still meet stakeholder expectations. This includes making necessary adjustments based on feedback and any changes in requirements to maintain alignment throughout the system's lifecycle.

System documentation

System documentation refers to the collection of records and documents that contains the configuration, architecture, design, and operational procedures of a system. In the context of security and risk management, especially within frameworks like NIST, system documentation is essential to ensure that security requirements are met and to maintain compliance with relevant standards. Some of the examples of system documentation are mentioned as follows:

- **System security plan**: The **system security plan** (SSP) outlines the security requirements of a system and the controls in place to meet those requirements. It also defines the responsibilities and behaviour expected from individuals accessing the system. The plan serves as a structured approach to ensure cost-effective security protection and includes input from key managers, such as information owners, system owners, and the **senior agency information security officer (SAISO)**. The plan's structure can be customized to fit agency needs, as long as the main sections are clearly addressed.

Agencies should establish a policy for the system security planning process considering SSPs as live documents that need regular reviews, updates, and action plans for security controls. Procedures should define who is responsible for reviewing and maintaining the plans and ensuring they are up-to-date before the security certification and accreditation process begins. During certification, the SSP is reviewed and updated to ensure security controls match the system's FIPS 199 security category and that risks are properly identified.

- **Risk assessment**: Risk assessment documentation captures the findings from the process of identifying and evaluating potential security risks to a system. It details the threats, vulnerabilities, and possible impacts on the system's CIA. This documentation serves as a foundation for determining appropriate security controls, tracking risks, and supporting decision-making for risk mitigation strategies. It ensures that all identified risks are properly documented, assessed, and addressed in line with organizational security requirements.

- **Security categorization**: Security categorization, as defined by FIPS 199 and NIST SP 800-53, involves classifying a system based on its potential impact on CIA. This process helps to determine the appropriate level of security controls by evaluating the potential consequences of breaches and ensure that systems are adequately protected based on their sensitivity and criticality. The details are provided in next section, *Categorization of information system*.

System naming convention

A naming convention is a set of rules for creating names used to ensure consistency and clarity across systems. These rules can be formal or informal and can include guidelines, company policies, programming conventions, and other specifications. Naming conventions help ensure that names are clear, easy to understand, and concise, minimizing confusion and the effort needed for interpretation.

The naming convention in the context of ISO/IEC 11179-5:2015 the goal is to create names that clearly express the meaning of the item they represent, while being short enough to be practical. Good naming conventions help ensure that names are easy to understand, even without needing to refer to detailed definitions, and they work across different systems or contexts. Following are some guidelines for naming conventions:

- Use clear and descriptive names.

- Define a consistent pattern for naming systems or components.

- Include version information in the naming convention.
- Follow the principles of simplicity, consistency, and standardization.

Categorization of information system

Security categories help organizations assess the potential impact of events that could compromise their information and systems. These categories are crucial for understanding how different types of security incidents might affect the organization's mission, asset protection, legal obligations, daily operations, and individual safety. By categorizing information and systems based on their potential impact, organizations can better evaluate and prioritize risks.

Security categories should be used alongside vulnerability and threat information to conduct a comprehensive risk assessment. This approach ensures that organizations can effectively address and mitigate potential risks by considering both the impact of possible incidents and the existing vulnerabilities and threats they face.

System objective

The FISMA defines three key security objectives for safeguarding information and information systems which are as follows:

- **Confidentiality**: This involves maintaining authorized restrictions on access and disclosure of information, ensuring personal privacy and protecting proprietary data. A breach of confidentiality occurs when information is disclosed without proper authorization.

- **Integrity**: This objective focuses on protecting information from unauthorized modifications or destruction, and ensuring that information remains accurate and authentic. A loss of integrity happens when data is improperly altered or destroyed.

- **Availability**: This ensures that information and information systems are accessible and usable when needed. A loss of availability refers to disruptions that prevent timely access to or use of information or systems.

These objectives guide how organizations protect their data and systems, addressing potential risks and ensuring the reliable operation of their information infrastructure.

System purpose and functionality

System Purpose is a critical component that articulates the primary objectives for which a system is designed. It serves as a guiding principle that defines the specific problems the system aims to address and the value it offers to both users and the organization. Understanding the system's purpose is essential for ensuring that the design, implementation, and operation align with strategic goals.

There are three main elements of the system purpose as follows:

- **Business objectives**: This objective reflects the broader goals of the organization and serves as the rationale behind developing the system.

- **User needs**: This element focuses on the specific functionalities and features that users require to perform their tasks effectively.

- **Outcomes**: This element represents the actual benefits that the system delivers, and they help organizations measure the success of the system.

System functionality outlines the specific features and operations that a system performs to fulfil its defined purpose. At its core, functionality comprises of essential features such as data entry, processing, storage, and reporting, which are fundamental to the system's operation. These core features ensure that the system can efficiently manage and manipulate the data it handles. Additionally, user interactions and integration capabilities enhance overall system functionality.

Real-world use-cases

An **enterprise data warehouse (EDW)** is a central storage system where an organization gathers and manages large volumes of data from various sources, such as operational systems, external sources, and cloud platforms. It organizes and standardizes this data for analysis, reporting, and decision-making. The EDW makes this data accessible for **business intelligence (BI)** tools and is designed to handle growing amounts of data as the organization expands over time. Following is some of the real-world examples:

- **Ecommerce**: In the fast-moving ecommerce industry, data warehouse processes data instantly to provide insights into customer behavior, buying patterns, and website activity. This helps marketers offer personalized content, recommend products, and provide quick customer service.

- **Healthcare**: In healthcare, data warehouse improves care coordination by giving instant access to patient records, lab results, and treatment plans. They also allow real-time monitoring of patient vitals, enabling quick responses to any critical changes in a patient's condition.

System and system elements

When implementing the RMF, it is crucial to consider information systems within the context of the **system development lifecycle (SDLC)**. This approach ensures that security and privacy capabilities are integrated throughout the various stages of system development. By taking a comprehensive view of the SDLC, organizations can effectively address security and privacy risks, including those related to the supply chain and vendors.

The RMF helps to establish a logical connection between architectural and engineering concepts and the practical implementation of security measures. This ensures that risks are managed at every stage of the system's lifecycle from initial design through deployment and operation. The goal is to incorporate security and privacy considerations into the system from the outset, adapting to changes and challenges as they arise.

ISO 15288 provides an engineering framework that supports this approach by detailing how an information system interacts with its operational environment. This framework helps organizations understand and manage the complexities of integrating security and privacy measures throughout the entire lifecycle of the system. Recognizing these interactions ensures that all potential impacts and dependencies are considered, which can prevent issues and enhance system integration. This comprehensive approach supports effective risk management, ensuring that the system functions smoothly within its broader environment and meets its intended objectives.

There is a total six lifecycle stages in ISO/IEC 15288 as shown in the following figure:

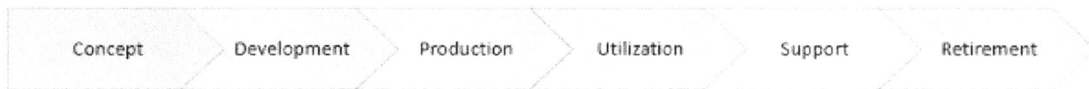

Figure 4.2: Lifecycle stages in ISO/IEC 15288

Let us see the stages in detail:

- **Concept**: Concept is the first stage that defines the system's purpose, goals, and feasibility, establishing a clear understanding of what the system should achieve and how it aligns with stakeholder needs.

- **Development**: Development is the second stage that designs, builds, and integrates the system based on the concept and requirements defined in the concept phase.

- **Production**: Production is the third stage that deploys the system for operational use.

- **Utilization**: Utilization is the fourth stage that operates and uses the system according to its intended purpose.

- **Support**: Support is the fifth stage that provides ongoing support and maintenance to ensure the system continues to meet its requirements over its operational life.

- **Retirement**: Retirement is the last stage that decommissions the system at the end of its lifecycle, ensuring a smooth transition to any replacement systems and a proper disposal of system components.

System interfaces

System interfaces are critical components that define how a system interacts with its users and other software applications, facilitating communication and functionality:

- **User interfaces**: User interfaces are the various ways in which users interact with the system. These interfaces include web portals, where users can access system features and data through a browser, applications that provide a graphical or **command line interface** (**CLI**), and other interactive elements. User interfaces are designed to be intuitive and user-friendly, enabling efficient navigation and operation of the system. By clarifying user interfaces, organizations ensure that end-users can effectively engage with the system and perform their tasks seamlessly.

- **Application interfaces**: Application interfaces on the other hand, refer to the mechanisms through which other software applications communicate with the system. This often involves **application programming interfaces** (**APIs**), which provide a set of protocols and tools for integrating and interacting with the system. Application interfaces are crucial for enabling interoperability between systems, allowing for data exchange and functionality extension. By defining these interfaces, organizations facilitate smooth integration with other software, ensuring that systems can work together efficiently and meet broader operational needs.

Together, user and application interfaces play a vital role in the system's overall functionality and user experience, ensuring both human and machine interactions are well-defined and effective.

Information level tier

NIST SP 800-37 provides guidance on managing information system risks but emphasizes that effective risk management extends beyond the system level. It stresses the need for a comprehensive approach that involves the entire organization. To manage information security risks effectively, all levels of the organization must be engaged, like:

- Individual employees play a crucial role in developing, implementing, and operating information systems, contributing to the overall risk management effort.

- Project and mid-level managers are responsible for overseeing these activities and ensuring that risk management practices are followed.

- Senior leaders are essential for providing strategic direction, setting goals, and ensuring that risk management principles are integrated into the organization's broader mission.

For risk management to be truly effective, it must be embedded in every aspect of the organization's operations and aligned with its strategic objectives. This holistic integration ensures that risk management is not just a set of isolated activities but a fundamental part of the organization's culture and processes. The following figure shows the organization tiers to manage risk effectively:

Figure 4.3: *Information tier*

Let us look at the organizational tiers in detail:

- **Organization level (Tier 1)**: At the organizational level (Tier 1), risk management is addressed from an enterprise-wide perspective through a robust governance structure and a comprehensive risk management strategy. This strategy includes the following several key components:

  - **Assessment of risks**: Organizations need processes for evaluating information system-related security risks and other relevant risks. Typically, these processes adhere to NIST SP 800-30, which outlines methods for performing system level risk assessments.

  - **Evaluation of risks**: After identifying risks, procedures are needed to assess their significance and prioritize them accordingly. NIST SP 800-30 provides guidance on how to prioritize these risks effectively.

  - **Mitigation of risks**: The strategy should outline corrective actions and mitigation measures to address the identified risks. NIST SP 800-53 offers a broad set of security controls that can be used to guide these mitigation efforts.

  - **Acceptance of risk**: Organizations must define their risk tolerance and determine the level of risk they are willing to accept. NIST SP 800-39 provides guidance for establishing an organization's risk appetite.

  - **Monitoring risk**: A continuous monitoring plan is essential to keep track of risk as information systems and their environments evolve. Regular monitoring helps manage new and changing risks.

  - **Risk management strategy oversight**: The strategy should include details on the oversight needed to ensure that the risk management practices are properly implemented and followed. These components together ensure that risk management is systematically integrated into the organization's overall operations and governance framework.

- **Mission/business process level (Tier 2)**: At Tier 2, risk decisions made at the organizational level (Tier 1) drive how mission and business process risks are managed. The business tier focuses on the core activities related to the organization's mission and business processes, closely linked to the enterprise architecture. Key activities include the following:

  o **Identifying core missions and business processes**: Organizations need to define their primary missions and business processes, including those of subordinate elements, to understand their essential functions.

  o **Prioritizing missions and processes**: Missions and business processes are prioritized based on their importance to the organization's goals and objectives. This prioritization helps allocate resources effectively and manage risks according to their impact.

  o **Defining information needs and flows**: Determining how information flows within the organization and between external entities is crucial. This includes mapping out how information is exchanged, processed, and stored, which aids in identifying potential vulnerabilities and ensuring secure information handling.

  o **Information categorization**: At this stage, information is categorized based on its sensitivity and the impact that a loss of CIA would have. This categorization helps in determining the appropriate level of protection required for different types of information.

  o **Developing an information protection strategy**: A comprehensive strategy for protecting information is developed, integrating general security requirements into all core missions and processes to ensure consistency and coverage.

  o **Specifying authority for risk management**: The authority and responsibilities for assessing, evaluating, mitigating, accepting, and monitoring risks are clearly defined for subordinate organizations, such as bureaus or divisions.

These activities ensure that risk management is aligned with the organization's mission and business processes, promoting effective protection and support for critical functions.

- **Information system level (Tier 3)**: Tier 3 of the RMF focuses on managing risks at the information system level. This tier builds on the decisions and strategies established in the higher tiers (Tier 1 and Tier 2), impacting the selection and implementation of security controls for individual systems. NIST SP 800-37 which is central to this tier, provides detailed guidance on this process, integrating well with the broader FISMA-related guidance.

At Tier 3, organizations allocate security control components according to the information security architecture developed in Tier 2. This involves applying system-specific, hybrid, or common controls as outlined in NIST SP 800-53, which details management, operational, and technical security controls. These controls should be traceable to the organization's established security requirements to ensure they are effectively addressed during system design, development, and implementation. Key activities include the following:

- o **Linkage to SDLC**: At this tier, there is a strong connection between risk management and SDLC. Risk management activities are integrated into each phase of the SDLC to ensure that security considerations are embedded from the design and development stages through to deployment and maintenance.

- o **Selection of security controls**: Based on the system's categorization and risk assessment, appropriate security controls are selected. These controls are chosen to mitigate identified risks and ensure that the system meets its security requirements.

- o **Security control allocation and implementation**: Security controls are then allocated and implemented according to the system's architecture. This may involve implementing system-specific controls, utilizing hybrid controls, or leveraging common controls shared across multiple systems.

- o **Security control assessment**: Once implemented, security controls are assessed to verify their effectiveness. This assessment helps determine if the controls are functioning as intended and if they adequately address the risks associated with the system.

- o **Risk acceptance**: After assessing the controls, any residual risks that cannot be mitigated are evaluated for acceptance. The organization must decide whether these risks are acceptable based on its risk tolerance and business objectives.

- o **Continuous monitoring**: Ongoing monitoring of the information system is crucial to ensure that security controls remain effective over time. This includes tracking changes, identifying new risks, and ensuring that controls continue to meet the system's security requirements.

By following these steps, organizations ensure that information systems are protected effectively throughout their lifecycle, aligning with both internal security policies and external regulatory requirements.

Data classification

Data classification is the process of categorizing data based on its sensitivity and the level of protection it requires. The effective data classification is crucial for minimizing risks and ensuring that sensitive information is adequately protected. For example, FIPS 199 provides a structured approach required for classifying *U.S. government* data, ensuring that data is properly categorized based on its sensitivity and protection needs. The data classification schemes are not solely concerned with protecting data from unauthorized disclosure, rather, data classification processes address all three primary system security objectives: CIA.

This broader approach ensures that data is not only protected from unauthorized access but also maintained accurately and accessible when needed. By applying these classification schemes, organizations can effectively manage and safeguard their data across various security dimensions. The example of data classification is shown in *Table 4.1*:

Data sensitivity	Definition	Example	Classification
High	Information that must be closely safeguarded and is restricted to use. If compromised or destroyed, the impact on the organization or individuals would be catastrophic.	Financial records, intellectual property.	Restricted
Medium	Information related to the day-to-day operations of the company and intended for internal use only, and if compromised or destroyed, would not have a catastrophic impact.	Incident report, emails and documents without confidential information.	Internal use
Low	Information that can be disseminated to the public following management review.	public website content, marketing material.	Public

Table 4.1: Data classification

The **Cybersecurity Maturity Model Certification** (**CMMC**) framework aims to protect government information from unauthorized access. It focuses on securing two types of data:

- **Controlled Unclassified Information (CUI)**: This is sensitive data that is not classified but still needs protection, like information related to national defense, financial records, or critical infrastructure.

- **Federal contract information (FCI)**: This is data provided by or created for the U.S. government under contract that isn't meant for public release. It is less sensitive than CUI, but still needs to be carefully protected.

Federal Risk and Authorization Management Program (*FedRAMP*) authorization has three impact levels for cloud providers:

- **Low impact**: The data is publicly available but still important for agency operations. Loss or damage could affect agency performance and constituents.

- **Moderate impact**: The data is more sensitive and could cause serious harm to the agency or its constituents, such as financial losses or privacy breaches.

- **High impact**: Loss or damage of this data could have catastrophic effects, including company reputation or loss of privacy (e.g., health records).

System boundary

Identifying the appropriate boundaries for organizational information systems presents a significant challenge for system owners, authorizing officials, the **chief information officer** (**CIO**), and the **chief information security officer** (**CISO**). System boundaries are crucial as they establish the scope of protection for an information system, encompassing all associated people, processes, and technology components. This collaborative approach helps address the risk management implications of boundary definitions and ensures that they are aligned with mission objectives, technical requirements, and programmatic costs. By integrating these considerations, organizations can maintain robust information security while optimizing resource use.

The definition of system boundaries is a critical part of the initial categorization step in RMF, which must be completed before developing the SSP. Properly defining these boundaries helps in determining the scope of security measures and controls required. If the boundaries are set too broadly, they can lead to excessive complexity and a larger number of components, complicating risk management efforts. On the other hand, overly restrictive boundaries can result in a higher number of systems, increasing security costs and potentially reducing overall efficiency. Balancing these considerations is essential to managing risks effectively, while optimizing resource allocation and maintaining security.

As information systems evolve, it is crucial to periodically reassess system boundaries to ensure they remain relevant and effective. This review is part of the monitoring step in RMF and ensures that system components and subsystems are aligned with current needs and risks. NIST guidance emphasizes that while defining system boundaries, organizations should not be unduly constrained, but should tailor boundaries to fit their mission and business operations effectively.

NIST's updated guidance on system authorization, offers organizations flexibility in defining system boundaries, without imposing a strict framework. However, it highlights the following three key considerations for setting these boundaries effectively:

- **Management control**: Systems should generally fall under the same direct management control. This ensures cohesive oversight and accountability. However, in cases where multiple systems are managed separately, they may still be considered part of a larger, integrated system if they function as subsystems within a more complex framework.

- **Mission and function**: Systems typically support similar mission or business functions and share basic operating characteristics and information security requirements. This alignment helps ensure that the security measures and controls applied are consistent with the system's objectives.

- **Operating environment**: Systems should reside within the same general operating environment. If a system is distributed across various locations, these locations should have similar operating environments to maintain consistent security practices and control measures.

By considering these factors, organizations can define system boundaries that align with their operational and security needs while maintaining flexibility in their approach.

Simple system

In the context of NIST, a simple system refers to an information system with straightforward simple configurations, operations, and interactions. Such systems typically involve fewer components, are easier to manage, and have well-defined boundaries.

The key characteristics are:

- **Limited components**: The system includes a small number of components (hardware, software, network elements) with minimal interactions.

- **Clear boundaries**: The system's operational boundaries are well-defined, making it easier to identify and manage system components.

- **Predictable behavior**: The system's operations are predictable, and interactions between components follow simple cause-and-effect patterns.

- **Low complexity**: The system's architecture and configuration are relatively simple, often with minimal customization or integration.

- **Security controls**: Simple systems can often be managed using standard security controls and procedures. NIST SP 800-53, security and privacy controls for information systems and organizations, provides guidelines that can be directly applied.

- **Documentation**: Documenting the system's configuration, data flows, and security measures is relatively straightforward. Regular updates and reviews are essential but manageable.

- **Risk management**: Risk management for simple systems involves assessing and mitigating straightforward threats. The NIST RMF can be applied with less complexity.

Complex system

Complex systems, according to NIST, involve multiple interacting components, often with complex configurations, numerous interfaces, and dynamic interactions. Managing the security of complex information systems can be challenging due to the intricacies involved in applying security controls. To address this challenge, NIST guidance recommends breaking down complex systems into more manageable subsystems. By decomposing an information system, each subsystem can have its own distinct boundary, allowing for more targeted application of security controls. This approach not only helps in meeting security requirements but also supports cost-effective risk management.

System owners should collaborate with the authorizing official, CISO, information security architect, and information system security engineer to assess the purpose and function of the information system. This collaborative effort ensures that the decomposition aligns with the system's objectives and security needs. Additionally, when dividing a complex system into subsystems, it is crucial to ensure that these subsystems can work together both securely and functionally, maintaining overall system integrity and effectiveness.

The key characteristics are:

- **Multiple interactions**: Complex systems involve numerous components that interact in non-linear ways, making behavior less predictable.

- **Dynamic configuration**: The system's configuration and operational environment may change frequently, introducing new variables and interactions.

- **High interdependency**: Components are highly interdependent, and changes in one part of the system can have cascading effects throughout the entire system.

- **Emergent properties**: The system exhibits behaviors or properties that arise from the interactions of its components, which cannot be easily predicted from the components alone.

NIST considerations

NIST emphasizes several key considerations to address privacy and security for complex systems. Here is a summary of these considerations.

- **Advanced security controls**: For complex systems, security controls need to be more sophisticated and adaptive. NIST SP 800-53 and NIST SP 800-37, guide for applying the RMF to Federal Information Systems, provide frameworks for managing these complexities.

- **System interdependencies**: Understanding and managing interdependencies require detailed mapping and continuous monitoring. Tools and techniques from NIST SP 800-160, systems security engineering, can be utilized to address complex interactions.

- **Risk management**: Complex systems necessitate a more comprehensive risk management approach. NIST's RMF involves detailed risk assessments and continuous monitoring to adapt to changing threats and vulnerabilities.

The following figure shows the complex system by taking an example of **local area network** (**LAN**) network system in the organization:

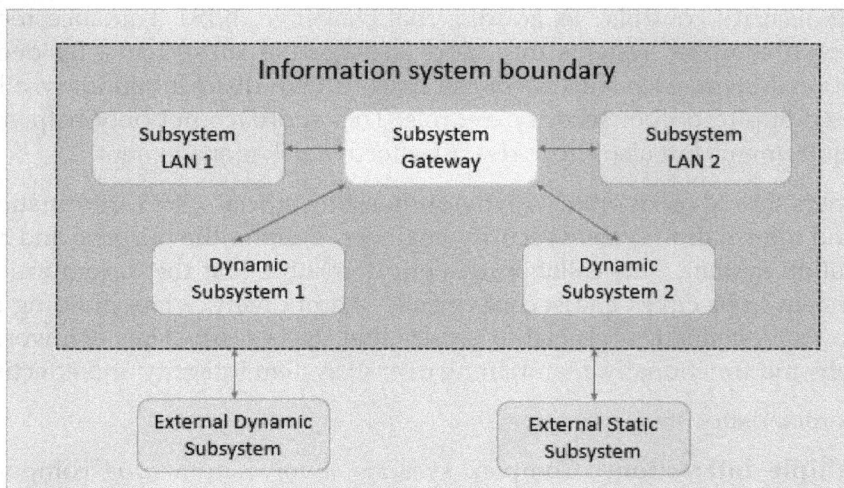

Figure 4.4: Information system boundary

Security control selection and allocation for complex information systems are significantly influenced by the system's overall security architecture. This architecture is designed to manage and monitor communications across various subsystem boundaries and to implement system-wide common controls that address the security needs of each subsystem through inheritance. NIST guidance recommends categorizing each subsystem to facilitate precise and effective security control selection. This method ensures that while the overall system remains categorized based on its highest risk level, each subsystem can be targeted with specific controls that address its unique requirements.

This is crucial for selecting appropriate interconnection security controls that can address potential vulnerabilities arising from these interactions. In cases where subsystems have different security policies or are managed by distinct organizational entities, additional controls are needed to ensure secure interconnections and enforce access policies.

To effectively test the security controls in a complex system, it is efficient to combine assessments of individual subsystems and focus on the interface issues between them. This method not only optimizes the assessment process by aligning it with each subsystem's security categorization, but also allows for the reuse of assessment results at the system level, enhancing cost-effectiveness.

Dynamic subsystem

While the addition of a dynamic subsystem may not usually alter the external boundary of the overall information system, it does impact the internal dynamics. Specifically, the integration of new subsystems can affect interactions and dependencies among existing subsystems within the system boundary. Consequently, the security controls for these internal interactions must be reassessed to ensure that the entire system remains secure and that all subsystems function cohesively. This ongoing adjustment helps maintain the integrity of the system's security posture as it evolves.

Ideally, subsystems should be defined during the initial phase of a system's lifecycle and incorporated into the system's categorization process. This early identification allows for comprehensive planning and integration of security controls from the outset. However, in practice, subsystems are often introduced or identified after the system's initiation. When new subsystems are added during the design phase, it is crucial that the security plan reflects these changes and incorporates appropriate controls for each new subsystem.

When dynamic subsystems are owned by external providers through contracts, licensing agreements, or other arrangements—the organization must carefully evaluate the impact of these subsystems on the existing information system. This involves assessing the capabilities of the new subsystems and conducting a thorough security impact analysis. Such an analysis examines how the new subsystems interact with other parts of the system, their interfaces, and their connections to other systems.

The security impact analysis helps identify potential vulnerabilities and allows for the adjustment of existing security controls as needed. By updating the system design and incorporating these changes into the security plan, organizations can ensure that the integration of new subsystems does not compromise the overall system security. This approach allows for the dynamic addition or removal of subsystems, without necessitating a complete reassessment of the entire information system, provided the new subsystems adhere to predefined constraints and assumptions.

External subsystem

NIST defines external subsystems as components or subsystems that are beyond the direct control of the organization that owns the primary information system. These external subsystems can include various forms of computing services, such as cloud-based solutions or third-party services, which are used to process, store, or transmit the organization's information. They may be provided by external entities, whether public or private, and often come into play through contracts or service agreements.

Since these subsystems are not directly managed by the owning organization, they present unique challenges in terms of security and risk management. Organizations must carefully evaluate and manage the security implications of integrating such external subsystems, ensuring that appropriate controls are in place to protect their information and maintain compliance with security requirements.

Under the FISMA and *Office of Management and Budget* (*OMB*) policy, external subsystems must adhere to the same security standards as those maintained internally by government agencies. This ensures that the security of all systems, whether managed internally or by external service providers, meets federal requirements. Government agencies depend on a robust level of trust established through their relationship with these external entities.

Challenges in external subsystem

Trust in external service providers is often built on positive experiences from long-term relationships or the provider's proven track record in addressing issues effectively. However, establishing and maintaining this trust can be challenging due to several factors highlighted by NIST guidance.

The rapid evolution of external subsystems can also create difficulties. As external systems change swiftly, it becomes challenging for organizations to continuously ensure that these systems meet security requirements. Furthermore, when integrating critical external services into existing organizational systems on a tight timeline, there may not be sufficient opportunity to thoroughly evaluate the effectiveness of the security controls in place. These factors can complicate the trust dynamic and underscore the need for careful management and oversight in relationships with external service providers.

NIST guidance points out several factors that can complicate the level of trust issue, which are as follows:

- Lack of clarity in the delineation between what is owned by the external entity and the organization. For example, an agency-owned platform is used to execute application software developed by an external provider. For instance, when an agency uses an external provider's software on its own platform, distinguishing responsibilities can be problematic. Additionally, the organization may face limitations in controlling certain aspects of the service provider's operations, such as specifying the location for data storage, which could impact compliance and security.

- Limits on the control the organization has over the external provider (for example, inability to specify a geographical location for the storage of its information).

- Possible rapid change of external subsystems, making it difficult or impossible for the organization to gain assurance that security requirements are being met by the external provider.

- Need for incorporation of critical externally provided subsystems or services into existing organizational systems rapidly, thereby restricting the ability to properly assess the effectiveness of necessary controls.

NIST guidelines address both simple and complex information systems by providing a framework for security controls and risk management. Here is a simplified explanation of how these guidelines apply.

NIST framework is built on a flexible approach that allows organizations to tailor security controls according to their specific needs, ensuring that each system receives the appropriate level of protection. Organizations can utilize the structured RMF to assess risks, categorize systems, and select relevant controls. Additionally, NIST promotes the principle of continuous improvement, encouraging organizations to regularly monitor and reassess their security measures.

NIST guidelines empower organizations to strengthen their security posture while effectively addressing the unique requirements of their information systems. This robust framework not only promotes compliance with standards and regulations but also fosters a culture of security awareness that is essential for long-term resilience.

Conclusion

In this chapter, we explored the scope of the information system, focusing on its purpose and functionality. We detailed the types of information that are processed, stored, or transmitted by the system, highlighting the importance of managing these aspects to mitigate risks effectively. The chapter also examined the concept of system boundaries, emphasizing their role in maintaining robust information security by clearly defining what is included within and outside the system.

Furthermore, we addressed stakeholder and system requirements, illustrating how these requirements contribute to the effective development of the system. In the next chapter, we will learn about the personal data information types, examining their specific characteristics and implications for data governance. We will also discuss the security categorization of information, highlighting how it influences the implementation of appropriate security measures. Additionally, we will explore various data security frameworks that provide guidelines for protecting sensitive information effectively.

Key terms

- **Use-case of a simple system**:
    - o **Standalone applications**: A single application running on a personal computer with minimal integration with other systems.
    - o **Basic network configurations**: A small office network with a few computers connected to a central server.
- **Use-case of a complex system**:
    - o **Enterprise systems**: Large-scale ERP systems that integrate various business processes across different departments.
    - o **Cloud computing environments:** Complex cloud infrastructures with multiple services, platforms, and third-party integrations.
- SSP is a formal document outlining system scope, components, boundaries, and security controls.
- High-water mark methodology is a process for assigning the highest impact level to a system based on its most sensitive data.
- Prepare step (NIST SP 800-37 Revision 2) is organizational readiness activities for risk management and system scoping.

- Baseline controls are minimum mandatory controls applied to systems (e.g., FIPS 200 requirements).

- Inherited controls are controls shared across systems, particularly in hybrid or cloud environments.

- Data tagging and labeling are the techniques for classifying and managing sensitive information.

- Continuous monitoring is ongoing evaluation of system security and compliance using NIST SP 800-137 guidance.

- Organizational tiered risk management is NIST's three tiers structure (organization, mission, system) for managing risk comprehensively.

Join our book's Discord space

Join the book's Discord Workspace for Latest updates, Offers, Tech happenings around the world, New Release and Sessions with the Authors:

https://discord.bpbonline.com

CHAPTER 5

System Categorization and Control

Introduction

This chapter focuses on the types of information related to personal data, emphasizing the importance of implementing effective data governance practices. The chapter outlines the frameworks established by the *Federal Information Processing Standards (FIPS) 199* and *200*, which provide guidelines for information categorization and helps organizations determine the necessary security controls based on the impact levels of different data types.

Additionally, the chapter discusses the **Data Protection Impact Assessment (DPIA)**, a structured process designed to identify and evaluate potential risks associated with data processing activities. The chapter also highlights various legal frameworks and regulations like *Health Insurance Portability and Accountability Act (HIPAA)*, *General Data Protection Regulation (GDPR)*, etc., that support the protection of personal data, reinforcing the need for organizations to prioritize data security and privacy in their operations.

Structure

The chapter covers the following main topics:

- Information types
- Security categorization of information

- Federal Information Processing Standards
- Data Protection Impact Assessment
- Health Insurance Portability and Accountability Act
- General Data Protection Regulation

Objectives

By the end of this chapter, you will gain a comprehensive understanding of personal data types and their impact on organizational governance. You will explore the security categorization of different information types and information systems, along with the specifications outlined in FIPS 199 and 200. Additionally, you will learn about the DPIA, which helps in managing effective data protection measures. You will also understand important personal data regulations, including HIPAA and GDPR, providing you with the knowledge needed to navigate the complexities of data governance and compliance.

Information types

There are various types of information serving different purposes including **personally identifiable information (PII)**, **protected health information (PHI)**, financial information, **intellectual property (IP)** information etc. Understanding these information types helps organizations to implement appropriate data governance and security measures. We will focus on personal data types particularly PII, PHI, financial information, and IP information.

Personally identifiable information

PII includes any data that can identify an individual, such as names, addresses, social security numbers, phone numbers, email addresses, and financial information. The importance of PII has increased with the evolution of the internet, e-commerce, and online communication, etc., as PII is essential for various applications like creating online accounts, making financial transactions, etc.

However, unauthorized access or exposure to PII can lead to serious issues, including identity theft, fraud, and privacy violations. As more people share their information online, the risk of misuse has grown, highlighting the need for organizations to implement strong data protection measures. Protecting PII is crucial, not only for maintaining user trust but also for complying with laws that safeguard individuals' privacy rights.

Types of PII records:

- **Direct identifiers** are unique personal identifiers, such as passport numbers, driver's license numbers, and biometric data.
- **Indirect identifiers** are combinations of data fields that can identify someone, like gender, ZIP code, and date of birth together.

Protected health information

PHI specifically relates to sensitive health-related data, including patient records, medical histories, treatment details, and insurance information. The importance of PHI has grown alongside the rise of **electronic health records** (**EHRs**) and the overall digitization of the healthcare industry. In today's healthcare systems, PHI is essential for enabling providers to deliver efficient, patient-centric care. However, protecting PHI is critical due to serious consequences that can arise from breaches, such as medical identity theft, unauthorized disclosure, and misuse of health-related information.

Financial information

The financial information provides various categories of data that require strict security measures to protect against unauthorized access or tampering. This includes transactional data (such as sales and payment records), accounting data (such as general ledger entries and payroll), financial reports (such as income statements and balance sheets), and budgets/forecasts. Additionally, sensitive financial information like tax records, bank details, and credit card information must be safeguarded through encryption, access control, and compliance with regulations such as *Sarbanes-Oxley* (*SOX*) *Act*. Ensuring the **confidentiality, integrity, and availability** (**CIA**) of this financial data is critical in maintaining business trust and legal compliance.

Intellectual property

An IP refers to sensitive data related to an organization's intangible assets, such as patents (inventions and processes), trademarks (brand names, logos, and symbols), copyrights (creative works like software, literature, and music), and trade secrets (confidential business information). This type of information is critical to prevent unauthorized access, theft, or infringement that could harm organization's reputation. There are strong security measures that can be implemented including encryption, access control, and compliance with IP protection laws and regulations. These controls are essential for safeguarding these valuable assets from breaches and unauthorized exploitation.

Key differences of PII and PHI

The following table summarizes the key differences between PII and PHI:

	PII	**PHI**
Scope	PII includes a wide variety of identifying details, such as names, addresses, and social security numbers.	PHI is specifically focused on health-related information, like medical records and treatment histories.
Regulations	PII is governed by various data protection laws, such as GDPR and CCPA.	PHI is specifically regulated under HIPAA, which sets stringent standards for handling health information.
Industry use-case	PII is utilized across multiple sectors, such as finance and retail.	PHI is exclusive to healthcare settings, focusing solely on health-related information.
Risks	Unauthorized access to PII can lead to identity theft, fraud, and privacy invasions in various contexts.	Breaches of PHI can have serious consequences, including identity theft, unauthorized medical treatments, and violations of patient privacy rights.
Security measures	PII requires general data protection strategies, like encryption, access controls, and privacy policies.	PHI demands more stringent security measures due to regulatory compliance, which includes audits, training, and breach notification procedures.

Table 5.1: PII and PHI comparison

Security categorization of information

The **security category** (**SC**) can be applied to both information types and information system, as shown in the following figure:

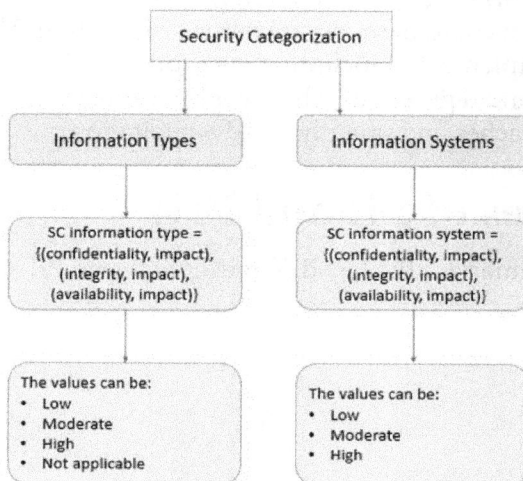

Figure 5.1: Security categorization

Security category of information types

The SC of an information type applies to both user and system information and can encompass data in electronic or non-electronic formats. This categorization helps in assessing the appropriate security measures for an information system by evaluating the potential impact on each security objective CIA associated with the information type. Essentially, establishing the correct SC involves determining the potential impact of a breach for each of these security objectives, ensuring that the information is protected according to its level of sensitivity and importance.

The SC of an information type is expressed in the following format:

SC information type = {(confidentiality, impact), (integrity, impact), (availability, impact)}

Here, each aspect of the SC CIA is assigned an impact value that can be LOW, MODERATE, HIGH, or **NOT APPLICABLE** (**NA**). This format helps in clearly defining the level of protection needed for each security objective associated with the information type.

Example:

For an organization managing public information on its web server, the SC of the information type would be determined as follows: Since there is no potential impact from a loss of confidentiality, the confidentiality requirement is deemed NA. However, there is a moderate potential impact from both a loss of integrity and a loss of availability. Therefore, the resulting SC is expressed as:

SC public information = {(confidentiality, NA), (integrity, MODERATE), (availability, MODERATE)}

Security category of information system

The SC of an information system involves a more detailed analysis, as it must consider the security categories of all information types within the system. To establish the SC for the system, you must evaluate the potential impact values for each security objective CIA. These values should be the highest levels, known as the **high-water mark**, among the security categories assigned to the various types of information present in the system. This approach ensures that the system's security measures are adequately aligned with the most critical security needs of all the information it handles.

The SC of an information system is expressed in the following format:

SC information system = {(confidentiality, impact), (integrity, impact), (availability, impact)}

This is where the potential impact values for CIA are categorized as LOW, MODERATE, or HIGH. This format provides a clear framework for defining the overall security requirements of the system based on the highest impact levels associated with each security objective.

Example:

Consider an information system used for large acquisitions in a contracting organization. This system handles both sensitive, pre-solicitation phase contract information and routine administrative information. To determine the SC of this system, you would first assess the potential impact of a loss of CIA for each type of information.

Given the security categories for the different types of information handled by the acquisition system, the resulting SC for the entire system is determined by identifying the highest potential impact values for each security objective.

The security categories for the information types are:

- **SC contract information**: *{(confidentiality, MODERATE), (integrity, MODERATE), (availability, LOW)}*

- **SC administrative information**: *{(confidentiality, LOW), (integrity, LOW), (availability, LOW)}*

To determine the SC of the acquisition system, you select the highest impact value for each security objective from these categories:

- **Confidentiality**: The highest impact value is MODERATE (from both contract and administrative information).

- **Integrity**: The highest impact value is MODERATE (from contract information).

- **Availability**: The highest impact value is LOW (from all types).

Thus, the resulting SC for the information system is:

SC acquisition system = {(confidentiality, MODERATE), (integrity, MODERATE), (availability, LOW)}

This reflects the maximum potential impact values for each security objective based on the information types resident in the acquisition system.

> **Note: The value of NA cannot be assigned to any security objective in the context of establishing a SC for an information system.**

Assigning security categorization and impact level

The methodology for assigning security impact levels and categorizing information types and systems is crucial for ensuring that organizations meet their mission and business objectives effectively. Based on the guidelines outlined in FIPS 199, this process helps organizations systematically evaluate the potential impact of data breaches and security incidents. Familiarity with FIPS 199 is assumed, as it serves as the foundation for these categorizations.

The security categorization process involves four key steps, which guide organizations in determining the appropriate level of security controls needed. These steps assess the nature of the information being handled, the potential risks associated with its exposure, and the implications for organizational operations. By following this structured approach, organizations can align their security measures with their specific mission requirements and ensure compliance with federal standards. The following figure outlines the security categorization process steps:

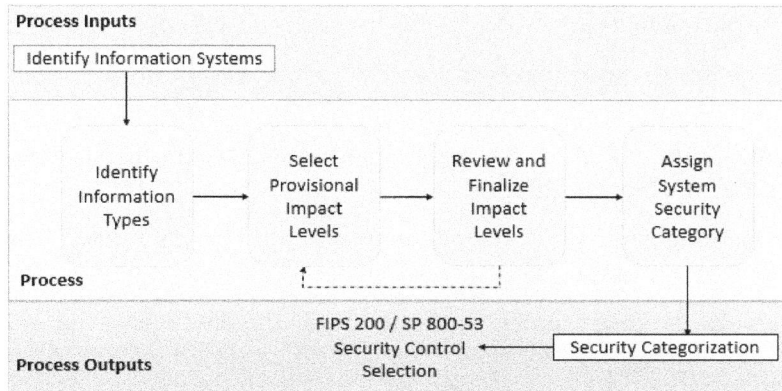

Figure 5.2: *Security categorization process*

Let us look at the steps in detail:

1. **Step one**: Identify information types:

   This is the first step where organizations should identify all the relevant information types associated with their systems, including data that is input, stored, processed, or output. The first step in aligning federal information and systems with security objectives and impact levels is to create an information taxonomy, which serves as a catalog of these information types.

2. **Step two**: Select provisional impact levels:

   In this step, organizations should assign initial impact levels based on the information types identified in *Step one*. These provisional impact levels reflect the original ratings for CIA of each information type before any modifications are made.

3. **Step three**: Review and finalize impact levels:

   In this step, organizations should assess and finalize the provisional security impact levels for each information type. To do this, organization should evaluate whether the provisional levels are suitable based on the organization's context, mission, usage, and data sharing. After evaluating provisional levels organization should make necessary adjustments and document all changes along with the reasons for those adjustments.

4. **Step four**: Assign system SC:

   After selecting and adjusting the security impact levels for each information type, the next step is to assign a system SC based on the overall information types. This involves the following:

   o Reviewing the security categorizations of all identified information types.

   o Determining the system security categorization by finding the highest impact level (high-water mark) for each security objective (CIA).

   o Adjusting these levels if needed, using the guidance available in FIPS section.

   o Assigning the overall impact level based on the highest value from the security objectives.

   o Documenting all decisions and determinations related to the security categorization.

The impact levels of management and support information used across various organizations are influenced by the associated mission-based information. When organization information is linked to very sensitive or critical mission data, it may signify a higher impact level compared to when the same information is used with less critical data. This relationship underscores the importance of context in assessing information security.

Moreover, information systems are designed to process a diverse array of information types, each with varying security impact levels. Not all types of information pose the same risks; the compromise of certain data may threaten system functionality and the overall mission of the agency more significantly than others.

NIST guidance on security categorization

The second step in the **Risk Management Framework** (**RMF**) is categorize. The purpose of the categorize step is to help risk management by identifying the potential impact on operations and assets if the CIA of systems is lost. The following figure shows the second step of *National Institute of Standards and Technology* (*NIST*) RMF:

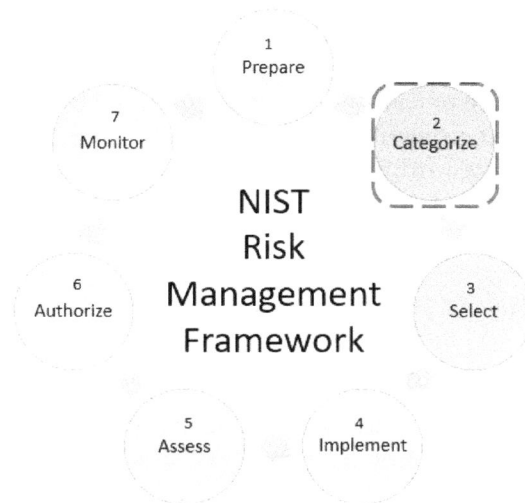

Figure 5.3: *RMF steps*

The categorization step helps to prioritize security measures and ensures that the organization understands the consequences of any security breaches. The following figure shows the task associated with categorization step:

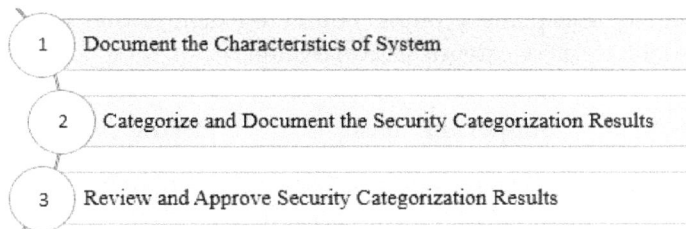

Figure 5.4: *Control categorization tasks*

Here are the details of all categorization tasks:

- **Task 1**: Document the characteristics of system:

  The system characteristics are documented in security and privacy plans, including relevant attachments or other sources from the **system development lifecycle (SDLC)**. These plans are updated as new information becomes available or system characteristics change, with details aligned to the system's security categorization and risk assessments. The level of detail in these plans is based on the system's risk and security needs. Examples of descriptive information that may be included are the system name, version, purpose, architecture, information types, components, users, physical processes, interconnections, laws/regulations, and maintenance agreements, among others. The following table shows the roles to document characteristics of the system:

Primary responsibility	Supporting roles	SDLC phase	References
System owner	Authorizing official or authorizing official designated representative, information owner or steward, system security officer, system privacy officer.	New: Initiation Existing: Operations/ maintenance	NIST SP 800-18; NIST CSF

Table 5.2: Roles to document characteristics of system

- **Task 2**: Categorize and document the security categorization results:

    Security categorization involves assessing the potential impact of losing CIA of information on organizational operations, assets, individuals, and the nation. Organizations can use FIPS 200 for a single impact level (for non-national security systems) or CNSSI 1253 for three separate impact values for CIA (for national security systems). This process is a collaborative effort between the system owner, information owner, and senior leaders to ensure categorization aligns with mission and business objectives. The decision is influenced by security and privacy risk assessments and is consistent with the organization's risk management strategy. The results guide the selection of security controls, which are documented in the system security and privacy plans. Following table shows the roles to categorize and document security categorization results.

Primary responsibility	Supporting roles	SDLC phase	References
System owner; information owner or steward	Senior accountable official for risk management or risk executive, chief information officer, senior agency information security officer, senior agency official for privacy, authorizing official or authorizing official designated representative, system security officer, system privacy officer	New: Initiation Existing: Operations/ maintenance	NIST SP 800-30; SP 800-39; SP 800-59; SP 800-60 v1; SP 800-60 v2; SP 800-160 v1; FIPS 199; FIPS 200 NIST CSF; CNSSI 1253

Table 5.3: Roles to categorize and document results

- **Task 3**: Review and approve security categorization results:

    For information systems that process PII, the senior agency official for privacy must review and approve the security categorization results before the authorizing official does. The authorizing official or their representative then ensures the chosen SC aligns with the organization's mission and business functions and is consistent across all systems. They work with the senior risk management official to confirm that the categorization fits the organization's risk management strategy and meets high-value asset requirements. If the categorization is not approved, the system owner must revise it and resubmit the results. Once approved, the security categorization is updated in the system registration information. The following table shows the roles to review and approve security categorization results:

Primary responsibility	Supporting roles	SDLC phase	References
Authorizing official or authorizing official designated representative, senior agency official for privacy	Senior accountable official for risk management or risk executive, chief information officer, senior agency information security officer	New: Initiation Existing: Operations/maintenance	NIST SP 800-30; SP 800-39; SP 800-160 v1; FIPS 199; NIST CSF

Table 5.4: Roles to review and approve results

Federal Information Processing Standards

The FIPS are a set of security requirements established by the *U.S. government* to ensure the protection and encryption of data. These standards are publicly available and endorsed by the *U.S. federal government*, with oversight provided by the NIST. Organizations, including government agencies, partners, and entities who seek to engage with the federal government, are mandated to comply with FIPS guidelines.

FIPS are tailored to address the various levels of data sensitivity and value. Private and government organizations have different classifications of data, as we have seen in previous chapters. As the classification of government data ranges from classified to top secret, the severity of the FIPS standards increases accordingly. This means that the standards imposed on how data is handled, protected, and transmitted becomes more stringent based on the secrecy and sensitivity of the information. Organizations must adhere to these standards to ensure that their practices, technologies, and personnel are equipped to manage and secure government information appropriately.

Key specifications of Federal Information Processing Standards

There are various key specifications of FIPS to ensure that federal data is protected through robust encryption methods, secure hashing, effective authentication mechanisms, and comprehensive security controls. The following table specifies some key specifications that align with the U.S. government's requirements for data protection and information security:

FIPS specifications	Description
FIPS 140	Security requirements for cryptographic modules
FIPS 180	FIPS 180: **Secure Hash Standard** (**SHS**)
FIPS 186	**Digital Signature Standard** (**DSS**)
FIPS 197	Announcing the **Advanced Encryption Standard** (**AES**)
FIPS 198	Keyed **Hash-based Message Authentication Code** (**HMAC**)
FIPS 199	Standards for security categorization
FIPS 200	Minimum security requirements
FIPS 201	**Personal identity verification** (**PIV**)
FIPS 202	SHA-3 standard: Permutation-based hash and extendable-output functions

Table 5.5: Key specifications of FIPS

We will focus on FIPS 199 and FIPS 200 in this chapter to ensure that minimum security requirements and standards for security categorization.

Introduction to FIPS 199 and FIPS 200

FIPS 200 (Minimum security requirements), is a mandatory federal standard established by NIST in response to the *Federal Information Security Management Act* (*FISMA*). This publication outlines essential security requirements that Federal Information Systems must meet to ensure adequate protection of federal data.

To comply with this standard, organizations must first determine the SC of their information system according to FIPS 199 (Standards for security categorization), which provides guidelines for categorizing federal information based on its impact level. Once the SC is established, organizations conclude the system's impact level as specified in FIPS 200. This impact level helps in tailoring the appropriate set of baseline security controls detailed in NIST SP 800-53. This publication offers a comprehensive set of security and privacy controls designed to safeguard Federal Information Systems and organizations. By following these guidelines, organizations can ensure that their information systems are secured, in accordance with federal requirements.

FIPS 199

FIPS Publication 199 focuses on establishing standards for categorizing information and information systems, which is the initial step in managing information security. This publication provides a common framework for classifying the security needs of Federal Information Systems based on their impact levels. By categorizing information and systems, it ensures a standardized approach to expressing and managing security requirements.

For the federal government, these categorization standards are crucial as they facilitate effective management and oversight of information security programs. They promote coordinated efforts across various sectors, including civilian, national security and law enforcement. This coordinated approach helps streamline information security practices, ensuring a unified strategy for protecting federal data and systems across diverse government functions and agencies.

Information system impact levels

FIPS Publication 199 defines three levels of potential impact—LOW, MODERATE, and HIGH that describe the consequences of a security breach involving a loss of CIA. These impact levels are intended to guide organizations in assessing the severity of potential risks associated with their information systems. The application of these definitions must be tailored to the specific context of each organization and considered within the broader scope of national interests. By evaluating potential impacts in this manner, organizations can ensure that their security measures are appropriately aligned with both their operational needs and the overarching security objectives of the nation:

- **LOW impact**: The potential impact is considered LOW if loss of CIA would only cause minor harm to organizational operations, assets, or individuals.

- **MODERATE impact**: The potential impact is considered MODERATE if loss of CIA could significantly harm organizational operations, assets, or individuals.

- **HIGH impact**: The potential impact is considered HIGH if loss of CIA could cause severe or catastrophic damage to organizational operations, assets, or individuals.

FIPS 200

FIPS 200 standard outlines the minimum security requirements for federal information and information systems across seventeen security-related areas. Federal agencies are required to comply with these minimum security requirements by implementing the relevant security controls specified in NIST SP 800-53. This ensures that agencies adopt a comprehensive approach to safeguarding sensitive information and maintaining the integrity and availability of their information systems. By adhering to these standards, federal agencies can effectively manage risks and protect against potential security threats.

Minimum security requirements

The minimum security requirements comprise 17 security-related areas focused at safeguarding the CIA of Federal Information Systems and the information they process, store, and transmit. These areas collectively represent a comprehensive and balanced information security program that addresses the management, operational, and technical aspects of protection. By covering a wide range of considerations, the requirements ensure that federal agencies can effectively mitigate risks and maintain robust security measures for their information and systems, thereby enhancing overall security posture.

The security-related areas include the following, as shown in the following table:

Security area	Description
Access control	• Organizations must restrict access to information systems to only authorized users and processes.
Awareness and training	• Organizations must ensure that managers and users of information systems understand the security risks related to their activities and the relevant laws. • Personnel are provided with adequate training to perform their information security duties effectively.
Audit and accountability	• Organizations must create, protect, and keep audit records of information systems to monitor and investigate any unlawful or unauthorized activity. • Ensure that the actions of individual users can be traced back to them for accountability.
Certification, accreditation, and security assessments	• Organizations must periodically assess the security controls in organizational information systems. Develop and implement plans of action designed to correct deficiencies and manage vulnerabilities.
Configuration management	• Organizations must create and maintain baseline configurations and inventories of their information systems. Establish and enforce security configuration settings.
Contingency planning	• Organizations must create, maintain, and effectively implement plans for emergency response and backup operations.
Identification and authentication	• Organizations must identify users, processes acting on their behalf, and devices, and authenticate (or verify) their identities.
Incident response	• Organizations must setup an incident handling capability for their information systems that includes preparation, detection, analysis, containment, recovery, and user response; and Track, document, and report incidents to the relevant officials or authorities.
Maintenance	• Organizations must carry out regular and timely maintenance on their information systems. Implement effective controls over the tools, techniques, and personnel involved in system maintenance.
Media protection	• Organizations must protect both paper and digital information system media. Restrict access to this information to authorized users sanitize or destroy media before disposal or reuse.

Security area	Description
Physical and environmental protection	• Organizations must restrict physical access to information systems and equipment to authorized individuals. Secure the physical environment and infrastructure for these systems; and ensure utilities are available for information systems; Protect systems from environmental hazards Implement suitable environmental controls in facilities housing information systems.
Planning	• Organizations must create, document, regularly update, and implement security plans for their information systems.
Personnel security	• Organizations must ensure that individuals are trustworthy and meet security criteria. Protect information and systems during and after personnel actions like terminations and transfers. Impose formal sanctions on personnel who do not comply with security policies and procedures.
Risk assessment	• Organizations must regularly assess the risks to their operations, assets, and individuals from the use of their information systems and the handling of organizational information.
System and services acquisition	• Organizations must provide enough resources to protect their information systems. Use system development processes that include information security. Enforce restrictions on software usage and installation Ensure that third-party providers implement proper security measures.
System and communications protection	• Organizations must monitor, control, and protect communications at the external and key internal boundaries of their information systems. • Use architectural designs, software development methods, and systems engineering principles.
System and information integrity	• Organizations must identify, report, and fix flaws in information and information systems. Protect against malicious code in key areas of their systems. Monitor security alerts and advisories related to their information systems.

Table 5.6: FIPS 200 security areas

Data Protection Impact Assessment

Most organizations collect, store, or use personal data in one form or another, and this can lead to various risks associated with the handling of their information. These risks can include the theft or accidental release of personal data, which may be exploited by hackers or unauthorized personnel. Additionally, individuals may not be sure about how their data is being used by employers and whether it is used for the intended purpose only.

To address these risks, a DPIA provides a structured process for identifying and evaluating potential risks related to the processing of personal data. The primary goal of a DPIA is to minimize these risks as early as possible, ensuring that appropriate measures are in place to protect personal data. By conducting DPIA, organizations can mitigate risks as well as demonstrate their compliance with the GDPR, reinforcing their commitment to data protection and privacy. This proactive approach is essential for maintaining trust with individuals whose data is being processed.

Benefits of Data Protection Impact Assessment

Conducting a DPIA significantly boosts awareness within the organization regarding the data protection risks associated with a project. By systematically identifying these risks, DPIA enables teams to better understand the potential implications for personal data handling, which can lead to better project design. This proactive approach allows the implementation of effective data protection measures from the outset.

Additionally, DPIA enhances communication about data privacy risks with relevant stakeholders, promoting transparency and collaboration. Organizations can build trust by clearly articulating the identified risks and the strategies in place to mitigate them. This will ensure that all parties involved are informed and aligned in their commitment to safeguarding personal data. Some of the benefits of conducting a DPIA are as follows:

- Ensures compliance with GDPR and avoids penalties.
- Builds public confidence through better communication about data protection.
- Protects user's data as per protection rights.
- Integrates data protection by design into new projects.
- Reduces operational costs by optimizing information flows and minimizing unnecessary data collection.
- Lowers data protection-related risks.
- Decreases costs and disruptions by incorporating safeguards early in project design.
- Lowers the chance of data breaches for systems, cookies, apps, and websites.
- Less risk of high costs for data breach recovery, fines, lawsuits, and lost business.
- Easier compliance with other data protection regulations.

Data Protection Impact Assessment process

A DPIA should be initiated early in a project's lifecycle, ideally before any data processing begins, and continue throughout the planning and development phases. This proactive approach ensures that data protection considerations are integrated from the start. The DPIA process typically includes several key steps, such as identifying the data to be processed, assessing the potential risks to individuals' privacy, evaluating the necessity and proportionality of the data processing, and implementing measures to mitigate identified risks. By following these steps, organizations can effectively manage data protection risks and ensure compliance with relevant regulations. The steps are mentioned in the following figure:

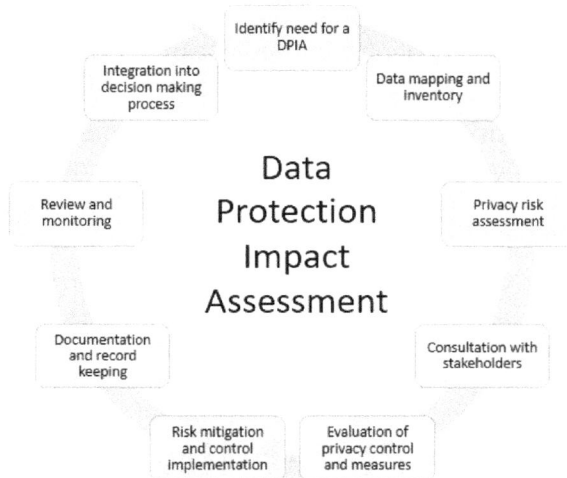

Figure 5.5: *DPIA steps*

Following is the breakdown of the key steps involved in conducting a DPIA:

- **Identification of the need for a DPIA**: The first step is to decide if a DPIA is necessary for a specific project, system, or data processing activity. This involves evaluating the potential risks to an individual's privacy rights and freedoms from the proposed processing.

- **Data mapping and inventory**: Organizations must identify and document the types of personal data being processed, the reasons for processing, the sources of data, and the data flows involved. This step helps clarify the scope and context of the processing activities.

- **Privacy risk assessment**: Conduct a detailed evaluation of the potential risks to individuals' privacy rights related to the processing activities. This includes considering factors like the type of data, the extent of processing, the context in which it occurs, and the possible consequences for individuals.

- **Consultation with stakeholders**: Involve relevant stakeholders, such as data subjects, **data protection officers** (**DPOs**), internal teams, and external experts, to gather their insights on potential privacy risks and ways to mitigate them.

- **Evaluation of privacy controls and measures**: Assess how well current privacy controls, security measures, and data protection policies work to reduce privacy risks. Identify any gaps or weaknesses that need to be addressed to ensure compliance with data protection regulations.

- **Risk mitigation and control implementation**: Create and put in place measures to effectively reduce identified privacy risks. This might include using privacy-enhancing technologies, adopting privacy-by-design principles, improving security controls, or changing data processing practices.

- **Documentation and record-keeping**: Keep a record of the DPIA process, including its scope, findings, recommendations, and decisions made. Ensure that this documentation is maintained according to regulatory requirements and internal policies.

- **Review and monitoring**: Regularly assess and monitor the effectiveness of the privacy controls and measures in place. This helps ensure compliance with data protection regulations and allows the organization to quickly address any new privacy risks or changes in processing activities.

- **Integration into decision-making processes**: Incorporate the findings and recommendations from the DPIA into the organization's decision-making processes. Ensure that privacy considerations are prioritized throughout the project or system lifecycle to reduce risks and protect individuals' privacy rights.

Health Insurance Portability and Accountability Act

The HIPAA of 1996 sets federal standards to protect sensitive health information from being shared without a patient's consent. The *U.S. Department of Health and Human Services* (*HHS*) created the *HIPAA Privacy Rule* to enforce these requirements. Additionally, the *HIPAA Security Rule* safeguards specific information covered by the HIPAA Privacy Rule.

Health Insurance Portability and Accountability Act rules

HIPAA legislation is essentially comprised of five rules, each of which lays out different requirements for HIPAA compliance. The rules are shown in the following figure:

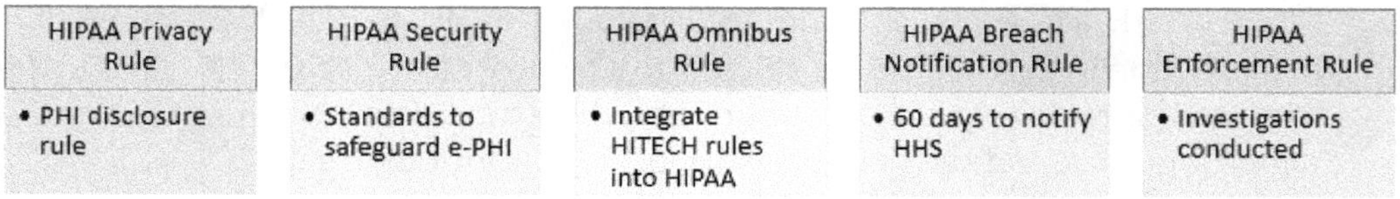

HIPAA Privacy Rule	HIPAA Security Rule	HIPAA Omnibus Rule	HIPAA Breach Notification Rule	HIPAA Enforcement Rule
• PHI disclosure rule	• Standards to safeguard e-PHI	• Integrate HITECH rules into HIPAA	• 60 days to notify HHS	• Investigations conducted

Figure 5.6: *HIPAA rules*

- **HIPAA Privacy Rule**: The HIPAA Privacy Rule establishes standards for how PHI can be used and disclosed by entities known as **covered entities**. These include healthcare providers, health plans, and healthcare clearinghouses that handle PHI. The privacy rule ensures that individuals' health information is treated with respect and confidentiality.

In addition to regulating the use of PHI, the privacy rule outlines individual's rights to understand and control how their health information is used. This includes the right to access their health records and request corrections. By balancing the need for healthcare providers to access information with the necessity of protecting individual privacy, the privacy rule promotes high-quality healthcare and safeguards public health. It allows for essential uses of health information while ensuring that the privacy of those seeking care is upheld.

- **HIPAA Security Rule**: While the HIPAA Privacy Rule protects all forms of PHI, the HIPAA Security Rule focuses specifically on a subset of this information known as **electronic-PHI (e-PHI)**. This includes any individually identifiable health information that a covered entity creates, receives, maintains, or transmits in electronic form.

  The HIPPA Security Rule establishes specific safeguards to ensure the CIA of e-PHI, addressing various aspects such as administrative, physical, and technical protections. However, it is important to note that the security rule does not cover PHI transmitted orally or in written form. This distinction motivates the need for enhanced security measures for electronic information, reflecting the increasing reliance on digital systems in the healthcare sector. By focusing on e-PHI, the security rule aims to mitigate risks associated with electronic data breaches and unauthorized access.

  To comply with the HIPAA Security Rule, all covered entities must:

  - Ensure the CIA of all e-PHI.
  - Identify and guard against potential security threats to the information.
  - Protect against unauthorized uses or disclosures of e-PHI.
  - Ensure that their workforce is trained and compliant with these requirements.

- **HIPAA Omnibus Rule**: The Omnibus Rule brought significant changes to HIPAA, largely implementing provisions from the *Health Information Technology for Economic and Clinical Health (HITECH) Act*. One of the key changes was the extension of HIPAA coverage to **business associates (BAs)**, which means that these third-party vendors who handle PHI are now also held accountable for compliance.

  Additionally, the Omnibus Rule established stricter guidelines regarding the use of PHI for marketing and fundraising. It prohibits organizations from using individuals' health information for these purposes without obtaining explicit authorization. This change enhances patient privacy and gives individuals more control over how their information is used.

  Furthermore, the Omnibus Rule introduced new penalty tiers for HIPAA violations, which are designed to reflect the severity and nature of the breaches. These penalties serve as a stronger deterrent against non-compliance, reinforcing the importance of safeguarding PHI and ensuring that all covered entities and business associates adhere to HIPAA regulations.

- **HIPAA Breach Notification Rule:** The Department of HHS requires notification in the event of a data breach involving PHI. If a breach affects 500 or more individuals, organizations must report it within 60 days of discovering the incident. For breaches involving fewer than 500 records, the notification deadline is extended to 60 days after the end of the calendar year in which the breach occurred.

  In addition to notifying HHS, organizations are also required to inform individuals whose personal information has been compromised within the same 60 day timeframe. This direct communication is crucial for individuals to understand the potential risks and take necessary precautions.

  If a breach impacts more than 500 individuals within a specific jurisdiction, the organization must also issue a media notice to a prominent news outlet in that area. This ensures that the public is informed and can take appropriate actions to protect their information, further enhancing transparency and accountability in handling health data breaches.

- **HIPAA Enforcement Rule:** If a violation of HIPAA occurs, the enforcement process is outlined in the HIPAA rules. Typically, a covered entity or business associate will agree to voluntary compliance, which may include receiving technical assistance from the *Office for Civil Rights (OCR)*. However, if non-compliance persists, the OCR has the authority to impose civil monetary penalties and mandate corrective action plans for both covered entities and business associates. Since 2009, state attorneys general have also been empowered to seek civil penalties in cases where a HIPAA violation leads to a data breach.

  These cases are referred to the *Department of Justice* for a criminal investigation. If the individuals are found guilty of wrongful disclosure, they could face severe penalties, including fines of up to $250,000 and potential imprisonment for up to ten years. This determines the seriousness with which HIPAA violations are treated and the commitment to safeguarding individuals' health information.

General Data Protection Regulation

The GDPR is recognized as the most stringent privacy and security law globally. Although it was created by the *European Union (EU)*, it applies to organizations around the world that target or collect data about individuals in the EU. GDPR is enforced since May 25, 2018, that imposes significant penalties for non-compliance, with fines that can reach tens of millions of euros.

The GDPR is an EU law that sets mandatory guidelines for how organizations and companies must handle personal data in a way that respects individual's privacy. Personal data comprise of any information that can directly or indirectly identify a living person. This includes various examples like names, phone numbers, and addresses, as well as indirect data, such as interests, purchase history, health information, and online behavior.

Processing data refers to a range of activities, including collecting, organizing, using, storing, sharing, disclosing, erasing, and destroying data. Since virtually every organization has employees and customers, they all process personal data and must comply with GDPR requirements. This means ensuring that any personal data they handle must comply to the principles outlined in the regulation and, hence protecting individual's rights and privacy.

Key terminology in General Data Protection Regulation

The GDPR introduces several key terminology concepts that are essential for understanding its framework and requirements. Following is some key terminology:

- **Personal data**: Personal data refers to any information that can identify an individual, either directly or indirectly. Examples include names, email addresses, location information, ethnicity, gender, biometric data, religious beliefs, web cookies, and political opinions.

- **Data processing**: This refers to any action taken on data, whether done manually or automatically. It includes activities like collecting, recording, organizing, storing, using, and deleting data.

- **Data subject**: This is the individual whose personal data is being processed. This can be your customers.

- **Data controller**: This is the individual or entity that decides how and why personal data is processed. If you own or work for an organization that handles data, this role applies to you.

- **Data processor**: This refers to a third-party that processes personal data on behalf of a data controller. The GDPR imposes specific rules on data processors, which can include cloud services like Google drive, email services etc.

Data protection principles

Any organization processing personal data must adhere to seven key protection and accountability principles outlined by the GDPR, which are as follows:

Data principles	Description
Lawfulness, fairness, and transparency	Data processing must be lawful, fair, and transparent to the individuals.
Purpose limitation	Data should only be processed for legitimate purposes that were explicitly communicated to the individual at the time of collection.
Data minimization	Only the minimum amount of necessary data must be collected and for the specified purposes.
Accuracy	Personal data must be kept accurate and updated as needed.

Data principles	Description
Storage limitation	Personally identifiable data can only be stored for as long as necessary to fulfil the specified purpose.
Integrity and confidentiality	Data processing must ensure appropriate security and confidentiality, using measures like encryption.
Accountability	The data controller must demonstrate compliance with all these principles, showing that they are taking the necessary steps to protect personal data.

Table 5.7: GDPR data protection principles

Conclusion

In this chapter, we examined the scope of information types related to personal data, identifying their specific characteristics and implications. We also discussed the security categorization of both information types and information systems, emphasizing how these classifications enhance organizational security measures. Additionally, we explored the data security framework designed to strengthen these protections and covered the DPIA process to effectively manage risks and ensure compliance with relevant regulations.

Moreover, we addressed important privacy and security regulations, including HIPAA and GDPR, outlining their standards and requirements. In the next chapter, we will learn about control categories and the various privacy data frameworks, building on our understanding of how to safeguard personal data effectively.

Key terms

- **Regulatory Frameworks for PII**: GDPR is a comprehensive regulation from the EU that applies to organizations around the world if they handle the data of EU residents.

- **Regulatory Frameworks for PHI**: HIPAA focuses on ensuring the confidentiality and security of PHI.

- **FIPS**: Primarily focuses on cryptographic standards and security requirements or systems.

- **FedRAMP**: Specifically addresses the security of cloud services used by federal agencies.

- **FedRAMP and CMMC**: Modern compliance frameworks for cloud systems and supply chain security.

- **Data minimization (GDPR)**: A principle requiring data collection and processing to be limited to what is strictly necessary.

CHAPTER 6

Introduction to Control Selection and Approval

Introduction

This chapter delves into the fundamentals of security controls, providing essential guidance for developing a robust security strategy and selecting appropriate controls. The chapter highlights the importance of the *Center for Internet Security (CIS) Benchmark* and the **CIS Critical Security Controls** (**CIS Controls**) in improving organizational security. In addition to security controls, the chapter outlines the *American Institute of Certified Public Accountants (AICPA)* **Privacy Management Framework** (**PMF**), which helps organizations integrate privacy considerations into their processes.

Furthermore, the chapter introduces the *National Institute of Standards and Technology (NIST)* Privacy Framework, designed to assist organizations in managing privacy risks efficiently. It highlights the key considerations related to the *European Union (EU)-United States (U.S.)* **Data Privacy Framework** (**DPF**), addressing compliance and data protection issues that arise from cross-border data transfers. Finally, the chapter covers privacy assessments, equipping organizations with the tools needed to analyze the privacy risks and take appropriate action.

Structure

The chapter covers the following main topics:

- Security control overview
- CIS Controls
- AICPA Privacy Management Framework
- Singapore Personal Data Protection Act
- NIST Privacy Framework
- Data Privacy Framework
- Privacy assessment overview

Objectives

By the end of this chapter, you will have a thorough understanding of security controls and their various types. You will explore the CIS Benchmark and its Controls, which are essential for strengthening organizational security. Additionally, you will learn about different PMFs, such as those established by AICPA, NIST, and the EU-U.S. DPF, gaining insights into how these frameworks guide effective privacy practices.

Furthermore, you will learn about the critical steps involved in implementing a Privacy Framework and the key elements related to data privacy. The chapter will also cover **Privacy Impact Assessments (PIAs)**, highlighting their significance in identifying and mitigating privacy risks. This comprehensive overview will equip you with the knowledge necessary to navigate the complexities of security and privacy management in today's data-driven landscape.

Security controls overview

Security controls are essential measures implemented by organizations to protect their information systems and data from various threats and vulnerabilities. These controls serve as safeguards that help mitigate risks, ensuring the **confidentiality, integrity, and availability (CIA)** of sensitive information. NIST SP 800-53 categorizes control into 20 control families, including areas such as access control, incident response, and security training. Each family addresses specific aspects of security, allowing organizations to create a comprehensive security strategy.

The effectiveness of security controls can be enhanced by classifying them into three types: **Managerial, operational, and technical**. The classification helps to address different aspects of security and allows for accountability, an efficient security strategy to manage all levels within an organization. Managerial controls focus on the governance and policies that guide security practices, operational controls involve day-to-day procedures and practices, while technical controls consist of automated systems and technologies that enforce security measures. This classification helps organizations allocate resources effectively and align their security initiatives with overall business objectives.

The managerial controls are necessary for creating a security-focused culture within an organization. Examples of managerial controls include security policies, risk management processes, security awareness training, incident response plans, etc. The operational controls are necessary for the day-to-day management and monitoring of security systems. Examples of operational controls include regular system backups, vulnerability management, network security monitoring, change management processes, etc. The technical controls are necessary to safeguard the organization's infrastructure, systems, and data. Examples of technical controls include firewalls, intrusion detection and prevention systems, encryption mechanisms, access control mechanisms, antivirus software etc.

In addition, frameworks like NIST SP 800-53 provide structured guidance on implementing security controls. They identify roles and responsibilities for control provision, ensuring accountability within the organization. NIST SP 800-53 provides guidance on classification for information systems into three categories based on responsibility for their provision:

- **System-specific controls**: This category includes controls intended for the protection of a specific information system only, and their implementation and maintenance are the responsibility of the system owner.

- **Common controls**: These include controls that are common to multiple information systems and fall under the responsibility of the common control provider for implementation.

- **Hybrid controls**: This category of controls includes those that have characteristics of both system-specific and common controls, with shared responsibility for their implementation.

Organizations should develop a process for assigning security controls to their information systems, ensuring alignment with their overall architecture and security strategies. According to NIST, this should be done across the entire organization and involve various personnel responsible for information security. This collaborative approach helps ensure that security measures are effectively integrated and managed. The key roles as per NIST SP 800-53 include the following:

- **Authorizing officials (AO)**
- System owners
- **Chief information security officer (CISO)**
- Enterprise architects
- Information security architects
- Risk executives

NIST guidance on allocating security controls encourages organizations to identify and implement common capabilities that can serve multiple information systems. This approach enhances efficiency and should be integrated into the overall information security architecture. System owners, using common controls provided by another system, must document these as inherited controls in their security planning. Identifying common controls promotes cost-effectiveness and consistency across the organization, simplifying risk management activities. Additionally, categorizing security controls as system-specific, hybrid, or common allows for clear assignment of responsibility and accountability for their development, implementation, assessment, authorization, and monitoring. The following figure highlights the security controls:

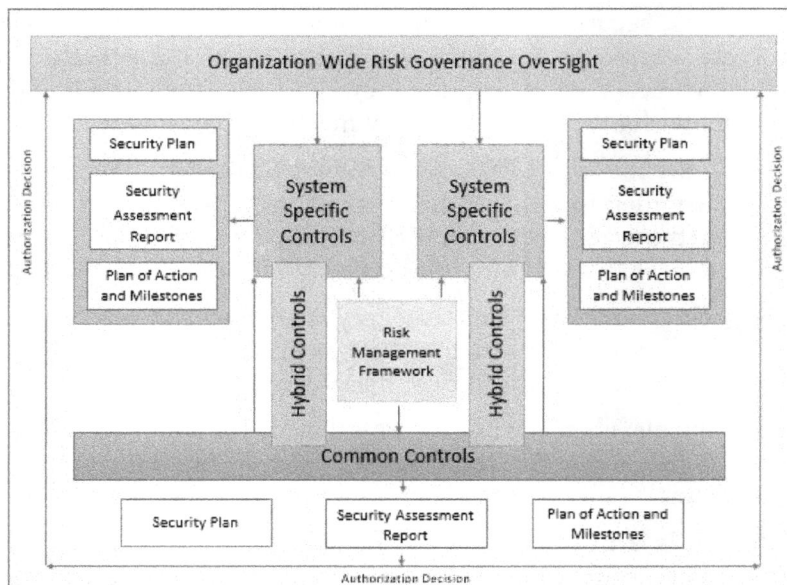

Figure 6.1: Security controls

Figure 6.1 shows how security controls are allocated within an organization using the **Risk Management Framework** (**RMF**). It provides senior leaders, including authorized officials, with important information about the current security status of information systems and the business processes they support. This process ensures that leaders are informed about the effectiveness of security measures and the risks related to those systems. This figure also highlights the correlation between common controls, system-specific controls, and hybrid controls.

Baseline and inherited controls

Baseline controls and inherited controls are terms used to describe different types of security measures that organizations apply to their systems. These security measures are important in environments like cloud, hybrid, or on-premises environments. These controls help to determine how security is managed, who is responsible, and what controls are shared across systems or inherited from third-party providers. Here is a breakdown of baseline and inherited controls in various environments:

Environment	Baseline controls	Inherited controls	Examples
Cloud	Security measures that the organization must implement directly to protect their own data and systems, regardless of the **cloud service provider** (**CSP**).	Controls are implemented by the cloud provider but benefit the organization.	Examples of baseline controls: Encryption of data at rest and in transit Examples of inherited controls: Network security (firewalls, intrusion detection)
On-premises	Security measures that the organization must apply to their internal systems.	Controls are inherited from third-party vendors who provide technology or services.	Examples of baseline controls: Access controls for physical systems Examples of inherited controls: Operating system security patches
Hybrid	Security measures that the organization applies to both on-premises and cloud-based systems to ensure security across the entire infrastructure.	Controls are inherited from both the cloud provider and the organization's on-premises vendors.	Examples of baseline controls: Incident response procedures Examples of inherited controls: Cloud network security

Table 6.1: Baseline and inherited controls

NIST control families

NIST has created a set of control families as part of its RMF and SP 800-53. These guidelines help organizations choose and implement security and privacy controls for Federal Information Systems. The control families are organized to cover different aspects of security and privacy. The following table provides a summary of the main NIST control families:

ID	Control family	Description
AC	Access Control	The Access Control is about controlling access to applications and information.
AT	Awareness and Training	The Awareness and Training control is the process of educating individuals within an organization about security risks, information systems, policies and procedures.
AU	Audit and Accountability	The Audit and Accountability provides controls regarding event logging and auditing.
CA	Assessment, Authorization, and Monitoring	The Assessment, Authorization and Monitoring covers the monitoring, maintenance and improvements of security and privacy controls.

ID	Control family	Description
CM	Configuration Management	The Configuration Management contains controls to manage, asses and improve configuration of software and systems.
CP	Contingency Planning	The Contingency Planning contains controls to prepare organizations for contingencies.
IA	Identification and Authentication	The Identification and Authentication family contains controls to protect the identity of users and devices.
IR	Incident Response	The Incident Response family contains controls that help with responding to significant incidents.
MA	Maintenance	The Maintenance controls handle all aspects of system maintenance, such as software updates, logging, and inspection tools.
MP	Media Protection	The controls in the Media Protection covers how media and files are used, stored, and safely destroyed.
PE	Physical and Environmental Protection	The controls in the Physical and Environmental Protection family covers how to protect physical locations.
PL	Planning	The Planning controls is about the creation and approach to cybersecurity and privacy related plans.
PM	Program Management	The Program Management contains controls to manage cybersecurity and privacy programs.
PS	Personnel Security	The different policies and procedures for managing employees are covered by the Personnel Security family of controls.
PT	PII Processing and Transparency	The controls in the **personally identifiable information (PII)** Processing and Transparency help protect sensitive data by putting an emphasis on privacy and consent.
RA	Risk Assessment	The Risk Assessment controls focus on identifying risks within the organizations and systems.
SA	System and Services Acquisition	The System and Service Acquisition controls focuses on security controls regarding the acquisition of systems and services.
SC	System and Communications Protection	The System and Communications Protection controls protects the edges of a system and makes sure that devices that work together are managed safely.
SI	System and Information Integrity	The System and Information Integrity controls focuses on keeping the integrity of the information system.
SR	Supply Chain Risk Management	The Supply Chain Risk Management controls include policies and procedures to mitigate risks in the supply chain.

Table 6.2: NIST control families

CIS Controls

The CIS Controls are a set of best practices for cybersecurity created by the CIS. Their primary goal is to help organizations identify, manage, and mitigate the most common cyber threats affecting their systems and networks. CIS Controls can effectively support cybersecurity programs for organizations of any size while simplifying the implementation process.

Each CIS Control is divided into CIS Safeguards, which are measurable actions that organizations can take to enhance their security posture. These safeguards provide clear guidance on steps to defend against a variety of cyber threats, including malware, ransomware, web application attacks, insider threats, and targeted intrusions. By following these actionable recommendations, organizations can better protect themselves against the evolving landscape of cyber risks.

CIS Controls v8.1 is the latest update in cybersecurity standards, aimed at strengthening organization security. CIS Controls v8.1 has refined and enhanced the controls, to better meet current cybersecurity challenges. Following is the list of CIS Controls:

- Inventory and control of enterprise assets.
- Inventory and control of software assets.
- Data protection.
- Secure configuration of enterprise assets and software.
- Account management.
- Access control management.
- Continuous vulnerability management.
- Audit log management.
- Email and web browser protections.
- Malware defenses.
- Data recovery.
- Network infrastructure management.
- Network monitoring and defense.
- Security awareness and skills training.
- Service provider management.
- Application software security.
- Incident response management.
- Penetration testing.

CIS Benchmark

The CIS Benchmarks are published by the CIS. The CIS Benchmarks provide essential secure configuration recommendations designed to harden various technologies within an organization's environment. These benchmarks help to build the robust cybersecurity strategy and mitigate the risk associated with cyberattacks. Each recommendation within the CIS Benchmarks aligns with the CIS Controls, ensuring a balanced approach to security best practices.

With over 100 CIS Benchmarks available for more than 25 vendor product families, organizations can easily access these valuable resources through free PDF downloads for non-commercial use. This extensive coverage includes security guidelines for a wide range of technologies, encompassing cloud provider platforms, cloud services, containers, databases, desktop and server software, mobile devices, network devices, and operating systems.

By implementing the CIS Benchmarks, organizations can strengthen their security posture, reduce vulnerabilities, and enhance their resilience against emerging threats. The structured recommendations serve as a practical framework for aligning security configurations with industry standards, ultimately contributing to a more secure operational environment.

Framework aligned with CIS Benchmark

There are several cybersecurity and risk frameworks that an organization needs to adapt, based on their business needs and regulatory requirements. CIS recognizes this and has created its Controls, Benchmarks, and other resources to be useful on their own or alongside other frameworks. Since the CIS Benchmarks are widely accepted as a hardening standard, many frameworks and standards reference them as a reliable resource for achieving compliance. The following figure shows some industry standard frameworks aligned with CIS Benchmarks:

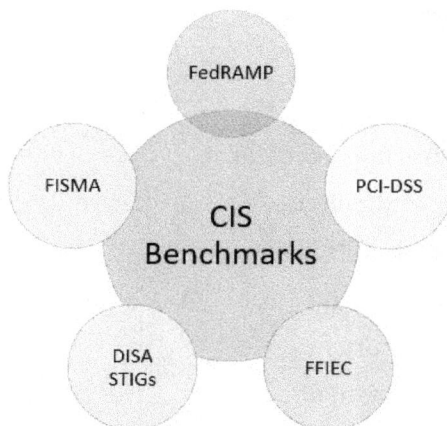

Figure 6.2: CIS Benchmark integration

Here is the detail of *Figure 6.2* explained in the following table:

Standards requirement	CIS Benchmark integration	Examples
Payment Card Industry Data Security Standard (*PCI DSS*) sets specific requirements for securing payment card information.	The CIS Benchmarks include specific hardening guidelines that align with PCI DSS requirements for securing payment card information.	Strong password policies
Federal Risk and Authorization Management Program (*FedRAMP*) is a U.S. government program that standardizes security assessments for cloud services.	The CIS Benchmarks provide specific security controls that can help meet FedRAMP's stringent cloud security requirements.	Limiting and monitoring administrative privileges
Federal Financial Institutions Examination Council (*FFIEC*) provides guidelines for financial institutions to protect data and perform risk management.	The CIS Benchmarks align with FFIEC's guidelines by offering actionable recommendations for system hardening.	Encryption, access controls
Defense Information Systems Agency (*DISA*) provides security standards for the *U.S. Department of Defense* (*DoD*) and contractors to secure information systems.	The CIS Benchmarks offer detailed, technical steps that align with DISA's requirements for system hardening.	Secure configurations for hardware and software
Federal Information Security Modernization Act (*FISMA*) requires *U.S. federal agencies* to secure their information systems and ensures compliance with standards set by NIST.	CIS Benchmarks complement FISMA by providing a framework for organizations to implement specific security controls that align with NIST's security requirements.	Continuous monitoring, audit logging

Table 6.3: *Framework aligned with CIS*

AICPA Privacy Management Framework

The AICPA PMF provides organizations with a comprehensive set of principles and guidelines to effectively incorporate privacy considerations into their processes, products, and services. This framework emphasizes a proactive approach to privacy management, helping organizations anticipate and address privacy risks before they become issues.

Privacy by Design, is the core of the framework that encourages organizations to integrate privacy measures from the outset of product and service development. By adopting this framework, organizations can ensure that privacy is an integral part of their operations rather than an afterthought. The framework is aligned with various privacy regulations and best practices, making it a valuable resource for organizations seeking to navigate complex compliance landscapes.

Additionally, the AICPA PMF promotes transparency and individual participation, ensuring that stakeholders are informed about how their personal data is collected and used. By fostering trust through clear communication and enabling individuals to exercise their privacy rights, organizations can enhance their reputation and build stronger relationships with customers. Overall, adopting this framework not only mitigates risks but supports a culture of respect for personal data within the organization. It contains nine components related to privacy which are detailed in the following table:

AICPA components	Description
Management	The entity clearly outlines, documents, and communicates its privacy policies and procedures, assigning responsibility and accountability for them.
Agreement, notice and communication	The entity creates formal agreements, informs data subjects, and provides choices when requesting their consent. This includes explaining why it needs and will use their personal information.
Collection and creation	The entity only collects and creates personal information for the purposes stated in its agreements and ongoing communications with data subjects.
Use, retention and disposal	The entity uses personal information only for the purposes stated in its agreements and for which data subjects have given consent. It keeps this information only as long as needed to fulfil those purposes or as required by law. Once the purposes are met, the entity securely disposes of the information.
Access	The entity allows data subjects to access their personal information and make updates or corrections when requested.
Disclosure to third-parties	The entity shares personal information with third-parties only for the purposes outlined in privacy agreements and notices, and only with the data subject's explicit consent.
Security for privacy	The entity protects personal information from unauthorized access, removal, changes, d estruction, and disclosure, both physically and digitally.
Data integrity and quality	The entity keeps personal information accurate, complete, and relevant for the purposes stated in the notice, ensuring it remains trustworthy in its interactions with data subjects.
Monitoring and enforcement	The entity monitors adherence to its privacy policies and has procedures in place to handle privacy complaints and disputes.

Table 6.4: *AICPA components*

AICPA Trust Services Criteria

The **System and Organization Controls 2 (SOC 2)** guidelines is designed around five key Trust Services Criteria established by the AICPA. These criteria are essential for developing a strong cybersecurity posture and helping organizations manage their security practices effectively. The five Trust Services Criteria are shown in the following figure:

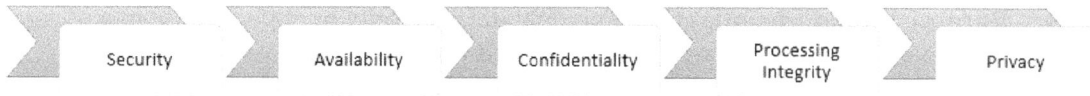

Figure 6.3: *Trust Services Criteria*

Following are the high-level details of Trust Services Criteria:

- **Security**: This involves protecting information from unauthorized access and vulnerabilities.

- **Availability**: Organizations must ensure that their systems are reliable and accessible to employees and clients when needed.

- **Processing integrity**: This criterion focuses on ensuring that systems function correctly and as intended.

- **Confidentiality**: Organizations need to safeguard confidential information by controlling who can access, store, and use it.

- **Privacy**: This involves protecting sensitive personal information from unauthorized access.

Singapore Personal Data Protection Act

The *Personal Data Protection Act* (*PDPA*) sets a fundamental standard for protecting personal data in *Singapore*, ensuring that individuals' privacy is respected across various sectors. It works alongside other specific laws, such as the *Banking Regulation Act* and the *Insurance Act*, to create a comprehensive regulatory framework.

The PDPA outlines several key requirements for the collection, use, disclosure, and management of personal data, helping organizations handle personal information responsibly and transparently. This framework is designed to safeguard individuals' rights while also facilitating responsible use of data by businesses.

Additionally, the PDPA establishes a national **Do Not Call** (**DNC**) Registry, allowing individuals to register their phone numbers to avoid unwanted telemarketing messages from organizations. This feature empowers consumers to take control of their privacy and limits unsolicited communication, enhancing overall data protection in Singapore.

PDPA obligations

The PDPA outlines several key obligations for businesses that handle the personal data of Singapore residents, which are as follows:

- **Consent obligation**: Businesses must obtain clear and informed consent from individuals before collecting, using, or sharing their personal data.

- **Purpose limitation obligation**: Personal data can only be collected for specific and legitimate purposes, clearly communicated to individuals.

- **Notification obligation**: Organizations must inform individuals how their personal data will be collected, used, and disclosed.

- **Access and correction obligation**: Individuals have the right to access their personal data and request corrections if it is inaccurate or incomplete.

- **Accuracy obligation**: Organizations must take reasonable steps to ensure that the personal data they hold is accurate, complete, and up-to-date.

- **Data protection obligation**: Appropriate security measures must be implemented to protect personal data from unauthorized access, use, or loss, reflecting the risks involved.

- **Retention limitation obligation**: Personal data should only be retained as long as necessary for its intended purposes or to meet legal requirements, avoiding indefinite storage.

- **Data transfer limitation obligation**: When transferring personal data to third-parties outside Singapore, businesses must ensure those parties provide similar protection as required by the PDPA.

- **Accountability obligation**: Organizations must show their commitment to data protection by establishing a data protection program, which may include appointing a **data protection officer (DPO)**.

- **Data breach notification obligation**: Since 2020, businesses must notify individuals if a data breach occurs that affects their personal data, highlighting the importance of data security and response protocols.

NIST Privacy Framework

The NIST Privacy Framework is designed to help organizations handle personal data, including government agencies and private companies, build customer trust and meet compliance requirements. It consists of three key components: Core, profiles, and implementation tiers.

The core outlines essential privacy protection activities that help organizations identify and manage privacy risks effectively. Profiles provide a customizable way for organizations to assess their current privacy practices against desired outcomes, enabling them to tailor their approach to specific needs and goals. Lastly, implementation tiers help organizations gauge their maturity in privacy risk management and facilitate the development of a strategic privacy program.

By integrating these components, the NIST Privacy Framework establishes clear connections between business objectives, organizational roles, and privacy protection efforts. This comprehensive approach improves privacy risk management, promoting accountability and transparency, which in turn builds greater trust with customers. The following figure shows the three different tiers of the NIST Privacy Framework:

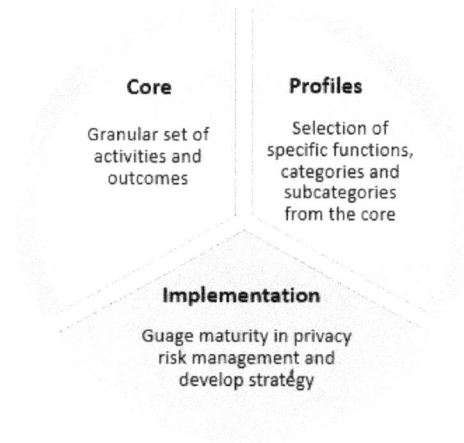

Figure 6.4: NIST Privacy Framework tiers

Core tier

The core tier consists of privacy protection activities and outcomes that help all levels of an organization communicate prioritized privacy efforts. It is organized into functions, categories, and subcategories, which work together effectively:

- **Functions**: Functions are the highest-level and organize essential privacy activities. They help organizations manage privacy risks by understanding data processing, enabling risk management decisions, connecting with individuals, and learning from past experiences. These functions should be performed simultaneously and repeatedly, fostering a proactive approach to evolving privacy challenges.

- **Categories**: Categories break down each function into related groups of privacy outcomes tailored to the program's specific needs.

- **Subcategories**: Subcategories further detail each category into specific managerial or technical activities, providing a set of outcomes that support achieving the objectives in each category, even though they may not cover every possible scenario.

The following figure represents the Privacy Framework's core structure:

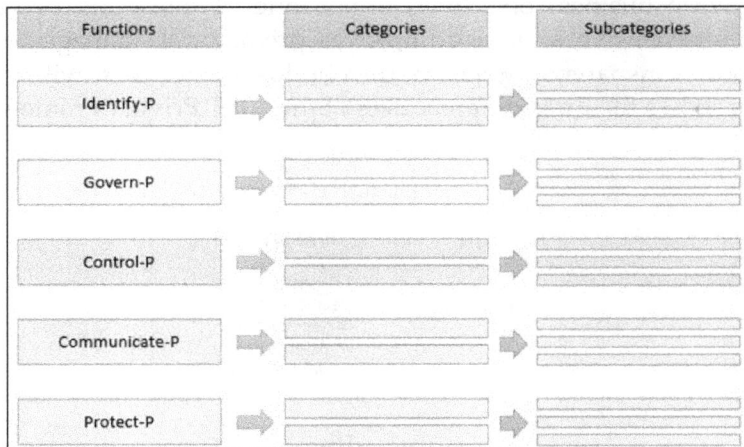

Figure 6.5: Privacy Framework core structure

The functions represent key activities for managing risks related to privacy events caused by cybersecurity threats. They help organizations develop strategies to understand, address, and reduce privacy risks from cybersecurity incidents. The five functions, namely, Identify-P, Govern-P, Control-P, Communicate-P, and Protect-P, are designed to address privacy concerns associated with data processing, which are shown in the following table:

Functions	Details
Identify-P	This function focuses on understanding privacy risks for individuals by cataloguing data processing activities, recognizing privacy interests, and conducting risk assessments to prioritize these risks.
Govern-P	This function focuses on establishing a governance structure to maintain an understanding of privacy risk management priorities. It includes setting privacy values and policies, complying with legal requirements, and determining risk tolerance to align efforts with the organization's strategy.
Control-P	This function develops activities that allow organizations and individuals to manage data effectively, focusing on detailed management to mitigate privacy risks.
Communicate-P	This function emphasizes clear communication between organizations and individuals about data processing practices and privacy risks, ensuring informed discussions on managing those risks.
Protect-P	This function focuses on implementing safeguards to protect data and prevent privacy incidents, highlighting the connection between privacy and cybersecurity risk management.

Table 6.5: Functions of NIST Privacy Framework

Profiles tier

Profiles consist of selected functions, categories, and subcategories from the core that an organization prioritizes to manage privacy risks effectively. They help illustrate both the current state and the desired future state of privacy activities:

- **Current profile**: This profile reflects the privacy outcomes the organization is currently achieving.

- **Target profile**: This profile outlines the outcomes necessary to meet the organization's privacy risk management goals.

Comparing these two profiles allows organizations to identify gaps and create action plans for improvement, including determining the resources needed, such as staffing and funding. By using profiles, organizations can develop a structured plan to reduce privacy risks in a cost-effective and prioritized way. Additionally, they facilitate communication about risk, both within the organization and with external partners, helping everyone understand and compare current and desired privacy outcomes.

The following figure shows the correlation between the core and profiles. An organization can start by creating a target profile to outline its desired privacy outcomes and then develop a current profile to identify gaps. Alternatively, it may assess its current activities first and then determine how to adjust them to meet the Target Profile, as shown in the following figure:

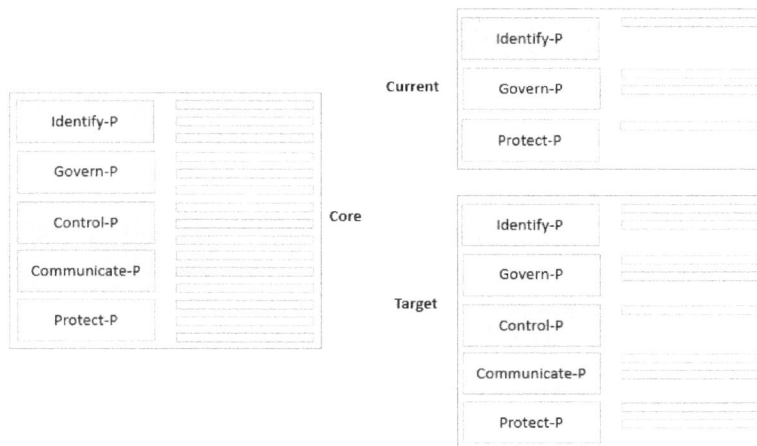

Figure 6.6: *Core and profiles correlation*

Implementation tier

Implementation tiers help organizations manage privacy risks by assessing their systems, practices, and resources across four levels. These tiers represent a maturity scale for handling privacy risks, with higher tiers indicating more advanced and effective practices:

- Partial (Tier 1)
- Risk informed (Tier 2)
- Repeatable (Tier 3)
- Adaptive (Tier 4)

Organizations should select tiers based on their target profiles, taking into account their current practices, how well they integrate overall risk management, their relationships within the ecosystem, and the training of their workforce. If existing methods are insufficient for managing privacy risks, advancing to a higher tier may be necessary.

While tiers serve as useful benchmarks for internal resource planning and evaluating progress in privacy risk management, the main goal is to achieve the outcomes outlined in the target profiles rather than focusing solely on the tier level.

Data Privacy Framework

The DPF program is designed to support cross-continent commerce by providing a reliable mechanism for transferring personal data from the *EU*, the *European Economic Area* (*EEA*), the *United Kingdom* (*U.K.*), *Gibraltar*, and *Switzerland* to the *US*.

To facilitate these data transfers, an adequacy decision must be established by the *European Commission* to ensure that personal data can move safely to a third country. The framework ensures that U.S. data processors comply with key data protection laws from the EU, U.K., and Switzerland, including the *General Data Protection Regulation* (*GDPR*) and the *Federal Data Protection Act* (*FDPA*). This compliance helps to protect an individual's privacy rights during international data exchanges.

The DPF program mainly consists of the following three key frameworks to account for each location:

- The EU-U.S. DPF
- The U.K. Extension to the EU-U.S. DPF
- The Swiss-U.S. DPF

EU-US Data Privacy Framework

The EU-U.S. DPF is designed to ensure compliance with EU data protection requirements when transferring personal data to organizations in the U.S. This framework represents the most recent solution for cross-border data transfers, following the invalidation of previous mechanisms like the Safe Harbor and Privacy Shield Frameworks by the *Court of Justice of the European Union* (*CJEU*).

By establishing a legal basis for data transfers, the EU-U.S. DPF aims to reconcile the differing data protection standards of the EU and the U.S. It facilitates smoother data exchanges while maintaining the necessary safeguards for individuals' privacy rights.

This framework not only helps organizations comply with regulations but also fosters trust in transatlantic data flows, benefiting both businesses and consumers.

Key elements of EU-US Data Privacy Framework

The EU-U.S. DPF includes key elements designed to protect personal data transferred between the EU and the U.S. The following figure represents the key components of the EU-US DPF:

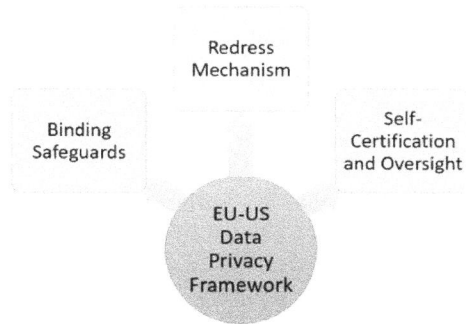

Figure 6.7: Components of EU-US DPF

Following are the details of the key components:

- **Binding safeguards**: A crucial feature of the framework is the introduction of binding safeguards. This rule limits U.S. intelligence agency's access to EU data to what is necessary for national security. This approach addresses concerns from the CJEU by adhering to principles of necessity and proportionality.

- **Redress mechanism**: To ensure accountability and address complaints, the framework includes a strong redress mechanism. Instead of the previous Ombudsman model, a new *Data Protection Review Court (DPRC)* has been established. This court has investigative powers and can propose remedies, giving individuals an effective way to address data privacy issues.

- **Self-certification and oversight**: U.S. organizations participating in the framework must go through a self-certification process, administered by the *U.S. Department of Commerce*. This department monitors compliance with the framework's principles, while the *U.S. Federal Trade Commission (FTC)* enforces these obligations, ensuring that companies meet their commitments.

Privacy assessment overview

Privacy assessments evaluate an organization's compliance with relevant laws, regulations, standards, and internal policies. These assessments can cover a wide range of areas, including employee awareness, monitoring regulatory changes, assessing data and systems, conducting risk assessments, managing incident responses, reviewing contracts, and ensuring overall program assurance through audits.

These assessments can be performed internally by the organization's audit function, the DPO, or specific business units. Alternatively, the assessment may be conducted by external third-parties. Privacy assessments can take place at scheduled intervals or be triggered by specific events, such as a security breach or a request from an enforcement authority.

There are three types of privacy assessments, namely privacy assessments, PIAs, and **Data Protection Impact Assessments (DPIAs)**. Sometimes these terms are used interchangeably, but they can also be distinguished from one another.

Privacy assessment

A privacy assessment is a broad evaluation process that examines how an organization collects, processes, stores, and protects personal data. This assessment covers various aspects of data handling practices to ensure that the organization's privacy policies align with relevant laws and regulations, such as the GDPR or the *California Consumer Privacy Act* (*CCPA*). The main purpose of a privacy assessment is to identify potential privacy risks, ensure compliance with applicable standards, and recommend strategies or safeguards to address any vulnerabilities. The scope of a privacy assessment is comprehensive and may include evaluating areas like data retention policies, user content and overall privacy management within the organization.

Privacy Impact Assessment

A PIA analyzes the privacy risks associated with processing personal information for a specific project, product, or service. For a PIA to be effective, it should not only identify these risks but also recommend actions or mitigations to avoid or minimize them. PIA requirements may emerge from organizational policies, laws, regulations, or directives from supervisory authorities.

PIA plays a crucial role in highlighting Privacy by Design, which emphasizes integrating privacy considerations into technology and systems from the design phase. PIA should be conducted early in the process, such as during the scoping phase of any project that involves collecting personal information to maximize effectiveness. These assessments are also important when new or revised industry standards, organizational policies, or laws are introduced or when changes in how personal information is handled create new privacy risks.

The following figure shows the fundamental steps of PIA:

Gather   Check   Risk   Produce   Action   Review

Figure 6.8: Steps of PIA

Conducting a PIA involves a structured process to ensure that privacy risks are identified and managed effectively. Here are the detailed steps typically involved in a PIA:

- **Gather**: Gather is the first step to collecting all relevant information necessary to perform the PIA. This includes the following:

    o **Project scope**: Define the objectives, scope, and context of the project, product, or service.

    o **Data inventory**: Document what types of personal data will be collected (for example, names, addresses, financial information).

    o **Processing activities**: Identify how data will be collected, stored, used, shared, and disposed of.

    o **Regulatory requirements**: Gather information on applicable laws and regulations (for example, GDPR, CCPA) to understand the legal obligations surrounding data privacy.

- **Check**: Check is the second step that evaluates the gathered information against the organization's privacy principles and policies. This typically involves:

    o **Compliance**: Ensure that the planned data processing activities align with the organization's privacy commitments and any relevant legal frameworks.

    o **Transparency**: Check that there are clear communications about how personal data will be handled.

    o **Purpose limitation**: Confirm that personal data is collected for legitimate purposes and not used beyond those purposes.

    o **Data minimization**: Ensure that only the necessary amount of personal data is collected.

- **Risk**: Risk is the third step, which involves conducting a thorough risk assessment to identify potential privacy risks associated with the data processing activities. This includes:

    o **Threat analysis**: Evaluate potential threats to personal data, such as unauthorized access, data breaches, or misuse of information.

    o **Vulnerability assessment**: Identify vulnerabilities in the current data handling practices or systems that could be exploited.

    o **Impact assessment**: Assess the potential impact on individuals, that is, if their personal data were compromised or misused.

    o **Mitigation strategies**: Develop strategies to mitigate identified risks.

- **Produce**: Produce is the next step that develops a PIA report to outline the findings and recommendations. This template should include:

- o **Executive summary**: A brief overview of the project and the PIA findings.

- o **Detailed findings**: A section summarizing the identified privacy risks, assessment results, and mitigation strategies.

- o **Action plan**: Specific recommendations for addressing the identified risks, along with assigned responsibilities and timelines for implementation.

- o **Stakeholder feedback**: Document any feedback or concerns raised by stakeholders during the consultation process.

- **Action**: Action is the fifth step to address identified risks and implement the recommended measures based on the PIA report. This may involve the following:

- o **Training**: Providing training to staff involved in data handling to ensure they understand privacy practices and responsibilities.

- o **Technical controls**: Implementing security measures such as encryption, access controls, or data anonymization.

- o **Policy adjustments**: Updating organizational policies and procedures to align with the findings of the PIA.

- **Review**: Review is the final step that focuses on regular review and adjusts the PIA to account for any changes in data processing activities, technology, or regulatory requirements. This involves the following:

- o **Monitoring changes**: Keeping track of any modifications to the project that could impact data privacy, such as new data sources or changes in processing methods.

- o **Periodic reassessments**: Conducting periodic reviews of the PIA to ensure that it remains relevant and effective in managing privacy risks.

Data Protection Impact Assessment

When an organization collects, stores, or uses personal data, individuals face various risks, like the theft of personal data or its unauthorized release, leading to potential identity theft or misuse. Additionally, individuals may be concerned about their data usage by the organization for purposes they are unaware of. A DPIA is a process designed to identify these risks and minimize them as early as possible. DPIAs are essential for managing risk and demonstrating compliance with the GDPR.

Under the GDPR, a DPIA is mandatory when processing activities are likely to pose a high risk to individuals' privacy. Failing to conduct a DPIA when required, conducting it incorrectly, or neglecting to consult the appropriate supervisory authority can result in significant penalties. These fines can reach up to 10 million euros or, for companies, up to two percent of their total global annual revenue from the previous financial year, whichever amount is greater.

While the term PIA is often used in broader contexts, a DPIA under the GDPR has specific requirements and triggers that organizations must follow. This distinction is crucial for ensuring that organizations are fully compliant with data protection regulations while safeguarding individuals' privacy rights.

Conclusion

In this chapter, we explored various types of security controls tailored to meet specific business requirements. We discussed the CIS Benchmark and the NIST control families, which provide essential guidelines for establishing effective security measures. Additionally, we examined the AICPA PMF and the Trust Services Criteria, along with the NIST Privacy Framework that guide organizations in managing privacy risks.

Moreover, we addressed DPFs in the context of cross-border regulations and privacy requirements, highlighting the importance of compliance in a global landscape. We also covered PIAs, emphasizing their role in enhancing the security posture of organizations.

As we move to the next chapter, we will focus on control scoping and selection, providing further insights into the implementation of security controls.

Key terms

- AICPA PMF has the following core capabilities.

    o The PMF contains nine privacy components.

    o The PMF aligns with the privacy principle of the SOC 2 TSC.

    o The adoption of PMF is voluntary.

- PIA focuses on broad assessment, considering overall privacy impact, and DPIA specifically focuses on the processing of personal data.

- CIS Benchmarks provide two levels of security settings:

    o Level 1 recommends essential basic security requirements that can be configured on any system and should cause little or no interruption of service or reduced functionality.

    o Level 2 recommends security settings for environments requiring greater security that could result in some reduced functionality.

- Baseline controls are the minimum mandatory controls applied to systems, as outlined in FIPS 200 and NIST SP 800-53 Revision 5.

- Inherited controls are shared across systems or inherited from organizational frameworks (e.g., cloud environments).

Join our book's Discord space

Join the book's Discord Workspace for Latest updates, Offers, Tech happenings around the world, New Release and Sessions with the Authors:

https://discord.bpbonline.com

CHAPTER 7
Evaluating and Selecting Controls

Introduction

This chapter provides an in-depth knowledge of control scoping guidance, emphasizing the optimization of organizational resources through a targeted focus on applicable controls. By discussing different control types, the chapter clarifies which controls are necessary for specific organizational purposes. It highlights the importance of selecting appropriate control baselines and tailoring them by identifying common control for security management.

In addition to traditional security controls, the chapter discusses compensating controls, which serve as alternatives to baseline controls, particularly useful for temporary implementations. The concept of overlay controls is also introduced, enabling organizations to adjust the initial baselines by adding or removing controls based on their unique needs and circumstances. Moreover, the chapter outlines the essential process of control selection documentation, which provides the necessary context for organizations to make informed authorization decisions regarding their systems. It also addresses the significance of systems of record notices, along with concepts of assurance and trustworthiness.

Structure

The chapter covers the following main topics:

- Control scoping guidance
- Control types and functions
- Control baselines
- Tailoring control baselines
- Compensating control
- Creating overlays
- System of record notice
- Assurance and trustworthiness
- Control selection

Objectives

By the end of this chapter, you will gain a comprehensive understanding of scoping guidance and the various types of controls essential for aligning with organizational business goals. Additionally, you will become familiar with the underlying assumptions of control baselines and the various parameters necessary to support the operations and processing of information.

You will also understand the concept of compensating controls, learning how these alternatives can aid organizations in efficiently managing risk. This chapter will provide you with insights into systems of record notices and overlays, enhancing your ability to support and refine initial baselines based on organizational needs. Furthermore, you will explore the privacy control catalogue as per *National Institute of Standards and Technology* (*NIST*) SP 800-53 Revision 5 standards. and the importance of documenting selected controls. This documentation will ensure that future evaluations are informed and contextualized, taking into account previous decisions and enabling a more robust approach to security management.

Control scoping guidance

Scoping guidance provides organizations with clear terms and conditions regarding the applicability and implementation of individual security controls outlined in the NIST SP 800-53 security control baselines. Various factors can influence how these baseline security controls are applied, and agencies must carefully consider these factors when implementing controls. **System security plans** (**SSPs**) should explicitly state which controls utilize scoping guidance and provide a detailed description of the considerations that influenced these decisions.

Furthermore, any application of scoping guidance must undergo review and approval by the authorizing official for the information system. This ensures that the security measures in place align with organizational policies and regulatory requirements, promoting a consistent approach to risk management and security compliance across the organization. By documenting and gaining approval for scoping guidance, an organization can enhance their security posture while effectively addressing specific operational needs.

Scoping considerations

The scoping guidance supports various considerations to customize the organization's security controls based on the specific context of their information systems. This also helps to optimize the organization's resources by focusing on applicable controls. The scoping considerations ensure that organizations comply with relevant regulations and standards. The following figure shows six important considerations for any organization:

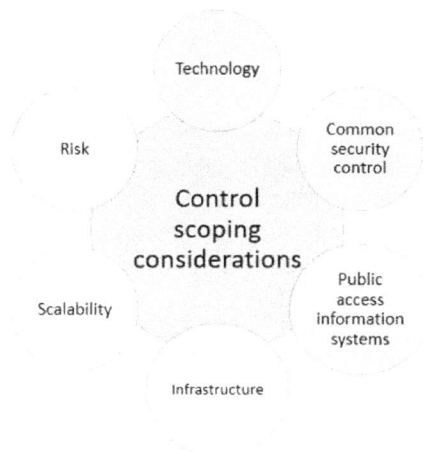

Figure 7.1: Scoping considerations

Let me briefly explain the various scoping considerations to ensure that the organization can select the appropriate security controls to drive the business goals:

- **Technology considerations**: Technology considerations are crucial in ensuring that the security controls are effectively tailored to an organization's specific information systems. Controls associated with particular technologies, such as wireless communication or **public key infrastructure** (**PKI**), are only relevant if those technologies are employed within the system. Furthermore, security measures should focus on the components of the information system that provide essential security capabilities in line with minimum requirements, ensuring a targeted and efficient approach to security.

  In situations where automated solutions are impractical, organizations can implement compensating controls through non-automated methods. This flexibility allows organizations to meet minimum-security requirements effectively, even when specific technologies or automated tools are not in place, ensuring robust protection tailored to their unique operational contexts.

- **Common security control considerations**: Common security controls are typically managed by an organizational entity separate from the information system owner. This structure allows for centralized oversight and management of these controls, ensuring consistency and efficiency across multiple systems. However, it remains essential that every control in the security control baseline is adequately addressed, either through the agency's implementation of common security controls or directly by the information system owner.

Despite the delegation of certain controls to a common control framework, the organization retains ultimate responsibility to ensure that all minimum-security requirements are met. This means that regardless of whether controls are classified as common or specific to a system, the organization must ensure that adequate security measures are in place to protect its information assets effectively.

- **Public access information system considerations**: The public access information systems require careful consideration and tailored application. Since these systems are designed for use by a broad range of users, including those who may not be part of the organization, certain controls may not be relevant. For example, personnel security controls, which are typically focused on verifying the identity and background of specific individuals, may not apply when users are accessing the system through public interfaces.

Furthermore, organizations must evaluate which security controls from established baselines are necessary for public access systems. Some controls like access controls and data protection measures, remain critical to safeguard the integrity and confidentiality of the information. By selectively implementing security controls that align with the nature of public access, organizations can create a secure environment that still allows users to interact with the system efficiently and safely.

- **Infrastructure considerations**: Infrastructure security controls, such as physical access controls and environmental safeguards, are essential for protecting information systems and their associated technology assets. These controls include measures like locks, security personnel, and systems for managing temperature, humidity, lighting, fire, and power, etc. However, their applicability is limited to the specific areas of the facility that directly support or protect the information system.

By focusing on the sections of the facility that house critical components, such as data centers, and networking nodes, organizations can create more efficient security environment. For example, the access control may differ for general areas of a facility and secure data center housing sensitive equipment. This strategic application of security controls not only helps to mitigate risks associated with unauthorized access or environmental threats, but also supports compliance with regulatory requirements.

- **Scalability considerations**: The scalability of security controls is crucial to accommodate the size and complexity of the organization implementing controls. This means that the organization can adjust the breadth and depth of their security measures according to their specific operational contexts and the sensitivity of the data. A smaller organization may require a different level of controls compared to a larger organization with more complex systems, ensuring that security measures are proportionate to the potential risks involved.

  Implementing a scalable approach requires discretion and careful consideration of the organization's unique environment and operational needs. Organizations can achieve a cost-effective, risk-based strategy that optimizes resource allocation by tailoring security controls to fit the specific circumstances.

- **Risk considerations**: Security controls that specifically support the core security objectives of **confidentiality, integrity, and availability** (**CIA**) can be adjusted to align with a lower baseline when certain criteria are met. However, it is crucial to ensure that any reduction in security controls does not compromise the overall security posture. This downgrading process is permissible only if it adheres to the *Federal Information Processing Standards* (*FIPS*) *199* security categorization, ensuring that the adjustments remain consistent with the established security objectives for CIA. This step is critical to maintaining the integrity of the overall security framework while ensuring compliance with federal standards.

Additionally, any decision to downgrade controls must be measured through a risk assessment conducted by the organization. This assessment helps to determine whether the reduction in control strength is justified based on the specific context and risks associated with the information system. By following these guidelines, organizations can make informed decisions about their security controls, allowing for a balanced approach that maintains necessary protections.

Control types and functions

As we have noticed, there are numerous types of controls available to organizations. These controls can generally be grouped into broad categories based on their intended type and function. However, the terminology may vary depending on the control framework you consult or the cybersecurity or risk expert you engage with, as different standards may categorize them in various ways. It is essential to understand three main types of controls, Administrative, technical, and physical based on NIST SP 800-53 Revision 5 standard:

- **Administrative controls**, sometimes referred to as **managerial controls**, focus on policies, procedures, and regulations that govern the organization's security practices.

- **Technical controls**, also known as **logical controls**, involve the technological measures used to protect information systems, such as encryption and access controls.

- **Physical controls**, or **operational controls**, are the tangible measures that protect the physical environment, including security guards, locks, and surveillance systems.

Understanding these categories will help you better navigate the complexities of security controls in the context of risk management.

Controls can also be categorized by their function, which refers to the purpose they serve and how they operate. The most common control functions include deterrent, preventive, detective, corrective, and compensating controls. Each type serves a distinct role in an organization's security strategy. The following table lists each control type function, its definition, and an example of the control:

Control function	Definition	Example
Deterrent	Deters individuals from performing policy violations or illegal acts.	Video surveillance, security guards, login warning banners, policies.
Preventive	Prevents policy violations or illegal acts.	Firewall rules, permission settings, perimeter fencing.
Detective	Detects or discovers policy violations or illegal acts.	Physical intrusion detection system, alarm system, integrity checks, audit logs.
Corrective	Temporarily corrects an immediate security issue.	System configured to shut down when attack occurs, facility lockdowns, security guards.
Compensating	Short term alternative solution when primary controls cannot be implemented for legitimate business reasons.	If the system lacks **multifactor authentication** (**MFA**), the compensating controls can be strict password policies and monitoring of login attempts.

Table 7.1: Control functions

Note: Different control functions can be found across all three control types: Administrative, technical, and physical. For instance, there are deterrent, preventive, detective, corrective, and compensating controls that can be categorized within each type. This leads to some significant overlap between the types and functions of controls. The control types and functions can overlap and they can also complement each other.

Let us take the example of a video surveillance system that serves both as a deterrent control (discouraging potential intruders by its mere presence) and as a detective control (identifying and recording unauthorized access when it occurs). Additionally, some experts may not clearly differentiate between certain functions, such as deterrent and preventive controls. Therefore, it is crucial to understand these distinctions to effectively design and implement a comprehensive security strategy that addresses various risks and vulnerabilities. Recognizing both the types and functions of controls will enable organizations to deploy a more robust security framework.

The following figure summarizes the relation between different type of controls. Deterrent and preventive controls are proactive security measures designed to stop or discourage security incidents before they happen. They are considered safeguards because they aim to prevent breaches by implementing firewalls, access control policies etc. On the other hand, detective, corrective, and compensating controls are reactive, as they respond to incidents that have already occurred or help to mitigate impact. These are considered countermeasures because they aim to identify, respond and recover from security threats:

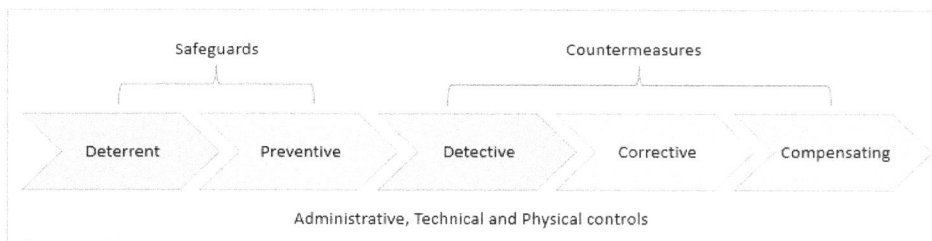

Figure 7.2: Control functions and types

Control baselines

Organizations always find challenges in selecting the appropriate security and privacy controls to protect their business functions while effectively managing risks. These controls must not only align with legal requirements and policies but also be tailored to the unique requirements of the organization. Organizations need a comprehensive understanding of their business priorities and the environments in which they operate, as controls need to be tailored. This understanding is essential for choosing the right controls that can ensure CIA of information, while also safeguarding individual privacy.

To facilitate the selection of these controls, the concept of a control baseline is introduced. A control baseline is a curated collection of controls designed to address the specific protection needs of an organization. Providing a foundational set of controls allows organizations to start with a generalized framework before tailoring it to meet their specific security and privacy requirements. This initial baseline is crucial for organizations to establish a systematic approach to risk management, enabling them to focus their efforts on the most pertinent threats and vulnerabilities.

Tailoring control baselines involves considering various factors, including threat landscapes, mission-critical requirements, and sector-specific regulations. Organizations must also factor in technological nuances, operating environments, and individual privacy interests, along with compliance and best practices. This tailored approach makes sure the chosen controls are both effective and cost-efficient, helping organizations protect their information and systems while supporting their overall business goals.

Selecting control baselines

Information security programs protect information and systems from unauthorized access and unwanted actions to ensure CIA. Privacy programs focus on managing risks to individuals related to the handling of **personally identifiable information (PII)** and ensuring compliance with privacy laws. When a system processes PII, both information security and privacy programs work together to manage risks to individuals and collaborate on categorizing security needs and selecting appropriate controls. Selecting control baselines involves choosing a set of security controls that align with an organization's specific needs, risk profile, and regulatory requirements. The control baseline serves as the foundation for securing systems and processes, ensuring they meet minimum-security standards.

Security control baseline

Organizations must first assess the criticality and sensitivity of information before selecting and tailoring the appropriate security control baselines for their systems. This assessment, known as **security categorization**, is outlined in FIPS 199. The results of this categorization play a crucial role in guiding the selection of security control baselines that effectively protect systems and sensitive information. The chosen controls should correspond to the potential adverse impacts on organizational operations, assets, and individuals that could result from a loss of CIA.

FIPS 199 requires organizations to categorize their systems as low-impact, moderate-impact, or high-impact based on the security objectives of CIA. Since the potential impacts on these objectives can vary for any given system, the high-water mark concept is employed to determine the overall impact level. This impact level directly informs the selection of the appropriate security control baseline. For example, if all security objectives CIA are considered low, the overall system impact would be low. If one or more of the security objectives are moderate, the overall system impact would be moderate, indicating that a breach could have more significant but manageable. Similarly, if one or more security objectives are high, the overall system impact would be high, meaning that any compromise would result in serious consequences for the system or organization.

Once the impact level is established, organizations can select the corresponding security control baseline. The selection process is based on the system's impact level as determined through security categorization. It is important to note that not all controls or enhancements listed in NIST SP 800-53 are included in the baselines. The term control baseline emphasizes that these controls serve as a foundational starting point from which organizations can customize their security measures by adding, removing, or modifying controls according to their unique needs.

Privacy control baseline

The privacy control baseline aims to address privacy requirements and manage risks associated with the processing of PII. The controls and enhancements included in this privacy baseline are marked, but it is important to note that not all privacy-related controls are part of this baseline. This framework serves as a starting point, allowing organizations to modify the controls by removing, adding, or customizing them according to the guidance.

To effectively tailor the privacy control baseline, organizations conduct privacy risk assessments that evaluate the nature of their PII processing and its potential impact on individuals. These assessments help organizations determine which controls are necessary based on applicable legal and policy requirements. For example, organizations may choose to remove certain controls that are not relevant to their requirements or specific legal context. However, if a privacy risk assessment indicates that certain controls could help mitigate identified risks, organizations may decide to retain or even enhance those controls.

Additionally, organizations have the flexibility to incorporate custom controls or enhancements to further address privacy risks specific to their information systems. These decisions are guided by the findings from their privacy risk assessments, ensuring that the control baseline is effectively tailored to meet the unique needs of the organization. This adaptive approach allows organizations to remain compliant while effectively managing privacy risks.

Control baseline assumptions

The assumptions made while establishing baselines take into account various factors related to the environments in which organizational information systems operate. These factors include legal and regulatory, the nature of the organization's operations, the specific functions of the systems, the types of threats, privacy data, and the kinds of information processed, stored, or transmitted. Clearly stating these assumptions is crucial in the risk framing step of the risk management process outlined in NIST SP 800-39 and emphasized in the prepare step of NIST SP 800-37. The key assumptions underlying the control baselines are as follows:

- **Persistence of information**: Information in organizational systems is typically long-lasting and remains accessible over time.

- **Multi-user operation**: Organizational systems are designed for multiple users to access them, either one after the other or at the same time.

- **Non-shareable information**: Certain information within organizational systems cannot be shared, even among users who have authorized access to the same system.

- **Networked environments**: Organizational systems operate in networked settings and serve general purposes.

- **Implementation capability**: Organizations possess the necessary structure, resources, and infrastructure to effectively implement the required controls.

Tailoring control baseline

This section describes the tailoring approach as discussed in NIST SP 800-53. Organizations begin a tailoring process after selecting an appropriate control baseline to better align the controls with their specific security and privacy requirements. This tailoring process is part of a comprehensive risk management strategy that encompasses framing, assessing, responding to, and monitoring information security and privacy risks. Tailoring decisions are influenced by various organizational or system-specific factors. Although the focus is on security and privacy considerations, these decisions often take into account other risk-related issues that organizations regularly face. Factors such as cost, schedule, and performance are crucial in determining which controls to implement and how to integrate them effectively into the organization's systems and operational environments. The tailoring process can include the following activities:

- Identifying and designating common controls in initial security control baselines.

- Applying scoping considerations to the remaining baseline security controls.

- Selecting compensating security controls, if needed.

- Assigning specific values to organization-defined security control parameters via explicit assignment and selection statements.

- Supplementing baselines with additional security controls and control enhancements, if needed.

- Providing additional specification information for control implementation, if needed.

Organizations rely on risk management guidance to inform their risk-based decision-making regarding the applicability of controls outlined in the baselines. The tailoring process aims to create cost-effective solutions that align with the organization's mission and business needs and also ensure that security and privacy protections are appropriate to the level of risk. Organizations have the flexibility to tailor controls either at the organizational level, a specific line of business or mission, at the individual system-level, or through a combination of both approaches.

All tailoring decisions, including the justifications for them, must be documented in the system security and privacy plans for the organization's systems. Documenting risk management decisions during the tailoring process is crucial for ensuring that organizational officials have the necessary information to make credible, risk-based decisions regarding security and privacy.

Tailoring guidelines in ISO/IEC 27002:2022

ISO/IEC 27002:2022 provides a comprehensive framework for information security controls and serves as a guide for organizations to implement an **information security management system** (**ISMS**). Tailoring controls within the context of ISO/IEC 27002:2022 means adjusting the standard's recommendations to suit the organization's business needs, regulatory requirements and operational environment. Organizations must first conduct a thorough risk assessment to identify their unique security threats, vulnerabilities, and risk appetite.

ISO/IEC 27002:2022 offers a catalogue of controls based on different aspects (e.g., organizational controls, technical controls, physical security). Tailoring process involves selecting and adapting these controls based on the risks identified during the assessment. All controls from catalogues will not apply to every organization or system and it needs to be customized to the organization's needs. For example, the standard control requires that organizations restrict access to privileged accounts. However, the tailored controls may differ based on cloud or on-premise environment. The tailored approach would be to add **Identity and Access Management** (**IAM**) tool or process to control the privileged access.

Identifying common controls

Common controls refer to security measures that can be inherited by one or more information systems within an organization. When an information system inherits a common control, it does not need to implement that control explicitly, as the security capability is provided by another entity. Therefore, when security controls require an information system to perform a specific function, it does not mean that every system in a larger, complex system has to implement that control on its own.

The decisions made by organizations, regarding which security controls are designated as common can significantly impact the responsibilities of individual system owners within a specific baseline. Furthermore, the selection of common controls can influence the overall resource expenditures of organizations. In general, the more common controls that are implemented, the greater the potential for cost savings, as these protective measures can be shared across multiple systems rather than being duplicated for each individual system. This approach not only enhances efficiency but also optimizes resource allocation within the organization.

NIST guidance on selecting security controls

The third step of the NIST **Risk Management Framework** (**RMF**) is to select which focuses on selecting, tailoring, and documenting the security and privacy controls needed to protect the information system and organization. These controls are chosen based on the level of risk to organizational operations, assets, and individuals:

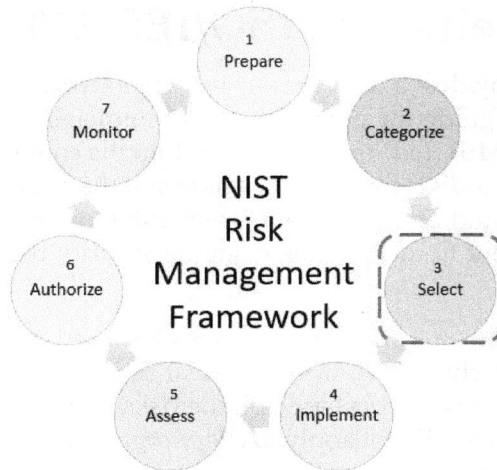

Figure 7.3: RMF steps

The selection process involves assessing the system's requirements, applying pre-defined control baselines, and tailoring them to meet specific needs, ensuring that the chosen controls effectively mitigate the identified risks. The following figure shows the task associated with the selection step:

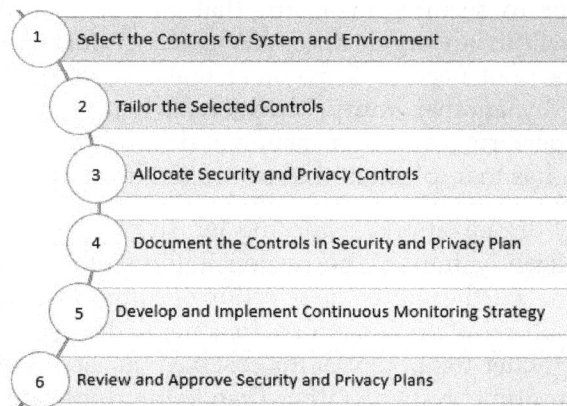

1. Select the Controls for System and Environment
2. Tailor the Selected Controls
3. Allocate Security and Privacy Controls
4. Document the Controls in Security and Privacy Plan
5. Develop and Implement Continuous Monitoring Strategy
6. Review and Approve Security and Privacy Plans

Figure 7.4: Control selection tasks

Let us look at the select process in detail:

- **Task 1**: Select the controls for system and environment:

  There are two main methods for selecting security and privacy controls: The baseline control selection approach and the organization-generated control selection approach. The baseline approach uses pre-defined sets of controls, like those in NIST SP 800-53B, tailored to an organization's needs based on factors like system security and privacy risks. The organization-generated approach allows an organization to choose its own controls for specialized systems, like medical devices, making it more flexible and cost-effective. Both methods require tailoring to fit specific requirements, and organizations follow a systems engineering process to ensure that security and privacy controls align with system lifecycle needs. The following table shows the roles to select controls for the system:

Primary responsibility	Supporting roles	SDLC phase	References
System owner, common control provider.	Authorizing official or authorizing official designated representative, information owner or steward, systems security engineer, privacy engineer, system security officer, system privacy officer.	New: Development/ acquisition Existing: Operations/ maintenance	NIST SP 800-30; SP 800-53; SP 800-53B; SP 800-160 v1; SP 800-161; FIPS 199; FIPS 200; NIST CSF

Table 7.2: Roles to select controls

- **Task 2**: Tailor the selected controls:

  The tailoring process includes identifying common controls, applying scoping considerations, selecting compensating controls, and adjusting control parameters. The level of justification for these decisions depends on the system's risk and impact level, with high-impact systems requiring more detailed justification. The tailoring process also considers factors like stakeholder needs, laws, policies, and the **system development lifecycle** (**SDLC**). Risk assessments guide the process and help to determine which controls are most appropriate. If common controls are not enough, additional controls may be added, or a higher level of risk may be accepted. The following table shows the roles to tailor the selected controls:

Primary responsibility	Supporting roles	SDLC phase	References
System owner, common control provider.	Authorizing official or authorizing official designated representative, information owner or steward, systems security engineer, privacy engineer, system security officer, system privacy officer.	New: Development/ acquisition Existing: Operations/ maintenance	NIST SP 800-30; SP 800-53; SP 800-53B; SP 800-160 v1; SP 800-161; FIPS 199; FIPS 200; NIST CSF

Table 7.3: Roles to tailor controls

- **Task 3**: Allocate security and privacy controls:

  Organizations categorize controls as system-specific, hybrid, or common, and assign them to the relevant system components (like machines, physical parts, or processes) that are responsible for security or privacy. Controls are allocated based on the organization's architecture and specific security and privacy needs, ensuring that only the necessary controls are applied to each system element. Common controls are provided at the organizational level and inherited by multiple systems, while hybrid controls serve both the system and organization. System-specific controls address unique needs and are only allocated where necessary. The following table shows the roles to allocate security and privacy controls:

Primary responsibility	Supporting roles	SDLC phase	References
Security architect, privacy architect, system security officer, system privacy officer	Chief information officer, authorizing official or authorizing official designated representative, mission or business owner, senior agency information security officer, senior agency official for privacy, system owner.	New: Initiation Existing: Operations/ maintenance	NIST SP 800-39; SP 800-64; SP 800-160 v1; NIST CSF

Table 7.4: Roles to allocate security and privacy controls

- **Task 4**: Document the controls in the security and privacy plan:

  Security and privacy plans describe the system's requirements and the controls chosen to meet them, detailing how each control is implemented, including inputs, expected behaviours, and outputs. These plans clarify the responsibilities of common control providers and how hybrid controls are shared between the system and provider. Organizations may develop a consolidated plan for both security and privacy or separate plans with cross-references. The senior agency official for privacy reviews and approves the privacy aspects before submission for authorization. Control selection and tailoring information are documented in systems engineering or lifecycledocuments to ensure traceability, and any potential privacy risks are noted and addressed. The following table shows the roles to document controls in security and privacy plan:

Primary responsibility	Supporting roles	SDLC phase	References
System owner, common control provider	Authorizing official or authorizing official designated representative, information owner or steward, systems security engineer; privacy engineer, system security officer, system privacy officer	New: Development/ acquisition Existing: Operations/ maintenance	NIST SP 800-18; SP 800-30; SP 800-53; SP 800-64; SP 800-160 v1; SP 800-161; NIST CSF; FIPS 199; FIPS 200;

Table 7.5: Roles to document controls

- **Task 5**: Develop and implement a continuous monitoring strategy:

  Continuous monitoring of controls is a key part of risk management, starting with a system-level monitoring strategy developed early in the SDLC. This strategy aligns with the organization's broader monitoring plan and outlines how often controls should be assessed, how changes to the system should be tracked, and how risk assessments and security/privacy reports should be handled. The strategy specifies monitoring frequency based on the system's importance and risk, must be approved by the authorizing official, and continues through the system's operational phase until disposal. The following table shows the roles to develop and implement monitoring strategy:

Primary responsibility	Supporting roles	SDLC phase	References
System owner, common control provider	Senior accountable official for risk management or risk executive, chief information officer, senior agency information security officer, senior agency official for privacy, authorizing official or authorizing official designated representative, information owner or steward, security architect, privacy architect; systems security engineer, privacy engineer, system security officer, system privacy officer	New: Development/ acquisition Existing: Operations/ maintenance	NIST SP 800-30; SP 800-39; SP 800-53; SP 800-53A; SP 800-137; SP 800-161; NIST CSF

Table 7.6: Roles to develop and implement monitoring strategy

- **Task 6**: Review and approve security and privacy plans:

  The authorizing official, with support from key leaders like the senior accountable official for risk management and other senior officers, reviews the security and privacy plans to ensure they meet the system's requirements. If any inconsistencies or gaps are found, they may suggest changes. Once the plans are complete, the authorized official approves them, marking an important step in the SDLC and risk management process. This approval allows the risk management process to move forward to the implementation phase, setting the stage for acquiring the system and completing further RMF steps. The following table shows the roles to review and approve security and privacy plans:

Primary responsibility	Supporting roles	SDLC phase	References
Authorizing official or authorizing official designated representative	Senior accountable official for risk management or risk executive, chief information officer, chief acquisition officer, senior agency information security officer, senior agency official for privacy	New: Development/ acquisition Existing: Operations/ maintenance	NIST SP 800-30; SP 800-53; SP 800-160 v1

Table 7.7: Roles to review and approve security plans

Compensating controls

Compensating controls serve as alternatives for specific controls that are part of the control baselines. Organizations select these controls when they need to tailor certain baseline controls due to various reasons while still requiring protection to mitigate risk to an acceptable level. The decision to use compensating controls is often made when the original baseline control is technically infeasible to implement, not cost-effective, or when its implementation could adversely impact the organization's mission or business functions.

In some cases, particularly for technology-related scoping considerations, compensating controls may be temporary solutions intended for use only until the system can be updated or modified to include the original controls. The primary goal of compensating controls is to provide equivalent or comparable protection to the systems, organizations, and individuals. Therefore, the selection of compensating controls follows the application of scoping considerations during the tailoring process, ensuring that these alternatives effectively address the identified risks and also align with the organization's overall security strategy. To use compensating controls, organizations should consider the following:

- Choose compensating controls from the control catalog in SP 800-53.

- Explain how these compensating controls meet security or privacy requirements and why the baseline controls could not be implemented.

- Consider adopting suitable compensating controls from other sources if the necessary ones are not available in SP 800-53.

- Evaluate and accept the security and privacy risks linked to using these compensating controls.

Supplementing control baselines

In certain cases, organizations may need to implement additional controls or control enhancements beyond those outlined in the control baselines. This need arises to address specific threats to the organization, its mission and business processes, and the systems it employs. Additionally, organizations may require extra controls to manage specific types of PII processing and the associated privacy risks, as well as to comply with various laws, policies, regulations, standards, and guidelines.

Conducting organizational risk assessments is crucial for determining the necessity and adequacy of the controls and enhancements included in the control baselines. These assessments provide valuable insights that inform decisions about additional protections needed to effectively manage risks. Organizations are encouraged to leverage the control catalog found in NIST SP 800-53, which offers a wide range of controls and enhancements, to supplement their existing control baselines and ensure comprehensive security and privacy measures are in place.

Control parameter values

Controls and control enhancements that include embedded parameters—such as assignment and selection operations, allow organizations to tailor specific aspects of these controls to meet their unique requirements. After considering scoping factors and selecting compensating controls, organizations should review the controls and enhancements for any assignment and determine the appropriate values for the identified parameters. These parameter values may be influenced by business needs, or they might be mandated by laws, executive orders, regulations, policies, standards, guidelines, or industry best practices.

Once organizations establish the parameter values for the controls and enhancements, these specified values become a permanent part of the controls. Consequently, this must be documented in relevant security and privacy program plans or in system security and privacy plans, as needed. Organizations may even specify these parameter values before selecting compensating controls and may influence whether compensating controls are necessary. Collaboration on the development of parameter values can result in significant benefits, especially for organizations that frequently work together or regularly exchange information. This collaboration helps ensure that the controls are effectively aligned with shared objectives and regulatory requirements:

- **Example 1**: The parameter values for the password policy can be as follows:
    - **Minimum password length**: Must be at least 12 characters.
    - **Password complexity**: Must include at least one uppercase letter, one lowercase letter, one number, and one special character.
    - **Password expiry**: Passwords must be changed every 90 days.
- **Example 2**: The parameter values for audit logging can be as follows:
    - **Log retention period**: Retain logs for a minimum of 365 days.
    - **Event types**: Capture event types such as record failed login attempts, changes to user permissions, etc.
    - **Log storage**: Store logs in a secure, centralized logging server.
    - **Review period**: The logs must be reviewed every 30 days.

Creating overlays

To meet the need for tailored security controls across different communities and specialized contexts, the concept of an overlay has been introduced. An overlay consists of a fully specified set of security controls, control enhancements, and supplemental guidance that arise from applying specific tailoring guidance to the foundational security control baselines. These overlays serve to enhance the initial baselines by allowing organizations to add or remove controls as necessary. They also provide clarity on how security controls apply to particular information technologies, computing environments, mission types, operating modes, industry sectors, and regulatory requirements.

Moreover, overlays establish community-wide parameter values for assignment and selection statements within security controls and control enhancements. They also extend supplemental guidance for security controls when needed. Organizations often resort to creating overlays when there are significant deviations from the fundamental assumptions that shaped the original security control baselines. If organizations align closely with these initial assumptions, the creation of an overlay may be unnecessary. However, if the baselines lack essential assumptions, an overlay can help fill those gaps by incorporating additional, relevant assumptions.

The process of developing overlays allows organizations to apply a structured approach to tailoring security controls, fostering collaboration and consensus among various stakeholders. This ensures that the resulting security plans for information systems receive broad support and are well-suited to address specific circumstances or conditions faced by the organization.

Overlays can be categorized into several useful types, tailored to address specific contexts and needs within different organizations. These categories include the following:

- **Communities of interest**: This encompasses sectors such as healthcare, law enforcement, financial services, transportation, energy, and collaborative partnerships. Each community may have unique security requirements that necessitate specialized controls.

- **Information technologies and computing paradigms**: Overlays can focus on specific technologies, including cloud computing, mobile devices, PKI, and cross-domain solutions. These overlays ensure that security controls align with the characteristics and risks associated with these technologies.

- **Environments of operation**: Different operational environments, such as space or tactical settings, may have unique security challenges that require tailored controls to protect information systems effectively.

- **Types of information systems and operating modes**: This category includes overlays for industrial and process control systems, single-user systems, and standalone systems. Each type may have distinct security needs based on its operation and potential vulnerabilities.

- **Types of missions and operations**: Overlays can be developed to address specific security requirements for various missions, such as emergency response, development, testing, and evaluation activities.

- **Statutory and regulatory requirements**: This includes overlays designed to comply with specific laws and regulations, such as the *Foreign Intelligence Surveillance Act* (*FISA*), the *Health Insurance Portability and Accountability Act* (*HIPAA*), and the *Privacy Act* (U.S. federal law). Ensuring compliance with these legal frameworks is crucial for organizations operating in regulated environments.

Multiple overlays can indeed be applied to a single security control baseline, leading to tailored baselines that may be either more or less stringent than the original controls. This flexibility allows organizations to adapt their security measures based on specific needs or circumstances.

Risk assessments play a crucial role in this process, as they provide the necessary information to evaluate whether the risks associated with implementing the tailored baselines align with the organization's or community's risk tolerance. This ensures that any modifications made through overlays do not exceed acceptable levels of risk.

However, using multiple overlays can lead to potential conflicts, especially if they suggest different applications or removals of security controls. In such cases, it is essential for the authorizing official or their designee to work closely with the business owner and/or information owner or steward to resolve these conflicts. This collaborative approach helps maintain the integrity and effectiveness of the security controls while ensuring compliance with the tailored requirements.

System of record notices

The *Privacy Act* of 1974 mandates that each organization (government agency) publicly disclose its systems of records through publication in the Federal Register. A system of records consists of a group of records controlled by the agency, from which information about individuals can be retrieved using the individual's name or another assigned identifier. This public notice, known as a **System of Records Notice** (**SORN**), outlines the purpose of the system, the authority under which it is maintained, and the types of records it contains. Additionally, the SORN details how the information can be routinely used and provides further insights into the system.

When proposing a new system or revising an existing one, board program office staff collaborate with board privacy program staff. The privacy program staff oversees the review of SORNs within the board, which includes legal counsel review and submission of the notice for evaluation by the *Office of Management and Budget* (*OMB*) and *Congress*, followed by its publication in the *Federal Register*.

After the notice is published, interested parties have 30 calendar days to submit comments on the proposed or revised system. If no changes are deemed necessary after this comment period, the system of records becomes official. However, if modifications are needed based on the feedback received, the board will revise the notice and republish it to reflect those changes. A SORN is intended to inform the public about key information like the following:

- The kind of personal information federal agencies maintain.

- How agencies limit the uses and disclosures of the information to only those compatible with the purpose for which the information was collected.

- How an individual might request access or seek redress to their information.

Assurance and trustworthiness

Assurance and trustworthiness in information systems are becoming critical components of organizational risk management strategies. Whether it is systems supporting major financial institutions, nuclear power plants, or military operations, these systems must be reliable, trustworthy, and resilient against increasingly sophisticated threats.

To grasp how organizations achieve this level of trustworthiness, it is essential to define trust itself. Trust can be understood as the belief that an entity, be it a person, process, information system, or system component, will behave predictably while performing specific functions in particular environments and under defined conditions. This foundational concept of trust underpins the assurance processes that organizations implement to ensure their systems are dependable and secure.

Implementing systems security and privacy engineering principles allows organizations to create trustworthy, secure, and resilient systems. This proactive approach helps to mitigate disruptions, hazards, and threats while also addressing potential privacy issues for individuals. Key examples of these principles include developing layered protections, establishing comprehensive security and privacy policies, and incorporating security and privacy requirements into the development process.

By adhering to these systems security and privacy engineering concepts, organizations can effectively build secure systems, components, and services while reducing risks to acceptable levels. This approach not only supports better risk management decisions but also helps address supply chain risks, like using tamper-resistant hardware in system designs. Ultimately, these principles contribute to a robust security posture that protects both organizational assets and individual privacy.

The principle of self-reliant trustworthiness emphasizes that systems should minimize their dependence on other systems to maintain their own trustworthiness. Under this principle, a system is considered trustworthy by default, with any external connections serving merely to enhance its functionality. If a system were to rely on an external entity to uphold its trustworthiness, it would become susceptible to both malicious and non-malicious threats that could compromise or degrade that essential connection.

One of the key advantages of self-reliant trustworthiness is that isolating a system can significantly reduce its vulnerability to attacks. By operating independently, the system is better protected from potential threats that might exploit weaknesses in external connections. This ensures that the system can maintain its integrity and performance even in scenarios where external connections are temporarily disrupted.

Control selection documentation

Organizations must carefully document the decisions made during the security control selection process, ensuring that each decision is supported by a clear rationale. This documentation is crucial for assessing the security implications for organizational information systems, particularly regarding their potential impact on mission and business functions. The finalized set of security controls, along with the rationale for their selection—including any specific restrictions on information system use should be captured in the organization's security plans. This thorough documentation of risk management decisions is essential for authorizing officials, as it provides them with the necessary context to make informed authorization decisions regarding the systems.

Without comprehensive documentation, the underlying understanding, assumptions, constraints, and justifications for risk management choices may be lost over time. This gap in information becomes particularly problematic when the state of the information systems or their operational environments changes, necessitating a revisit of the original risk decisions. Therefore, maintaining clear records is vital to ensure that future evaluations are informed and grounded in the context of previous decisions.

To facilitate this process, organizations can refer to a summarized flow of the security control selection process, which includes the initial selection of baselines and the subsequent tailoring of these baselines based on specific organizational needs. The security control guidance serves as a framework for systematically addressing security considerations and ensuring that all relevant decisions are documented for future reference. The following figure summarizes the security control selection and tailoring process along with documentation:

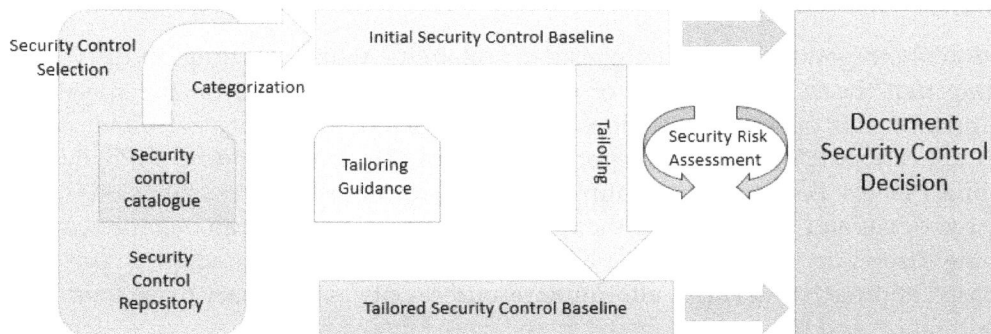

Figure 7.5: Security control workflow

The figure illustrates the process of selecting a security control baseline from a security control catalogue and customizing it (tailoring) to fit the specific needs and requirements of an organization. The security control catalogue is essentially a pre-defined list of controls that provide guidelines and standards for safeguarding an organization's systems and data. The security control repository, on the other hand, is a centralized database or system that stores and manages the controls that have been implemented within the organization. All these baselines and tailored security controls are documented.

As organizations work on fully specifying their security controls for their operational environments, they may encounter challenges that necessitate the introduction of additional supplemental controls. This adaptability is key, as the tailoring process is not a one-time event. Organizations are encouraged to revisit and refine the tailoring steps regularly, adjusting their approach based on ongoing assessments of risk and changing circumstances.

A SSP outlines the security measures for systems and applications within an organization. According to NIST, it is a formal document that describes the security requirements of an information system and the controls in place or planned to meet those requirements.

Other risk considerations

Organizational tailoring decisions regarding security controls are not made randomly. Usually, these decisions primarily focus on information security. However, they must also align with other risk factors to consider. Key factors such as cost, schedule, and performance play a significant role in determining which security controls are implemented within organizational information systems and their operating environments. For example, in military command and control systems, where human lives are often at risk, security controls must be balanced with operational needs.

Integrating the security control selection process, including tailoring activities into the overall RMF, is crucial, as outlined in NIST SP 800-39. This approach ensures that the security considerations are part of a comprehensive strategy that addresses various risk factors.

Additionally, organizations must consider scalability when selecting security controls, meaning that the implementation of controls should vary based on the specific needs and impact levels of the information systems involved. Scalability is influenced by the FIPS Publication 199 security categorizations and the corresponding FIPS Publication 200 impact levels. For example, contingency plans for high-impact systems might require extensive detail and length, while those for low-impact systems can be more concise. By applying discretion in how controls are scaled, organizations can adopt a cost-effective, risk-based approach to security, allocating resources only as necessary to achieve adequate risk mitigation and security.

Privacy control catalogue

The privacy control catalogue as mentioned in NIST SP 800-53 Revision 5, serves as a comprehensive framework for organizations to implement effective privacy controls aimed at protecting personal information. It outlines a structured approach to identifying, assessing, and mitigating privacy risks associated with the handling of personal data. This catalogue is particularly valuable in ensuring compliance with various privacy regulations and standards, helping organizations maintain trust with individuals whose data they process.

One of the primary components of the privacy control catalogue is governance and accountability. This includes establishing robust policies and procedures that guide the organization's privacy practices. Organizations must ensure that there are clear lines of responsibility and oversight mechanisms in place to monitor compliance with these policies. Effective governance helps foster a culture of accountability and awareness regarding privacy issues.

Risk assessment is another critical element in the catalogue where organizations are encouraged to conduct thorough assessments to identify and evaluate the risks associated with their data processing activities. This proactive approach enables organizations to prioritize their privacy controls based on the level of risk and to implement tailored measures to mitigate those risks effectively.

Conclusion

In this chapter, we explored the process of selecting security controls guided by scoping considerations and control functions. We identified common controls and outlined the assumptions that underpin control baselines, which support effective tailoring. Additionally, we examined compensating controls and the assignment of control parameter values to address the unique needs of organizations.

We also understood the concept of overlays and the significance of the system of record notice, particularly regarding the management of personal information and associated controls. Furthermore, we highlighted the importance of documenting the rationale behind selecting control baselines, ensuring alignment with business needs, and facilitating informed decision-making.

As we transition to the next chapter, our focus will shift to control enhancement and monitoring, as well as the establishment of service-level requirements. This will equip you with the necessary insights to ensure that security controls not only meet current needs but also adapt and evolve in response to emerging threats and organizational changes.

Key terms

- NIST SP 800-60 (Volumes 1 and 2) provides guidance for the assignment of security categories to information systems.

- NIST SP 800-37 provides guidance for the specific tasks of the RMF categorize step.

- NIST SP 800-53 Revision 5 is the most recent comprehensive guide for security and privacy controls while NIST SP 800-53B complements Revision 5 by providing specific baselines of controls.

- NIST SP 800-160-1 provides guidance on systems security engineering and the application of security design principles to achieve trustworthy systems.

- The additional assumptions that are not addressed in the control baselines include:

  o Insider threats exist within organizations.

- o Classified information is processed, stored, or transmitted by organizational systems.

- o **Advanced persistent threats (APTs)** exist within organizations.

- o Information requires specialized protection based on legislation, directives, regulations, or policies.

- o Organizational systems communicate with other systems across different security domains

- Compensating controls are not intended to bypass compliance with established requirements. Instead, they serve as alternative measures that provide effective security and privacy protections.

- Control enhancements are additional safeguards applied to address specific risks or high-impact systems (e.g., zero trust principles and data masking).

- SSP is a formal document outlining system boundaries, controls, and compliance requirements.

- Assurance refers to the confidence or certainty that an information system, process, or control will function as intended and meet security requirements.

- Trustworthiness is the inherent quality or characteristic of a system or entity that makes it reliable and deserving of trust.

Join our book's Discord space

Join the book's Discord Workspace for Latest updates, Offers, Tech happenings around the world, New Release and Sessions with the Authors:

https://discord.bpbonline.com

CHAPTER 8
Enhancing Security Controls

Introduction

This chapter provides a comprehensive exploration of control enhancement strategies aimed at maintaining and improving an organization's security posture. It emphasizes the importance of a continuous monitoring the program, which is essential for ensuring ongoing effectiveness of security controls within information systems. In addition to the control enhancement plan, the chapter also focuses on recovery strategies. It outlines a robust recovery plan designed to help organizations respond to incidents effectively while maintaining an expected level of service.

Furthermore, the chapter addresses the significance of monitoring compliance, which involves evaluating system performance and conducting timely reviews of security controls. It discusses various audit strategies and types of audits, highlighting their critical role in thoroughly evaluating security measures. Moreover, the chapter delves into vulnerability management, emphasizing its importance in effectively managing risks within IT environments. Additionally, the chapter outlines **key performance indicators (KPIs)** and **key risk indicators (KRIs)** that are essential for measuring and understanding various metrics related to security controls..

Structure

The chapter covers the following main topics:

- Control enhancement
- Security continuous monitoring
- Recovery plan
- Monitoring compliance
- Vulnerability management
- Performance and risk monitoring

Objectives

By the end of this chapter, you will have a thorough understanding of control enhancement strategies, providing you with the tools to strengthen security measures. You will learn about the key components of a continuous security program, ensuring long-term protection for your systems. Additionally, you will become familiar with the importance of **service level agreements (SLAs)** and the best practices for implementing record recovery controls to safeguard critical data.

Furthermore, this chapter will equip you with valuable knowledge on monitoring compliance and effective audit strategies to maintain regulatory adherence. You will also gain insight into vulnerability management processes and the best approaches to identify, assess, and mitigate security risks. Finally, you will explore performance and risk monitoring techniques, empowering you to proactively manage and improve your organization's security posture.

Control enhancement

The control enhancement plan serves as a comprehensive roadmap that outlines the steps needed to enhance security measures, prioritize improvements, and optimize risk management efforts. By keeping pace with new vulnerabilities, emerging threats, and regulatory changes, organizations can ensure ongoing compliance and resilience against evolving risks.

One of the primary advantages of this strategy is its proactive approach to risk management. It enables organizations to identify and mitigate potential risks before they escalate, ensuring that security controls remain effective and responsive to incidents. This proactive approach is crucial for safeguarding the organization's critical assets, data, and systems, forming a fundamental part of a robust risk management program.

Furthermore, a well-structured enhancement strategy significantly reduces overall risk exposure. By continually refining and bolstering security controls, organizations can minimize both the likelihood and impact of security incidents. This not only protects the organization's reputation but also fosters customer trust and supports financial stability.

Additionally, the strategy promotes a culture of security awareness and accountability among employees. When staff are educated about security risks and understand their role in mitigating them, they are more likely to adhere to established policies and procedures. This heightened awareness can help prevent incidents stemming from human error or negligence, which are often among the most frequent and costly types of security breaches. Overall, a security control enhancement strategy plan is vital for fostering a resilient and security-conscious organizational environment.

Control enhancement strategy

A robust security control enhancement strategy plan within the **Risk Management Framework** (**RMF**) is critical for maintaining and improving an organization's security posture. The following key elements are integral to developing an effective plan, as shown in following figure:

Figure 8.1: *Control enhancement strategy plan*

The following key elements are explained in detail:

- **Continuous monitoring and assessment of security controls**: Continuous monitoring is a crucial part of a strategy that involves regularly evaluating the effectiveness of security controls to ensure they are functioning as intended. This includes collecting and analyzing security-related data, reviewing system logs, and conducting periodic assessments. By employing automated tools and metrics, organizations can detect anomalies, assess compliance, and promptly address any issues that arise. This proactive approach helps maintain an adaptive security environment where controls can be adjusted based on the latest threat intelligence.

- **Identification and remediation of vulnerabilities and weaknesses**: A vital component of any security enhancement strategy is the ongoing identification and remediation of vulnerabilities. This involves conducting vulnerability assessments and penetration testing to uncover weaknesses in systems and processes. Once identified, these vulnerabilities must be prioritized based on risk level, and timely remediation efforts must be implemented. Establishing a systematic process for tracking vulnerabilities from identification through resolution ensures that the organization remains vigilant and responsive to potential threats.

- **Training and awareness programs for employees**: Employee training and awareness are essential for fostering a security-conscious culture within the organization. Regular training sessions should cover topics such as recognizing phishing attempts, following secure practices for data handling, and understanding the importance of compliance. The awareness campaigns can utilize various formats, such as workshops, e-learning modules, and simulated exercises, to engage employees effectively. By equipping staff with the knowledge and skills needed to recognize and mitigate security risks, organizations can significantly reduce the incidence of human errors, which often lead to security breaches.

- **Incident response planning and testing**: An effective incident response plan is crucial for ensuring a swift and coordinated reaction to security incidents. The plan should outline roles and responsibilities, communication protocols, and escalation procedures. Regular testing of the incident response plan through tabletop exercises and simulations helps to assess the readiness of the response team and identify areas for improvement. By preparing for potential incidents, organizations can minimize damage and recovery time, thereby protecting critical assets and maintaining operational continuity.

- **Regular review and updating of the security control enhancement plan**: The security landscape is continually evolving, making it necessary for organizations to regularly review and update their security control enhancement plan. This includes assessing the effectiveness of current controls, incorporating lessons learned from incidents, and adapting to changes in technology and threat landscapes. A structured review schedule ensures that the plan remains relevant and aligned with organizational goals, facilitating ongoing improvement in security practices.

- **Alignment with the organization's overall risk management program and objectives**: For a security control enhancement strategy to be truly effective, it must align with the organization's broader risk management program and objectives. This involves ensuring that security measures support overall business goals and risk appetite. Collaboration among different departments, such as IT, legal, and compliance, is essential to create a cohesive approach to risk management, where security enhancements are integrated into all facets of organizational operations.

- **Compliance with regulatory requirements**: Lastly, adherence to regulatory requirements is a fundamental aspect of any security control enhancement strategy. Organizations must stay informed about relevant laws and regulations such as *General Data Protection Regulation* (*GDPR*), *Health Insurance Portability and Accountability Act* (*HIPAA*), or *Payment Card Industry Data Security Standard* (*PCI DSS*) that govern data protection and privacy. Regular audits and assessments should be conducted to ensure compliance, which not only mitigates legal risks but also reinforces trust among customers and stakeholders. By embedding compliance into the security enhancement strategy, organizations can create a more robust and trustworthy security framework.

In summary, a comprehensive security control enhancement strategy plan encompasses continuous monitoring, vulnerability management, employee training, incident response planning, regular reviews, alignment with risk management objectives, and compliance with regulations. By integrating these elements, organizations can effectively enhance their security posture, reduce risks, and foster a culture of security awareness.

Control enhancement implement plan

In NIST SP 800-53 Revision 5, security control enhancements are discussed as part of the control tailoring process. These enhancements are detailed in the security control families (like access control, audit, accountability, etc.) where organizations can choose additional measures to strengthen security beyond the baseline controls. Implementing a security control enhancement strategy plan within the RMF is a systematic process that involves several critical steps. Each step is designed to ensure that security controls are effectively enhanced to protect sensitive information and mitigate potential risks. *Figure 8.2* shows the implementation process:

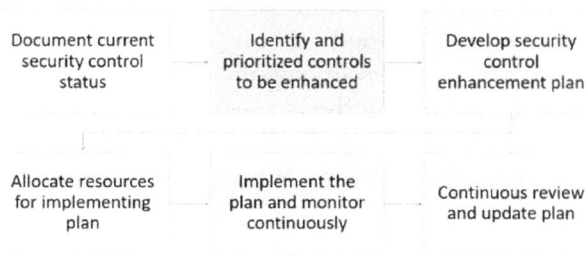

Figure 8.2: *Control enhancement implementation process*

Following is the detailed breakdown of the implementation process:

- **Document the current security control implementation status**: The first step is to conduct a thorough assessment of the existing security controls. This involves documenting the current implementation status, including what controls are in place, their effectiveness, and any gaps or weaknesses identified during previous assessments. Utilizing tools like security audits, risk assessments, and compliance checks can provide valuable insights into the current security posture. This documentation serves as a baseline for identifying areas needing enhancement.

- **Identify and prioritize the security controls to be enhanced**: Once the current status is documented, the next step is to identify which security controls require enhancement. This involves evaluating the effectiveness of existing controls against current threats, vulnerabilities, and regulatory requirements. Controls should be prioritized based on factors such as risk exposure, potential impact on the organization, and compliance obligations. A risk assessment matrix can help in this prioritization, ensuring that the most critical areas are addressed first.

- **Develop a security control enhancement plan**: After prioritizing the controls, organizations should develop a detailed enhancement plan. This plan should outline specific timelines for implementation, clear goals, and measurable objectives. Each enhancement should have defined success criteria to evaluate effectiveness post-implementation. Additionally, the plan should incorporate KPIs to track progress. This structured approach ensures that all stakeholders have a clear understanding of what needs to be achieved and by when.

- **Allocate resources for implementing the plan**: Implementing the enhancement plan requires adequate resource allocation, including budgetary considerations and human resources. Organizations need to identify the financial resources necessary for acquiring new technologies, tools, or services that may be needed for the enhancements. Furthermore, assigning the right personnel whether in-house teams or external consultants—ensures that the implementation is managed effectively. A clear budget and resource plan will help in tracking expenditures and managing project costs.

- **Implement the plan and monitor progress regularly**: With resources allocated, organizations can proceed to implement the enhancement plan. This phase involves executing the defined actions, deploying new technologies, and strengthening existing processes. Regular monitoring of progress is essential during this phase to ensure that the implementation stays on track. Organizations should establish regular check-ins and status updates to assess progress against the defined timelines and objectives, allowing for any necessary adjustments to be made promptly.

- **Continuously review and update the plan**: The security landscape is dynamic, and thus, the enhancement plan must be regularly reviewed and updated to remain effective. This includes evaluating the outcomes of implemented controls, analyzing any incidents or breaches, and reassessing risks. Organizations should establish a schedule for these reviews, such as quarterly or bi-annually, to ensure that the plan aligns with evolving organizational objectives and the threat landscape. Continuous improvement is key to maintaining a robust security posture.

It is crucial that the security control enhancement strategy plan is developed in collaboration with all relevant stakeholders, including IT personnel, security professionals, compliance officers, and management. Engaging these stakeholders ensures that the plan addresses all potential security risks and aligns with organizational goals. Additionally, conducting regular training and awareness programs for employees is essential. These programs should inform staff about the enhancements, their roles in the implementation process, and best practices for maintaining security.

Zero trust architecture

Zero trust is a cybersecurity framework that operates on the principle that no entity, whether inside or outside the network, should be trusted by default. It requires continuous evaluation of trust based on identity, context, and behavior before granting access to any resource. The goal of **zero trust architecture** (**ZTA**) is to protect organization resources and data by ensuring that access is strictly controlled and security is maintained throughout the entire system. This may include identity management, access controls, operations, endpoints, hosting environments, and interconnecting infrastructure.

Traditionally, enterprises focused on perimeter defense, where authenticated users inside the network were often trusted with access to a wide range of resources. However, this approach created vulnerabilities, particularly with lateral movement—where attackers, once inside the network, could move freely and access additional resources. Zero trust aims to address this challenge by requiring constant verification, limiting lateral movement, and enforcing access policies that are based on real-time evaluations of user behavior, device health, and other contextual factors. This significantly reduces the risk of unauthorized access or attacks, even if an attacker manages to breach the perimeter.

Let us take the example of identity and access management. Traditional access controls grant users access based on roles or trusted IP addresses. ZTA verifies identity with **multifactor authentication** (**MFA**) and adjusts access in real-time based on user behavior, location, device health and other contextual data.

The NIST SP 800-207 outlines three core models for ZTA: Enhanced identity governance, micro-segmentation, and software-defined perimeters. These models serve as foundational approaches for organizations to adopt zero trust principles. Enhanced identity governance focuses on robust authentication and authorization mechanisms, while micro-segmentation involves dividing networks into smaller, more manageable segments. Software-defined perimeters create dynamic, identity-centric boundaries around resources.

Data masking

Data masking is a technique that creates a version of data that looks similar to the original data but hides sensitive information. This masked data can be used for activities like software testing or user training without exposing the real data. Data masking helps organization by allowing access to the information while safeguarding sensitive data. Methods like character shuffling, substitution, or encryption can be used, but the masked data cannot be reversed to reveal the original sensitive information. Here are some common data masking techniques to protect sensitive data within the organization:

- **Encryption**: Encryption is one of the most secure data masking techniques used to protect sensitive data. It involves converting original, readable data into an unreadable format using a cryptographic algorithm.

- **Data pseudonymization**: This technique replaces original data, like names or emails, with a pseudonym or alias. This method is reversible, so the data can be re-identified later if needed.

- **Data anonymization**: This technique protects sensitive information by removing identifiers that could link data back to an individual or entity. The goal is to make the data completely unidentifiable, ensuring privacy while still allowing for analysis or use in non-sensitive contexts.

- **Redaction**: This technique involves permanently removing sensitive information from a dataset or document. The sensitive data such as names, social security numbers, addresses, or financial information are either blacked out or replaced with placeholder text (e.g., XXXX) to hide the original value.

- **Shuffling**: This technique scrambles data within a dataset, keeping the original values but swapping them between different elements.

Data labeling and tagging

Data labeling and tagging are important practices outlined in ISO/IEC 27002:2022, which provides guidelines for information security management. Organizations should develop an organization-wide information labeling procedure that adheres to the information classification scheme:

- **Data labeling**: Data labeling is the process of categorizing data based on its classification level, such as confidential, internal, or public. Labeling helps organizations to identify the level of protection needed for the data and ensures the right security measures are applied throughout its lifecycle.

- **Data tagging**: Data tagging is similar to labeling, but involves adding metadata or tags to data to track specific attributes or characteristics. Tags can be used to store additional information about data, such as its classification, usage, or ownership. Some organizations use automated tools to tag data to ensure consistent and accurate tagging.

Data labeling and tagging plays an important role in an organization. Following is some of the advantages:

- **Compliance**: Regulations like GDPR, HIPAA, and PCI DSS require organizations to classify and protect sensitive data, and proper labeling and tagging help meet these requirements.

- **Data lifecycle management**: Labeling and tagging allow organizations to manage data throughout its lifecycle, ensuring that data is handled correctly during storage, transfer, or deletion.

- **Security and access control**: Labeling and tagging helps to protect sensitive data by restricting access based on its classification.

Security continuous monitoring

A continuous monitoring strategy is essential for maintaining the effectiveness of security controls within information systems. This strategy is designed to assess and understand the security state of a system over time, allowing for timely adjustments in response to changes in both the system itself and its operational environment. By implementing a robust monitoring framework, organizations can ensure that security measures remain effective and relevant, thereby reducing vulnerabilities and enhancing overall risk management.

The development of a monitoring plan for security controls is a collaborative effort involving several key stakeholders, including the system owner, common control provider, risk executive, authorizing official, chief information officer, senior information security officer, information owner, and information systems security officer. To facilitate effective monitoring, the strategy emphasizes the use of automated tools that enable near-real-time assessment of risks. This approach not only streamlines the monitoring process but also allows for immediate response to emerging threats. Key components of the strategy include the oversight of inherited controls, configuration management, security impact analysis of proposed changes, and regular reporting on the security status to management. These elements ensure that all aspects of the system's security posture are considered and continuously evaluated.

The strategy also outlines specific security controls to be monitored, detailing the frequency of monitoring and the assessment methods to be employed. Controls are prioritized based on their criticality and volatility, ensuring that those with the highest risk potential are closely observed. The frequency of monitoring for inherited controls varies depending on the trustworthiness of the provider, while risk assessments help in selecting which controls to focus on and determining their monitoring frequency. This structured approach ensures that the security posture remains aligned with the organization's risk management goals.

Approval of the monitoring strategy typically falls to the **authorizing official** (**AO**) or **authorizing official designated representative** (**AODR**) as part of the overall security plan. Continuous monitoring is vital throughout the system's lifecycle, accommodating dynamic subsystems that may arise after initial development. The examples of dynamic subsystem can be cloud services, third-party API integration, etc. that may change or evolve after initial system design. By aligning monitoring efforts with a risk acceptance framework, organizations can prevent unnecessary reauthorization when subsystems change.

Continuous monitoring program

According to NIST SP 800-37, an effective continuous monitoring program is essential for managing the security of Federal Information Systems. This program should encompass several critical components to ensure comprehensive oversight and risk management as shown in the following figure:

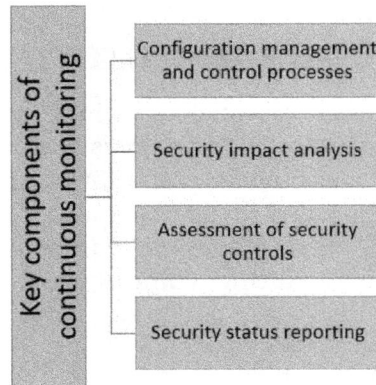

Figure 8.3: *Components of continuous monitoring*

There are four key components explained briefly:

- **Configuration management and control processes**: Configuration management involves maintaining the integrity of the system's configurations throughout its lifecycle. This includes establishing baseline configurations, monitoring changes, and ensuring that any modifications are documented and approved. Effective configuration management helps prevent unauthorized changes that could introduce vulnerabilities.

- **Security impact analyses**: Conducting security impact analyses is crucial for evaluating the potential effects of proposed or actual changes to the information system and its operational environment. This analysis helps identify risks associated with changes, ensuring that security implications are considered before modifications are implemented. It allows organizations to proactively address potential weaknesses that could be introduced by system changes.

- **Assessment of security controls**: A comprehensive assessment of selected security controls is necessary to evaluate both those employed within the system and those inherited from other systems (including dynamic subsystems). This assessment involves verifying that controls are functioning as intended and remain effective in mitigating risks. It also requires monitoring for any changes in the environment that could impact control effectiveness.

- **Security status reporting**: Regular reporting on the security status of the information system to appropriate organizational officials is vital for informed decision-making. These reports should provide insights into the current security posture, highlight any identified vulnerabilities, and recommend actions for remediation. Effective communication ensures that management is aware of security issues and can prioritize resources accordingly.

The continuous monitoring program should clearly define how each control will be monitored and establish a monitoring frequency. This frequency should be determined based on the volatility of the security controls, which refers to how long a control is expected to remain effective before needing a review. More volatile controls that are likely to change frequently should be monitored more often, while stable controls may require less frequent assessments.

Continuous monitoring, as per NIST SP 800-137, is the ongoing process of gathering, analyzing, and addressing security and privacy risks, vulnerabilities, and threats in real-time. The guidelines in NIST SP 800-137 help organizations to create and manage a continuous monitoring program, originally intended for federal systems, but can be applied by any organization that aims to improve its security monitoring practices.

Recovery plan

A recovery plan is essential for organizations to document and maintain strategies for effective business recovery processes. It outlines the approved methods for implementing recovery actions following a disruption, such as a cyber incident. NIST SP 800-53 emphasizes the importance of recovery-related controls applicable to all federal systems, while NIST SP 800-34 defines the recovery plan as a critical component of a cyber incident response plan, focusing specifically on recovery strategies.

Some key components of a recovery plan are:

- **SLAs**: The recovery plan should detail relevant service agreements, including commitments regarding service availability, maximum allowable downtime, and guaranteed bandwidth. This may involve contracts with external support teams that can assist the organization during significant recovery efforts, ensuring that recovery actions can be executed efficiently.

- **Authority**: It is crucial to document the names and contact information of management personnel authorized to activate the recovery plan. This ensures that decision-makers are readily identifiable and can take swift action when needed.

- **Recovery team membership**: The plan must include a list of designated recovery team members, along with their contact information. These individuals should be familiar with the plan, having reviewed and practiced its execution to ensure readiness during a real incident.

- **Specific recovery details and procedures**: This section should document system-specific recovery activities, including technical details and diagrams where applicable. It outlines the exact steps the recovery team must take, such as restoring applications and activating alternate processing methods, like backup servers or failover sites.

- **Out-of-band communications**: The recovery plan should establish protocols for communication among critical stakeholders during a recovery scenario, ensuring that communication can occur outside of the production systems, which may be compromised or monitored by adversaries.

- **Communication plan**: Clear notification and escalation procedures must be defined, especially for systems that impact users outside the organization. Involvement of legal, public relations, and human resources personnel is essential to manage expectations and coordinate information disclosure related to the incident and recovery efforts.

- **Offsite storage details**: The plan should specify arrangements for storing critical records or media at offline or offsite locations. This is particularly important in light of ransomware threats that can encrypt data and demand payment for decryption keys.

- **Operational workarounds**: If the system cannot be restored within the designated **recovery time objective (RTO)**, the plan should outline approved workaround procedures to maintain operational continuity.

- **Facility recovery details**: Information related to the resilience of physical facilities, such as office locations or data centers, should be included. This may cover personnel notification processes, alternate location information, and communication circuit (internet connection, telephone lines) details.

- **Infrastructure, hardware, and software**: The recovery plan must detail access to necessary infrastructure, hardware, and software to facilitate the recovery process. This may include systems for recovery networks, messaging systems, and staging environments for validating recovered data. In summary, a well-structured recovery plan is crucial for organizations to effectively respond to and recover from disruptions. By addressing the outlined components, organizations can ensure they are prepared to manage incidents and minimize downtime, ultimately safeguarding their operations and data integrity. This proactive approach enhances resilience and enables a swift recovery, reducing the impact of potential cyber incidents.

Service level requirement

Service level requirements (SLRs) are specific expectations set by the customer regarding the quality, availability, and performance of a service. These requirements are defined during the service design phase and form the foundation for creating SLAs between the service provider and the customer. SLR detail key aspects of the service, including performance metrics, responsibilities, and expectations, ensuring both parties understand and agree on the service deliverables.

SLRs are based on the customer's business needs and are documented to define how the service will meet those requirements. For example, an SLR for email service might specify the required storage capacity. Once the SLR is documented, it leads to the creation of service level targets, which outline the specific goals that must be met to fulfil the requirements.

This process often involves collaboration with other operational processes, like incident or problem management, and should include measurable service targets to avoid future misunderstandings.

The key elements of SLRs define the parameters that ensure a service meets the customer's expectations and needs. These elements include:

- **Service description**: A clear and detailed description of the service, including its scope, limitations, and functionalities.

- **Service success criteria**: Establishing clear metrics or goals that define what constitutes a successful service delivery.

- **Availability**: Specifies the required uptime and acceptable downtime, along with maintenance schedules.

- **Response**: Outlines the expected response and resolution times for service requests, inquiries, and incidents.

- **Planned service interruptions**: Identifying any scheduled maintenance or disruptions to service and how they will be communicated.

- **Security**: Specifies the security measures and protocols necessary to protect the service and its data.

- **Compliance**: Specifies legal, regulatory, or standard compliance requirements relevant to the service.

- **Business continuity**: Outlining strategies and measures in place to ensure that the service continues to operate in the event of disruptions or disasters.

Service level agreement

A SLA is a formal document that defines the expected level of service between a service provider and a client. Within the context of a recovery plan, SLAs play a crucial role in ensuring that the organization understands its commitments and the specific expectations for service delivery during and after a disruption. Here is a detailed breakdown of the key elements and considerations related to SLAs in recovery plans:

- **Scope of services**: This section of the SLA outlines what is included and excluded in the agreement. It should clearly describe the services being provided, such as recovery services and incident support. Additionally, it is important to specify any services or situations that are not covered by the SLA to prevent any misunderstandings between the parties involved.

- **Performance metrics**: This section outlines key standards for service delivery. It defines the expected uptime for services (e.g., 99.9% uptime) and explains how this will be measured and reported. It also sets benchmarks for response times to incidents or service requests, indicating how quickly the service provider should react. Additionally, it specifies the maximum time allowed for resolving issues, which is crucial for ensuring smooth operations.

- **RTO and recovery point objectives (RPO)**: RTO is the longest acceptable time that a service can be down after a disruption before it seriously affects the organization. RPO, on the other hand, defines the maximum acceptable amount of data loss in terms of time, specifying how recent backups need to be to minimize any potential data loss.

- **Support levels**: This section outlines the different levels of support available, such as tier 1 and tier 2, along with the specific service commitments for each level. It also defines the escalation procedures for how issues will be advanced through the support hierarchy if initial attempts to resolve them do not meet expectations.

- **Monitoring and reporting**: This section explains how service performance will be tracked, including the tools and methods used to ensure compliance with SLA metrics. It also specifies how often performance reports will be created and shared with stakeholders, such as monthly or quarterly.

- **Penalties and remedies**: This section outlines the penalties for not meeting SLA obligations, which may include service credits or financial penalties. It also defines the actions that will be taken to address SLA violations and ensure that corrective measures are put in place.

- **Review and amendment process**: This section sets a schedule for regularly reviewing the SLA to keep it relevant and aligned with business needs. It also outlines the procedure for making changes to the SLA, emphasizing that any amendments require mutual agreement between the parties involved.

- **Termination clauses**: This section outlines the conditions under which either party can end the SLA, such as breaches of contract or changes in business circumstances. It also includes an exit strategy, detailing how the transition will be managed to minimize disruptions to services if the SLA is terminated.

Incorporating robust SLAs into recovery plans is vital for ensuring that organizations have the necessary support and commitments from service providers during and after incidents. By clearly outlining expectations, performance metrics, and remediation processes, SLAs enhance the organization's ability to maintain operational continuity and recover effectively from disruptions. Regular review and adjustment of SLAs will further ensure that they remain aligned with evolving business needs and technological changes.

Importance of SLAs in recovery plans

The following table explains the benefits of SLA in recovery plans:

Benefits	Description
Clarity of expectations	SLAs provide clear expectations regarding service delivery, which is essential for effective incident management and recovery.
Accountability	SLAs promote accountability and ensure that both parties are aware of their responsibilities by formalizing the commitments of the service provider.
Risk management	SLAs help organizations manage risks by defining acceptable service levels, enabling proactive planning for potential disruptions.
Performance evaluation	SLAs provide a framework for evaluating service provider performance, allowing organizations to make informed decisions regarding service contracts.

Table 8.1: Benefits of SLA

Record recovery control

Record recovery refers to the processes used to restore critical data and records after events like system failures, disasters, or security breaches. It is a key part of disaster recovery and business continuity planning. NIST provides guidelines for effective record recovery, such as in NIST SP 800-34, which offers strategies for backing up data, recovering lost records, and ensuring critical information is available to resume operations. The guidance emphasizes having a structured plan for data backup and recovery to minimize business disruption and ensure compliance. NIST SP 800-53 also outlines the following security and privacy controls for federal systems to support record recovery practices:

- **Data backup**: Regular backups of critical records and systems are essential for ensuring that data is securely stored in reliable locations. These backups enable rapid recovery in the event of data loss or system failure, minimizing downtime and ensuring business continuity.

- **Recovery strategy**: A clear and well-defined recovery strategy is crucial to ensure that critical records can be restored quickly. The strategy should be based on thorough risk assessments and business needs, ensuring that the most important data is prioritized during recovery efforts.

- **Testing**: Regular testing of recovery plans is essential to verify that they are effective in real-world scenarios. Ongoing testing helps identify weaknesses or gaps in the recovery process, ensuring that organizations can respond efficiently in the event of an actual disruption.

- **Data integrity**: Ensuring the integrity of recovered data is vital to prevent corruption or inaccuracies. Verifying that the data is accurate and intact during the recovery process helps avoid potential issues that could affect business operations or compliance.

Monitoring compliance

Monitoring compliance is a crucial aspect of maintaining the integrity and security of information systems. It involves regularly assessing whether systems adhere to established standards, policies, and regulatory requirements. Effective compliance monitoring includes ongoing evaluations of system performance, timely reviews of security controls, and audits to identify potential vulnerabilities. By continuously tracking compliance, organizations can ensure that corrective actions are implemented swiftly, risks are mitigated, and any deviations from compliance are addressed proactively.

The compliance-tracking process should include several key capabilities:

- **Vulnerability scanning**: Automated tools should regularly scan systems for vulnerabilities at regular intervals. Sensitive systems should be scanned weekly, while all systems should be scanned at least quarterly. Additionally, physical checks (inspection and physical verification) should be conducted to verify security practices like verification of biometric system and documentation reviews like audit trails and access logs should be conducted to ensure compliance.

- **Recertification tracking**: The process must track when systems need recertification to prevent accreditations from expiring. The **chief information security officer (CISO)** should also monitor systems that have been denied accreditation to ensure they stop processing data.

- **Monitoring accepted risks**: The CISO should keep a list of risks accepted by authorities that will not be mitigated. This helps ensure these risks do not affect other systems and allows for reassessment if circumstances change.

- **Tracking environmental changes**: The process must monitor any changes in system environments to identify new protection needs, closely linking this to incident response efforts.

- **Tracking audit findings**: The CISO should maintain visibility of security-related findings from audits and ensure they are integrated into remediation plans.

- **Reviewing security documentation**: The process should ensure that security documentation is reviewed and updated annually by system owners to reflect any changes in the system or its security measures.

- **Validating corrective action**: After system owners report that corrective actions are complete, the process must allow for spot checks to confirm that these actions effectively address the weaknesses and prevent them from recurring.

Audit strategies

An audit is fundamentally a systematic assessment, and in the context of the CGRC exam, this definition focuses on evaluating the security controls of an information system. An information system encompasses a specific combination of people, computers, processes, and information. Therefore, when we talk about an information system's security audit, we are referring to a thorough evaluation of the security measures applied to these interconnected components.

Understanding this definition is vital for several reasons. By clearly identifying what constitutes an information system, we can ensure that the audit strategies comprehensively address all relevant elements. Each component, like people, technology, processes, and information, plays a crucial role in the overall security posture. Ignoring any part can lead to vulnerabilities that compromise the system as a whole.

Information system security audit process

The information security audit process involves several key steps to ensure a thorough evaluation of an organization's security measures. The following figure shows the audit process from end-to-end:

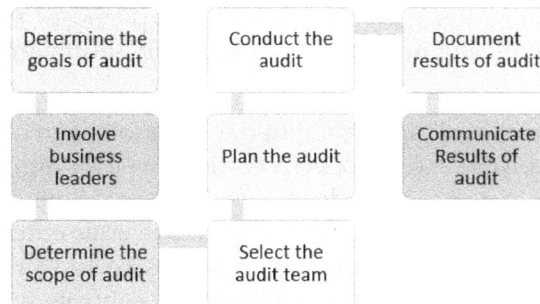

Figure 8.4: Audit process

The process is detailed as follows:

- **Determine goals**: The first step is to clearly define the goals of the audit, as everything else depends on this foundational element. Understanding the objectives ensures that the audit is focused and effective.

- **Involve business leaders**: Engaging the appropriate business unit leaders is crucial. Their input helps identify and address the specific needs of the business, ensuring that the audit aligns with organizational priorities.

- **Determine scope**: Establishing the scope of the audit is essential, as it is not feasible to test every aspect of the system. A well-defined scope helps concentrate efforts on the most critical areas.

- **Choose the audit team**: Select an audit team based on the goals, scope, budget, and available expertise. This team may consist of internal staff or external professionals, depending on the requirements of the audit.

- **Plan the audit**: Develop a detailed plan to ensure that all goals are met within the specified time frame and budget. A comprehensive plan helps guide the audit process and keeps it on track.

- **Conduct the audit**: Execute the audit according to the established plan, carefully documenting any deviations. This documentation is vital for accountability and future reference.

- **Document results**: After the audit, thoroughly document the findings. The information generated is both valuable and volatile, and proper documentation ensures that it is preserved for analysis and action.

- **Communicate results**: Finally, share the results with the relevant leaders in the organization. Effective communication of the findings is crucial for fostering a strong security posture and ensuring that necessary improvements are made.

Types of audits

There are several types of audits, each serving different purposes and focusing on various aspects of an organization. The most common types of audits are internal and external audits.

Internal audits: An internal audit is an unbiased evaluation of an organization's functions and operations, offering an objective perspective on how well the organization is performing. The internal audits aim to assess the effectiveness of operations and identify areas that require improvement. To mitigate risks and enhance overall efficiency, businesses must implement internal controls, along with various processes and procedures. The primary purpose of an internal audit is to regularly review these controls and processes, providing strategic recommendations to boost productivity and operational effectiveness.

By conducting internal audits as a best practice, organizations can build trust with customers and stakeholders, demonstrating their commitment to transparency and accountability. Many organizations have started automating their audit processes to increase efficiency. This automation not only streamlines the audit workflow but also enhances the accuracy and consistency of evaluations, enabling organizations to respond more swiftly to potential issues and improve their overall operational integrity.

Internal auditors play a crucial role in conducting regular audits within an organization. Organizations typically have the option to employ an internal audit team or outsource these services. Regardless of the approach taken, internal auditors may operate independently and are not part of any other teams within the organization. This separation is essential, as it allows them to maintain an objective perspective when assessing the company's functions and operations. By remaining independent, internal auditors can effectively identify areas for improvement and provide unbiased insights that contribute to the organization's overall efficiency and risk management.

External audits: An external audit is an independent evaluation of an organization's functions, operations, financial statement and reliability of security and privacy controls conducted by an external auditor. The primary purpose of this audit is to review the accuracy and integrity of the reported financial information, ensuring that it complies with established accounting standards and regulations. These audits are particularly beneficial for external stakeholders, including investors, shareholders, and the general public.

The external audits contribute to overall transparency and accountability within the business environment. They help identify any discrepancies or issues in financial reporting, which can then be addressed by the company. This not only safeguards the interests of external parties but also fosters trust in the organization, ultimately benefiting its reputation and long-term success.

The external auditors provide an unbiased opinion on the organization's financial statements, with their primary responsibility being towards the stakeholders and not the organization. Engaging external auditors offers several advantages over using an internal team. Firstly, external auditors often have extensive experience testing various information systems across different organizations. This broad exposure allows them to bring valuable knowledge and insights that an internal team may not possess, even if some internal auditors have prior experience.

Another key benefit of third-party auditors is their lack of familiarity with the organization's internal dynamics and politics. Since they have no personal connections or agendas, their focus is solely on identifying flaws. This objectivity can enhance their effectiveness in testing, especially compared to internal personnel who may have been involved in implementing the controls and might unintentionally overlook issues. Overall, external auditors provide a fresh perspective and a level of impartiality that can be crucial for a thorough assessment.

Key areas of audit

To effectively perform their roles, both internal and external auditors concentrate on several key areas during their audits. Each of these focus areas plays a crucial role in ensuring the overall health and integrity of an organization's operations and financial reporting. The following figure shows the key areas of audit that will help the organization to perform the audits:

Figure 8.5: Key areas of audit

Following are the details of key audit areas that help organization to focus on appropriate controls:

- **Effectiveness of internal controls**: One of the primary responsibilities of auditors is to assess the effectiveness of internal controls within the organization. Internal controls are processes and procedures designed to ensure the reliability of security and privacy controls, financial reporting, compliance with laws and regulations, and the efficiency of operations. Auditors evaluate these controls to determine whether they are functioning as intended and whether they mitigate risks effectively. This includes examining the design and implementation of controls, testing their operational effectiveness, and identifying any weaknesses or gaps that could expose the organization to risks.

- **Regulatory compliance**: Another critical area of focus for auditors is regulatory compliance. Organizations are subject to various laws and regulations depending on their industry and jurisdiction. Auditors review policies and procedures to ensure that the organization is adhering to these legal requirements. This includes evaluating compliance with financial regulations, data protection laws, environmental regulations, and industry-specific standards. By identifying areas of non-compliance, auditors help organizations avoid legal penalties, financial losses, and reputational damage.

- **Enhancing operational efficiency**: Auditors also assess the operational efficiency of the organization. This involves analyzing processes to identify inefficiencies, redundancies, and areas for improvement. By evaluating how resources are utilized, auditors can suggest ways to streamline operations, reduce costs, and enhance productivity. This focus on operational efficiency not only helps improve the organization's bottom line but also ensures that resources are allocated effectively to achieve strategic objectives.

- **Financial integrity**: Financial integrity examine the accuracy and completeness of financial statements, verifying that the reported information is a true reflection of the organization's financial position. This involves testing transactions, reviewing accounting policies, and assessing the overall financial reporting process. By identifying errors or discrepancies, auditors help maintain the integrity of financial data, which is essential for decision-making by management, investors, and other stakeholders.

- **Fraud detection**: Finally, auditors play a crucial role in fraud detection. They evaluate the effectiveness of the organization's fraud prevention and detection mechanisms, looking for signs of potentially fraudulent activity. This includes analyzing financial records, conducting interviews, and reviewing transaction patterns for irregularities. Auditors also assess the overall control environment to determine whether there are adequate safeguards in place to deter fraud. By identifying vulnerabilities, auditors help organizations strengthen their defenses against fraudulent activities, protecting assets and preserving stakeholder trust.

The comparison of internal and external audits can be seen in the following table:

	Internal audit	**External audit**
Definition	Internal audits are conducted by an organization to assess and improve its functions and operations.	External audits are conducted to review the accuracy and truthfulness of a company's security and privacy controls, financial statements.
Frequency	Performed on a regular basis.	Performed once a year.
Perspective	Historical and future.	Primarily historical.
Auditors	Auditors can be part of the organization or a third-party serving the needs of the company.	Auditors are not related to the company in any way and are part of certified audit firms.
Obligation	Internal audits are not mandatory.	External audits are mandatory.
Focus	Continuous improvement and meeting strategic goals.	Fair reporting of financials or other compliance matter.
Audience	The reports are used by the management to improve their operations.	The report is used by stakeholders to assess the accuracy of a company's financial information.

Table 8.2: Internal vs external audit

Vulnerability management

Vulnerability management is a vital process for identifying, assessing, remediating, and mitigating security vulnerabilities within software and computer systems. This proactive approach is essential for managing risk in IT environments, as unaddressed vulnerabilities can lead to damaging cyberattacks and data breaches. By systematically addressing vulnerabilities, organizations can safeguard their critical assets and maintain the integrity of their operations.

A typical vulnerability management process involves continuous scanning of IT assets to detect vulnerabilities. Once identified, the risks associated with these vulnerabilities are evaluated, allowing organizations to prioritize their remediation efforts based on the severity of the risks. The primary goals of vulnerability management include reducing attack surfaces, enhancing the organization's overall security posture, ensuring compliance with regulatory requirements, and minimizing business risks. By focusing on these objectives, organizations can create a more resilient cybersecurity framework.

It is important to note that vulnerability management differs from patch management, although the two processes overlap. Vulnerability management takes a comprehensive view of identifying vulnerabilities across IT systems and devising strategies for resolution, while patch management focuses specifically on implementing fixes for known bugs and security holes through software updates provided by vendors. Many practitioners consider patch management to be a component of the broader vulnerability management process, as effective patching is critical for addressing identified vulnerabilities.

Furthermore, vulnerability management is distinct from risk management, even though both are interconnected. While vulnerability management focus on identifying and rectifying technical security gaps, risk management encompasses a broader initiative that addresses potential cybersecurity threats and other risks that could impact business operations. Risk management involves assessing various types of risks, including operational, strategic, and compliance risks, to develop a holistic approach to safeguarding the organization.

Performance and risk monitoring

Performance and risk monitoring means regularly checking how well systems, processes, or projects are meeting their goals. It includes KPI, which tracks key metrics for business goals and efficiency, and KRI, which helps identify risks early so that organizations can manage and prevent issues before they affect performance.

Key performance indicators

KPIs are essential tools for measuring and understanding the effectiveness of control measures within an organization. These indicators can encompass a wide range of metrics, from how frequently a firewall successfully blocks malicious incoming traffic to how often an organization's continuity of operations plan is tested and exercised. By providing quantifiable data, KPIs enable organizations to assess their control performance and identify areas for improvement.

The definition of performance can vary significantly from one organization to another. It is crucial for each organization to establish performance goals that align with its specific objectives, risk appetite, and tolerance levels. This tailored approach ensures that the KPIs are relevant and meaningful, reflecting the unique context and priorities of the organization. The effective use of KPIs not only helps organizations track their security controls but also facilitates informed decision-making. By regularly monitoring these indicators, organizations can adjust their strategies and resource allocations to enhance their overall security posture.

KPIs are most effective when they follow the S.M.A.R.T. criteria. This means KPIs should have the following characteristics:

- **Specific**: Clearly defined and focused on a particular goal.
- **Measurable**: Quantifiable to track progress and performance.
- **Attainable**: Realistic and achievable within the given resources and constraints.
- **Relevant**: Aligned with organizational objectives and priorities.
- **Timely**: Measured within a set time frame to ensure timely decision-making.

Key risk indicators

KRIs serve as vital metrics for organizations, similar to KPIs, in assessing the likelihood of risks that may exceed the defined risk appetite. These indicators help organizations monitor potential threats and vulnerabilities, allowing them to respond proactively. However, not all risk indicators hold equal importance; KRIs are specifically designed to predict significant levels of risk with a high degree of accuracy based on established thresholds.

While KPIs focus on the performance of specific controls, KRIs provide insights into the potential risks facing the organization. By identifying KRIs, organizations can better understand their risk landscape and make informed decisions regarding resource allocation and risk management strategies. By continuously monitoring these indicators, organizations can assess whether they are operating within their acceptable risk levels and take corrective actions when necessary.

The ISO 31000:2018 risk framework provides key criteria for selecting KRIs. These criteria include the following:

- **Impact**: A KRI should have a high impact, meaning that it can significantly affect the organization's risk profile if it changes.

- **Effort to implement, measure, and report**: The best KRIs are those that are easiest to measure and report on, minimizing the complexity of tracking.

- **Reliability**: A KRI should be reliable, meaning it consistently predicts an outcome and provides accurate insights.

- **Sensitivity**: The indicator should be sensitive enough to detect variations in risk levels, ensuring it reflects changes in the risk environment effectively.

Conclusion

In this chapter, we explored the control enhancement strategy aimed at improving security controls and mitigating risks. We examined the continuous monitoring program, which plays a crucial role in overseeing risk management and ensuring that security controls remain effective over time. Additionally, we discussed the importance of recovery plans and SLAs, which help maintain essential services even during disruptions. Our focus also extended to monitoring compliance, including various audit strategies and types of audits that are vital for evaluating the effectiveness of security measures.

Furthermore, we delved into vulnerability management and the various metrics that can be used to measure performance and assess risks. By understanding these elements, organizations can strengthen their security posture and better prepare for potential threats. As we transition to the next chapter, our focus will shift to control implementation guidelines, where we will explore different types of controls and the process of configuration identification. This next step will build upon the foundational knowledge established in this chapter, guiding you in effectively implementing the strategies discussed.

Key terms

- The control enhancements section provides security capability to build in additional but related functionality to a basic control and to increase the strength of a basic control.

- The broader continuous monitoring activity within an organization is implemented through the execution of three major foundational elements:

  o Organizational governance

  o Continuous monitoring strategy

  o Continuous monitoring program

- Signing a nondisclosure agreement is almost always a prerequisite before a third-party team is permitted to audit an organization's systems.

- **The SLA usually includes two components**: Services and management. Service elements include specifics of services provided, and management elements include definitions of measurement, reporting processes, contents and frequency, dispute resolution process, etc.

- Vulnerability assessment refers to the systematic evaluation of a system, network, or application to identify security weaknesses or vulnerabilities.

- Vulnerability management is an ongoing, proactive process that encompasses the identification, evaluation, treatment, and reporting of vulnerabilities over time.

- The identification and remediation of technical vulnerabilities are means for mitigating operational risk, but they do not fully constitute the activities of risk management.

- Data masking is a strategy to obscure sensitive data for testing and non-production environments.

- Data tagging and labeling are techniques for classifying information based on sensitivity and handling requirements.

- Continuous monitoring is ongoing assessment of control effectiveness to maintain compliance and address emerging risks.

- High-water mark methodology is a principle used in security categorization to assign the highest impact level among data types.

CHAPTER 9

Introduction to Implementing Controls

Introduction

This chapter provides an overview of control implementation guidelines based on industry standards such as *National Institute of Standards and Technology (NIST)*, *Center for Internet Security (CIS)*, and *International Organization for Standardization (ISO)/International Electrotechnical Commission (IEC) 27001:2022*. It highlights the importance of adopting various types of security controls to strengthen an organization's security strategy and manage risks effectively. By focusing on these well-established standards, the chapter ensures that security controls are clearly defined and can adapt to the evolving threat landscape, helping organizations stay secure.

The chapter also discusses the creation of a **plan of action and milestones (POA&M)** to track and address any security gaps identified during assessments. It outlines the steps for developing this plan, helping organizations monitor progress and implement necessary changes. Additionally, the chapter covers configuration identification, which is critical for documenting and managing **configuration items (CIs)** throughout their lifecycle. This practice ensures better control and oversight of configurations, strengthening the organization's overall security posture.

Structure

The chapter covers the following main topics:

- Control implementation guidelines
- NIST control structure
- CIS Control implementation guidelines
- ISO or IEC 27001:2022 control implementation guidelines
- Control types identification
- Plan of action and milestones
- Configuration identification

Objectives

By the end of this chapter, you will gain a solid understanding of control implementation guidelines, including industry standards like NIST, CIS, and internal ISO/IEC 27001:2022. You will learn about different types of security controls—technical, management, and operational which are crucial for building a strong security framework.

Additionally, you will become familiar with the components and objectives of a POA&M. This will guide you in creating an effective POA&M strategy, conducting risk assessments, and integrating these plans with industry standards. The chapter will also help you master the configuration identification process, ensuring you can track and manage system changes to maintain a robust security posture.

Control implementation guidelines

Security control implementation guidelines provide a structured approach for effectively applying security measures within an organization. It is essential to align the implementation with established industry standards and best practices, such as NIST and ISO frameworks, ensuring consistency and effectiveness. Tailoring controls to the specific context and risk profile of the organization is crucial, as not every control needs to apply to every system. The control guidelines help identify the required configuration settings for the systems and ensure that the controls are implemented according to current industry standards.

There are three major approaches that can be applied to implement the controls for security and privacy, including **common, system-specific, and hybrid** approaches. These models determine the scope and responsibility for implementation, assessment, and monitoring of controls that enable organizations to choose an approach that best suits their security and privacy requirements. The common control approach allows controls to be shared across multiple systems. The controls would be developed and maintained by a different entity from the system or program using them. Common controls may bring some cost savings and efficiency, though they also include some risks: A single point of failure is one of these. Normally, common controls refer to physical, personnel, or technological aspects like authentication and access controls.

Controls implemented for a single system reside with the system owner and **authorizing official** (**AO**). This can be customized to meet the needs of the system but can also be very risky if controls do not function well with other common controls. A hybrid control combines common and system-specific elements: A part of it is shared across systems, and a part is unique to certain systems. In hybrid controls, the common control portion of the control rests with the provider, while the specific portion relates to the system owner.

The approach to be followed for implementation depends upon the context of the organization and thus requires careful planning and coordination, preferably early in the **system development lifecycle** (**SDLC**). If a control is to be inheritable, the organization should ensure that the parameters of the control are compatible with the needs of the inheriting entity. Control parameters if misaligned, may lead to the control failure in addressing the system-specific risks despite the same control identifiers.

NIST control implementation strategy

NIST SP 800-53 Revision 5 provides 20 sets of controls that should be carefully implemented based on organization needs. The implementation necessitates strategic planning with appropriate consideration of resourcing, funding, and timelines for the implementation activity. Implementation will involve guidelines and considerations for effective resourcing, funding, incorporating timelines, and assessing effectiveness.

Context and requirements

Before implementation, an organization should understand what needs protection and why: System boundary definition, categorization of information systems impact levels-in accordance with FIPS 199 (low, moderate, or high) which will assist in determining the required security controls. Organizations should ensure regulatory requirements such as *Federal Information Systems Management Act* (*FISMA*), *Health Insurance Portability and Accountability Act* (*HIPAA*), or *General Data Protection Regulation* (*GDPR*) that may influence how the security controls will be implemented.

Resourcing

NIST SP 800-53 Revision 5 implementation needs adequate human and technological resources. From a human resource perspective, the process should be led by a project manager or implementation lead with experience in NIST frameworks and knowledge of the security requirements within the organization. Control owners will be responsible for managing specific controls and may come from existing staff or new hires. **Subject Matter Experts** (**SMEs**) may be required in areas such as security, privacy, compliance, and incident response. Training of staff at all levels is very necessary for everyone to know their role in maintaining security and privacy. Technologically, the organization should be equipped with firewalls, encryption, IAM solutions, and SIEM systems, among others. If using cloud computing, the cloud provider must also meet necessary controls and integrate with the organization's security systems.

Funding

Proper funding is a must for the effective implementation of NIST SP 800-53 Revision 5. This will cover costs regarding personnel salary of the project manager and SMEs, and technological costs that include but are not limited to SIEM systems and access management solutions. Besides these, training programs and continuous monitoring and maintenance services will also involve expenses. This funding may either come from within, through internal budgets for areas such as IT or security, or via grants, especially for public sector organizations. A cost-benefit analysis will be justified to support this investment in comparing the cost of possible security breaches against the cost required to implement and maintain controls NIST SP 800-53 Revision 5.

Timelines

The implementation timeline of NIST SP 800-53 Revision 5 is determined by organization's size, complexity, and current security posture. Generally, there are four phases:

- **Initiation phase**: This includes the current security posture assessment, definition of system boundaries, system categorization, control tailoring, and control owner assignment.

- **Planning and design phase**: Develop the implementation plan for technical, operational, and privacy controls, tool procurement, and policy and training plan development.

- **Implementation phase**: This includes controls implementation, evaluations, testing, training, and the start of documentation.

- **Review and continuous improvement (ongoing)**: Perform regular effectiveness monitoring, quarterly or semi-annual reviews of controls and find areas for improvement.

Effectiveness

Controls should be continuously tested after implementation to ensure that they indeed work as designed and change with emerging challenges. This will include continuous monitoring in which security events are tracked, mostly using tools like SIEM systems, which allow the detection of events that are anomalous. Also, regular audits by internal auditor and third-party auditors will help appraise the performance of controls, while ongoing risk assessment will identify new threats. Key performance includes incident response time, control compliance rate, and employee training completions. The program progress should also be documented and reported to senior management for transparency and continuous improvement.

Implementing NIST security controls

The system owner or **common control provider** (**CCP**) bears the responsibility for implementing security controls outlined in the security plan for the information system. Ideally, this implementation occurs during the development or acquisition phases of a new or modernized system. By integrating security controls at this stage, organizations can ensure that security measures are embedded into the system's architecture from the outset, minimizing vulnerabilities and enhancing the overall security posture. This proactive approach not only streamlines the implementation process but also fosters a culture of security awareness. The following table shows the roles and responsibilities for implementing controls:

SDLC phase	Primary responsibility	Supporting roles	References
Development/ acquisition implementation	**Information system owner** (**ISO**) or CCP	**Information owner** (**IO**)/**information steward** (**IS**), **Information system security engineer** (**ISSE**)	FIPS Publication 200, NIST SPs 800-30, 800-53, 800-53A, **Committee on National Security Systems** (**CNSS**) Instruction 1253

Table 9.1: Roles and responsibilities to implement controls

Here is a simplified and detailed breakdown of the key points regarding the implementation of security controls:

- **Alignment with architecture**: When implementing security controls, it is essential that they align with the organization's overall enterprise and information security architecture. This ensures consistency and effectiveness across systems.

- **Selective control allocation**: Security controls do not need to be applied to every subsystem within a system. It is important to prioritize security controls based on risk and necessity.

- **Best practices**: Using established best practices is crucial when implementing security controls. This includes following methodologies from system and software engineering, as well as principles of security engineering and secure coding techniques.

- **Configuration settings**: The system owner must ensure that the mandatory configuration settings for technology products are implemented in line with federal and organizational policies.

- **Security engineering process**: Information system security engineers should follow a robust security engineering process to define and refine security requirements. These requirements must be effectively integrated into the technology products and systems.

- **Utilizing evaluated products**: Organizations should aim to use technology products that have been independently tested or validated. This reduces the risk of vulnerabilities and enhances trust in the products being used.

- **Meeting assurance requirements**: The system owner must meet minimum assurance requirements when implementing security controls. These requirements help ensure that controls are correctly applied and effective.

- **Consideration of additional measures**: For high-value systems, or those likely to be targeted by advanced cyberattacks, additional assurance measures should be implemented to bolster security.

- **Integration of controls**: The implementation must consider how to integrate both common controls and system-specific controls, including how they interface with each other.

- **Coordination with CCPs**: ISSEs and **information system security officers** (**ISSOs**) should work with CCPs to determine the best way to apply common controls to the system.

- **Management and operational controls**: Some management and operational controls may not need to be formally integrated into technology products, but their application should still be considered.

- **Operational and technical control needs**: Implementing certain operational and technical controls might require additional components or services to ensure that common controls can be effectively utilized.

- **Reviewing common controls**: If the system owner has postponed selecting common controls, this decision should be re-evaluated during the implementation phase to see if they are appropriate at this stage in the SDLC.

- **Assessing common controls**: The system owner should check the adequacy of common controls by reviewing authorization packages prepared by CCPs to ensure they meet security requirements.

- **Identifying compensating controls**: If common controls do not fulfil the system's security needs, the system owner must identify compensating or supplementary controls to address any weaknesses.

- **Initial security assessments**: System owners can start conducting initial **security control assessments** (**SCAs**) during system development and implementation, a process known as developmental testing and evaluation.

- **Early detection of issues**: Conducting these assessments early allows for the identification of deficiencies and provides a cost-effective way to make necessary corrections.

- **Reporting issues for resolution**: Certain issues found during assessments may need to be escalated to AOs for early resolution, especially if they could affect risk acceptance.

- **Using assessment results**: The results from initial SCAs can be valuable for later system authorization, helping to save time and avoid redundant assessment activities.

This comprehensive approach ensures that security controls are effectively implemented, aligned with organizational policies, and capable of addressing potential vulnerabilities.

NIST control structure

NIST SP 800-53 classifies controls into 20 different families to be more easily selected and implemented. Each family specifies a security or privacy category, and each family is labelled by a unique two-character code; for example, **personnel security** (**PS**). Controls can also be policies, procedures (manually or automated), individual actions, or a combination of these. Each family contains both base controls and control enhancements. Base controls offer general protection, while control enhancements add more specific functionality or stronger protection, especially in environments needing higher security. Organizations may apply control enhancements if they face greater risks or need additional protection. Following are 20 control families. The details of each family controls are provided in *Chapter 10, Deploying Security and Privacy Control*, under key components of NIST SP 800-53:

ID	Control Family	ID	Control Family
AC	Access Control	PE	Physical and Environmental Protection
AT	Awareness and Training	PL	Planning
AU	Audit and Accountability	PM	Program Management
CA	Assessment, Authorization, and Monitoring	PS	Personnel Security
CM	Configuration Management	PT	PT PII Processing and Transparency
CP	Contingency Planning	RA	Risk Assessment
IA	Identification and Authentication	SA	System and Services Acquisition
IR	Incident Response	SC	System and Communications Protection
MA	Maintenance	SI	System and Information Integrity
MP	Media Protection	SR	Supply Chain Risk Management

Figure 9.1: NIST SP 800-53 Revision 5 control families

NIST privacy considerations

NIST SP 800-53 Revision 5 consists of a holistic set of security controls that also includes consideration of privacy. It, therefore, gives guidelines that can help an organization manage the risks involved in the release of personal information about individuals. Organizations should implement privacy controls with the purpose of managing privacy risks, data exposure, and compliance with legal and regulatory requirements about privacy. Actually, in practice, it addresses privacy in a number of security control families. Herein are some important privacy considerations within the NIST SP 800-53 Revision 5:

- **System and communications protection**: Controls for privacy emphasize the protection of sensitive personal data both during transmission and storage. The implementation of encryption ensures confidentiality for data so that personal information is not disclosed to unauthorized parties.

- **Access control**: Organizations should set strict control policies that allow only authorized personnel and a certain number of personnel to access information. It means that role-based access control and the principle of least privilege are to be applied to provide employees with a minimum level of access.

- **PIA**: In cases where an agency proposes new systems or technologies that process personal information, NIST recommends the use of a PIA. This is said to help in ascertaining, beforehand, possible associated privacy risks and mitigation strategies in terms of protecting privacy.

- **Audit and accountability**: Auditing should be periodically conducted to ensure compliance with privacy policies; it needs to verify whether data protection measures are followed. Logging and accountability mechanisms permit an organization to trace how applications access and use personal data, thus enabling the detection of possible breaches and follow-up actions.

- **Incident response**: NIST provides the organization with preparation for responding in case any kind of privacy incident has taken place. It covers the definition of processes for reporting and mitigating privacy breaches, notification of affected persons, and data protection in the case of a breach.

- **PII processing and transparency**: NIST ensures the significance of transparency in the processing of PII. The organizations should provide the individual with notice about how the collection, use, storage, and sharing of PII are performed through appropriate privacy notices. It grants transparency to the individuals for making decisions on their data and helps to keep the privacy regulations intact. **Cybersecurity Framework (CSF)** integration with NIST SP 800-53 Revision 5.

NIST SP 800-53 Revision 5 is developed to complement the NIST CSF, providing detailed guidelines on how to implement security measures. CSF organizes cybersecurity into five core functions: Identify, protect, detect, respond, and recover. The NIST SP 800-53 Revision 5 supports these five core functions through specific controls. It allows an organization to adopt a consistent methodology for risk management by which cybersecurity and privacy become integrated in the alignment of security and privacy controls with the CSF. Here is the mapping with examples:

CSF functions	NIST SP 800-53 Revision 5 controls
Identify: Understand and manage cybersecurity risk by identifying the assets, data, and systems that need protection.	NIST SP 800-53 Revision 5 supports this function with controls that enable an organization to define the scope of the systems, perform risk assessments, and identify threats and vulnerabilities. Key controls are Risk Assessment (RA); System and Communications Protection (SC); and Access Control (AC).
Protect: Implement safeguards to ensure critical infrastructure can perform its primary functions.	NIST SP 800-53 Revision 5 provides appropriate controls in terms of data protection, access control, configuration management of systems, and protective controls to prevent unauthorized access. Key controls are Access Control (AC), Media Protection (MP), and System and Communications Protection (SC).
Detection: Monitor for cybersecurity events, detecting potential anomalies or intrusions.	NIST SP 800-53 Revision 5 provides relevant controls to support continued detection and monitoring of events. Key controls are Audit and Accountability (AU), Incident Response (IR), and System and Information Integrity (SI) that help and provide the ability to identify and detect, in real-time, cybersecurity threats.
Respond: Take actions to respond to detected cybersecurity events, which include limiting damage and recovering from the incident.	NIST SP 800-53 Revision 5 supports the respond function with controls for incident response planning, reporting, and coordination. Key controls are Incident Response (IR) family that guide an organization through responding properly to security breaches for mitigating their effects.
Recover: Implement recovery plans and processes to restore systems and services after a cybersecurity event.	NIST SP 800-53 Revision 5 supports the recovery function through controls in the Contingency Planning (CP) family. These controls provide a framework for organizations to create contingency plans that will allow for the continuation of operations.

Table 9.2: CSF mapping with NIST SP 800-53 Revision 5

CIS Control implementation guidelines

The CIS and **Critical Security Control** (**CSC**) represent a prioritized set of actions designed to provide organizations with a robust defence-in-depth strategy against the most common cybersecurity threats. These controls are developed through a collaborative effort among cybersecurity experts and are recognized globally as essential best practices for securing systems and networks. By focusing on the most prevalent attack vectors, the CIS Controls offer organizations a practical framework for enhancing their security posture.

Each of the 18 CIS Controls encompasses a series of specific safeguards tailored to address particular security functions. In total, there are 153 safeguards that organizations can implement to improve their defences. These safeguards are designed to guide organizations in identifying and addressing vulnerabilities systematically. The organizations may be of varying sizes and complexities often struggle to initiate their security efforts; the CIS Controls provide a clear starting point. By prioritizing actions, the CIS Controls help organizations effectively allocate their attention and resources to where they can have the most significant impact on reducing risk. This structured approach not only simplifies the implementation process but also enhances the overall cybersecurity resilience. The following figure shows the 18 CIS Controls:

01 Inventory and Control of Enterprise Assets	05 Account Management	09 Email and Web Browser Protection	13 Network Monitoring and Defense	17 Incident Response Management
02 Inventory and Control of Software Assets	06 Access Control Management	10 Malware Defenses	14 Security Awareness and Skills Training	
03 Data Protection	07 Continuous Vulnerability Management	11 Data Recovery	15 Service Provider Management	18 Penetration Testing
04 Secure Configuration	08 Audit Log Management	12 Network Infrastructure	16 Applications Software Security	

Figure 9.2: CIS Controls

Implement CIS security controls

The CIS Controls are structured into **implementation groups (IGs)**, each featuring a distinct set of safeguards tailored to the specific needs of different organizations. These IGs provide a straightforward framework that enables organizations of various sizes and complexities to focus their limited security resources while still benefiting from the CIS Controls program, its community, and associated tools and resources.

These IGs are defined based on three key attributes:

- **Data sensitivity and criticality of services**: This attribute considers the nature of the data the organization handles and the importance of the services it provides. Organizations managing highly sensitive information or critical services will require more stringent security measures.

- **Expected level of technical expertise**: This aspect assesses the technical skills and expertise of the organization's staff or contracted personnel. Organizations with a higher level of technical proficiency can implement more advanced controls effectively.

- **Resources and expertise dedicated to cybersecurity**: This attribute evaluates the resources—both human and financial—that the organization has allocated to cybersecurity efforts. Organizations with more resources can pursue a broader range of controls and implement them more comprehensively.

By organizing the CIS Controls into these IGs, organizations can select and prioritize safeguards that align with their specific circumstances, enhancing their ability to address cybersecurity challenges effectively.

CIS IG category

The CIS Controls are categorized into three distinct IGs, each featuring a tailored list of safeguards based on a specific criteria. These criteria include the sensitivity of the data handled and the criticality of the services provided by the organization, the expected technical expertise of the staff or contractors, and the resources dedicated to cybersecurity efforts. The categories can be seen in the following figure:

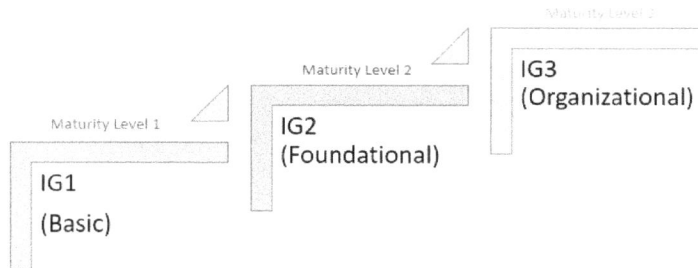

Figure 9.3: *CIS category and maturity levels*

The three IGs are as follows:

- **IG1—basic**: This group includes fundamental controls aimed at helping organizations assess their current security posture and implement straightforward improvements. It is roughly equivalent to level 1 maturity.

- **IG2—foundational**: This group provides more advanced guidance, helping organizations enhance their security measures. It aligns with level 2 maturity.

- **IG3—organizational**: This group focuses on controls that require changes to organizational policies to improve and sustain cybersecurity practices. It corresponds to level 3 maturity.

By categorizing controls into these IGs, organizations can adopt a tailored approach to security that aligns with their unique needs and capabilities, facilitating a more effective cybersecurity strategy.

ISO or IEC 27001:2022 control implementation guidelines

ISO/IEC 27001:2022 provides a comprehensive framework for implementing an **information security management system (ISMS)**, which is crucial for safeguarding sensitive information. Here is key control implementation guidelines based on ISO/IEC 27001:2022:

- **Understand context and scope**: Begin by defining the context of your organization, including internal and external factors that affect information security. Clearly outline the scope of the ISMS, identifying the boundaries and applicability of security controls.

- **Conduct a risk assessment**: Perform a thorough risk assessment to identify potential threats and vulnerabilities to your information assets. This process helps prioritize risks and determines which controls are necessary to mitigate them effectively.

- **Establish information security policy**: Develop an overarching information security policy that outlines your organization's commitment to information security. This policy should provide direction and support for the ISMS, ensuring alignment with business objectives.

- **Define roles and responsibilities**: Clearly assign roles and responsibilities for information security within the organization. This includes appointing a management representative to oversee the ISMS and ensure accountability across departments.

- **Select and implement controls**: Based on the results of the risk assessment, select appropriate controls from Annex A of ISO/IEC 27001:2022, which includes 114 controls across various domains. Tailor these controls to fit the specific needs and risks of your organization.

- **Document processes and procedures:** Create detailed documentation for the ISMS, including policies, procedures, and guidelines for implementing the selected controls. This documentation should be easily accessible and regularly updated.

- **Training and awareness**: Conduct training sessions to raise awareness about information security among employees. Ensure that staff understand their roles in maintaining security and the importance of compliance with the established policies and controls.

- **Monitor and review**: Continuously monitor the performance of the ISMS and the effectiveness of implemented controls. Regularly review and assess the risk environment to adapt to new threats and changes within the organization.

- **Conduct internal audits**: Implement a schedule for internal audits to evaluate the ISMS's compliance with ISO/IEC 27001:2022 standards. This helps identify areas for improvement and ensures ongoing adherence to the established controls.

- **Management review**: Periodically review the ISMS at the management level to assess its overall performance and alignment with organizational objectives. Use this review to make informed decisions about necessary changes or enhancements to the ISMS.

- **Continual improvement**: Foster a culture of continual improvement within the ISMS. Encourage feedback, learn from incidents, and adapt policies and controls based on evolving risks and organizational needs.

By following these guidelines, organizations can effectively implement the ISO/IEC 27001:2022 standard, enhancing their information security posture and protecting critical assets.

Control types identification

In information security, controls are classified based on their function. This functional classification helps in understanding how each type of control contributes to the overall security posture of an organization. The main functional types of security controls are:

- **Preventive controls**: These controls aim to prevent security incidents before they occur. Examples include firewalls, antivirus software, antimalware software, and access control mechanisms.

- **Deterrent controls**: These controls might not physically or logically block access, but they psychologically discourage an attacker from trying to breach a system. Examples include warning signs, security policies, and the presence of security personnel.

- **Detective controls**: These controls are crafted to identify and document any attempted or accomplished intrusion. A detective control functions when an attack is in progress. Examples are **intrusion detection systems** (**IDSs**), log monitoring, and audits.

- **Corrective controls**: These controls mitigate damage or restore systems after a security breach. Examples include backup and restore procedures and patch management systems.

- **Compensating controls**: These are alternative controls used when principal controls are not feasible. They provide a comparable level of security. Examples include additional monitoring or manual processes in place of automated tools.

- **Directive controls**: These controls are designed to direct, confine, or control subjects' actions to force or encourage compliance with security policies, best practices, or **Standard Operating Procedures** (**SOPs**). Examples include security policy statements, signs, and guardrails.

Organizations should consider a combination of technical, management, and operational security controls while implementing recommended controls to mitigate risk. This approach enhances the effectiveness of security measures across IT systems and the organization as a whole. Properly utilized security controls can prevent, limit, or deter damage from potential threats, thereby protecting the organization's mission and assets.

The process of selecting appropriate controls involves evaluating various options to bolster the organization's security posture. The organizations must weigh the various trade-offs carefully, considering factors such as cost, complexity, and the potential effectiveness of each control type. A well-balanced strategy that integrates technical, management, and operational controls can lead to a more robust and resilient security environment, effectively addressing the diverse range of threats organizations face. The following figure shows the three control types:

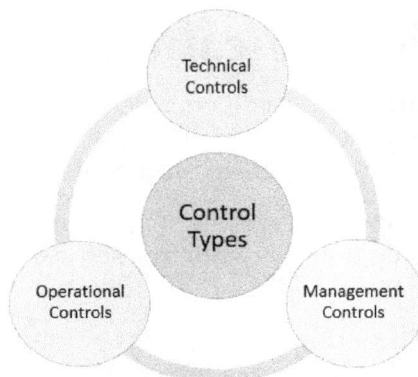

Figure 9.4: Control types

The following section provides a high-level overview of the control categories.

Technical security controls

Technical security controls play a crucial role in mitigating risks by providing targeted protection against specific types of threats. These controls can range from straightforward measures to complex systems, incorporating various components such as hardware, software, and firmware. The effectiveness of these controls relies on their ability to work cohesively to safeguard critical and sensitive data, as well as essential IT system functions.

Technical controls can be categorized into three major groups based on their primary purpose:

- **Supporting controls**: The supporting controls are the foundation of IT security capabilities. These controls are generic measures that must be in place to enable the implementation of other controls. Without these foundational elements, the effectiveness of more specialized controls may be compromised.

- **Preventive controls**: Preventive controls are designed to prevent security breaches before they occur. These measures proactively address vulnerabilities and mitigate potential threats, reducing the likelihood of incidents that could compromise data integrity and availability.

- **Detect and recover controls**: Detect and recover controls are essential for identifying and responding to security breaches. These controls focus on detecting incidents when they occur and facilitate recovery efforts to restore systems and data.

Management security controls

Management security controls play a vital role in an organization's overall security strategy, along with technical and operational controls to manage and mitigate risks effectively. These controls are primarily focused on establishing the framework for information protection through policies, guidelines, and standards that guide the organization in achieving its goals. These policies define the organization's security approach, outline roles and responsibilities, specify acceptable use of information systems, and detail how to manage information security risks. By setting clear guidelines, management controls help ensure that everyone in the organization understands their responsibilities and expectations regarding information security. Management security controls can be categorized into three main types: preventive, detection, and recovery controls:

- **Preventive controls**: These controls are designed to prevent security incidents before they occur. Preventive measures include risk assessments, security training, and the establishment of security policies that dictate acceptable behaviors and practices. For example, an organization might implement mandatory security awareness training for all employees to reduce the risk of human error, which is often a significant factor in security breaches. Additionally, preventive controls may involve access controls that restrict who can access sensitive information, ensuring that only authorized personnel have the ability to view or modify critical data.

- **Detection controls**: Detection controls are focused on identifying security incidents as they happen. These controls often include monitoring systems, logging activities, and conducting regular audits. For example, the use of IDS can alert an organization to potential breaches, allowing for immediate investigation and response. Regular security audits and assessments help organizations identify vulnerabilities before they can be exploited. By implementing robust detection controls, organizations can enhance their ability to respond quickly to incidents, minimizing potential damage.

- **Recovery controls**: Recovery controls are essential for restoring normal operations after a security incident has occurred. These controls include disaster recovery plans, business continuity planning, and incident response strategies. A well-defined incident response plan outlines the action steps following a breach, including roles and responsibilities, communication strategies, and recovery procedures. This ensures that the organization can quickly recover from an incident, minimizing downtime and preserving the integrity of its operations. Additionally, business continuity planning helps ensure that critical functions can continue during and after a disruption, safeguarding the organization's mission.

Integration with technical and operational controls

Management security controls are most effective when integrated with technical and operational controls. While management controls establish the policies and frameworks necessary for security, technical controls implement the technology needed to enforce these policies. For example, if a management policy requires strong authentication methods, technical controls might include multi-factor authentication systems that ensure compliance.

Operational controls, on the other hand, involve the day-to-day procedures and practices that support the implementation of management policies. This could include regular training sessions for employees or scheduled security reviews. By aligning management controls with technical and operational measures, organizations can create a holistic approach to information security that significantly reduces the risk of loss and protects their critical missions.

Operational security controls

An organization's security standards must establish a comprehensive set of controls and guidelines to ensure effective enforcement of security procedures related to its IT assets and resources. These standards provide a framework for managing risks and protecting sensitive information aligning with the organization's goals and mission. Management plays a critical role in overseeing the implementation of these security policies. They are responsible for ensuring that appropriate operational controls are established and maintained, facilitating adherence to the defined security standards. This oversight includes the regular reviews of security practices, assessment of compliance, and adjustments as necessary to address emerging threats or changes in the operational environment.

Operational controls are based on foundational requirements like technical controls and industry best practices. They aim to address weaknesses that could be targeted by potential threats. These controls are essential for maintaining a robust security posture and include measures that protect the organization from various types of security incidents. By establishing clear security standards and effective operational controls, organizations can ensure that their security practices are well-integrated, consistently applied, and capable of adapting to the evolving threat landscape.

To ensure consistency and uniformity in security operations, it is crucial that step-by-step procedures and methods for implementing operational controls are clearly defined, documented, and regularly maintained. This documentation acts as a reference for employees and stakeholders, helping to ensure that security protocols are followed accurately and consistently across the organization. Examples of operational controls might include access management procedures, incident response plans, and user training programs. Each of these controls should be designed to mitigate specific risks while ensuring that all personnel understand their roles and responsibilities in maintaining security. Regular training and updates are essential to keep staff informed about changes in procedures and emerging threats.

Plan of action and milestones

The POA&M is a crucial component of the security authorization package, along with the security assessment report and the **system security plan** (**SSP**). POA&M describes the specific tasks necessary to rectify weaknesses or deficiencies identified during SCAs, as well as to address any residual vulnerabilities within the information system. This structured document ensures that the organization has a clear roadmap for improving its security posture.

The POA&M serves multiple purposes for the AO. It acts as a monitoring tool to track the progress of remediation efforts for the weaknesses or deficiencies highlighted during assessments. By clearly outlining the tasks, the POA&M allows the AO to maintain oversight and ensure that the necessary actions are being taken to improve the system's security.

Each POA&M outlines several critical components, like the following:

- **Goals**: Goals define the broader targets that an organization aims to achieve through the implementation of the POA&M. While objectives are specific and measurable, goals provide a high-level framework that guides the overall direction of the POA&M. They support the decision-making process and ensure that all activities align with the organization's mission and strategic priorities. For example, a goal might be to enhance the organization's cybersecurity posture, while specific objectives could detail the exact vulnerabilities to be addressed.

- **Identified tasks**: These tasks may include software updates, configuration changes, or implementing new security measures. Tasks are the specific activities required to accomplish the established goals and objectives. Each task should be clearly defined and prioritized based on its importance and urgency. Identifying tasks involves breaking down broader objectives into actionable steps, which helps to create a detailed implementation plan. This plan outlines what needs to be done, by whom, and when, thereby ensuring a systematic approach to achieving the desired outcomes.

Establishing timelines for each task is crucial for effective project management. These timelines help allocate resources efficiently and provide accountability, as responsible individuals can be held accountable for completing tasks within the designated periods.

- **Recommendations for completion**: The POA&M provides guidance on whether tasks should be completed before the information system goes live or if they can be addressed afterward. This distinction helps prioritize actions based on the level of risk they pose to the organization.

- **Metrics and resources**: To evaluate the success of a POA&M, metrics should be established. Metrics provide quantitative and qualitative measures of progress, enabling organizations to assess their performance against the defined objectives. These metrics help to identify areas that may need additional focus our resources and allow for timely adjustments to the plan.

  Finally, outlining the resources required for completing the tasks is essential. This includes not only personnel and funding but also technology and other support necessary for successful implementation. By ensuring that the necessary resources are allocated, organizations can enhance their capacity to meet their security objectives and milestones.

- **Milestones**: Milestones are critical checkpoints within the POA&M that signify significant progress toward achieving the overall objectives. Each milestone represents a key event or achievement that indicates a shift in direction or completion of a major task. By setting milestones, organizations can measure progress more effectively and ensure that they remain on track.

  Milestones also serve as motivational markers for teams, providing a sense of accomplishment as they reach each target. For instance, a milestone could be the completion of a vulnerability assessment, which would indicate readiness to implement remediation measures.

- **POA&M items**: Within the context of milestones, POA&M items refer to the specific tasks and milestones that need to be completed to achieve a particular goal or objective. These items can encompass a wide range of activities, such as:

  o   Completing a training program for staff on cybersecurity best practices

  o   Implementing new software solutions to address identified vulnerabilities

  o   Conducting regular security audits to ensure compliance with standards

  By listing these POA&M items, organizations can ensure that all necessary tasks are identified, assigned, and tracked effectively. This systematic approach helps maintain accountability and progress, making it easier to manage complex projects.

- **Scheduled completion dates**: The POA&M specifies target completion dates for each milestone, providing a timeline for when tasks should be finalized.

This scheduling helps to ensure accountability and facilitates timely updates to stakeholders regarding the status of remediation efforts.

Overall, the POA&M not only aids in addressing immediate security deficiencies but also promotes a culture of continuous improvement in information security management. By providing a clear, structured approach to identifying and rectifying vulnerabilities, the POA&M plays a vital role in enhancing an organization's overall cybersecurity resilience.

Objectives of a plan of action and milestones

The objectives of a POA&M represent the specific outcomes that an organization aims to achieve within a defined timeframe. By adhering to these requirements, organizations can set realistic and achievable objectives that provide a solid foundation for their action plans. These objectives should adhere to the S.M.A.R.T. criteria, mentioned as follows:

- **Specific**: Objectives must be clear and unambiguous, focusing on a particular area of improvement.

- **Measurable**: There should be criteria in place to assess progress and determine whether the objectives have been met.

- **Achievable**: Objectives should be realistic, taking into account the organization's capabilities and resources.

- **Relevant**: The objectives should align with the organization's broader goals and priorities.

- **Time-bound**: Each objective must have a specific deadline for completion.

A list of POA&M items include:

Items	Description
POA&M identifier	A unique identifier assigned to each POA&M item for tracking purposes.
Name of the control	The specific control or action that needs to be implemented to address the weakness or deficiency.
Name of the weakness/deficiency	A concise description of the weakness or deficiency that needs to be addressed.
Weakness/deficiency description	A more detailed explanation of the weakness or deficiency, including its impact on the organization.
Asset identifier	The identifier of the asset or system related to the weakness or deficiency.
Date of identification	The date that the weakness or deficiency was first identified.
Resources required to address the issue	An estimate of the resources (time, money, personnel, etc.) needed to address the weakness or deficiency.

Items	Description
Planned milestones	Specific milestones or targets for addressing the weakness or deficiency.
Planned resolution date	The date by which the weakness or deficiency is planned to be fully addressed.
Milestone changes	Any changes to the planned milestones or targets.
Vendor dependencies	Any dependencies on vendors or third-party providers that may impact the resolution of the weakness or deficiency.
Risk rating	A quantitative assessment of the level of risk posed by the weakness or deficiency.
Adjusted risk rating	Any adjustments made to the risk rating based on new information or changed circumstances.
Operational requirement assessment	An assessment of whether addressing the weakness or deficiency is necessary to meet the organization's operational requirements.
Supporting documents	Any documents or evidence that support the identification or resolution of the weakness or deficiency

Table 9.3: POA&M items

Prepare the plan of action and milestones

The POA&M is one of the three key documents within the security authorization package, alongside the security plan and the SCA. This trio of documents forms the foundation of an organization's approach to information security, ensuring a systematic method for identifying, managing, and mitigating risks associated with information systems.

The AO plays a critical role in overseeing the implementation of the POA&M. The AO uses the document to monitor progress in correcting weaknesses identified during the SCA. This ongoing oversight helps ensure that the organization remains focused on addressing vulnerabilities and enhances the overall security of the information system. The following table shows the roles and responsibilities to prepare POA&M:

Primary responsibility	Supporting roles	SDLC phase	References
ISO or CCP	IO/IS, ISSO	Implementation	NIST SPs 800-30, 800-53A, *Office of Management and Budget (OMB)* Memorandum 02-01

Table 9.4: Roles and responsibilities to prepare POA&M

Following are some key considerations while preparing for the POA&M:

- **Documentation and compliance**: The development of a POA&M is guided by various legal and regulatory frameworks, including applicable laws, executive orders, directives, policies, standards, and guidance. These documents ensure that the POA&M is not only a practical tool for remediation but also compliant with national and organizational security standards.

  Note: The weaknesses that are remediated during the assessment phase or prior to the submission of the authorization package to the AO do not need to be included in the POA&M. This allows organizations to focus on tracking outstanding vulnerabilities that require action.

- **Strategy for developing POA&Ms**: Organizations are encouraged to define a clear strategy for developing POA&Ms to facilitate the prioritized mitigation of risks. This strategy should be consistent throughout the organization and align with its overall **Risk Management Framework** (**RMF**). A well-defined strategy ensures that POA&Ms are:

  o Based on the security categorization of the system, which helps determine the level of risk associated with various vulnerabilities.

  o Focused on specific weaknesses in security controls that have been identified during assessments.

  o Prioritized based on the importance of these weaknesses, enabling the organization to allocate resources effectively.

  o Aligned with the organization's proposed approach to risk mitigation, providing a clear path forward for remediation efforts.

- **Risk assessment and prioritization**: A critical aspect of developing an effective POA&M is the integration of risk assessment into the prioritization process. The risk assessment informs which weaknesses should be addressed first based on factors such as:

  o The potential impact of each vulnerability on the organization's operations and data integrity.

  o The likelihood of exploitation of the identified weaknesses.

  o The resources required to remediate each issue effectively.

By leveraging risk assessment findings, organizations can ensure that their remediation efforts are not only targeted but also efficient, maximizing the use of available resources and minimizing exposure to risk.

In summary, the POA&M is an essential document in the security authorization package, providing a comprehensive plan for addressing identified weaknesses in security controls. By detailing specific actions, required resources, milestones, and completion dates, the

POA&M serves as a roadmap for remediation. The oversight provided by the AO and the adherence to relevant regulations ensure that the organization is committed to maintaining a robust security posture. A strategic approach to developing POA&Ms, informed by risk assessments, allows organizations to prioritize their efforts effectively, ultimately enhancing their overall security and compliance.

POA&M integration with standards

The POA&M is required by the FISMA as a formal corrective action plan for addressing specific weaknesses in an organization's information systems. These weaknesses can arise from vulnerabilities in software, hardware, or operational processes. The POA&M serves as a structured, version-controlled document that plays a crucial role in managing risks. It is typically used along with security control frameworks like the NIST RMF or the **Cybersecurity Maturity Model Certification** (**CMMC**). Additionally, the *Federal Risk and Authorization Management Program* (*FedRAMP*) mandates that **cloud service providers** (**CSPs**) maintain POA&Ms to track their compliance with security standards. Maintaining a current and comprehensive POA&M is essential for organizations to identify, mitigate risks, and meet regulatory requirements. Failure to do so could lead to the loss of authorization to operate an information system.

POA&Ms are vital for achieving regulatory compliance as they provide a systematic approach to address deficiencies or noncompliance issues identified during audits or assessments. Each POA&M outlines a specific plan of action detailing the steps needed to correct deficiencies, along with associated milestones that establish time frames for completion. This structured approach ensures that corrective actions are implemented promptly, thereby minimizing the risk of non-compliance and potential regulatory penalties. Regulatory agencies often require organizations to submit POA&Ms as part of their compliance reporting, demonstrating their commitment to addressing identified weaknesses and continuously enhancing their compliance posture.

Configuration identification

The configuration identification process is a fundamental component of configuration management in software engineering, primarily focused on the selection and documentation of **configuration items** (**CIs**). The configuration administrator plays a crucial role in this process by carefully selecting CIs based on their significance within the software system. Once selected, the administrator records the identifying characteristics of each CI, ensuring that detailed information is maintained for effective management. By establishing mechanisms to track changes such as additions, modifications, and deletions, developers can maintain a clear record of the state of the system. This documentation not only supports the production of desired outcomes but also helps to identify and verify any failures during the development process.

As a key component of configuration management, configuration identification plays a vital role in various processes, including change version control, release management, and overall change management. It fosters improved collaboration and communication among team members, enhancing the effectiveness of modifications made to the system. Additionally, by providing insights into the software's evolution over time, configuration identification enables better decision-making, allowing teams to respond more effectively to changes and challenges that arise during development.

Configuration identification in risk management

Configuration identification plays a vital role in risk management and compliance efforts, especially under frameworks like NIST. The following demonstrates some ways:

- **Asset inventory and control**: Configuration identification helps to identify, document, and track all hardware, software, and firmware components of system within an organization's infrastructure. This provides necessary asset inventories in both risk management and compliance.

- **Security baselines**: By establishing and maintaining the configuration of systems, configuration identification ensures alignment of components with security baselines imposed by NIST standards, such as NIST SP 800-53 Revision 5. This prevents unauthorized changes that might lead to vulnerabilities.

- **Change management**: Configuration identification facilitates effective change control processes wherein configuration changes are qualified for any risks and compliance against standards before actual implementation. In that perspective, it also underpins risk mitigation to meet the NIST requirements of continuous monitoring and security.

- **Audit and traceability**: Configuration identification provides an updated record at any moment regarding systems and their constituent components in place, and hence proof for compliance is made easier where audits are held. It ascertains that problems and other forms of vulnerabilities can be traced from the beginning and are critical in assessing and mitigating risks.

- **Incident response**: If the incident is identified and documented early, it helps in quickly assessing which systems are affected, streamlining faster response and ensuring minimal impact on compliance requirements.

Configuration identification process

The configuration identification process is a comprehensive framework that ensures effective documentation, control, and support of CIs throughout their lifecycle. This process encompasses several key activities, as shown in the following figure:

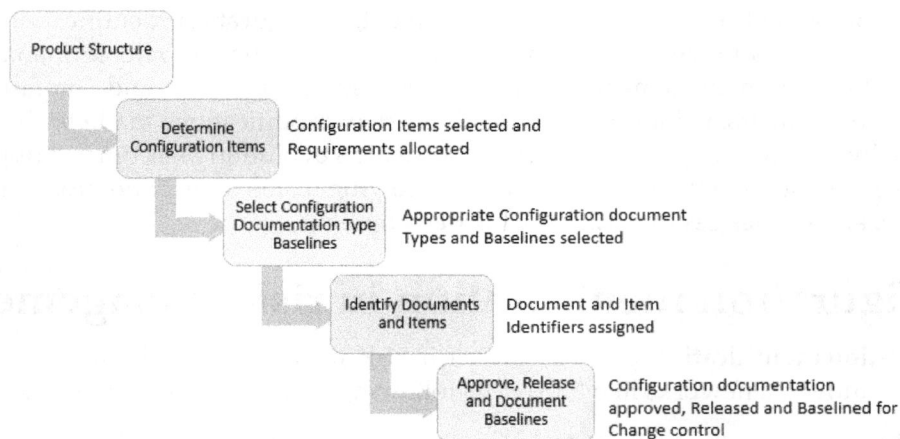

Figure 9.5: Configuration identification steps

Here are the details of the configuration identification process:

- **Selecting configuration items**: The first step involves identifying CIs at the appropriate levels of the product structure. This selection is crucial for ensuring that each item is adequately documented and controlled. By focusing on the right levels, the process facilitates effective oversight and management of the items and their associated documentation.

- **Determining required documentation**: For each selected CI, it is essential to define the types of configuration documentation needed. This documentation should outline the CI's performance, and functional and physical attributes, including both internal and external interfaces. Proper configuration documentation serves as a foundational resource for various activities, such as developing and procuring software.

- **Establishing configuration control authority**: Identifying the appropriate configuration control authority for each configuration document is critical. This authority must align with logistic support planning for the associated CI, ensuring that all documentation is managed consistently and effectively. By establishing clear control authority, organizations can streamline the approval process for changes and maintain integrity in the documentation.

- **Issuing identifiers**: A vital aspect of configuration identification is issuing unique identifiers for both the CIs and the associated configuration documentation. These identifiers allow for efficient tracking and retrieval of information, minimizing the risk of errors and enhancing overall management.

- **Maintaining configuration identification**: The ongoing maintenance of configuration identification for CIs is necessary to ensure effective logistics support for items in service. This includes regularly updating documentation and records to reflect any changes in the CIs or their status, which helps in planning and managing resources efficiently.

- **Releasing configuration documentation**: Once the configuration documentation has been developed and reviewed, it must be officially released. This step signifies that the documents are now authoritative and can be used for reference, training, and operational purposes.

- **Establishing configuration baselines**: Finally, the last process involves establishing configuration baselines for the control of CIs. A configuration baseline serves as a reference point for managing changes and helps ensure that any alterations are systematically documented and approved.

Conclusion

In this chapter, we explored control implementation guidelines to identify the necessary configuration settings for systems, aligning with key industry standards. We examined various types of security controls, such as technical, management, and operational, that are essential for managing risk and enhancing an organization's security posture. This comprehensive understanding equips organizations to implement effective measures that safeguard their assets.

We also discussed the strategy behind creating templates POA&M, which are crucial for tracking remediation efforts and ensuring that security deficiencies are addressed promptly. Additionally, we delved into the configuration identification process, which supports improved decision-making. This process enables organizations to respond more effectively to changes and challenges that may arise during development, ensuring they remain agile and resilient.

As we transition to the next chapter, our focus will shift to configuration control, including implemented control and privacy control standards. This next phase will build upon the foundation established in this chapter, emphasizing the importance of maintaining effective oversight and compliance in an ever-evolving security landscape.

Key terms

- NIST SP 800-53 lists 20 families of controls that provide operational, technical, and managerial safeguards to ensure the privacy, integrity, and security of information systems.

- The system owner should assess the adequacy of common controls by referring to the authorization packages prepared by CCPs.

- NIST SP 800-53B includes three security control baselines (one for each system impact level: low-impact, moderate-impact, and high-impact), as well as a privacy control baseline that is applied to systems irrespective of impact levels.

- A POA&M is a remediation plan that outlines the steps necessary to address and remediate the identified risks and vulnerabilities in an information system.

- On the other hand, *Defense Federal Acquisition Regulation Supplement* (*DFARS*) SSP is a broader and more comprehensive plan that outlines the policies and procedures for protecting sensitive information and systems.

- Configuration identification is responsible for collecting information about CIs and their relationships, and for loading this information into configuration management.

Join our book's Discord space

Join the book's Discord Workspace for Latest updates, Offers, Tech happenings around the world, New Release and Sessions with the Authors:

https://discord.bpbonline.com

CHAPTER 10

Deploying Security and Privacy Controls

Introduction

This chapter offers a detailed overview of configuration management to ensure that an organization can effectively track changes without compromising its security posture. It emphasizes the importance of **security-focused configuration management (SecCM)** in managing risks, ensuring that any system modifications or updates do not introduce vulnerabilities or weaken existing defenses. By maintaining control over configurations, organizations can safeguard the integrity and security of their systems.

In addition to configuration management, the chapter highlights the implementation of security controls based on industry standards such as *National Institute of Standards and Technology (NIST) Special Publication (SP) 800-70, Security Technical Implementation Guides (STIGs)*, and *NIST SP 800-53*. It also discusses privacy control guidelines to protect sensitive personal information. Furthermore, the chapter explores the frameworks provided by *International Organization for Standardization (ISO)/International Electrotechnical Commission (IEC) 27001:2022* to guide control implementation, ensuring organizations comply with regulatory requirements and maintain a robust security and privacy posture.

Structure

The chapter covers the following main topics. Each topic will have respective sub-topics:

- Configuration management or control
- Implementation of controls
- Privacy control guideline
- NIST SP 800-53
- ISO/IEC 27001:2022

Objectives

By the end of this chapter, you will have a solid understanding of the configuration management process, including the phases of SecCM. You will learn how to implement security controls based on industry standards, ensuring your organization's systems are secure and resilient. Additionally, the chapter will introduce you to essential privacy control guidelines, helping you to protect sensitive data and maintain privacy compliance.

The chapter also covers key industry frameworks such as NIST SP 800-53 and ISO/IEC 27001:2022, providing you with the knowledge to align security practices with organizational goals and manage risks effectively. With this comprehensive approach, you will be equipped to implement industry best practices, comply with regulations, and enhance your organization's overall security and privacy posture.

Configuration management or control

Configuration management and configuration control are essential processes for effectively tracking and approving changes within an information system. These processes involve identifying, controlling, and auditing all modifications related to hardware, software, networking, or other components that could impact system security. By maintaining a structured approach to changes, organizations can ensure the integrity of their systems and safeguard the trusted environment throughout the system's design, development, and operational phases.

The primary security objective of configuration management is to ensure that changes do not inadvertently weaken the system's security posture. For example, it helps to prevent outdated or vulnerable versions from being deployed as the production environment, thereby protecting against potential security breaches. Additionally, configuration management allows for the precise rollback to earlier system versions if new implementations prove faulty, minimizing disruptions and reducing the risk of introducing new vulnerabilities. This rollback capability is vital for maintaining a secure and stable operational state.

Another key aspect of configuration management is to ensure that all system changes are accurately reflected in up-to-date documentation. This documentation helps to mitigate the impact of changes on the overall system and provides clear guidance to stakeholders, ensuring consistency across teams. By maintaining current records, organizations are better equipped to understand the implications of system modifications, provide effective training, and ensure compliance with security standards and regulations. The configuration management process also involves identifying and tracking individual **configuration items (CIs)**, documenting their functional capabilities, and understanding their interdependencies.

To streamline and enforce configuration management, organizations typically use specialized tools that help track changes and monitor configurations in real time. These tools alert administrators about configuration issues or unauthorized changes, allowing for proactive intervention. This monitoring ensures that configurations stay aligned with organizational standards and policies, minimizing risks related to configuration drift.

For administrators and software developers, understanding how changes to one CI affect other system components is essential for maintaining system stability and making informed decisions. Configuration management is also a critical tool for business leaders, as it supports governance, security, and compliance efforts, ensuring that IT practices are aligned with organizational goals and regulatory requirements. In many cases, configuration management is formalized within frameworks like the **Information Technology Infrastructure Library** (**ITIL**), which offer structured approaches to service asset and configuration management.

Practical example: Consider a simple example of a data center with numerous servers, each providing essential resources such as compute power, storage, and physical networking capabilities. These resources are provisioned to create a clearly defined operating environment that supports various services and applications, such as network firewalls, **operating systems** (**OSs**), web portals, websites, databases, APIs, **customer relationship management** (**CRM**) systems, and countless other business platforms.

Each business platform deployed within this environment must be carefully configured to use specific resources such as storage volumes, **virtual machines** (**VMs**) or containers. These configurations are vital to ensure that the platform functions correctly and can access the appropriate resources. Moreover, most business platforms are interdependent and must work together to support the broader business processes. These interdependencies must be carefully configured to ensure smooth communication and functionality between the systems. Any misconfiguration could lead to performance issues or even failures in business operations.

Configuration management process

The configuration management process involves several critical steps to ensure that an organization's systems are properly tracked, controlled, and maintained throughout their lifecycle. Each step plays a vital role in ensuring the integrity, security, and stability of the system:

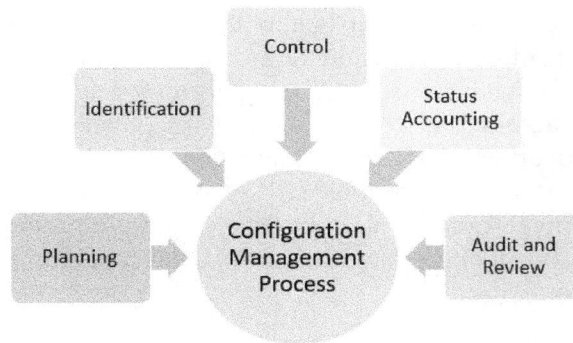

Figure 10.1: *Configuration management process*

Following are the details of the configuration management process:

- **Planning**: The first step is planning, where the scope and objectives of the configuration management process are defined. This includes identifying which CIs need to be managed and determining the roles and responsibilities of the team members involved in the process.

- **Identification**: Once the planning phase is complete, the identification step begins. This involves identifying the CIs that require management and creating a baseline configuration, which represents the current state of each CI. Each CI is assigned a unique identifier, and its attributes, such as software version, hardware specifications, and relationships with other CIs, are documented.

- **Control**: The control phase focuses on managing changes to the CIs. This includes defining clear change management processes and implementing procedures to evaluate, approve, and track changes. The control process ensures that no unauthorized or untracked changes are made to the system, maintaining stability and preventing configuration drift. All proposed changes are evaluated for their impact on the system before they are implemented.

- **Status accounting**: In this phase, the status of each CI is tracked over time. This includes maintaining a record of all changes made, the current version of each CI, and its relationship with other CIs. Status accounting helps maintain an audit trail of modifications, providing transparency and accountability in the configuration management process. It allows organizations to trace back any issues or changes to their root causes.

- **Audit and review**: The final step is to perform periodic audits and reviews of the configuration management process to ensure its effectiveness. This step involves verifying that all CIs are correctly identified and properly controlled and that change management procedures are being followed. The accuracy of the CI status records is also confirmed, ensuring that the system's integrity is maintained and that any deviations from the planned configuration are addressed.

By following these steps, organizations can ensure that all system components are consistently identified, documented, controlled, and tracked throughout their lifecycle. This structured approach guarantees that the changes are made in a controlled manner, minimizing risks, enhancing security, and ensuring the system remains reliable and compliant with organizational standards.

Security-focused configuration management

SecCM is a specialized approach to configuration management that prioritizes the security of system configurations while also managing associated risks. It extends the general principles of configuration management by specifically addressing the security requirements of an organization's systems and infrastructure. SecCM integrates the management of security configurations into the broader organizational processes, aiming to secure systems while enabling business operations. SecCM plays a critical role in ensuring that the configurations of systems and networks are secure, reducing vulnerabilities, and facilitating risk management in both information security and IT governance.

NIST provides guidelines, particularly publications like NIST SP 800-53 and NIST SP 800-128, to help organizations integrate security controls into their configuration management processes. The core objective of SecCM is to ensure that security requirements such as hardening system settings, securing user privileges, and enforcing access controls are systematically defined, implemented, and maintained throughout the system's lifecycle. This involves managing and controlling configurations, ensuring that all system components remain secure, and tracking any changes that could potentially affect security.

Some key aspects of SecCM are as follows:

- **Integration with organizational processes**: SecCM integrates SecCM requirements into broader organizational processes. These processes may include business functions, applications, products, and information systems. By aligning SecCM with existing configuration management practices, organizations can ensure that security considerations are addressed along with general operational requirements, ensuring a more cohesive and comprehensive risk management approach.

- **Identification and recording of security-critical configurations**: SecCM involves the identification and documentation of configurations that have a direct impact on the security posture of systems and the organization. This includes hardware, software, network configurations, and system settings that affect security. For example, configurations related to firewalls, user access controls, and system updates need to be carefully monitored and maintained to prevent security gaps.

- **Security risk consideration in initial configuration approval**: Before any system configuration is approved and implemented, SecCM ensures that security risks are considered. This includes evaluating potential vulnerabilities, assessing threats, and determining the potential impact of configurations on system security. For example, default settings or weak passwords may be identified as security risks that need to be addressed before deployment.

- **Analysis of security implications of configuration changes**: SecCM also includes the analysis of changes to system configurations to evaluate their security implications. Every time a configuration is altered, it must be assessed to understand how the change could impact the system's security. This ensures that new vulnerabilities are not inadvertently introduced and that the overall security posture is maintained or enhanced.

- **Documentation of approved/implemented changes**: Finally, SecCM requires the detailed documentation of all approved and implemented configuration changes. This documentation includes what changes were made, why they were necessary, who authorized them, and how they were tested for security. Maintaining thorough records helps with auditing, troubleshooting, and ensuring compliance with organizational security policies.

Phases of security-focused configuration management

SecCM involves a structured set of activities organized into four major phases: Planning, identifying and implementing configurations, controlling configuration changes, and monitoring. These phases work together to ensure the security of system configurations, reduce vulnerabilities, and support the overall management of organizational risk:

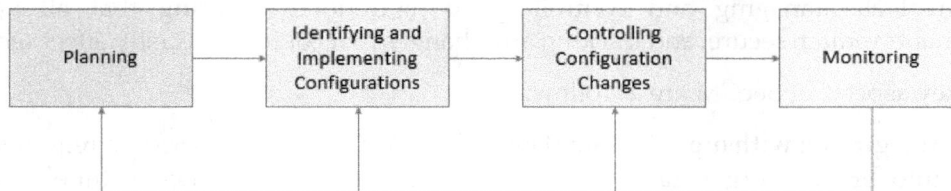

Figure 10.2: Phases of SecCM

They ae explained as follows:

- **Planning**: Planning is the foundational phase of SecCM. In this phase, security requirements are defined, and a strategy is developed for managing configurations securely. Effective planning ensures that security considerations are integrated into every aspect of configuration management and that all stakeholders are aligned on security objectives. Key activities in this phase include the following:

  o **Establishing security baselines**: Define secure configuration baselines that align with organizational security policies, industry standards, and regulatory requirements (e.g., NIST, *Center for Internet Security (CIS) Benchmarks*).

  o **Risk assessment**: Conduct a risk assessment to identify potential security threats and vulnerabilities related to system configurations.

- Defining roles and responsibilities: Establish clear roles and responsibilities for managing system configurations and security.

- Developing a configuration management policy: Create a policy that outlines the procedures for secure configuration management, including the approval process for changes and the criteria for selecting secure configurations.

- **Identifying and implementing configurations**: In this phase, SecCM focuses on identifying which configurations are critical to the security of the system and implementing those configurations in line with the established security baselines. This phase involves:

  - Identifying security-critical configurations: Identify all system components that directly impact the security posture of the system.

  - Implementing secure configurations: Once security-critical configurations are identified, the next step is to implement them.

  - Configuration testing: After configurations are implemented, testing must be conducted to verify that the system works as expected and that security controls are properly enforced.

- **Controlling configuration changes**: This phase of SecCM ensures that any modifications to system configurations are carefully managed to avoid introducing new vulnerabilities or compromising security. This phase includes the following:

  - Change management process: Establish a formal process for managing configuration changes. This includes reviewing and approving changes to configurations before they are implemented.

  - Security impact analysis: Before implementing any changes, assess the security implications of the proposed configuration changes.

  - Approval and documentation: Ensure that all configuration changes are authorized by the appropriate stakeholders and are well-documented.

  - Version control: Implement version control for configuration files and settings, ensuring that previous versions of configurations can be easily restored in case of issues or security breaches.

- **Monitoring**: The monitoring phase involves continuous oversight of system configurations to ensure that the configurations remain secure over time. This phase ensures that security configurations are maintained and any unauthorized changes are detected promptly. Key activities in the monitoring phase include:

  - Continuous monitoring: Regularly monitor the configurations of systems, applications, and networks for compliance with security baselines.

  - Vulnerability scanning and detection: Use automated tools to conduct regular vulnerability scans and configuration audits.

- o **Incident detection and response**: In case of any unauthorized configuration changes or security breaches, the monitoring phase includes detecting these events and responding promptly.

- o **Ongoing risk assessment**: As threats and vulnerabilities evolve, ongoing risk assessments are needed to ensure that the configuration management process remains up-to-date and effective at mitigating new risks.

Implementation of controls

Control implementation is a critical phase in the security lifecycle where specific security measures, or controls, are configured, customized, and deployed into the system to address identified risks and vulnerabilities. At this stage, the focus is on securing the system's environment by applying preventive, detective, and corrective controls to reduce the attack surface and mitigate potential threats. These controls can include technical configurations, access management policies, encryption settings, and network defenses. One of the core activities during this stage is system hardening, which involves disabling unnecessary services, applying patches, configuring firewalls, and ensuring that only the essential functionalities are enabled to minimize vulnerabilities.

In addition to securing the system, control implementation requires careful documentation of the baseline configurations. This documentation ensures that security configurations are consistent and aligned with established security standards and regulatory requirements. Furthermore, the documented baseline configurations are crucial for change management processes, ensuring that any modifications to the system are controlled and traceable and do not inadvertently introduce new risks.

A well-implemented control framework also supports operational efficiency by streamlining security operations, reducing the need for reactive interventions, and providing clarity on how security measures should be maintained and monitored over time. It facilitates troubleshooting by offering clear guidance on the expected system configurations and behaviors, enabling quicker identification and resolution of security-related issues.

During the implementation of security controls, organizations typically rely on a variety of guides, checklists, and benchmarks to ensure that they are covering all relevant security aspects and adhering to industry best practices. These resources provide a structured approach to configuring and deploying controls effectively, helping to standardize the process and ensure that all critical areas are addressed. Let us explore some of the most commonly used guides and frameworks.

NIST guidance on implementing security controls

The fourth step of the NIST **Risk Management Framework** (**RMF**) is focused on putting in place the security and privacy controls outlined in the system and organizational security plans. The following figure shows the fourth step of the NIST RMF:

Figure 10.3: NIST RMF steps

During this phase, the necessary controls are implemented, and the specific details of their implementation are documented in a baseline configuration. This ensures that the controls are properly integrated into the system and aligned with the organization's security and privacy requirements, providing a clear reference for ongoing management and future assessments. The following figure shows the task associated with the implementation step:

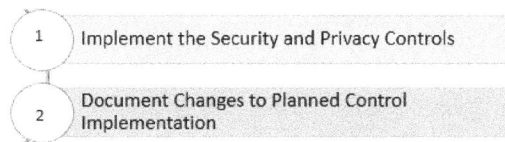

Figure 10.4: Implementation steps

The tasks are explained in detail:

- **Task 1**: **Implement the security and privacy controls**: During the implement step of the NIST RMF, organizations deploy the security and privacy controls outlined in their plans, ensuring they align with enterprise architecture and security standards. The process follows best practices, such as using security engineering methodologies, and is guided by risk assessments to evaluate the cost, benefits, and risks of different technologies or policies. Mandatory configuration settings are enforced, and third-party validated products, like commercial off-the-shelf software, are used where applicable. Collaboration between system security engineers and **common control providers** (**CCPs**) ensures the correct integration of controls, and if necessary, additional controls are added or risks accepted with organizational approval. Early control assessments during development and implementation identify deficiencies, preventing later-stage delays and costs while supporting the authorization process. The following table shows the roles to implement the security and privacy controls:

Primary responsibility	Supporting roles	SDLC phase	References
System owner; CCP	Information owner or steward; security architect; privacy architect; systems security engineer; privacy engineer; system security officer; system privacy officer; enterprise architect; system administrator	New: Development/ acquisition; implementation/ assessment Existing: Operations/ maintenance	NIST SP 800-30; SP 800-53; SP 800-53A; SP 800-160 v1; SP 800-161; FIPS 200

Table 10.1: Roles to implement security and privacy controls

- **Task 2: Document changes to planned control implementation**: Sometimes, controls cannot be implemented exactly as described in the security and privacy plans, so the plans are updated to reflect the actual implementation. These updates include revised descriptions of the controls, detailing changes to inputs, behavior, and outputs, which support control assessments. Documenting these as implemented details is essential for tracking changes, ensuring authorization, and understanding their impact on the system's security and privacy posture. The following table shows the roles to document changes in planned control implementation:

Primary responsibility	Supporting roles	SDLC phase	References
System owner; CCP	Information owner or steward; security architect; privacy architect; systems security engineer; privacy engineer; system security officer; system privacy officer; enterprise architect; system administrator	New: Development/ acquisition; implementation/ assessment Existing: Operations/ maintenance	NIST SP 800-53; SP 800-128; SP 800-160 v1

Table 10.2: Roles to document changes

Security Technical Implementation Guide

STIGs are the authoritative documents that provide detailed technical guidance on how to securely configure IT products and systems. They are designed to help organizations harden their systems against security vulnerabilities, ensuring that IT environments are configured to meet security standards and compliance requirements. STIGs are widely used across both governmental and private sectors, especially in industries where security is critical, such as defense, healthcare, and finance.

Following are the key aspects of STIGs:

- **Configuration and hardening**: STIGs provide highly detailed instructions on how to configure IT systems securely. STIGs cover aspects such as disabling unnecessary services, enforcing strong password policies, applying encryption, and ensuring that only authorized users have access to sensitive data.

- **Security controls**: STIGs specify the implementation of security controls across various domains, including access control, system auditing, patch management, network security, and incident response. The goal is to ensure that the system is resilient to common threats and exploits by maintaining robust defenses across all layers of the IT environment.

- **Compliance and auditing**: STIGs are often used as a benchmark for compliance and auditing, particularly for organizations that need to meet specific regulatory or contractual obligations. For example, *Department of Defense* (*DoD*) contractors and federal agencies must comply with the relevant STIGs to meet federal cybersecurity requirements and to pass security assessments or audits.

- **Tools and validation**: STIGs often come with automated tools and checklists to help organizations verify that systems have been correctly configured. For example, DISA provides tools like the **Security Content Automation Protocol** (**SCAP**) and STIG viewers that allow organizations to automate compliance checks and easily assess whether their systems meet the defined security standards.

Control implementation considerations

When implementing security controls in an information system, organizations must consider various factors to ensure that controls are effectively deployed and integrated into the overall system environment. These considerations help guarantee that controls are not only functional but also aligned with security objectives, compliance requirements, and organizational needs. Following are key considerations to keep in mind during the control implementation phase:

- **System security plan**: Implement controls as described in the **system security plan** (**SSP**) to ensure consistency with defined security requirements.

- **Consistency with architecture**: Ensure control implementation aligns with the organization's enterprise architecture and system security architectures.

- **Best practices**: Use established security engineering methodologies, principles, and best practices when implementing controls.

- **Risk assessments**: Use risk assessments to guide decisions on cost, benefit, and risk trade-offs when selecting control technologies or policies.

- **Mandatory settings**: Ensure mandatory security settings are applied on system elements as per federal and organizational procedures.

- **Third-party evaluation for off-the-shelf products**: For off-the-shelf products, select those tested, evaluated, or validated by independent third-party assessment facilities (e.g., certified testing labs).

- **Integration and assurance**: Focus on how products are integrated into the system while ensuring that integration maintains security and system functionality.

- **Quality assurance**: Address **quality assurance (QA)** requirements before integrating products into the system to verify the design, development, and implementation of controls.

- **Confidence in controls**: QA activities should build confidence in the controls effectiveness, ensuring they operate as intended and meet security requirements.

Privacy control guideline

Privacy control guidelines refer to the set of rules, policies, or best practices designed to protect an individual's personal information and ensure that it is collected, used, stored, and shared in a secure and transparent manner. These guidelines are typically followed by organizations, businesses, or digital platforms to maintain trust with their users, comply with legal and regulatory requirements, and minimize risks related to data security and privacy.

Privacy controls, distinct from general data security measures, specifically target the protection of sensitive personal information. As defined by NIST, privacy controls include administrative, technical, and physical safeguards that ensure compliance with privacy requirements and manage risks. Privacy controls play a crucial role in safeguarding individuals rights by mitigating the risks of unauthorized access, breaches, and malicious use of data. The following figure shows the privacy control guidelines framework:

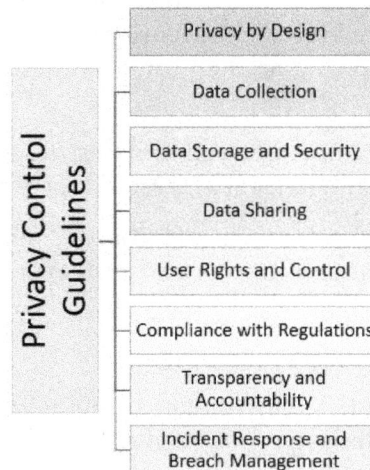

Figure 10.5: Privacy control guidelines

Here are the general guidelines for privacy controls:

- **Privacy by design**:

- o **Privacy by default**: Design products, services, and systems with privacy as a core component. This means making privacy settings the default configuration for users.

- o **Risk assessments**: Conduct PIA for new projects or products that involve handling personal data to assess risks and ensure compliance with privacy regulations.

- **Data collection**:

  - o **Minimize data collection**: Only collect the personal information that is necessary for the intended purpose.

  - o **Transparency**: Clearly inform users about what data is being collected, how it will be used, and why it is needed.

  - o **Consent**: Obtain explicit consent from individuals before collecting or processing sensitive data and ensure they can easily withdraw consent at any time.

  - o **Data anonymization**: When possible, anonymize or pseudonymize data to reduce risks in case of data breaches.

- **Data storage and security**:

  - o **Encryption**: Use strong encryption methods for storing and transmitting personal data.

  - o **Access controls**: Implement strict access controls to ensure that only authorized personnel can access sensitive data.

  - o **Regular audits**: Perform regular audits and security assessments to ensure that data is being stored securely and privacy policies are being followed.

  - o **Data minimization**: Avoid storing data longer than necessary. Implement retention policies and securely delete data that is no longer required.

- **Data sharing and third-parties**:

  - o **Third-party agreements**: Ensure that third-party vendors or partners who handle data on your behalf comply with the same privacy and security standards.

  - o **Data transfers**: If data is transferred across borders, ensure that the transfer complies with relevant data protection laws (e.g., *General Data Protection Regulation (GDPR)*, *California Consumer Privacy Act (CCPA)*).

- **User rights and control**:

  - o **Access to data**: Provide individuals with the ability to access, correct, or delete their personal data and offer a clear process for doing so.

- o **Opt-out and deletion**: Allow users to easily opt-out of data collection or marketing efforts and ensure they can permanently delete their personal data if desired.

- o **Data portability**: Enable users to download their data in a usable format (e.g., CSV, JSON) and transfer it to another service if they choose.

- **Compliance with regulations**:

  - o **Data protection laws**: Adhere to applicable data protection regulations, such as:

    - GDPR for EU residents.

    - CCPA for California residents.

    - *Health Insurance Portability and Accountability Act (HIPAA)* for healthcare data.

    - *Children's Online Privacy Protection Act (COPPA)* if applicable.

  - o **Regular compliance checks**: Stay up-to-date with changes in privacy laws and ensure ongoing compliance through periodic reviews.

- **Transparency and accountability**:

  - o **Privacy notices**: Provide clear and easy-to-understand privacy policies and terms of service that outline how data will be collected, used, and protected.

  - o **Employee training**: Regularly train employees and contractors on privacy policies, data protection best practices, and their responsibilities regarding personal data.

- **Incident response and breach management**:

  - o **Incident response plan**: Create and regularly update an incident response plan to manage data security incidents, including a detailed process for investigation and remediation.

  - o **Breach notification**: Have a clear protocol for notifying individuals and relevant authorities (e.g., regulatory bodies) in the event of a data breach.

NIST SP 800-53

NIST SP 800-53 is a foundational document that provides a set of detailed security guidelines and controls for Federal Information Systems, but its scope extends well beyond government agencies. This publication developed by the NIST, is part of a broader national initiative to improve the security posture of U.S. information systems. It serves as a comprehensive framework for establishing security and privacy practices, offering organizations a structured approach to mitigate risks and comply with legal and regulatory requirements.

The publication organizes security and privacy controls into categories that make it easier for organizations to adopt appropriate measures based on their specific risk assessments. Each control is supported by detailed implementation guidelines, enabling organizations to tailor their practices to their unique operational needs and risk environments. This adaptability makes NIST SP 800-53 a valuable resource for any organization seeking to establish or enhance its security infrastructure, regardless of size or sector.

One of the key strengths of NIST SP 800-53 is its holistic approach, addressing both technical controls and organizational procedures to create a robust security framework. It aligns with other NIST publications and emphasizes the integration of privacy considerations into the overall risk management strategy. This approach ensures that organizations not only address cybersecurity threats but also safeguard personal and sensitive data. Furthermore, NIST SP 800-53 encourages continuous monitoring, which helps organizations stay current with evolving threats. It also stresses the importance of employee training and awareness programs that foster a security culture within the organization.

Implementing NIST SP 800-53

Implementing NIST 800-53 Revision 5 effectively requires a strategic, methodical approach and strong leadership commitment to ensure that the framework is integrated across the organization. The following figure highlights the critical steps of implementing NIST SP 800-53 controls:

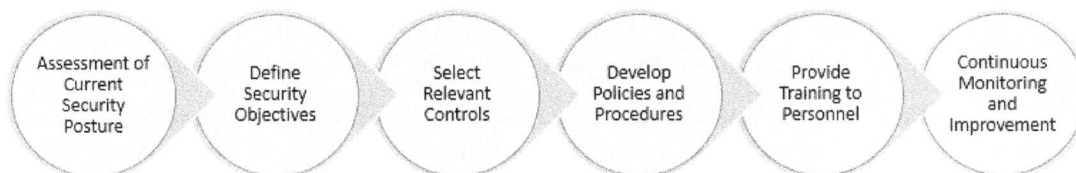

Figure 10.6: NIST SP 800-53 implementation steps

The following steps outline an effective pathway for integration:

- **Assessment of current security posture**: The first step in implementing NIST 800-53 is to assess the organization's existing security posture. This includes conducting a thorough review of current security controls, policies, and practices to identify areas of strength and weakness. The assessment must involve mapping existing controls to the NIST 800-53 framework to identify any gaps in compliance or areas where controls are not sufficiently mitigating risks. This process typically involves:

  o Conducting risk assessments to determine potential threats, vulnerabilities, and the impact of security incidents.

  o Auditing existing security controls to evaluate their effectiveness and determine whether they align with the required NIST controls.

- o Identifying any regulatory or compliance gaps, particularly in areas such as privacy, data protection, and cybersecurity.

- o Engaging stakeholders across the organization to gather input from key departments like IT, legal, compliance, and operations.

- **Define security objectives**: Once the current security posture has been assessed, the next step is to define clear security and privacy objectives that align with both the organization's mission and applicable regulatory requirements. These objectives should involve the following:

  - o Addressing specific risks identified during the assessment and align with the organization's business goals.

  - o Ensuring compliance with legal and regulatory requirements such as GDPR, HIPAA, or the CCPA, depending on the industry.

  - o Balancing security with operational needs to avoid overly restrictive controls that could hinder business performance or user productivity.

- **Select relevant controls**: With security objectives in place, the next step is to select and tailor appropriate controls from the NIST 800-53 catalogue. This step involves choosing controls that specifically address the risks and compliance gaps identified during the assessment phase and customizing them based on the organization's operational needs. The NIST 800-53 catalogue contains over 900 controls, grouped into 20 control families, covering areas such as access control, incident response, and system and communications protection. The selection process should involve:

  - o **Prioritizing controls based on risk level**: High-risk areas may require more stringent or complex controls, while lower-risk areas may be addressed with simpler measures.

  - o **Considering operational impact**: Controls should be feasible to implement and maintain, balancing security needs with business efficiency.

  - o **Adapting controls to specific organizational contexts**: For example, a healthcare organization might need to focus heavily on controls related to data encryption and patient privacy, while a financial institution might prioritize transaction security and fraud detection.

- **Develop policies and procedures**: After selecting the relevant controls, organizations must develop comprehensive policies and procedures that integrate the NIST 800-53 controls into daily operations. Policies should clearly define the expectations for security practices, compliance requirements, and the responsibilities of all stakeholders. Procedures should outline step-by-step guidance on how controls will be implemented, monitored, and enforced. The policy development phase should involve:

- Establishing clear roles and responsibilities for all the stakeholders across the organization, including IT personnel, security teams, compliance officers, and end-users.

- Documenting specific procedures for implementing and maintaining security controls. For example, access control protocols, incident response steps, data retention policies.

- Ensuring alignment with regulatory requirements. The policies should be designed to ensure ongoing compliance with industry standards and government regulations.

- **Train personnel**: A key element of effective implementation is ensuring that the personnel are trained on the importance of security controls and their specific roles in maintaining compliance. This step involves the following:

  - Developing a training program that includes both general security awareness and specific training on the new policies and procedures.

  - Conducting ongoing training sessions to keep all stakeholders up-to-date on evolving security threats, new regulatory requirements, and any changes to internal policies or controls.

  - Measuring the effectiveness of training through tests, feedback, and periodic assessments to ensure that employees understand their responsibilities and can effectively execute security practices.

- **Continuous monitoring and improvement**: The final step in the NIST 800-53 implementation process is to establish continuous monitoring mechanisms to evaluate the effectiveness of the selected controls and identify areas for improvement. Continuous monitoring is essential because the threat landscape is constantly evolving, and security controls must be regularly assessed and adjusted to remain effective. This step involves:

  - Implementing real-time monitoring tools to track system activity, user behavior, and potential security incidents. This might include network **intrusion detection systems** (**IDS**), **security information and event management** (**SIEM**) platforms, and automated vulnerability scanners.

  - Conducting periodic audits and assessments to ensure that controls are being properly implemented and remain aligned with organizational objectives and compliance requirements.

  - Establishing a feedback mechanism to capture lessons learned from security incidents, audits, and ongoing monitoring.

  - Regularly reviewing and updating controls based on changes in the organization's operations, the regulatory landscape, and the cybersecurity environment.

Key components of NIST SP 800-53

The NIST SP 800-53 Revision 5 framework organizes security and privacy controls into 20 families, ensuring that all aspects of an organization's security posture are covered. These families help organizations establish a holistic approach to managing risks, mitigating threats, and ensuring compliance with both security and privacy requirements. Following is some of the key control families in the NIST SP 800-53 framework:

- **Access Control (AC)**: This family includes controls that regulate who can access systems and data, enforcing authorization protocols to ensure that only authorized individuals have access to sensitive resources. AC mechanisms may include user authentication (passwords, biometrics), **role-based access control** (**RBAC**), and least privilege principles to minimize the potential for unauthorized access.

- **Awareness and Training (AT)**: These controls focus on educating personnel about security threats, policies, and best practices to ensure that the employees understand their roles in maintaining system security and data privacy. AT initiatives may include regular security training sessions, phishing simulations, and updates on emerging threats, helping employees recognize potential risks and respond appropriately.

- **Audit and Accountability (AU)**: This control family is focused on establishing mechanisms for tracking and recording computer activities, ensuring accountability for actions taken within information systems. Audit controls ensure that all access, changes, and data interactions are logged, enabling the organization to monitor system behavior and detect any suspicious or unauthorized activity.

- **Assessment, Authorization, and Monitoring (CA)**: This set of controls is designed to evaluate and validate the effectiveness of security controls and assess the overall security posture of systems. Assessment involves testing and reviewing security measures to identify any weaknesses or gaps. Authorization ensures that systems are approved for use based on their security posture. Monitoring involves ongoing surveillance of system activities and risks to detect and mitigate threats in real time.

- **Configuration Management (CM)**: The controls in this family focus on managing and documenting changes to system configurations that prevent vulnerabilities and unauthorized access. CM processes ensure that any changes to systems, whether software updates, patches, or hardware modifications are properly tested, authorized, and tracked.

- **Incident Response (IR)**: This family includes controls that define how an organization responds to security incidents, helping to ensure that incidents are addressed effectively and with minimal impact. IR plans include procedures for identifying, containing, and mitigating security breaches, as well as for communicating with stakeholders, including affected parties and regulatory bodies.

ISO/IEC 27001:2022

ISO/IEC 27001:2022 is the leading international standard focused on information security management, designed to help organizations protect their information assets and manage risks related to the security of data. ISO/IEC 27001:2022 is published by the ISO in partnership with the IEC. This standard sets out the criteria for establishing, implementing, maintaining, and continually improving an **information security management system** (**ISMS**). This system ensures that organizations have a structured approach to managing sensitive company data, safeguarding it from potential threats like cyberattacks, data breaches, and insider threats.

At its core, ISO/IEC 27001 is designed to ensure that an organization has implemented an effective system for managing the security of its information, encompassing both digital and physical data. The implementation of ISO/IEC 27001:2022 helps businesses address information security through a comprehensive framework, including risk assessment, controls, incident management, and continuous improvement. ISO/IEC 27001:2022 is applicable to organizations of all sizes and across various sectors, making it a versatile standard. The certification process involves a rigorous assessment by an external body, and organizations must demonstrate that they have established security policies, defined roles and responsibilities, conducted risk assessments, and implemented security controls to protect data.

ISO 27001:2022

ISO 27001:2022 is the latest version of ISO 27001 standard. ISO 27001:2022 introduces a revised set of Annex A controls, reducing the total from 114 to 93 and restructuring them into four main groups. Here is a breakdown of the control categories:

Control group	Number of controls	Examples
Organizational	37	Threat intelligence, **information and communication technology** (**ICT**) readiness, information security policies
People	8	Responsibilities for security, screening
Physical	14	Physical security monitoring, equipment protection
Technological	34	Web filtering, secure coding, data leakage prevention

Table 10.3: ISO 27001:2022 control categories

The clauses 4-10 of the ISO 27001:2022 outlines the key elements that organizations must address to build a comprehensive ISMS, but they do not specify individual controls. Instead, they focus on setting the strategic and organizational foundations for security management. The following figure shows the clauses of ISO 27001:2022:

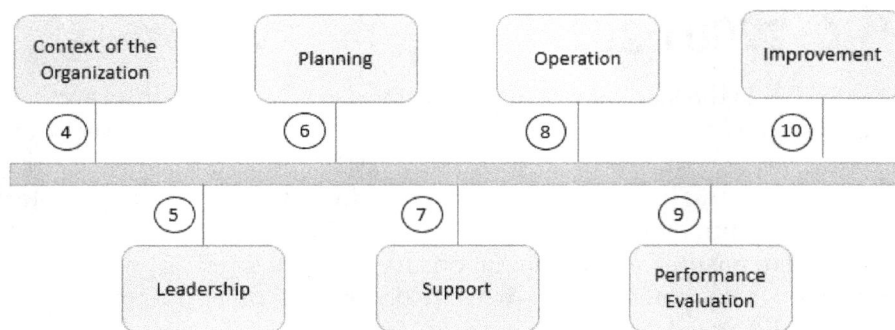

Figure 10.7: Clauses of ISO 27001:2022

Here is the breakdown of what each of these clauses addresses:

- **Clause 4—context of the organization**: This clause emphasizes the need for organizations to understand the internal and external factors that can affect their ISMS. It requires organizations to:

  o Define the scope of the ISMS, considering both internal and external issues that could impact information security.

  o Identify interested parties (such as customers, employees, and regulatory bodies) and their requirements regarding information security.

  o Establish the boundaries of the ISMS, clarifying which parts of the organization or its processes will be covered.

- **Clause 5—leadership**: Clause 5 emphasizes the critical role of top management in establishing and supporting the ISMS. It requires:

  o Clear leadership commitment to information security.

  o The appointment of a dedicated ISMS manager or team responsible for overseeing the implementation and ongoing maintenance of the ISMS.

  o Ensuring that information security objectives align with the organization's overall strategic goals.

  o Communication of the importance of effective information security to all employees.

- **Clause 6—planning**: Clause 6 outlines the requirements for risk assessment and the setting of information security objectives. It ensures that the ISMS is not only reactive to risks but also proactive in defining clear goals. Key elements include:

  o Conducting a thorough risk assessment to identify information security threats and vulnerabilities.

- Setting objectives to address identified risks and drive continual improvement in security measures.

- Planning for risk treatment strategies and the implementation of necessary security controls.

- **Clause 7—support**: Clause seven focuses on the resources, competence, awareness, and communication necessary to implement and maintain the ISMS effectively. This includes:

  - Ensuring that the appropriate resources (human, financial, technological) are available for the ISMS.

  - Providing training and awareness programs to ensure that all employees understand their roles in maintaining security.

  - Establishing effective communication channels for sharing information related to information security within the organization.

- **Clause 8—operation**: Clause 8 addresses how the ISMS will be implemented, monitored, and controlled to ensure it is effective in managing security risks. This involves:

  - Implementing the planned security controls.

  - Ensuring that the ISMS operates according to the defined security policies and procedures.

  - Monitoring the effectiveness of the controls and taking corrective actions when needed.

- **Clause 9—performance evaluation**: Clause 9 outlines the processes for monitoring, measurement, analysis, and evaluation of the ISMS. This includes:

  - Regularly assessing the effectiveness of the ISMS through audits, reviews, and risk assessments.

  - Monitoring security performance to ensure that security objectives are being met.

  - Evaluating the ISMS's overall effectiveness and identifying opportunities for improvement.

- **Clause 10—improvement**: Clause 10 focuses on the continuous improvement of the ISMS. It ensures that the organization is not static in its approach to information security but instead seeks to:

  - Correct any issues identified during audits or evaluations.

  - Continually improve the performance of the ISMS through lessons learned and feedback.

Key elements of ISO 27001:2022

ISO 27001:2022 certification emphasizes a comprehensive, risk-based approach to improve information security management. The key elements of ISO 27001 are described as follows:

- **ISMS framework**: The ISMS framework is the foundation of ISO 27001:2022. It provides a systematic structure of policies, procedures, and controls designed to manage information security risks. Clause 4.2 of ISO 27001:2022 specifically outlines the need for an ISMS that aligns organizational goals with security protocols. This alignment helps foster a culture of security awareness and compliance across the organization, ensuring that all employees, from top management to operational staff, understand their roles in protecting information assets.

- **Risk evaluation**: A core element of ISO 27001:2022 is the process of risk evaluation, which involves systematically identifying, assessing, and prioritizing potential security threats to the organization's data. This risk-based approach ensures that security measures are not only adequate but tailored to address the specific risks an organization faces. Risk evaluations help to determine the likelihood and potential impact of various threats, such as cyberattacks, data breaches, or natural disasters. By identifying risks early on, organizations can implement targeted controls to mitigate them.

- **ISO 27001 controls (Annex A)**: Annex A of ISO 27001:2022 provides a comprehensive set of controls designed to address various aspects of information security. These controls are categorized into 14 groups, covering a wide range of security domains such as access control, cryptography, physical security, incident management, and business continuity. Implementing these controls is essential for protecting the confidentiality, integrity, and availability of sensitive data. For example:

  - AC measures ensure that only authorized personnel can access critical systems and data.

  - Cryptography controls protect data during transmission and storage, ensuring its confidentiality and integrity.

  - Incident management procedures define how to detect, respond to, and recover from security incidents.

By adopting these controls, organizations ensure that their ISMS effectively mitigates risks, meets compliance requirements, and safeguards sensitive information from a range of threats. Regular audits and assessments of these controls help organizations stay ahead of new security challenges and continuously improve their information security posture.

Conclusion

In this chapter, we explored the critical aspects of configuration management and the best practices for implementing security controls to effectively manage risks. We also examined the importance of privacy control guidelines to ensure the secure handling of sensitive data. By understanding these foundational elements, we can better protect information systems and mitigate potential vulnerabilities.

Additionally, we understood industry standard frameworks like NIST SP 800-53 and ISO/IEC 27001:2022, highlighting key components and demonstrating how these standards can guide organizations in securing their systems and maintaining compliance. As we move into the next chapter, our focus will shift to the risk management lifecycle and the process of documenting security controls to ensure ongoing risk mitigation and system integrity.

Key terms

Some of the most common types of configuration management tools include:

- **Source control management (SCM) tools**: These tools track changes to source code, manage versioning, and facilitate collaboration. Examples are Git, Subversion, and Perforce.

- **Build management tools**: These tools automate the build process, including compiling code, running tests, and generating deployable artifacts. Examples are Jenkins and TeamCity.

- **Continuous integration (CI) tools**: CI tools automate the integration of code changes into a shared repository, run tests, and report any issues. Examples include Jenkins, and Bamboo.

- **Deployment automation tools**: These tools automate the deployment process, including environment configuration, artifact deployment, and rollback procedures. Examples are Ansible, Puppet, and Chef.

- There are two major tasks to be performed during the implementation phase of NIST RMF. task 1: Control implementation and task 2: Update control implementation information.

- ISO 27001:2022 integrates risk evaluation into the ISMS, involving risk assessment, risk treatment, and continuous monitoring.

- Data anonymization involves removing or encrypting sensitive information in a data set so as to protect individuals' privacy without impacting data storage and use.

- **Data loss prevention (DLP)** is a privacy control aimed primarily at detecting and avoiding instances in which data is leaked, inappropriately accessed, or inadvertently destroyed.

- Configuration control is the process of controlling modifications to hardware, firmware, software, and documentation to protect the information system against improper modifications before, during, and after system implementation.

CHAPTER 11
Documenting Security Controls

Introduction

This chapter provides a comprehensive overview of risk governance, focusing on the key elements required for effective risk management within an organization. It emphasizes the importance of understanding the risk management lifecycle, which ensures that risks are continuously identified, assessed, and addressed throughout the organization's operations. The chapter further explores the residual risk calculation process, providing a clear methodology for evaluating the remaining risks after mitigation efforts are implemented.

Additionally, the chapter highlights the use of a risk register, an essential tool for documenting and tracking identified risks, their potential impacts, and the response strategies in place. It underscores the importance of maintaining a proactive risk management approach. Moreover, the chapter delves into various risk treatment strategies, outlining the steps organizations should take to effectively address risks. These strategies include risk avoidance, reduction, transfer, and retention, each tailored to the specific nature of the risk and the organization's objectives.

Structure

The chapter covers the following main topics:

- Risk governance
- Risk management lifecycle
- Security assessment
- Residual risk
- Reducing residual risk by SDLC
- Risk register
- Risk treatment

Objectives

By the end of this chapter, you will gain a strong understanding of the risk governance framework, which is essential for fostering a robust risk culture within an organization. You will learn about the risk management lifecycle, a comprehensive approach to manage risks from identification to mitigation, ensuring that risks are addressed at every stage. This chapter will also introduce you to the concepts of inherent risk and residual risk, helping you understand the importance of applying mitigating controls to reduce risks to acceptable levels.

Furthermore, this chapter will outline the key components of a risk register, demonstrating how it serves as a critical tool for tracking, documenting, and managing risks proactively. You will also explore various risk treatment methodologies and learn how to develop an effective risk treatment plan to address and manage identified risks. Through this chapter, you will gain practical insights into managing risks in a structured and efficient way, aligning risk management practices with organizational goals to ensure sustainable success.

Risk governance

Risk governance refers to the framework and processes through which an organization manages its risks in a structured, accountable, and effective manner. It involves the oversight, decision-making, and accountability mechanisms for identifying, assessing, mitigating, and monitoring risks at all levels of the organization. Risk governance ensures that the organization's risk management practices are aligned with its strategic objectives, regulatory requirements, and stakeholders' interests and that risk-related decisions are made in a transparent and consistent way.

Some key elements of risk governance are as follows:

- **Governance structure**: Risk governance is a clear structure that defines roles, responsibilities, and reporting lines for managing risk. This typically includes the board of directors, executive leadership, risk committees, and other relevant stakeholders. The board is ultimately responsible for overseeing the organization's risk management efforts, while senior management ensures that these efforts are executed at the operational level. Following are the examples of risk governance structure:

Governance role	Responsibilities
Board	Provides policy, oversight and review of risk management.
Audit and risk committee	Overseas regular review of risk management activities.
Chief executive officer	Drives culture of risk management and signs off on annual risk attestation.
Risk manager	Continuously improving risk management policy, strategy and supporting framework.
Managers	Ensure staff in their business units comply with the risk management policy and foster a culture where risks can be identified and escalated.
Staff and contractors	Comply with risk management policies and procedures.

Table 11.1: Risk governance structure

- **Risk Management Framework** :
    - A robust Risk Management Framework provides the foundation for identifying, assessing, and managing risks across the organization. This includes policies, procedures, tools, and methodologies for dealing with risks. It typically integrates with other management systems (such as strategic planning, compliance, internal controls, and financial management) to provide a holistic approach to risk governance.
    - Frameworks such as ISO 31000, *Committee of Sponsoring Organizations* (*COSO*) **enterprise risk management** (**ERM**), or the COSO internal control framework provide guidelines and standards for managing risk effectively across organizations.

- **Risk appetite and tolerance**:
    - Risk governance involves setting clear parameters around the organization's risk appetite (the level of risk the organization is willing to take) and risk tolerance (the acceptable variation in performance relative to risk). These

concepts are critical for ensuring that risk management activities align with the organization's strategic objectives, financial capacity, and operational priorities.

o The board and executive leadership play key roles in defining risk appetite and tolerance, which guide the decisions made at all levels of the organization.

- **Risk identification and assessment**:

  o One of the key functions of risk governance is to ensure that risks are systematically identified, assessed, and prioritized. This requires understanding both internal (e.g., operational, financial, and cultural) and external risks (e.g., market changes, economic conditions, legal and regulatory risks).

  o Risk assessments should be regularly conducted to evaluate the likelihood, impact, and potential consequences of various risks on the organization's strategic objectives, operations, and reputation.

- **Risk mitigation and treatment**:

  o Once risks are identified and assessed, risk governance ensures that appropriate treatment plans are developed. This involves deciding on the most effective strategies (e.g., avoidance, reduction, transfer, or acceptance) for managing risks and then implementing these strategies across the organization.

  o Risk treatment is integrated into the organization's operations, with clear responsibilities and timelines for mitigating or managing risks.

- **Monitoring and reporting**:

  o An effective risk governance framework includes mechanisms for continuously monitoring and reviewing the organization's risk landscape. Regular reporting allows the board and management to stay informed about the status of key risks, the effectiveness of risk treatment measures, and emerging threats.

  o **Key risk indicators (KRIs)** are often used to monitor risk levels, meanwhile reporting should be structured to ensure that senior leaders are alerted to critical risks in a timely manner.

- **Compliance and legal oversight**:

  o In many organizations, risk governance is also closely tied to compliance efforts, ensuring that risks related to legal, regulatory, and ethical requirements are appropriately managed.

o Effective governance also ensures that risk management practices are aligned with legal and regulatory frameworks, such as *Sarbanes-Oxley (SOX) Act*, *General Data Protection Regulation (GDPR)*, and other relevant compliance standards.

- **Stakeholder communication**:

    o Transparent communication with stakeholders, both internal and external, is a critical component of risk governance. This ensures that stakeholders understand the organization's risk profile, how risks are being managed, and how risk governance aligns with overall strategic goals.

    o Regular communication of the organization's risk strategy and performance is often done through annual reports, investor briefings, and sustainability disclosures.

Risk management lifecycle

The risk management lifecycle is a continuous, dynamic process that helps organizations identify, assess, and mitigate risks that could impact their operations. It begins with understanding both internal activities (such as organizational practices, systems, and processes) and external threats (like cyberattacks, natural disasters, or regulatory changes) that could introduce risks to the organization. Recognizing the nature of these risks is the first step in creating a resilient and secure operational framework. This ongoing process does not have a defined start or end but evolves with the organization's needs and the changing threat landscape.

Once risks are identified, the next phase of the lifecycle is risk assessment. This involves analyzing the potential impact and likelihood of each risk, considering factors such as financial consequences, reputational damage, or operational disruptions. During this phase, organizations assess various solutions for reducing or eliminating identified risks. These solutions might include implementing new security controls, adjusting processes, or enhancing employee training. After thorough analysis, decision-making follows, where the organization decides on the appropriate course of action of whether to accept, transfer, mitigate, or avoid the risk altogether. The lifecycle continues with the implementation of chosen solutions, followed by monitoring and review to ensure that the measures are effective and that new risks are continuously identified and addressed. The following figure shows the risk management lifecycle from identification untill monitoring:

Figure 11.1: *Risk management lifecycle*

Here is the explanation of the risk management lifecycle process:

- **Risk identification**: Risk identification is the crucial first step in the risk management process. It involves systematically recognizing potential threats or opportunities that could impact an organization or project. Identifying these risks early allows teams to mitigate or capitalize on them effectively. Different types of risks require distinct approaches to management, and these risks can generally be categorized into strategic, operational, financial, and hazard risks:

  o **Strategic risks**: These risks are linked to changes in the business environment, shifts in market dynamics, or alterations in an organization's long-term strategy. For example, the emergence of new competitors, technological advancements, or regulatory changes can disrupt a company's market position or strategic direction.

  o **Operational risks**: These risks stem from the day-to-day activities of an organization. This includes failures in critical business processes, systems, or resources, as well as human errors or lapses in internal controls.

  o **Financial risks**: These risks are tied to the economic and financial aspects of an organization. They encompass fluctuations in market prices, interest rates, credit risks, and currency exchange rates, which could affect profitability, cash flow, or the organization's financial stability.

  o **Hazard risks**: These are associated with physical events such as natural disasters (earthquakes, floods), accidents, or other external events that could cause significant damage to an organization's assets or operations.

Here are the main techniques and approaches used during this phase:

o   **Documentation review**: Documentation review involves a detailed analysis of project documents, contracts, historical data, and relevant records to identify potential risks. By examining past projects and contractual clauses, organizations can gain valuable insights into issues that may have arisen in similar situations, helping to predict and mitigate future risks.

o   **Brainstorming sessions**: Brainstorming sessions are a collaborative approach where project team members, stakeholders, or cross-functional groups come together to generate ideas about potential risks, both positive and negative, that could impact the project. This process encourages creative thinking and diverse perspectives, enabling the identification of a wide range of possible risks.

o   **Checklists**: Checklists are standardized lists of known risks derived from past projects or industry standards designed to ensure comprehensive coverage of potential risk areas. By using these checklists, project teams can systematically assess and address common risks that may be easily overlooked, particularly in industries with well-established risk patterns.

o   **SWOT analysis**: **strengths, weaknesses, opportunities, and threats** (**SWOT**) analysis is a strategic planning tool used to assess an organization or project's SWOT. This analysis helps identify both internal and external factors that could present risks or opportunities, enabling teams to develop informed strategies.

o   **Expert interviews**: Expert interviews involve consulting **Subject Matter Experts** (**SMEs**) with deep knowledge in specific areas to identify risks that may not be immediately apparent through general risk identification methods. By leveraging their specialized expertise, organizations can uncover niche or technical risks that could otherwise be overlooked.

•   **Risk analysis**: Risk analysis is the process of evaluating identified risks to understand their likelihood, impact, and severity. It helps prioritize which risks need immediate attention and resources. Key factors in this stage include:

o   **Probability assessment**: This involves determining the likelihood of each risk occurring, using historical data, expert judgment, and statistical methods. It helps in estimating how probable a risk is based on past trends or available evidence.

o   **Impact assessment**: Here, the potential consequences of each risk on project objectives (such as cost, quality, schedule, or reputation) are assessed. This step considers how much damage or disruption each risk could cause if it materializes.

o   **Risk prioritization**: Risks are prioritized based on both their probability and impact. This enables the team to focus resources and mitigation efforts on the most critical and high-priority risks, ensuring the best use of available resources.

- o **Qualitative and quantitative analysis**: Risk analysis uses both qualitative techniques (such as risk matrices or expert judgment) and quantitative methods (like Monte Carlo simulations or decision tree analysis). Qualitative methods provide a broad overview, while quantitative methods provide more detailed, data-driven insights into the likelihood and potential financial impact of each risk.

- **Risk mitigation planning**: Risk mitigation planning is the process of developing strategies and actions to reduce or manage the impact of identified risks, ensuring that an organization can continue pursuing its objectives while minimizing potential disruptions. The strategies for mitigating risks will vary based on the type of risk and the organization's risk tolerance and goals.

Key components of risk mitigation strategies include the following:

- o **Risk tolerance**: This involves determining the level of risk the organization is willing to accept without negatively affecting its objectives. Understanding risk tolerance helps in deciding which risks require attention and which can be managed more casually.

- o **Risk avoidance**: This strategy involves changing the scope, requirements, or approach of a project to completely eliminate a risk. For example, a project might be redesigned or a particular feature omitted to avoid a potential risk, such as a technology failure or regulatory compliance issue.

- o **Risk transference**: This involves shifting the burden of the risk to a third-party, often through mechanisms like insurance, outsourcing, or contractual agreements. For example, a company might transfer financial risk-related to property damage to an insurance provider or use contracts to shift responsibility for delivery delays to a supplier.

- o **Risk mitigation**: This strategy focuses on reducing the likelihood or impact of a risk through proactive measures. It may involve developing contingency plans, building redundancy into systems or processes, improving operational procedures, or implementing safety measures to minimize exposure to risk.

- o **Risk acceptance**: In some cases, organizations may choose to accept the risk as it is, acknowledging its existence and potential consequences without taking specific action. This decision is often made when the cost of mitigation is higher than the potential impact of the risk or when the risk falls within the organization's acceptable tolerance level.

Based on impact, likelihood, and tolerance, you have four primary risk responses to choose from as shown in figure:

Figure 11.2: Risk response

- **Risk management implementation**: Risk management implementation is the stage where risk management plans are put into action, ensuring that risks are actively monitored, mitigated, and managed throughout the project or organizational process. Key elements of this stage include:

    o **Stakeholder engagement**: It is crucial to involve stakeholders throughout the implementation process to ensure their buy-in and support. Engaging stakeholders helps align risk management efforts with the expectations and interests of key parties, increasing the likelihood of successful risk mitigation.

    o **Communication strategies**: Clear and consistent communication channels are established to disseminate information about risks and mitigation strategies. Effective communication ensures that all relevant parties are informed of potential risks, the actions being taken to address them, and any changes in risk status.

    o **Monitoring and control**: Mechanisms must be implemented to continuously monitor identified risks and the effectiveness of mitigation strategies. This can include regular progress reviews, performance indicators, and risk assessments to ensure that risks are being managed as planned and that mitigation efforts are on track.

    o **Adaptation and adjustment**: Risk management plans should remain flexible and adaptable. As new information becomes available or circumstances change, the risk management plan should be adjusted to address emerging risks or shifts in existing ones. This ongoing adaptation ensures that the organization remains proactive in managing risks throughout the project lifecycle.

The following figure shows the common risk management strategies:

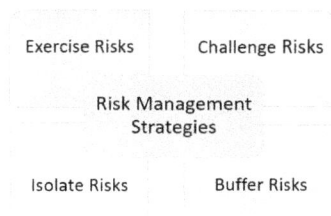

Figure 11.3: Risk management strategies

The exercise risk involves simulating risk scenarios through tabletop exercises to test responses and prepare for potential threats. The challenge risk focuses on proactively identifying and addressing risks before they escalate. The buffer risk entails creating contingency plans to manage the impact of identified risks, ensuring the organization can recover smoothly. The isolate risk aims to contain or minimize the impact of specific risks by implementing controls that limit their spread or severity.

- **Risk monitoring and review**: Risk monitoring and review is an ongoing process that ensures the effectiveness of risk management plans throughout the lifecycle of a project or operation. This stage involves regularly assessing and adjusting risk strategies to address new challenges and opportunities. Key components include:

  - **Regular reviews**: Periodic reviews of the risk management plan are conducted to evaluate its alignment with project objectives, ensuring that risks are still being appropriately managed as conditions evolve. These reviews also help identify any new risks that may arise during the course of the project.

  - **Performance metrics**: Establishing specific metrics to measure the success of risk mitigation efforts helps track progress and effectiveness. These metrics can include the frequency and impact of risk events, the timeliness of mitigation actions, and the cost-effectiveness of risk management strategies, highlighting areas where improvements may be needed.

  - **Risk reporting**: Regular reports are provided to stakeholders, offering updates on risk trends, any new or emerging risks, and the overall status of risk management activities. Transparent communication keeps all parties informed and ensures that risk management efforts remain aligned with stakeholder expectations.

  - **Lessons learned**: Capturing lessons learned from past risk management experiences is vital for continuous improvement. By analyzing what worked well and what did not, teams can apply these insights to future projects, avoiding past mistakes and enhancing risk management practices.

  - **Root cause analysis**: When risk events occur, conducting a root cause analysis helps identify underlying systemic issues that contributed to the risk materializing. This deeper understanding allows for corrective actions to be taken, ensuring that similar risks are less likely to recur in the future.

Security assessment

Organizations need to ensure that control assessors have the necessary skills and technical expertise to effectively evaluate system controls, including system-specific, hybrid, common, and program management controls. These assessors should have a good understanding of risk management and be familiar with the specific hardware, software, and firmware components in use. Control assessments are carried out as part of the system's initial authorization, ongoing monitoring, and annual evaluations, as well as throughout the **system development lifecycle** (**SDLC**) and security engineering processes.

The purpose of these assessments is to verify that security and privacy requirements are met, identify system weaknesses, and support informed decision-making. Assessments can be conducted at various stages of the SDLC, such as during design reviews and when controls are implemented. Regular assessments help ensure that vulnerabilities are mitigated and that controls are working as expected. Organizations can create a single consolidated security and privacy assessment plan or maintain separate plans, depending on the structure. A coordinated approach to assessments can reduce redundancies and costs, especially when multiple organizations are involved.

To maintain system security and privacy throughout the lifecycle, organizations may also use activities like vulnerability scanning and system monitoring. Assessment results are documented in reports, which help determine if the controls are working as intended. These reports are shared with relevant stakeholders, such as authorizing officials and senior security officers, to ensure that decisions are made based on accurate information. Additionally, assessment results can be reused and supplemented over time, ensuring that controls remain effective and that the organization remains compliant with security and privacy requirements.

Configuration deviations

National Institute of Standards and Technology (*NIST*) configuration settings recommend that organizations need to identify, document, and approve any deviations from established configuration baselines to maintain security and privacy in systems. Here is simplified breakdown of how it works:

- **Identify deviations**: Organizations should be in a position to monitor their systems to identify deviations from the set of configuration settings. These may be caused by changes during system updates, patches, or if certain settings were changed for operational requirements.

- **Document deviations**: When a deviation is identified, it should be documented in detail. It should contain the nature of changes, the reason for the deviation, implications on security or privacy, and how it would affect the compliance of the system against the set security and privacy requirements.

- **Approval of deviations**: Any deviation should not be applied until approved by interested stakeholders. Approvals will imply that the deviation is understood and justified in terms of security and privacy policies of the organization, as well as risk mitigation strategies identified and implemented accordingly.

Residual risk

Residual risk refers to the remaining risk after mitigation or transfer efforts have been applied to reduce the impact or likelihood of an original risk. It represents the portion of the risk that could not be fully eliminated through the risk treatment strategies. For example, if a threat originally had a 10% probability of occurring and mitigation efforts reduce this to 1%, the residual risk is the remaining 1%. The relationship between the original, mitigated, transferred, and residual risks can be summarized by the following formula:

Figure 11.4: Calculation of residual risk

In most cases, risk treatment does not eliminate all risk; instead, it reduces it to an acceptable level. For example, implementing security controls might reduce the likelihood of a cyberattack but will not entirely eliminate the risk of a breach. While management often implicitly accepts the remaining residual risk, it is a best practice to formally acknowledge this acceptance by documenting it in a risk register or decision log. This documentation helps ensure that the decision to accept the residual risk is deliberate, transparent, and aligned with organizational risk tolerance. Let us see how to calculate residual risk.

To calculate residual risk, an organization follows a systematic approach that accounts for both the inherent risks in a process or system and the effectiveness of mitigating controls implemented. Here is how you can calculate residual risk step-by-step:

1. **Calculate the inherent risk factor**: Inherent risk refers to the level of risk that exists in a process or system before any mitigation efforts (such as controls or safeguards) are applied. It is a measure of the natural risk posed by a situation or event without taking any preventive measures into account. The most important aspect is to assess the likelihood and impact.

    a. **Assess the likelihood**: How probable is the risk occurring?

    b. **Assess the impact**: If the risk occurs, what is the potential damage or consequences?

Typically, an organization can use a risk matrix or a risk assessment scale to score inherent risk. For example:

* **Likelihood**: 1 (low) to 5 (high)
* **Impact**: 1 (low) to 5 (high)

The inherent risk factor is often calculated by multiplying likelihood and impact (or using other scoring systems specific to the organization).

$$Inherent\ risk = Likelihood \times Impact$$

2. **Identify acceptable levels of risk**: Once the inherent risk has been identified, an organization needs to determine what level of risk is acceptable to the organization. Acceptable risk is the amount of risk the organization is willing to tolerate, considering factors like cost, resource constraints, and the potential impact of the risk.

This will depend on factors such as:

   a. **Risk tolerance**: The level of risk the organization can accept without negatively affecting its objectives or operations.

   b. **Regulatory or legal limits**: Certain industries may have specific acceptable risk levels defined by law or regulation.

Typically, acceptable risk levels are defined in terms like:

   a. **Low**: Risk is very unlikely to cause significant harm.

   b. **Medium**: Risk may cause some harm, but it is manageable.

   c. **High**: Risk could have a severe impact and needs immediate action.

Assign weights for all mitigating controls: Mitigating controls are actions, policies, or procedures implemented to reduce the likelihood or impact of identified risks. These can include safety measures, security protocols, insurance, or other safeguards.

For each mitigating control, an organization need to do the following:

   a. **Identify the control**: What measures have been implemented?

   b. **Assess its effectiveness**: How well does the control reduce the likelihood or impact of the risk?

Assign each control a weight based on its effectiveness. The weight could range from:

   a. **0 (no mitigation)**: The control does not reduce the risk.

   b. **1 (partially effective)**: The control reduces risk but does not eliminate it.

   c. **2 (highly effective)**: The control significantly reduces risk.

The weighted effectiveness of each control should be considered in relation to the inherent risk.

3. **Calculate the residual risk**: Residual risk is the remaining risk after mitigating controls have been applied. It accounts for any risks that still exist after all reasonable mitigation efforts. The organization can subtract the weighted control effectiveness values directly from the inherent risk score to calculate the residual risk, which is shown as follows:

Residual risk = Inherent risk – Mitigated risk – Transferred risk

If the residual risk is equal to or lower than the risk tolerance threshold, then organization are within the acceptable risk range. For example, if the acceptable risk threshold is 8 (on a scale from 1 to 25), and the residual risk after controls is 6, organization are within tolerance because $6 \leq 8$.

Documenting residual risk

Residual risk documentation within ISO 27001 is a very important aspect of ISMS. ISO 27001 requires identifying, assessing, treating, and constantly monitoring information security risks. Residual risk refers to those risks that remain after mitigation has been applied. Proper recording of the residual risks should be done in order to allow for transparency and accountability in the demonstration of commitment to information security management. Documenting residual risk helps organization in following ways:

- **Risk assessment and treatment**: The risks that remain after applying controls are usually the ones for which acceptance is considered and are called **residual risks**. Documenting them means that the organization is fully aware of the remaining risks and has made an informed decision to accept them instead of just ignoring them.

- **Management review and decision**: Documenting residual risks gives top management a very fair view of the residual risks, thus helping in making of informed decisions about the acceptance of such risk, its further mitigation, or its transfer.

- **Compliance evidence**: The organization should document its risk treatment decisions and justify the acceptance of the residual risks. This document should be evidence during audits to prove that compliance was followed in accordance with the ISO 27001 standard.

- **Continual improvement**: Documentation of residual risk provides a track of changes and improvements over a period of time. ISO 27001 is based on the principle of continual improvement, so recording residual risks will help the organization understand if the risk treatment processes are working effectively and allow them to make adjustments in further risk management cycles.

- **Accountability and transparency**: Residual risk should be documented to allow transparency within the organization about the level of risk being accepted. It provides very clear audit trails for compliance purposes to support accountability in the management of risks at every level.

Reducing residual risk by SDLC

The security controls should be assessed and implemented in earlier phase of SDLC to minimize residual risks by addressing vulnerabilities during design and development. Identifying and mitigating the risks early on will help organizations to integrate security into the foundation of the system, rather than retrofitting it after development is complete. This way, potential weaknesses are addressed before they become bigger, complex and more expensive to fix. In this regard, early implementation of controls leads to a more secure end product. Early integration decreases the chances of architectural, code-level, and design-level security flaws, reducing the residual risks after applying controls.

Secondly, it encourages cost and resource efficiency. It is also easy to introduce measures in the phase of planning and designing rather than afterward, at considerably less expense. This further aids in responding effectively to strict standards and guidelines related to specific industries by baking security requirements from the beginning of a system lifecycle. By reducing vulnerabilities from the outset, organizations not only protect their systems but also enhance stakeholder confidence, ease incident response processes, and ensure a smoother path toward meeting both business and security objectives.

Risk register

All types of organizations face a broad range of risks, from cybersecurity and financial to operational, legal, reputational, privacy, safety, strategic, and supply chain risks. Identifying which risks are most critical and ensuring that high-priority risks, such as cybersecurity and supply chain disruptions, receive the appropriate level of attention can be challenging. Organizations must not only recognize the full spectrum of potential risks, but also allocate resources effectively to mitigate them.

This is where risk registers play a pivotal role. A risk register serves as a vital tool for senior leaders and decision-makers, allowing them to document, track, and manage the risks faced by the organization. By providing a comprehensive view of both existing and emerging risks, a risk register helps to prioritize those that could have the most significant impact on the organization's ability to meet its objectives. It acts as an organized, accessible repository for risk information, ensuring that no critical risks, such as cybersecurity vulnerabilities or supply chain interruptions, are ignored. For organizations committed to maintaining a robust risk management process, creating and maintaining a risk register is a crucial step in ensuring effective and proactive risk management.

Risk register integration

A risk register can be seamlessly integrated into any risk management methodology an organization follows. Many widely recognized frameworks, such as those provided by the COSO, the *Office of Management and Budget* (*OMB*), and the *International Organization for Standardization* (*ISO*), document established processes for ERM. These frameworks outline a similar, systematic approach: Identifying the context, assessing risks, analyzing risk, estimating risk importance, executing a risk response, and continually monitoring changes over time. A risk register is integral to this process, serving as a tool to track and communicate risk information across all stages of risk management, providing the essential input for decision-makers to act on.

The importance of a risk register becomes even clearer in the context of cybersecurity. The NIST, in its latest document, *Integrating Cybersecurity and Enterprise Risk Management*, observed that many organizations do not assess or manage cybersecurity risks with the same consistency as other types of risks. NIST's guidance aims to improve the quality of cyber risk data that organizations gather and provide to management, ensuring that decision-makers can take informed actions to mitigate potential cybersecurity threats. By integrating cybersecurity risk management into the broader Risk Management Framework , NIST seeks to enhance the organization's ability to protect its assets while supporting its core business objectives.

Layers of risk register

In risk management, it is common to maintain multiple layers of risk registers to address different levels of risks within an organization. These layers help to ensure that the risks are captured, categorized, and managed according to their scope and impact. Typically, organizations maintain three primary types of risk registers: Entity-level risk, program-level risk, and asset-level risk, seen in the following figure:

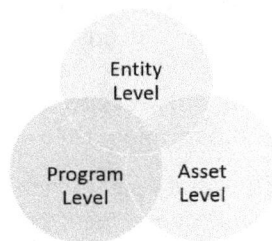

Figure 11.5: Risk register levels

Let us look at them in detail:

- **Entity-level risk register**: At the entity-level, the risk register captures risks that have the potential to affect the entire organization. These are broad, overarching risks that can influence the organization's strategic direction, financial health, and long-term sustainability. Examples include:

  o **Workforce-related risks**: Risks associated with talent retention, employee turnover, or workforce shortages.

  o **Macroeconomic risks**: Broad economic risks tied to business cycles, such as recessions, inflation, or shifts in global trade.

  o **Cultural risks**: Risks that stem from the organization's culture, such as poor communication or lack of diversity, that can affect organizational effectiveness.

- **Program-level risk register**: The program-level risk register is focused on specific business processes or programs within the organization. These risks are more tactical and relate to the day-to-day operations or initiatives aimed at achieving the organization's goals. Examples of risks at this level include:

- **Effectiveness of vulnerability management**: If the IT department is neglecting in applying security patches or updates to software and systems. This creates a risk that needs to be documented and mitigated.

- **Identity management**: Poor management of user access rights, such as failure to properly handle employee onboarding, access requests, and offboarding, can lead to security vulnerabilities or unauthorized data access.

- **Bring your own device (BYOD) risks**: Without adequate controls over employee's personal devices, there is a risk of critical data leakage, especially if devices are not properly secured or if sensitive data is accessed via insecure networks.

- **Asset-level risk register**: The asset-level risk register focuses on individual assets or groups of assets, capturing risks associated with the physical or digital resources that are vital to the organization's operations. These risks tend to be more specific and technical, often identified using automated scanning tools or regular asset audits. Examples include:

  - **Misconfiguration of critical devices**: Improperly configured servers or network devices could lead to security vulnerabilities or system downtime.

  - **Missing critical patches**: Unpatched software or firmware on key systems can expose the organization to cyberattacks or operational failures.

  - **Unmanaged devices**: New devices that connect to the network without proper oversight can present security risks if they are not adequately secured or monitored.

While each risk register focuses on a different level of the organization, effective communication between these layers is essential for comprehensive risk management. The entity-level risk register provides the strategic context within which program-level and asset-level risks should be understood. For example, a program-level risk like vulnerability management may escalate to the entity-level if it is found to have a widespread impact on the organization's reputation or finances. Similarly, a failure at the asset-level (e.g., a critical system being compromised due to a missing patch) may be reported up to the program-level to ensure that appropriate mitigation strategies are implemented across the organization.

To ensure a cohesive risk management strategy, there should be clear reporting structures that allow for a seamless flow of information between levels. Program managers should report high-priority risks to senior leaders, while asset owners should alert the risk management team about technical risks that may affect overall business continuity. This collaborative approach helps keep all levels aligned and ensures that the organization can respond to risks promptly and effectively, reducing exposure to potential threats across its operations.

Risk register record

At a minimum, each risk entry should include a clear description of the risk, an assessment of its likelihood of occurring, an evaluation of its potential impact from a cost perspective, a ranking of the risk's priority relative to others, the chosen response (mitigation, transfer, acceptance, or avoidance), and the identification of the risk owner responsible for managing and monitoring the risk. The following table shows the content of the risk register:

Risk register element	Descriptions
ID (risk identifier)	A sequential numeric identifier for referring to risk in the risk register.
Priority	A relative indicator of the criticality of this entry in the risk register, either expressed in ordinal value (e.g., 1, 2, 3) or in reference to a given scale (e.g. high, moderate, low).
Risk description	A brief explanation of the risk scenario (potentially) impacting the organization and enterprise.
Current likelihood	An estimation of the probability, before any risk response, that this scenario will occur.
Current impact	Analysis of the potential benefits or consequences that might result from this scenario if no additional response is provided.
Current exposure rating	A calculation of the probability of risk exposure based on the likelihood estimate and the determined benefits or consequences of the risk.
Risk response type	The risk response (sometimes referred to as the **risk treatment**) for handling the identified risk.
Risk response description	A brief description of the risk response. For example, implement software management application XYZ to ensure that software platforms and applications are inventoried.
Risk owner	The designated party who is responsible and accountable for ensuring that the risk is maintained in accordance with enterprise requirements.
Status	A field for tracking the current condition of the risk.

Table 11.2: Risk register components

Risk treatment

Risk treatment refers to the set of strategies, actions, and approaches an organization selects to address and respond to identified risks, with the goal of reducing or managing those risks to an acceptable level. It encompasses all the tactics used to mitigate, transfer, accept, or avoid risks in order to achieve the desired outcome—whether that is minimizing the likelihood of the risk event occurring, reducing its potential impact, or both.

However, risk treatment should not be viewed in isolation. It is inherently a part of the broader risk management process, which is a continuous and integrated approach that includes identifying, assessing, and responding to risks across an organization. Effective risk treatment requires a deep understanding of the organization's objectives, the nature of the risk, and the broader context in which the risk exists. This holistic perspective ensures that treatment strategies align with the organization's overall goals and risk appetite.

Risk treatment steps

The risk treatment process involves a structured approach to addressing identified risks, ensuring that the chosen strategies are effective in minimizing the potential impact of those risks while aligning with the organization's overall objectives. The process can be broken down into the following five main steps, each of which is crucial for ensuring the correct logistics and effectiveness of the risk treatment strategy:

- **Brainstorming and selecting the right risk treatment option**: The first step involves generating a range of possible strategies to address the identified risk. This typically involves brainstorming sessions with relevant stakeholders, such as risk managers, department heads, or subject matter experts. The goal is to identify and evaluate different risk treatment options based on factors, like cost, feasibility, effectiveness, and alignment with the organization's goals. Options typically include risk avoidance, risk reduction (mitigation), risk sharing (transfer), or risk acceptance. Once a range of options is identified, the most appropriate treatment strategy is selected based on the organization's risk appetite and the nature of the risk.

- **Planning and use of options chosen**: After selecting the most suitable risk treatment options, the next step is to develop a detailed plan for implementation. This plan should specify the actions to be taken, resources required, timelines, and responsibilities. For instance, if the chosen strategy is risk mitigation, the plan might outline the specific security measures to be implemented, the personnel responsible, and the deadlines for completing these actions. This step ensures that the risk treatment options are not only theoretical but also practically actionable and that clear instructions are in place for executing the response.

- **Examining the effectiveness of the chosen tactics**: Once the risk treatment measures are implemented, it is crucial to assess their effectiveness in managing the risk. This may involve monitoring the risk over time, gathering feedback from stakeholders, and conducting assessments or audits. The aim is to determine whether the chosen tactics are successfully reducing the likelihood or impact of the risk. If, for example, the mitigation strategy was to implement a new cybersecurity protocol, an organization might review system logs or conduct penetration testing to ensure the new protocol is effective at preventing breaches. Regular assessments are vital to ensure that the organization is not blind to new or evolving risks.

- **Deciding whether the level of residual risk is acceptable or not**: After evaluating the effectiveness of the risk treatment actions, the next step is to assess the residual risk that remains after treatment measures have been applied. At this stage, decision-makers must determine if the level of residual risk is within the organization's risk tolerance. If the residual risk is deemed acceptable based on the organization's risk appetite, then the treatment process can be considered complete. However, if the residual risk exceeds the acceptable threshold, further actions must be taken.

- **Implementing new risk treatment activities (if necessary)**: If the residual risk is not acceptable, additional steps must be taken to reduce it further. This may involve implementing more stringent mitigation strategies, reallocating resources, or employing new tactics to bring the residual risk within an acceptable range. For example, if a cybersecurity mitigation tactic (such as a firewall update) did not fully reduce the risk, the organization might opt for additional measures like **multifactor authentication** (MFA), staff training, or more frequent security audits. The process is iterative, and the risk treatment activities are adjusted until the residual risk is adequately controlled.

Risk treatment strategies

When addressing risks, it is important to recognize that there is no one-size-fits-all solution. Each threat or risk needs to be evaluated on its own merits, and the treatment strategy should be tailored to fit the specific circumstances and potential impact of that risk. Risk treatment involves applying the most appropriate approach to manage the risk, which may vary depending on the type of risk, the organization's goals, and its available resources. To ensure the correct strategy is chosen, a detailed analysis must be conducted, considering factors such as the organization's overall risk strategy, available resources, objectives, and the cost-benefit trade-off of each option:

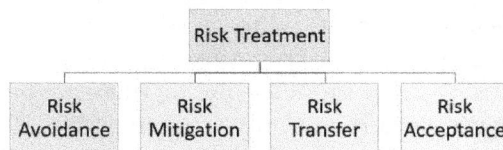

Figure 11.6: Risk treatment options

Here are the four primary risk treatment options commonly used:

- **Risk avoidance**: Risk avoidance involves changing the course of action or modifying plans to eliminate the risk entirely. This is usually the most drastic response and is applied when the potential impact of the risk is too great or when the risk can be entirely prevented by altering the current strategy. For example, an organization might decide to discontinue a high-risk business activity, such as a particular product line or market expansion, if the associated risks (e.g., regulatory uncertainty, high financial cost) are deemed unacceptable. While risk avoidance is effective at removing a threat, it may not always be feasible or desirable, especially if the activity is critical to the organization's success.

  Example: A company that faces a significant environmental risk in one of its manufacturing plants may decide to avoid the risk by moving its operations to a location with less environmental threat.

- **Risk reduction (mitigation)**: Risk reduction (or mitigation) focuses on reducing the likelihood or impact of a risk, rather than eliminating it entirely. This approach is often used when the risk is unavoidable but can be controlled to some extent. The goal of risk reduction is to lessen the impact or probability of the risk occurring through preventive measures, controls, or contingency planning. For example, a company might implement enhanced cybersecurity measures to reduce the risk of a data breach, such as encrypting sensitive information, conducting regular security audits, and providing employee training on phishing scams.

  Example: An organization may mitigate the risk of data loss by implementing regular backups, employing encryption, and using multi-factor authentication.

- **Risk transfer**: Risk transfer involves shifting the responsibility for managing or bearing the risk to another party. This is often achieved through contracts, insurance, or outsourcing. By transferring the risk, an organization can protect itself from the financial or operational consequences of a potential risk event. Insurance is a common method of transferring risk, as it helps mitigate the financial impact of incidents like natural disasters, product liability claims, or employee injuries. Similarly, outsourcing certain business functions to third-parties (such as IT services or logistics) can transfer the operational risks associated with those functions.

  Example: A company might transfer the risk of property damage due to fire by purchasing insurance, or it may transfer cybersecurity risk by outsourcing data management to a specialized provider.

- **Risk retention**: Risk retention (also known as **risk acceptance**) involves acknowledging the existence of a risk and choosing to live with it, usually because the cost of mitigation is higher than the potential impact of the risk. This strategy is often applied when the probability or impact of the risk is deemed low or when the organization has the resources and capacity to absorb the impact if the risk materializes. Essentially, the organization accepts the risk and assumes the consequences should the event occur but typically keeps it under review. This is a common approach for low-level risks that are unlikely to affect the organization's overall operations or reputation.

  Example: A small company might accept the risk of occasional minor hardware failures, choosing not to invest heavily in a backup system because the cost of such a system outweighs the potential disruptions.

Conclusion

In this chapter, we explored the concepts of risk governance and the risk management lifecycle, providing a structured approach for identifying, assessing, and mitigating risks within an organization. We also examined how to calculate residual risks and the importance of minimizing inherent risks through effective risk management strategies and controls. This chapter also highlighted the role of the risk register, explaining how it serves as a vital tool for organizations to track, document, and proactively manage risks, ensuring that risks are continuously monitored and addressed.

Additionally, we explored various risk treatment methodologies, understanding how to implement strategies such as risk avoidance, reduction, transfer, and retention to mitigate identified risks. As we transition into the next chapter, our focus will shift to control assessment objectives and audit scope, where we will explore the processes for evaluating the effectiveness of controls and determining the scope of audits to ensure comprehensive risk management across the organization.

Key terms

- Inherent risk is the amount of risk within an IT ecosystem in the absence of controls and residual risk is the amount of risk that exists after cybersecurity controls have been implemented.

- Residual risks could be caused by ineffective security controls or by the security controls themselves—these are known as **secondary risks**.

- A risk register and a risk matrix are similar tools. Both assess the level of risk and are key to any contingency plan or risk management plan. However, there are differences. For one, the risk matrix is a visual tool. It charts each risk and maps it on a grid.

- Risk mitigation is a proactive approach that can basically be done anytime, while risk treatment is reactive, something that is done only during the risk assessment and after a risk has been identified.

- KRI is a highly probable indicator designed to accurately predict an important level of risk based on a defined threshold.

- NIST RMF is the overall risk management methodology published and promulgated by NIST in SP 800-37.

- Risk assessment is the process of identifying and assessing various factors, including threats, threat actors, vulnerabilities, assets, and likelihood, to determine their impact on the organization.

- Risk appetite is the organization's overall acceptable level of risk for a given business venture.

- Risk capacity is the amount of loss that an organization can incur without seriously affecting its ability to continue as an organization.

- Risk factor is any factor that may contribute to an increase or decrease in risk; risk factors could be external or internal, and they could affect either likelihood or impact should a risk event actually occur.

CHAPTER 12

Introduction to Control Assessment and Audit

Introduction

This chapter offers a comprehensive overview of the control assessment objective, emphasizing the importance of evaluating the effectiveness of existing controls. It explores the security assessment plan and assessment procedure in detail, focusing on the systematic evaluation of specific controls and potential enhancements. This structured approach ensures that controls are not only in place but also functioning as intended, providing an effective safeguard against risks. By outlining clear procedures for assessing the adequacy of controls and their improvement, the chapter ensures that security measures remain robust and relevant.

Furthermore, the chapter highlights the significance of defining the audit scope and careful audit planning to ensure a smooth and efficient workflow. It details the various stages of the audit process, explaining the roles and responsibilities of all involved stakeholders. Key activities in each phase of the audit are also discussed, ensuring clarity in the execution of audit tasks. By focusing on proper planning and clear role definition, the chapter ensures that audits are conducted systematically, with a focus on achieving accurate, actionable results and maintaining compliance.

Structure

The chapter covers the following main topics:

- Control assessment objective
- Stakeholder roles and responsibilities
- Assessment procedure
- Security assessment plan
- NIST SP 800-53 mapping to ISO/IEC 27001
- Audit scope
- Audit planning
- Audit stages
- Evidence

Objectives

By the end of this chapter, you will have a solid understanding of the control assessment objectives that will assist in creation of a security assessment plan tailored to specific needs. You will also learn about the assessment procedures based on the *National Institute of Standards and Technology (NIST) Special Publication (SP) 800-53* standard, which provides a comprehensive framework for evaluating the effectiveness of security controls. This knowledge will enable you to apply structured assessment methods to ensure security measures are robust and aligned with best practices.

Additionally, this chapter will introduce key aspects of the audit process, helping you understand the essential components of audit planning and scope. You will learn how to define the boundaries and objectives of an audit to ensure thorough and effective evaluations. The chapter will also outline the various stages of the audit process, highlighting the roles and responsibilities of all stakeholders involved. This will equip you with the knowledge to manage and participate in audits effectively, ensuring the process is structured and the outcomes are actionable.

Control assessment objective

The objective of a control assessment is to rigorously test the effectiveness of existing controls to ensure that they are functioning as intended and are not vulnerable to failure. This process helps to identify the potential weaknesses or gaps in the controls that could pose a risk to the organization. By proactively testing controls, organizations can evaluate their overall risk exposure, detect areas that require additional monitoring, and make necessary improvements to their security posture. Regular testing, rather than waiting for audit cycles, is crucial to prevent vulnerabilities from going undetected, which could lead to costly security breaches or compliance failures.

Internal control testing is a critical component of risk management, as it enables an organization to maintain a high level of security and compliance. It helps ensure that risk management strategies are continuously updated and that controls remain effective against evolving threats. This ongoing assessment process allows organizations to identify and address potential control deficiencies before they compromise the organization's operations, reputation, or regulatory standing.

Following is the detailed breakdown of the security control assessment objective:

- **Determine the effectiveness of security controls**: The main goal of a security control assessment is to check if the security measures in place are effectively reducing the identified risks. This involves testing the controls to ensure they are properly configured, working as intended, and are able to address the risks they were designed to manage.

- **Ensure compliance with standards**: The assessment ensures that the security controls meet the required standards of the NIST, *International Organization for Standardization (ISO)*, *Payment Card Industry Security Standards Council (PCI DSS)*, or *General Data Protection Regulation (GDPR)*. This helps organizations avoid legal, financial, and reputational issues by confirming that the controls are up to date with compliance requirements.

- **Verify control implementation and coverage**: The assessment checks if the correct controls are applied across all relevant areas of the organization, ensuring both technical and administrative controls are in place to protect all system components and business processes.

- **Evaluate control testing and monitoring**: Security controls need to be tested and monitored over time to stay effective. The assessment reviews how well these controls are continuously tested and monitored through tools like audit logs and vulnerability assessments to stay ahead of emerging threats.

- **Identify weaknesses and areas for improvement**: The assessment identifies any gaps or weaknesses in the security controls, such as outdated systems or overlooked risks. It provides recommendations for improvement to strengthen security and address any vulnerabilities.

- **Ensure risk mitigation**: A key part of the assessment is to ensure that the controls are successfully reducing risks to acceptable levels. If the risks remain too high, corrective actions are recommended to modify or strengthen the controls.

- **Support continuous improvement**: Security control assessments help improve security practices over time by identifying areas for enhancement. This ongoing process helps organizations to stay proactive against new threats, improve incident response, and adapt their risk management strategies to maintain a strong security posture.

Scope of control assessment

The scoping of assets within risk management deals with the identification of assets, which could be physical, digital, human, or reputational, that are vital to the organization to determine the degree of protection necessary for each. This is usually determined through a risk assessment, in which each asset is assessed based on its criticality, sensitivity, and the possible consequences of compromise. For business-critical assets, which includes core IT systems, customer data, and proprietary information, robust protective measures would involve such options as encryption, access controls, and disaster recovery protocols.

Risk assessment is an integral part of the system security plan and involves the review of the whole set of controls within the system's security plan. Ideally, these controls are informed by an organization's minimum-security standards. The process of risk assessment enhances and evolves these standards for applicability with the unique risk profile for any given organization. The security plan not only documents the controls that have been applied but also allows for the addition of controls in the future and highlights weaknesses or gaps that need to be addressed.

The test plan, developed by the certification test team from the security plan is to validate that the controls are implemented as mentioned. This plan would evaluate the sufficiency of the existing controls and confirm that those planned controls will be implemented by the scheduled timeline. It further verifies that all controls marked not applicable are indeed irrelevant and performs an analysis to determine whether management justifications in support of the acceptance of identified risks are valid. Certification testing covers all control families from NIST SP 800-53 to identify potential flaws in design, implementation, or operation. The testing should be thorough enough to assess how well the security mechanisms enforce the system's security policy. It also ensures that the security documentation is complete and accurate, confirming alignment with the defined controls. Ultimately, the scope should be comprehensive enough to validate the system's security posture and address any gaps or weaknesses.

Stakeholder roles and responsibilities

There are different stakeholders involved in the control assessment process to ensure that assessments are comprehensive and effective in securing an organization. As outlined in NIST SP 800-53 Revision 5, some of these stakeholders are system owners, auditors, assessors, and other key personnel involved in the assessment and management of security controls. Here are the key roles and their responsibilities are highlighted as follows:

- **System owners**: The system owner is responsible for ensuring that the system operates securely and within all requirements of compliance. Responsibilities include the following:
  - Oversee monitoring and maintenance of the controls of security.
  - Provide oversight of an assessment of security controls and submit documentation where needed.

  - Take action on any identified vulnerabilities or other weakness in the system's security posture.

- **Security control assessor**: The security control assessor assesses the efficiency of the security controls implemented within the system. Responsibilities include the following:

  - Assess the effectiveness and efficiency of the design and implementation of security controls.

  - Test and collect audit evidence to prove if controls operate as expected.

  - Prepare an assessment report, which states the results of the assessment, findings, vulnerabilities, and recommendations for improvements.

- **Auditors**: Auditors review the implementation of security controls and their effectiveness, mostly directed toward regulatory requirements and compliance in line with generally accepted standards for the industry. Responsibilities include:

  - Provide in-depth analysis of the system and organizational processes for compliance with applicable laws and regulations.

  - Conduct documentation reviews, interviews with stakeholders, and test to check on the suitability and effectiveness of controls.

  - Audit and provide recommendations for corrective actions needed based on the identification of non-compliances or weaknesses.

- **Authorizing official (AO)**: The authorization official is responsible for accepting the risk related to the operational aspects of the information system. Responsibilities include:

  - Review the result of the security assessment and approve the final authorization of the system.

  - Approve or disapprove system's operation based on knowledge of residual risk, along with the effectiveness level of security control.

  - Approve the security authorization package consisting of the assessment report, control documentation and mitigation strategy plans.

- **Information security officer**: The information security officer ensures the organization's security policies are being followed and oversee the implementation of security controls. Responsibilities include:

  - Support security controls implementation in ensuring that implementation is in line with the organizational information security framework.

  - Coordinate with system owners and assessors on the effectiveness of controls and the determination of security issues.

  - Lead the development of risk management strategies and policies.

- **Risk manager**: The risk manager is responsible for identifying, assessing and mitigating information systems-related risks. Responsibilities include:

    o Coordinate with the system owners, assessors, and other stakeholders to ensure that the risks have been identified and dealt with accordingly.

    o Oversee the preparation and implementation of risk response plans in line with findings from the assessment.

    o Assess residual risks and ensure they are within the acceptable threshold of the organization.

Assessment procedure

The assessment procedures outlined in NIST SP 800-53 Revision 5 provides a structured approach to evaluating the effectiveness of an organization's security controls and form the foundation for building an effective assurance case. An assurance case is essentially a structured argument, supported by evidence, that justifies the security posture of a system. The procedures in NIST SP 800-53 are designed to assess the implementation and performance of security controls to ensure that they are operating as intended.

The assessment procedures in NIST 800-53 Revision 5 focus on evaluating the effectiveness of security measures across four main areas: Specifications, mechanisms, activities, and individuals. Each of these areas represents a critical aspect of security that needs to be assessed to ensure the system is adequately protected. The following figure shows the four ways of assessment procedure:

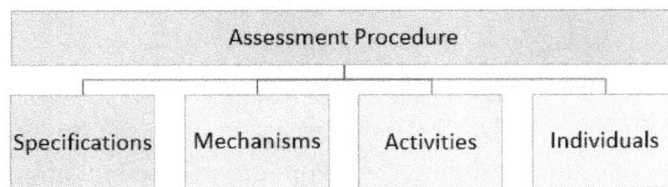

Figure 12.1: Security assessment procedure

Following is the breakdown of each area:

- **Specifications**: This area focuses on the documentation that defines the system's security posture. It includes policies, procedures, plans, system security requirements, functional specifications, and architectural designs. These documents establish the framework within which security controls are designed and implemented. The assessment will evaluate whether these specifications align with best practices, security standards, and organizational requirements. For example, an assessor might examine whether the system's security requirements are documented in a security plan or if the system architecture accounts for all necessary security controls.

- **Mechanisms**: This area refers to the specific hardware, software, or firmware safeguards and countermeasures that the organization has employed to protect the system. These mechanisms may include firewalls, encryption, access control systems, intrusion detection systems, antivirus software, and other technical solutions. The assessment will evaluate whether these mechanisms are correctly implemented and whether they are functioning as expected to provide the necessary protection against potential threats. For example, an assessment might include verifying that encryption is being applied to sensitive data both at rest and in transit or ensuring that firewalls are properly configured to block unauthorized access.

- **Activities**: The activities involved in a system's protection include the ongoing processes and actions that contribute to maintaining security over time. This may involve system maintenance tasks, monitoring activities, incident response procedures, and other protective actions. Examples of activities that will be assessed include system backup processes, patch management, and network traffic monitoring. The assessment will examine whether these activities are being regularly performed as intended and whether they are effective in maintaining the security of the system. For example, the assessor might verify that system backups are regularly conducted and tested for integrity or check if network traffic is being continuously monitored for unusual or malicious activity.

- **Individuals**: This area pertains to the people within the organization who are responsible for applying the specifications, mechanisms, and activities. This includes system administrators, security personnel, and other individuals who are directly involved in managing the security measures of the system. The assessment will evaluate whether these individuals are adequately trained, follow established procedures, and are fulfilling their responsibilities to protect the system. For instance, assessors might review the qualifications of personnel performing critical tasks such as system configuration or incident response and assess whether they follow proper protocols to mitigate security risks.

Development and approval of assessment plan

The development and approval of an assessment plan are considered important steps in ensuring that the assessment of security controls is comprehensive, aligned with organizational goals, and meets compliance requirements. Identification of the scope and objectives of the process starts with regulatory requirements, risk management priorities, and organization-specific goals. The assessment plan should identify what particular management controls will be assessed, the methods to be employed, and who should be involved in the assessment process.

The assessment plan should be aligned with the organizational goals, broader security strategy, and objectives such as asset protection, information confidentiality, and reduction of operational risks. Additionally, it is supposed to incorporate other ongoing security initiatives and assure an alignment with the organization's Risk Management Framework

. This is to ensure that the assessment contributes towards the overall organizational security posture.

Another important factor to consider in formulating the assessment plan is the requirements for compliance. The plan will ensure the assessment addresses relevant laws, regulations, and standards to which the organization must adhere. It includes requirements for such frameworks like NIST, GDPR, *Health Insurance Portability and Accountability Act* (*HIPAA*), and any particular industry-specific requirements. Additionally, the assessment plan outlines how the verification of such standards with respect to the compliance of the organization is fulfilled and how the findings are documented and taken care.

Upon compilation, it needs review and approval from responsible stakeholders, including system owners, security officers, and/or other responsible personnel. This will ensure that the plans are realistic and commensurate with organizational goals but at the same time in line with compliance regulations and requirements. Confirming resources against the timeline/methodology will deliver the desired outcomes through this. The approved assessment plan then provides a roadmap for actually performing the security control assessment, supporting ongoing risk management and compliance requirements within the organization.

Alignment with organizational risk priorities

The scope can also be aligned with the priorities of risk in organizations through an understanding of risk appetite and tolerance. The mitigation strategy would be stronger for high-priority assets, which are the most vital assets to an organization's mission, reflecting low organizational tolerance for disruption of these assets. Assets that are considered less critical may have only minimal protections. The scope is not static and shall evolve with changes in the business environment, emerging threats, and shifts in organizational goals that ensure the organization's risk management efforts remain focused on its most important assets and aligned with its overall strategy.

Security assessment plan

The security assessment plan is a crucial document that outlines the specific controls and control enhancements to be evaluated based on the goals of the assessment and the controls already implemented as described in the system security plan. This plan defines the scope of the assessment, clarifying whether the assessment will be comprehensive or partial. It also distinguishes whether the assessment is intended to support initial pre-authorization activities for new or significantly modified systems or if it will focus on ongoing evaluations of operational systems. The plan helps ensure that the assessment is aligned with the system's current security posture and organizational requirements.

Additionally, the security assessment plan details the procedures to be followed for each control being assessed. These procedures are generally derived from NIST SP 800-53A or other available assessment frameworks and are customized as necessary to meet specific organizational or system requirements. The plan includes the selection of appropriate assessment methods and the objects to be assessed and assigns attributes such as depth and coverage to each method, ensuring that all relevant aspects of the system's security controls are thoroughly evaluated. By tailoring the approach to the system's unique needs, the plan ensures that the assessment is both effective and efficient in identifying potential security risks and vulnerabilities.

The process of developing a security assessment plan involves several detailed actions to ensure the assessment is thorough, efficient, and tailored to the system's needs. The following figure shows the action plan for security assessment:

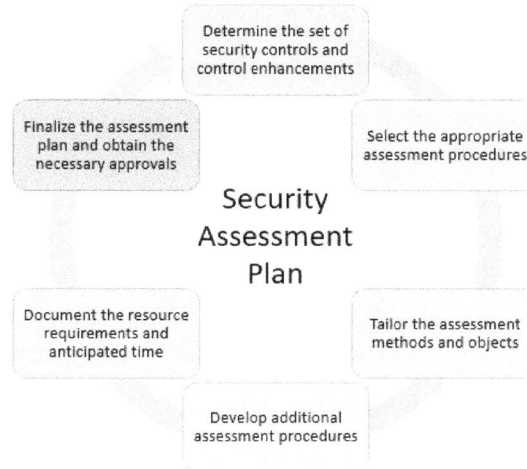

Figure 12.2: Security assessment plan

Before initiating a security control assessment, the security control assessor submits the assessment plan for approval by system owners, AOs, or other designated organizational officials. This plan must provide sufficient detail to clearly outline the scope of the assessment, the schedule for its completion, the individuals responsible for various tasks, and the specific procedures to be used for assessing each control. System owners rely on this plan to allocate the necessary resources for the assessment, including personnel who will provide documentation, participate in interviews, or facilitate access to the system, as well as those who will carry out the assessment itself.

Following is a breakdown of these actions:

- **Determine the set of security controls and control enhancements**:
    - Identify and select the security controls and enhancements that are relevant to the system being assessed.
    - Ensure that the selected controls align with the system's security requirements and the organization's risk management objectives.
    - Consider both implemented and planned controls as specified in the system security plan.

- **Select the appropriate assessment procedures**:
  - Choose assessment procedures based on the specific controls within the scope, ensuring they are appropriate for the security level and objectives.
  - Take into account organizational factors, such as minimum assurance levels or specific compliance requirements that guide how controls should be assessed.
  - The procedures should be designed to validate that the controls are functioning as intended and meet security objectives.

- **Tailor the assessment methods and objects**:
  - Customize assessment methods and objects to meet the particular needs of the agency or system under review.
  - Assign appropriate depth and coverage to each assessment method to ensure a thorough evaluation. Depth refers to the level of detail in testing, while coverage refers to the extent of the system evaluated.
  - Tailoring ensures that the assessment is aligned with the unique security posture and operational environment of the organization or system.

- **Develop additional assessment procedures**:
  - Identify any security controls or requirements that are outside the scope of the controls provided in NIST SP 800-53 or other relevant control catalogs.
  - Develop additional procedures to assess these controls or address specific security requirements that are not covered in the standard catalog.
  - This ensures that the assessment is comprehensive and includes all relevant security measures.

- **Document the resource requirements and anticipated time**:
  - Estimate and document the resources (personnel, tools, time, etc.) required to complete the assessment.
  - Plan the assessment timeline and consider ways to streamline the process by sequencing or consolidating procedures, reducing duplication of effort, and ensuring an efficient assessment process.
  - Resource documentation helps to allocate the right resources and manage the assessment process effectively.

- **Finalize the assessment plan and obtain the necessary approvals**:
  - Review and finalize the security assessment plan, ensuring all procedures, resources, and timelines are clearly defined.

    o   Submit the plan for approval by relevant stakeholders, such as system owners, AOs, or security managers, to ensure buy-in and support for the assessment.

    o   Once approved, the plan is ready for execution, ensuring a structured and well-supported approach to assessing security controls.

Assessment results applicability

In essence, risk management is an activity of information gathering, a way to conduct an as-implemented evaluation of the status of a system or its common controls. The process in itself does not create security or privacy outcomes but instead provides great insight with valuable information on the current effectiveness and gaps within the security measures. This seeks to evaluate the alignment of the system against established controls and identify those weaknesses or deficiencies that may carry risks.

The risk assessment results provide an organization with the most cost-effective way to carry out the assessment process. These results assist in decision-making based on an organization's maturity in the current state of risk management, available resources, and the organization's risk tolerance. NIST SP 800-53A Revision 5 provides a good starting point to define procedures to ensure consistency in the application of security and privacy controls. However, this is a flexible process in that one can mold it to suit factors such as organizational policies, operational needs, known vulnerabilities, and system dependencies. The information from these assessments can be used for various number of key purposes, including:

- **Determining weaknesses**: The assessment identifies security and privacy-related weaknesses associated with the system and its operational environment and ensures that any shortcomings are documented for future action.

- **Prioritization of risk responses**: Identification of weaknesses and gaps will, therefore, enable the organization to prioritize risk response activities by focusing on the most important areas that have to be given immediate attention.

- **Confirmation of issue resolution**: Assessment confirms whether or not previously identified weaknesses have been addressed to ascertain that corrective actions taken are appropriate and effective.

- **Supporting monitoring**: The results can keep informed about security and privacy for ongoing monitoring toward situational awareness and keeping the organizations responsive toward emerging threats.

- **Supporting authorization decisions**: Assessment results should be effective in making informed authorization decisions of a system, supporting the process for granting or renewing system certifications.

Validation of controls

Validation is a very important process that will help in ensuring the effectiveness of controls in practice. The first step is to establish clear objectives for each control, including measurable metrics and **key performance indicators** (**KPIs**) to monitor performance. Then, evaluate the design and implementation of each control to ensure that they appropriately address the identified risks and cover all necessary areas, including policies, processes, and technology.

Next, perform all the tests that include penetration testing, vulnerability scanning, and exercises to ensure controls work as intended. Continuous monitoring shall be performed through automated tools like SIEM systems for tracking performance and reviewing logs. In this way, controls can be kept updated and effective toward the security goals of the organization.

NIST SP 800-53 mapping to ISO/IEC 27001

Mapping NIST SP 800-53 Revision 5 controls against the controls contained in ISO/IEC 27001:2022 is useful in helping an organization to understand whether the security measures under one framework satisfy the intent of controls of the other framework. However, it is important to note that perfect mappings are not always achieved. The actual implementation of controls in each framework may differ due to differing organizations' needs and contexts.

For a control to effectively meet the mapping criteria, it needs to reach a similar state of security. At the same time, organizations should be highly cognizant that controls cannot be treated as exactly equivalent just because a mapping between frameworks is provided. Differences may still exist based on how both frameworks address any given security concern. Here are some examples of potential mapping issues that show some of these differences:

- **Example one**: NIST SP 800-53 contingency planning and ISO/IEC 27001 **information and communication technology** (**ICT**) readiness for business continuity have similar goals, but their functionality and focus differ slightly.

- **Example two**: Privacy controls were integrated into the NIST SP 800-53, Revision 5, control set to address privacy requirements for the processing of **personally identifiable information** (**PII**) and thus are included in the mapping table; however, ISO/IEC 27001 does not specifically address privacy beyond the inherent benefits provided by maintaining the security of PII.

Audit scope

The audit scope is a critical component of the audit planning process, as it defines the boundaries of the audit. It outlines what aspects of an organization, system, or process will be examined and, just as importantly, what will be excluded from the audit. Establishing a clear and well-defined scope ensures that the audit is focused, manageable, and aligned with the objectives of the organization or stakeholders involved.

The scope can be shaped around several factors, including particular products or services, which might be under review to assess their compliance with regulatory standards or internal policies. It can also apply to specific locations, where the audit examines practices and processes in particular geographic areas or offices. Similarly, the scope can focus on departments, targeting an in-depth review of how specific areas of the organization are operating, from finance to IT or human resources.

A risk-based approach in defining the audit scope involves focusing on identifying and addressing those areas that pose the highest potential risk to the organization. This includes an assessment of risks based on their likelihood and potential impact so that audit resources are directed to the most critical areas. High-risk areas, such as sensitive data protection or compliance with key regulations, are prioritized in order to ensure that the audit can identify vulnerabilities that could have significant consequences if left unaddressed. By focusing on high-risk areas, auditors can be most effective in assessing the sufficiency of controls and risk mitigation processes. This would be one way of performing a targeted audit that would yield meaningful insight into the efficiency of security, privacy, and operational processes.

Alignment of scope and assets

Compliance scope and asset alignment ensure that critical resources are effectively protected besides meeting regulatory and security requirements. The organization can focus on key systems, data and processes that need protection to tailor the security measures for particular risks related to compliance standards. Here are few examples to demonstrate scope and asset alignment.

Example 1: For GDPR, the scope includes systems that manage PII data in terms of storage, processing, and communication. The key assets to protect and store PII data include data management systems, encryption mechanism, access control and network infrastructures. The compliance requires that security measures such as encryption, access controls need to be implemented to meet the GDPR standards on privacy and security.

Example 2: For NIST **Cybersecurity Framework** (**CSF**), the scope includes protection of critical IT assets, such as servers, networks, endpoints, and cloud services from cyber threats. It would include key assets such as network infrastructure, application servers, databases, and user authentication systems. The compliance demands the security of these assets along the five areas: Identify, protect, detect, respond, and recover through a risk assessment, secure configuration, monitoring, and incident response procedures.

Example 3: For HIPAA compliance, the scope includes systems that create, receive, maintain and transmit **protected health information** (**PHI**) such as electronic health records, medical devices, and communication systems. The key assets include PHI, medical device data, and access controls. Compliance requires these assets to be protected by encryption, access controls, secure storage, regular audits, breach response plans and awareness trainings.

Audit planning

Audit planning is a critical first step in the audit process, serving as the foundation for a successful audit. When executed effectively, it ensures that the entire audit workflow runs smoothly and efficiently. A well-thought-out audit plan helps streamline the subsequent stages of the audit, including fieldwork, data analysis, issue management, and reporting. The planning phase enables auditors to define clear objectives, establish a comprehensive scope, and prioritize resources, all of which contribute to a more focused and effective audit.

An essential part of audit planning is identifying the key risks and controls that the audit should address. This ensures that all critical areas are covered, and nothing is overlooked. By understanding the key risks to the organization, such as, operational, or security compliance-related risks, the audit can focus on the areas that matter most. Likewise, identifying the relevant controls, processes, and procedures helps auditors evaluate whether the organization's security, compliance, and operational measures are functioning as intended.

Key components of audit planning

There are a few important processes in planning an information security audit that involves proper resource allocation, scheduling, and defining deliverables:

- **Resource allocation**: Resource allocation refers to appropriate allocations of personnel, tools, and budget for the success of the audit. The team should be composed of qualified auditors with extensive experience in cybersecurity, risk management, and corresponding compliance frameworks, such as NIST or ISO 27001. Also, auditors need to be equipped with the required tools, including security scanners, vulnerability testing software, and compliance checklists to perform their job effectively.

- **Scheduling**: Scheduling is another vital component of audit planning that details the timeline for the whole audit process. There should be a schedule of work developed with timelines regarding various audit stages: risk assessments, control testing, interviews, and document reviews. Scheduling must also consider the availability of key personnel whose input may be needed for system access, interviews, or data collection.

- **Deliverables**: Defining deliverables in the audit plan provides clarity with information like what the audit will deliver and what the expected outcome of the audit is. This includes the description of the scope to be audited: Security controls, regulations, and risk management processes. The most common deliverables would be findings in a report on vulnerabilities, weaknesses in security posture, and points of non-compliance that need recommendations.

The audit plan should also include follow-up actions like remediation plans and future audits to ensure that the identified issues are fixed and the security posture is enhanced.

Key steps in audit planning

There are various steps involved in planning audit. The following are the essential steps in audit planning:

- **Identify the audit purpose and scope**: The first step in audit planning is to identify the audit purpose which includes the reason for conducting the audit, such as compliance verification, risk assessment, or performance evaluation. Once the purpose is clear, the scope of the audit is defined. The scope determines the boundaries of the audit, specifying what will be included and excluded. This can include specific departments, systems, processes, or timeframes that the audit will focus on.

- **Define the audit objectives and criteria**: Next, auditors need to define the objectives of the audit. These objectives should align with the purpose of the audit and provide clear goals, such as evaluating the effectiveness of internal controls or ensuring compliance with relevant laws and regulations. Additionally, criteria should be established. These criteria are the standards, policies, regulations, or best practices that will be used to evaluate the organization's processes, controls, or performance.

- **Select the audit methods and techniques**: The audit methods and techniques are chosen based on the audit's objectives, scope, and criteria. Common audit methods include interviews, surveys, document reviews, observations, and testing. Sampling techniques may be used to select representative items or transactions for review. The goal is to determine the most effective way to gather evidence and evaluate the areas of interest, ensuring that the methods selected provide accurate and reliable results.

- **Identify the audit resources and roles**: Effective audit planning requires the identification of the resources needed for the audit. This includes the allocation of personnel, such as auditors with specific expertise, as well as any technological tools or systems required for data analysis and documentation. It is also important to define roles and responsibilities for each team member, ensuring that everyone understands their tasks and duties during the audit process.

- **Plan the audit schedule and activities**: Once the audit resources and roles are identified, a detailed schedule should be created. The schedule includes key milestones, deadlines for specific audit activities, and timelines for reporting findings. It helps ensure that the audit is completed on time and that necessary resources are available at each stage of the audit process. The schedule also provides a timeline for interim progress reports and the final audit report.

- **Establish a communication plan**: Effective communication is key to a successful audit. The audit plan should include a communication strategy outlining how information will be shared among the audit team, the organization, and any relevant stakeholders. This could involve regular meetings, status updates, and reports during the audit process.

- **Review and approve the audit scope template**: Finally, before the audit begins, it is essential to review and approve the audit scope template. This document outlines all the planning elements, including the audit purpose, scope, objectives, criteria, methods, resources, and schedule. Approval from relevant stakeholders, such as senior management or the audit committee, ensures that the audit plan is aligned with organizational goals and that the resources, timing, and focus are appropriate.

Systematic approach to audit planning

Every audit is a systematic approach to testing samples of evidence to measure compliance against a designated standard. The systematic approach follows a structured, continuous improvement cycle often referred to as the **Shewhart cycle** or **plan-do-check-act** (**PDCA**) **cycle**, which is used for the ongoing improvement of processes and systems. The cycle in the following diagram is iterative, meaning it repeats over time to drive continuous improvement:

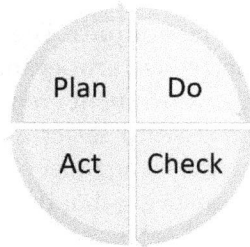

Figure 12.3: Systematic audit approach

Here is a breakdown of how to implement each step in the context you have described, with an emphasis on process improvement:

- **Plan**: The first step in the audit process is to determine whether there is a clear plan or method in place. This involves evaluating if the process or system has defined procedures, standards, and methods that outline how objectives are to be achieved. Additionally, it is important to assess whether management has communicated the significance of the objective, typically through policies, goal-setting, and resource allocation. The auditee should also have broken down broad objectives into specific tasks or procedures, making them actionable. Evidence to support this includes documents such as policies, outlines, flowcharts, meeting notes, and other written materials that clarify what needs to be done to meet the goal.

- **Do**: In the do step of the audit, the focus shifts to verifying whether the plan, procedure, or method is being followed as designed. This involves assessing whether the team or individual is executing the plan correctly and whether the actual work output aligns with the expectations set forth in the plan. The auditor compares the deliverables to the original objectives to identify any discrepancies or deviations. Evidence to look for includes status reports, meeting records, logs, training documentation, and other records that demonstrate the activities are being carried out as intended and that the work is meeting the expected standards.

- **Check**: In this step, the focus is on evaluating whether the process is being effectively monitored to ensure it operates as expected. This involves verifying whether there are mechanisms in place to track performance, detect issues, and maintain quality. The auditor should look for evidence of quality control measures, peer reviews, inspections, or audits that assess performance against established metrics or criteria. It is also important to review KPIs and determine how deviations are handled, including corrective actions or adjustments based on performance data. Evidence to support this step includes quality control logs, deviation reports, non-compliance records, audit findings, and documentation of corrective actions or peer reviews.

- **Act**: In this step, the auditor focuses on analyzing any discrepancies between the expected outcomes outlined in the plan and the actual results. If differences or issues are identified, corrective actions must be taken to address them. This could involve revising the plan, changing procedures, providing additional training, or enhancing monitoring processes to ensure better performance in the future. The goal is to learn from the issues discovered during the check phase and take the necessary steps to correct the process. Evidence to support this includes action plans, corrective action logs, updated procedures, revised policies, or any documentation showing that changes were made to resolve identified problems and improve the process.

Audit stages

When performing an audit, there are ten key stages that auditors need to be aware of and fully understand. Each stage requires specific roles and responsibilities to ensure the audit is thorough, effective, and compliant with relevant standards. The following figure represents the key stages of the audit:

Figure 12.4: *Audit stages*

Following is a detailed breakdown of each of the ten stages:

- **Approving the audit charter or engagement letter**: The first stage of the audit process involves formalizing the audit's objectives, scope, and responsibilities. This is typically done through the audit charter (for internal audits) or engagement letter (for external audits). The audit charter or engagement letter outlines the following:

  o The purpose of the audit.

  o The scope and objectives.

  o The roles and responsibilities of both the auditors and the auditee.

  o The methodology to be used.

  o The timeline for the audit.

  o Any legal or ethical considerations.

  This document must be approved by relevant parties, such as senior management or the audit committee, to ensure everyone is aligned and the audit proceeds with clear expectations.

- **Preplanning the audit**: Preplanning is the stage where auditors prepare for the audit by gathering initial information and developing a strategy. This involves:

  o Understanding the organization's environment and context.

  o Identifying relevant regulations and standards that the audit should comply with.

  o Reviewing previous audits, reports, and the risk environment.

  o Establishing initial communication with the client.

  o Setting up logistics, such as access to systems and personnel.

The goal of preplanning is to establish a roadmap for the audit, ensuring the team is fully prepared to carry out the audit efficiently.

- **Performing a risk assessment**: Risk assessment is a critical part of audit planning, helping auditors focus their efforts on areas of higher risk. Auditors evaluate:

    o **Inherent risk**: The likelihood that a risk exists before controls are considered.

    o **Control risk**: The risk that the controls in place may not prevent or detect errors or fraud.

    o **Detection risk**: The risk that the auditor may not detect material misstatements during the audit.

By identifying and assessing these risks, auditors can prioritize the areas that need more attention, allocate resources appropriately, and determine which audit techniques are most effective for each risk area.

- **Determining whether an audit is possible**: In this stage, auditors assess whether the audit can be conducted given the conditions and constraints. Factors that may affect the audit's feasibility include the following:

    o Availability of required documentation or access to systems.

    o Management's willingness to cooperate.

    o Adequate resources (personnel, time, budget).

    o Legal or regulatory barriers.

If an audit is not possible due to these constraints, auditors must assess alternative solutions or modify the scope of the audit.

- **Performing the actual audit**: This is the core stage where auditors implement the audit plan. This involves:

    o **Executing audit procedures**: Implementing the methodologies defined during the planning stages, such as testing, interviews, and data reviews.

    o **Coordinating with management**: Communicating with management and staff to obtain necessary access and information.

    o **Monitoring progress**: Ensuring that the audit is being conducted on schedule and within the scope.

The goal is to collect sufficient evidence and evaluate the effectiveness of the controls, systems, and processes under review.

- **Gathering evidence**: In this stage, auditors collect sufficient and appropriate evidence to support their findings and conclusions. Evidence may be gathered through the following:

- o   **Document reviews**: Policies, procedures, operations maintenance records, etc.

- o   **Interviews**: Discussions with key personnel to understand processes and controls.

- o   **Observations**: Watching operations in action to verify compliance with standards.

- o   **Data sampling**: Selecting transactions or items to analyze in detail.

The quality of the evidence collected will directly impact the reliability and credibility of the audit results.

- **Performing audit tests**: Audit tests are conducted to assess the validity of the information gathered and the effectiveness of the controls in place. These may include:

  - o   **Substantive tests**: To detect material misstatements or irregularities in the data.

  - o   **Control tests**: To evaluate the adequacy and effectiveness of internal controls.

  - o   **Analytical procedures**: To assess patterns or inconsistencies in data through statistical or trend analysis.

The types of tests depend on the audit's objectives, the risk assessment, and the areas of focus identified earlier.

- **Analyzing the results**: Once evidence has been gathered and tests completed, auditors analyze the data to form conclusions. This involves:

  - o   **Assessing control effectiveness**: Determining whether the controls in place are functioning as intended.

  - o   **Identifying discrepancies or weaknesses**: Recognizing any gaps, inefficiencies, or potential risks.

  - o   **Comparing with criteria**: Ensuring that the findings align with established criteria, such as regulations or best practices.

The analysis of results should provide the foundation for drafting the audit findings and recommendations.

- **Reporting the results**: After analyzing the results, auditors compile their findings into an audit report. This document includes:

  - o   **Audit objectives and scope**: Recap of what was covered and why.

  - o   **Methodology and evidence**: Explanation of how the audit was conducted and the evidence gathered.

o **Findings**: Detailed results, including any issues identified, weaknesses, or non-compliance.

o **Recommendations**: Suggestions for corrective actions or improvements.

o **Conclusions**: Overall assessment of the audited areas.

The audit report is shared with senior management, the board of directors, or other relevant stakeholders, depending on the type of audit.

- **Conducting follow-up activities**: After the audit is complete, it is essential to monitor the implementation of the recommendations and corrective actions. This involves:

    o **Tracking progress**: Ensuring that management is taking the necessary steps to address identified issues.

    o **Re-assessing controls**: Verifying that the corrective actions have been implemented effectively.

    o **Communicating results**: Updating stakeholders on the status of corrective actions and any remaining concerns.

Follow-up activities help ensure that the audit leads to tangible improvements and that the organization maintains a robust control environment.

Audit types

Audits can be classified into three general categories based on their objectives, scope, and level of trust involved. Each type of audit serves a unique purpose and helps organizations ensure the integrity of their processes, transactions, and systems. Here is an overview of the following three categories:

Audit type	Conducted by	Scope	Objective	Usage
Internal audits	Internal auditors within the organization	Restricted to internal operations and controls	Identify weakness, improve internal processes	Findings stay internal, not used for licensing or certification
External audits	A business auditor its suppliers or customers	Focus on business relationships and compliance with contracts	Ensure mutual compliance and performance	Findings shared between parties involved in the relationship
Independent audits	Third-party auditors	Broader scope, evaluating compliance with standards or regulations	Ensure compliance for certification, licensing, or approval	Findings used for licensing, certification, or public approval

Table 12.1: *Audit types*

The details of these categories are as follows:

- **Internal audits and assessments**: Internal audits are conducted within an organization by its own auditors or internal teams. These audits are typically part of the organization's self-assessment process and focus on evaluating internal operations, controls, compliance with policies, and the efficiency of processes. The scope of internal audits is generally restricted to the organization itself and is based on internal needs, such as risk management, performance evaluation, or compliance verification. The primary goal is to identify areas of improvement within the organization, ensure adherence to internal policies, and uncover inefficiencies or risks.

- **External audits**: External audits occur when a business audits its vendors, suppliers, or customers to ensure the integrity and accuracy of transactions, internal controls, compliance with regulations, and the performance of the relationship. The scope of an external audit is broader than internal audits, extending to the relationship between a business and its external entities (e.g., suppliers or customers). The purpose of an external audit is to verify that the other party (such as a vendor or supplier) is fulfilling their contractual obligations, ensuring that transactions are accurate, controls are in place, and risks are mitigated.

- **Independent audits**: Independent audits are conducted by third-party auditors who are not affiliated with either the organization being audited or its customers or suppliers. These audits are often used for licensing, certification, or product approval. Independent auditors have a broad, objective scope as they assess the compliance of an entity against established standards, regulations, or industry benchmarks. The goal of an independent audit is to provide an unbiased, objective evaluation of a company's compliance with regulations, standards, or contractual obligations. These audits often result in certification, licensing, or approval for public or industry recognition.

Evidence

When conducting an audit, the process of gathering evidence is similar to that of a detective gathering clues, requiring careful analysis of both high-value and low-value data. As an auditor, you must constantly assess the quality and quantity of the evidence collected to ensure it supports your findings effectively. This evidence can be discovered through a variety of methods, such as personal observations, reviewing internal documentation, using **computer-assisted audit techniques** (**CAAT**), or examining correspondence and meeting minutes. The goal is to gather relevant, reliable evidence that will help substantiate the audit's conclusions.

Examples of the various types of audit evidence include the following:

- Documentary evidence can include a business record of transactions, receipts, invoices, and logs.

- Data extraction, which uses automated tools to mine details from data files.

- Auditee claims, which are representations made in oral or written statements.

- Analysis of plans, policies, procedures, and flowcharts.

- Results of compliance and substantive audit tests.

- Auditor's observations of auditee work or re-performance of the selected process.

Evidence lifecycle

The evidence collected during an audit goes through seven essentials lifecycle phases, each critical to ensuring the integrity and validity of the audit findings. These phases include identification, collection, initial preservation storage, analysis, post-analysis preservation storage, presentation, and return of the evidence to the owner. Throughout this process, it is vital for the auditor to remain vigilant about the legal requirements surrounding evidence-handling, as mishandling or failing to maintain a proper chain of custody can lead to evidence being disqualified. This is particularly important in compliance audits, such as those for the *Sarbanes-Oxley (SOX) Act*, where proper evidence management ensures the audit's legitimacy. In addition to SOX, maintaining secure and compliant evidence-handling practices is essential for adhering to various industry regulations, as failure to do so could result in legal and reputational consequences.

The following figure shows the evidence lifecycle:

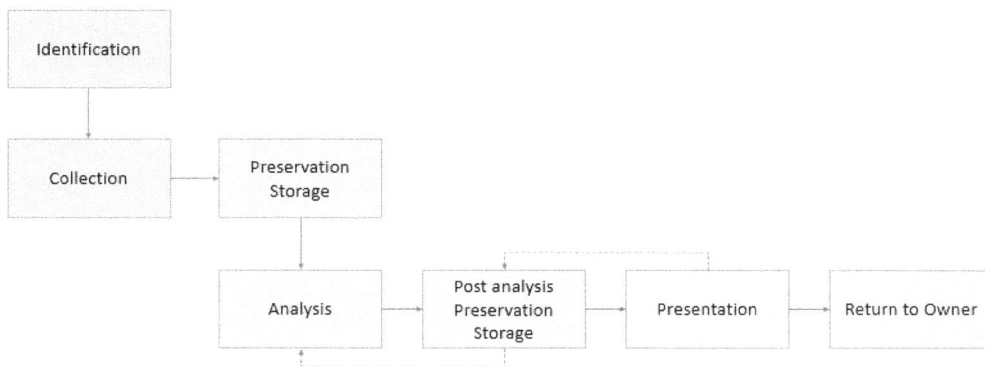

Figure 12.5: Audit evidence lifecycle

The seven phases of the evidence lifecycle ensure that evidence is handled securely and correctly throughout the audit or investigation process. Here is a brief overview of each phase:

- **Identification**: This is the initial phase where the evidence is identified and determined to be relevant to the audit or investigation. This includes recognizing potential pieces of evidence that could support the findings.

- **Collection**: During this phase, the evidence is gathered. It is important that evidence is collected systematically and carefully to prevent contamination, loss, or alteration. This may involve physical collection of documents or data extraction using tools and techniques.

- **Initial preservation storage**: Once collected, evidence must be properly preserved to ensure it remains intact and uncontaminated. This involves securing the evidence in a controlled environment, such as sealed containers or secure storage systems, to prevent tampering or degradation.

- **Analysis**: The evidence is then analyzed in this phase to determine its relevance and to extract valuable insights. The analysis might involve detailed data examination, document review, or testing to draw conclusions and support audit objectives.

- **Post-analysis preservation storage**: After analysis, evidence must be securely stored again to maintain its integrity. This ensures that it remains intact, in case it needs to be reviewed later or used in legal proceedings. It is critical to maintain a proper chain of custody during this phase.

- **Presentation**: In this phase, the evidence is presented in a clear and organized manner, typically as part of an audit report or during a legal or regulatory review. It must be structured to support the conclusions and findings of the audit or investigation.

- **Return of the evidence to the owner**: Once the audit or investigation is complete, the evidence is returned to its rightful owner unless it needs to be retained for legal purposes. This phase ensures that the evidence is properly handed back, with appropriate documentation, maintaining a clear record of the evidence's handling.

These phases ensure that evidence is managed with integrity, from identification to final return, maintaining its reliability and validity throughout the audit or investigation process.

Conclusion

In this chapter, we explored the objective of control assessment, focusing on determining the effectiveness of existing controls in safeguarding an organization's assets and data. We also delved into the development of a detailed security assessment plan and assessment procedure, providing guidance for organizations to create a tailored approach to evaluate their security measures. By understanding the assessment process, organizations can ensure their controls are not only in place but are functioning as intended to mitigate risks effectively.

Additionally, the chapter highlighted key concepts of audit, with an emphasis on the essential steps of audit planning. We explored how to define audit scope, set objectives, and ensure a structured approach to the process. The chapter also covered the stages of an audit, outlining the key activities and the roles and responsibilities of those involved. As we transition into the next chapter, our focus will shift to a more detailed exploration of control assessment and compliance checklists, which will serve as critical tools for ensuring ongoing adherence to security standards and regulations.

Key terms

- Control assessments are the testing of controls to ensure that they are implemented, operating, and functioning properly so an organization can meet security and privacy objectives.

- The subject of an audit is a broad definition, whereas the scope further defines exactly which processes, locations, and systems will be audited.

- Internal audits (or first-party audits) represent a self-declaration of conformity. A moderate level of independence may be demonstrated by the auditor having no responsibility in the activity being audited.

- External audits (or second-party audits) represent customers, vendors, or someone with interest in the activity being audited will conduct the audit.

- Independent external audits (or third-party audits) is the highest level of trust because the auditors are not related to the organization being audited. The conclusions of this audit can be used for licensing or industry certification.

- Integrated audit (or combined audit) occurs when two or more functions are being audited at the same time for the sake of efficiency.

- In a joint audit, two or more auditor organizations cooperate to audit a single auditee. This might occur because of the complexities of scope or tight deadlines.

- Conformity is the testing of evidence that proves that the auditee is ccomplishing their stated objectives. Minimum requirements have been met.

- Nonconformity is the testing that indicates that a violation exists that needs to be corrected. The violation found may be of minor or major significance. Nonconformities include system defects or missing control capabilities.

- Opportunity for improvement is a specific item found is not in violation but should be targeted as an opportunity for improvement. For example, if the level of work integration is low, fixing this issue could reduce waste or the amount of manual effort required.

- A bonded evidence storage facility might be used for storage when the evidence is used in legal cases lasting several years. An example would be a case of corporate fraud or theft.

Join our book's Discord space

Join the book's Discord Workspace for Latest updates, Offers, Tech happenings around the world, New Release and Sessions with the Authors:

https://discord.bpbonline.com

CHAPTER 13

Conducting Assessment and Audit

Introduction

This chapter provides a comprehensive overview of the key *National Institute of Standards and Technology* (*NIST*) compliance checklist, which is designed to help organizations identify any gaps in compliance and reduce the risk of data breaches. The chapter delves into the control assessment steps that assess the effectiveness of security systems, focusing on how to evaluate the implementation and management of security controls. The chapter also outlines the compliance verification process to ensure if the system aligns with the regulatory requirements and organization policies.

In addition to compliance and control assessments, this chapter covers the audit methodology and its crucial phases, emphasizing the importance of structured planning and evidence gathering to support compliance findings. The chapter also explores security testing techniques such as vulnerability scanning and penetration testing, which are essential for identifying weaknesses in systems and verifying their resilience against potential cyberattacks. Through these assessments and testing procedures, organizations can continuously strengthen their security posture.

Structure

The chapter covers the following main topics:

- Compliance checklist
- Compliance verification
- Audit methodology
- Vulnerability scanning
- Penetration testing

Objectives

By the end of this chapter, you will have a clear and thorough understanding of the compliance checklist, enabling you to support the business need for robust security measures and regulatory adherence. You will learn how to leverage these checklists to assess and close compliance gaps, ensuring that your organization meets the necessary standards to mitigate the risk of data breaches. The chapter will also guide you through the various phases of control assessment, focusing on how to evaluate the effectiveness of security controls.

Additionally, this chapter will introduce you to the audit methodology, providing insights into how audits are planned, executed, and reported to assess system security and compliance. You will gain practical knowledge on gathering audit evidence through techniques like document reviews, interviews, and observations. The chapter will also highlight essential security testing techniques, including vulnerability scanning and penetration testing, to help you identify and address vulnerabilities within your systems.

Compliance checklist

A compliance checklist is a useful tool that helps organizations follow the laws, regulations, and industry standards they are required to meet. It provides a clear guide for the steps and procedures needed to stay compliant. These checklists are customized to fit the specific needs of a business, considering its industry, location, and unique requirements. By using a checklist, businesses can effectively address risks and ensure they meet all necessary standards.

The checklist also serves as a reference to track compliance over time. It often includes actions like conducting audits, keeping accurate records, implementing security measures, and training employees on regulations. The checklist helps businesses identify any compliance gaps and reduce the risk of violations, data breaches, or fines. It may also include plans for corrective actions to fix problems if they arise, ensuring businesses can respond quickly to compliance issues.

The backbone of any good risk management strategy includes evidence validation and periodic reviews. Evidence validation means information that forms the basis for decisions has to be accurate, credible, and relevant, while periodic reviews give assurance that organizations periodically review systems, processes, and controls to keep up with emerging risks, regulations, and threats. Integrating evidence validation with routine reviews will enable an organization to keep a proactive compliance and risk management posture, hence being able to respond in appropriate time and take proper action whenever issues arise.

One key advantage of a compliance checklist is that it helps prevent compliance drift, where businesses unknowingly move away from required standards. This can happen due to changing regulations or business practices. A good checklist helps businesses stay on track by regularly reviewing and updating their processes to meet current standards. In the end, the checklist supports continuous improvement, helping businesses avoid costly mistakes and stay compliant.

Types of compliance and audit checklists

There are several types of compliance checklists that businesses can use to ensure adherence to various regulatory and industry standards. Each checklist is tailored to specific areas of compliance and the unique requirements of an organization. Some common types are shown in the following figure:

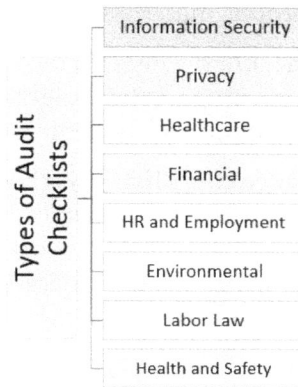

Figure 13.1: Audit checklists

Here is the detail of all checklists:

- **Information security compliance checklist**: This checklist ensures that businesses meet necessary security standards to protect sensitive data. It covers frameworks like *Service Organization Control 2 (SOC 2)*, *Payment Card Industry Data Security Standard (PCI DSS)*, *International Organization for Standardization (ISO) 27001*, and *NIST*, and includes tasks such as data encryption, network security, access control, incident response, and audit logging.

- **Privacy compliance checklist**: This checklist ensures that businesses comply with data privacy laws like *General Data Protection Regulation* (*GDPR*) and *California Consumer Privacy Act* (*CCPA*), covering consent management, data access controls, breach notifications, and handling personal data.

- **Healthcare compliance checklist**: This checklist is used by the healthcare organizations to ensure that they meet regulations regarding patient privacy and care. This includes compliance with *Health Insurance Portability and Accountability Act* (*HIPAA*) standards.

- **Financial compliance checklist**: This checklist is relevant for businesses in the financial sector. This checklist ensures compliance with regulations like the *Sarbanes-Oxley* (*SOX*) *Act*, **anti-money laundering** (**AML**) laws, and accounting standards such as *Generally Accepted Accounting Principles* (*GAAP*) or *International Financial Reporting Standards* (*IFRS*). It includes financial reporting, audits, and internal controls.

- **HR and employment compliance checklist**: This checklist ensures that businesses adhere to employment laws. This covers areas like fair hiring practices, workplace safety, wage and hour laws, anti-discrimination, employee benefits, and record-keeping requirements.

- **Environmental compliance checklist**: This checklist helps businesses to comply with environmental regulations, including waste management, pollution control, emissions standards, hazardous materials handling, and sustainability initiatives.

- **Labor law compliance checklist**: This checklist helps businesses to ensure that they follow labour laws protecting workers' rights. It covers areas such as working hours, wages, overtime pay, employee benefits, and workplace safety.

- **Health and safety compliance checklist**: This checklist helps businesses to comply with the safety regulations, such as *Occupational Safety and Health Administration* (*OSHA*) guidelines. It covers topics like workplace hazards, safety training, **personal protective equipment** (**PPE**), emergency procedures, and employee health programs.

Key NIST compliance checklist publications

NIST SP 800-53: This is a fundamental publication offering an exhaustive catalogue of security controls and guidelines designed to assist organizations in safeguarding their information systems. It provides detailed procedures and strategies to effectively manage Federal Information Systems while tailoring solutions according to an organization's specific risk levels. Although initially intended for federal agencies, its relevance extends to private entities as well, offering valuable security frameworks that help address evolving cyber threats and ensure data protection. This makes SP 800-53 an essential resource for businesses aiming to strengthen their security measures. Following are the steps in the NIST 800-53 compliance checklist for protecting sensitive data:

1. **Define the security control requirements**: Identify the specific security controls needed based on the organization's security needs and risk assessments.

2. **Assess the security environment**: Evaluate the existing security posture to understand the current security capabilities and any gaps.

3. **Select and tailor security controls**: Choose appropriate security controls from the NIST 800-53 catalogue and customize them to fit the organization's needs.

4. **Implement security controls**: Deploy the selected controls across the organization's information systems, ensuring they address identified risks and threats.

5. **Test and validate controls**: Conduct testing to ensure that the implemented controls are functioning effectively and provide the necessary protection.

6. **Document security measures**: Create detailed documentation to demonstrate that the security controls are in place and functioning as intended.

7. **Monitor and assess security controls**: Continuously monitor the effectiveness of security controls to ensure they remain operational and adjust as needed.

8. **Review and update policies**: Regularly review and update security policies, procedures, and controls to address new risks or regulatory changes.

9. **Train staff**: Provide ongoing training to employees to ensure they understand security protocols and their role in maintaining compliance.

10. **Prepare for audits and assessments**: Ensure readiness for internal or external audits by maintaining comprehensive records and supporting evidence of compliance.

NIST SP 800-171: This publication focuses specifically on safeguarding **Controlled Unclassified Information** (**CUI**) within non-federal systems. This publication provides critical guidance for organizations that manage sensitive data, ensuring its secure storage and transmission. By adhering to the standards set out in SP 800-171, organizations can mitigate the risk of compromising data that could potentially impact operations, assets, or individuals. Together, SP 800-53 and SP 800-171 serve as key NIST compliance checklists, offering organizations structured and comprehensive approaches to bolster their cybersecurity posture and meet regulatory requirements effectively. Following are the steps in the NIST 800-171 compliance checklist for protecting sensitive data:

1. **Assess the scope of the contract**: Understand the specific security requirements related to the contract and determine if the organization handles CUI.

2. **Identify whether to deal with CUI**: Determine if the data being handled falls under the category of CUI that requires protection.

3. **Classify the data**: Properly classify data to ensure it is handled according to its sensitivity level.

4. **Gather appropriate documentation**: Collect the necessary documentation that outlines current security measures and compliance efforts.

5. **Conduct a gap analysis**: Identify any gaps between current practices and NIST 800-171 requirements.

6. **Develop and test baseline controls**: Establish security controls and test them to ensure they meet the required standards.

7. **Gather the right evidence**: Collect evidence, such as logs and audit reports, to demonstrate compliance.

8. **Conduct continuous monitoring**: Implement ongoing monitoring to detect security risks and ensure compliance is maintained.

9. **Train employees**: Ensure employees are trained on security protocols and the importance of protecting sensitive information.

Compliance findings

Compliance findings are essential in the identification of weaknesses or gaps in controls that might lead to the exposure of the organization to risks in terms of data breaches or even legal issues. These findings are then analyzed for their severity to help prioritize the most critical risks that need immediate attention. In order to address those findings, corrective actions may be developed, such as enhancing access controls or developing mechanisms for encryption. Additionally, findings from compliance support continuous monitoring to ensure that corrective actions are effective and sustained over time. Finally, findings related to regulatory non-compliance guide the development of the risk response plan, ensuring the organization meets legal obligations and avoids potential penalties. The details with examples are provided in *Chapter 14, Developing Report and Risk Response* under topic *Audit findings*.

Risk mitigation activities address non-compliant findings by implementing corrective actions through control, such as process enhancement and regulatory compliance. In fact, these activities are very instrumental in reducing the likelihood or potential risk impact, such as security breaches or legal penalties. Once corrective actions have been implemented, previously identified non-compliant findings should be reassessed to ensure that changes have been effective in addressing the issues. Continuous monitoring and periodic reviews provide verification of the mitigation strategies, ensuring any new or recurring compliance gaps in these are brought up and quickly fixed.

NIST guidance on assessing security controls

The fifth step in the NIST **Risk Management Framework** (RMF) is assess where the security controls implemented within an information system are evaluated to determine their effectiveness in meeting the intended security requirements. This step involves conducting a thorough assessment of the system's security posture, identifying vulnerabilities or weaknesses, and verifying that the controls function as intended. The following figure shows the fifth step of NIST RMF:

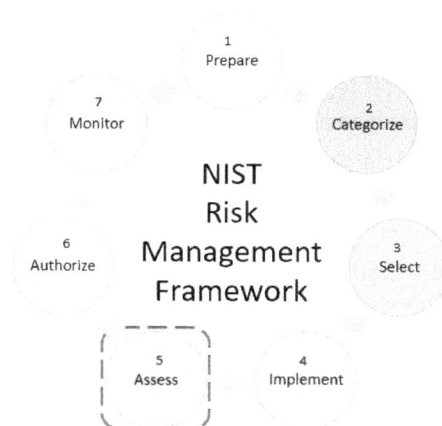

Figure 13.2: NIST RMF steps

The results of this assessment provide the necessary information for decision-makers to understand the system's risk level and whether additional corrective actions are required before the system can be authorized for operation. The assess step ensures that the system remains secure throughout its lifecycle and aligns with organizational security objectives. The following figure shows the task associated with assessment step:

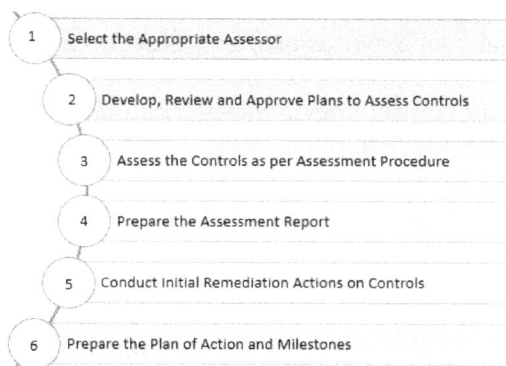

Figure 13.3: Assessment steps

Let us look at the steps in detail:

- **Task 1**: **Select the appropriate assessor**: When selecting control assessors, organizations must ensure they have the required technical expertise, independence, and knowledge of risk management, hardware, software, and firmware. The senior agency information security officer may manage the selection of assessors, considering collaboration between security and privacy control assessors, as both objectives may overlap. Organizations can choose self-assessments or hire independent assessors, who must be free from conflicts of interest to ensure impartiality. The authorizing official decides on the level of independence required, with input from key officials. The system privacy officer ensures privacy controls meet compliance and manages privacy risks, though the senior agency official for privacy remains accountable for the assessment results. The following table shows the roles in selecting the appropriate assessor:

Primary responsibility	Supporting roles	SDLC phase	References
Authorizing official or authorizing official designated representative	Chief information officer; senior agency information security officer; senior agency official for privacy.	New: Development/ acquisition; implementation/ assessment. Existing: Operations/ maintenance	NIST SP 800-30; SP 800-53A; SP 800-55; FIPS 199

Table 13.1: Roles to select the appropriate assessor

- **Task 2: Develop, review and approve plans to assess controls**: Control assessors create security and privacy assessment plans based on information from security and privacy plans, program management controls, and common control documentation. These plans can be integrated for both security and privacy controls, outlining roles, objectives, and procedures for different types of evaluations, such as testing, audits, or continuous monitoring. The plans must be reviewed and approved by the authorizing official to ensure they align with organizational goals, set expectations, and allocate resources efficiently. If controls are provided by external parties, organizations can request their assessment plans and results to verify control effectiveness. The following table shows the roles to develop, review and approve plans to assess controls:

Primary responsibility	Supporting roles	SDLC phase	References
Authorizing official or authorizing official designated representative; control assessor	Senior agency information security officer; senior agency official for privacy; system owner; common control provider; information owner or steward; system security officer; system privacy officer	New: Development/ acquisition; implementation/ assessment. Existing: Operations/ maintenance	NIST SP 800-53A; SP 800-160 v1; SP 800-161

Table 13.2: Roles to develop, review and approve plans

- **Task 3: Assess the controls as per the assessment procedure**: Control assessments check if security and privacy controls are properly implemented, functioning correctly, and achieving the desired results. These assessments, led by skilled assessors, identify weaknesses or risks in the controls. The senior agency official for privacy is responsible for assessing privacy controls before the system goes live and periodically afterward. Collaboration between assessors may be needed if controls address both security and privacy. Early assessments in the **system development lifecycle** (**SDLC**), such as during design reviews or testing, help identify issues early for cost-effective fixes. Assessments can also be done during procurement and, with automation, can speed up continuous monitoring. In agile environments, assessments are done at the end of each cycle for efficiency. The following table shows the roles to assess the controls as per assessment procedure:

Primary responsibility	Supporting roles	SDLC phase	References
Control assessor	Authorizing official or authorizing official designated representative; system owner; common control provider; information owner or steward; senior agency information security officer; senior agency official for privacy; system security officer; system privacy officer	New: Development/acquisition; implementation/assessment. Existing: Operations/maintenance	NIST SP 800-53A; SP 800-160 v1

Table 13.3: Roles to assess the controls

- **Task 4**: **Prepare the assessment report**: The results of security and privacy control assessments, including recommendations for fixing deficiencies, are documented in assessment reports prepared by assessors. These reports, which may cover both security and privacy controls, are crucial for the authorization process and help authorizing officials evaluate the effectiveness of controls and related risks. The level of detail varies depending on the type of assessment, such as testing, audits, or monitoring. Interim reports track assessment progress throughout the SDLC and contribute to the final report. Organizations may also create an executive summary to highlight key findings and recommendations, ensuring stakeholders can quickly grasp the most important issues. The following table shows the roles to prepare the assessment report:

Primary responsibility	Supporting roles	SDLC phase	References
Control assessor	System owner; common control provider; system security officer; system privacy officer.	New: Development/acquisition; implementation/assessment. Existing: Operations/maintenance	NIST SP 800-53A; SP 800-160 v1

Table 13.4: Roles to prepare the assessment report

- **Task 5**: **Conduct initial remediation actions on controls**: Security and privacy assessment reports document control deficiencies found during or after system development, which may pose risks, including supply chain risks. Based on these findings, the authorizing official, with input from system owners and stakeholders, may decide if risks are unacceptable and need immediate remediation. Some issues can be fixed quickly, while others may require more action. After initial remediation, assessors reassess the controls to verify their effectiveness and update the reports without altering the original results. The security and privacy plans are then updated to reflect the corrected controls. Organizations may also create an addendum to the reports, allowing system owners to respond and provide context or clarification, helping authorizing officials make informed risk management decisions. The following table shows the roles to conduct the initial remediation actions:

Primary responsibility	Supporting roles	SDLC phase	References
System owner; common control provider; control assessor	Authorizing official or authorizing official designated representative; senior agency information security officer; senior agency official for privacy; senior accountable official for risk management or risk executive (function); information owner or steward; systems security engineer; privacy engineer; system security officer; system privacy officer.	New: Development/ acquisition; implementation/ assessment. Existing: Operations/ maintenance	NIST SP 800-53A; SP 800-160 v1

Table 13.5: Roles to conduct initial remediations

- **Task 6**: **Prepare the plan of action and milestones**: The **plan of action and milestones (POA&M)** is part of the system authorization package and outlines steps to address control deficiencies found during assessments and monitoring. It includes tasks, required resources, milestones, and deadlines. The authorizing official reviews the POA&M to ensure remediation actions align with organizational priorities and approves any residual risks. Progress is tracked, and deficiencies accepted as residual risks are not included in the POA&M but remain documented in the assessment reports. Organizations follow a standardized process for creating POA&Ms, guided by risk assessments and prioritizing remediation based on severity, impact, and operational needs, ensuring resources are allocated to address critical risks. The following table shows the roles to prepare the POA&M:

Primary responsibility	Supporting roles	SDLC phase	References
System owner; common control provider	Information owner or steward; system security officer; system privacy officer; senior agency information security officer; senior agency official for privacy; control assessor; chief acquisition officer.	New: Implementation/ assessment. Existing: Operations/ maintenance	NIST SP 800-30; SP 800-53A; SP 800-160 v1

Table 13.6: Roles to prepare the POA&M

Compliance verification

The compliance verification methods are critical processes in evaluating the compliance, effectiveness, and security of systems and operations. They provide a structured approach to assess how well systems, activities, or processes meet specific requirements or standards. The three main assessment methods—examine, interview, and test serve different purposes and are applied based on the goals and context of the assessment:

- **Examine method**: The examine method involves review, inspection, or analysis of various elements, including specifications, mechanisms, or activities. This helps the assessor in following ways:

    o **Facilitate understanding**: The checking/analysis of documents, procedures, or system configurations enables the assessor to understand how a system or process works.

    o **Achieve clarification**: The examine method may highlight details that are not clear in a system or process.

    o **Gather proof**: The process helps in gaining good evidence to verify if the system meets the required standards or controls.

    Example: A compliance officer can check the system logs or configuration settings in the system to verify if the system meets cybersecurity standards.

- **Interview technique**: This technique involves one-to-one or even group conversations with individuals to acquire knowledge and insight regarding organizations. This can be helpful in the following ways:

    o **Facilitating understanding**: It provides a clear understanding of the practices or decisions behind certain practices that could be dangerous.

    o **Clarification**: Interviews help provide clarity for specific doubts either in the implementation of controls or in the process.

    o **Providing evidence**: Through interviews, assessors get firsthand information that acts like evidence of compliance and security in operations.

    Example: An assessor may interview the IT personnel in order to be enlightened on the security controls enforcement and maintenance across a network.

- **Testing method**: Exercising one or more objects under specified conditions whether activity or mechanism, to compare actual performance or behaviour with expected behaviour. This methodology assists in the following ways:

    o **Performance testing**: It determines directly whether or not the system functions as anticipated to meet basic security or operational requirements.

    o **Gaps identification**: Testing may reveal flaws in mechanisms or processes that may not be evident through review or discussion alone.

Example: A penetration test may be carried out to check whether the system is resilient to attacks and whether its security measures are appropriate.

Gathering and evaluating evidence

Evidence gathering and evaluation are core activities in the audit process for carrying out the objectives of the audit accurately and reliably. The process should start with a thorough understanding of the auditor regarding the audit's objectives, scope, and criteria. These understandings will be the guidelines in choosing the appropriate methods to collect the evidence, which may include document reviews, interviews, observations, and data analysis. Each of these methods is selected according to the nature of the audit, resource availability, and the type of information required.

Key steps of evidence validation:

1. **Verification of sources**: The basis of verification should be that evidence is obtained from reliable sources, such as logs, records, reports, or an interview with concerned personnel to ascertain that the assessment data is valid and free from falsification.

2. **Completeness and consistency**: Verification of evidence is needed for consistency among sources. Evidence inconsistent or incomplete can be reflective of operational failures or compliance. For example, multiple system logs should indicate the consistency of events or some other activities.

3. **Corroborating evidence**: Evidence has to be corroborated, which means it should be checked against other independent sources. For example, interview responses about a process can be verified against documented policies or system configurations to ensure that they correspond.

4. **Relevance**: Evidence must relate directly to the specific control, regulation, or objective being assessed. Irrelevant data should not be used for validating compliance or operational effectiveness.

5. **Data integrity**: It means that proof should not have been tampered with or damaged. This could be done by means of verifying the integrity of digital evidence using hash values or ensuring physical evidence remains unaltered.

Evidence validation methods

The selection of methods for gathering evidence depends on the audit's needs, resources, and information requirements. Common methods include:

- **Document reviews**: Auditors examine policies, procedures, security controls, and internal reports to gain insights into organizational operations, control mechanisms, and compliance.

- **Interviews**: Discussions with key personnel, such as management and staff, provide valuable firsthand insights into organizational practices, risks, and challenges.

- **Direct observations**: Observing operational processes helps auditors validate the information collected and assess how procedures are implemented in practice.

- **Evaluating audit evidence**: Once the evidence is gathered, auditors must assess it based on the following key criteria:

    o **Relevance**: Ensure that the evidence directly supports the audit's objectives and criteria.

    o **Reliability**: Assess the accuracy, completeness, and integrity of the data, as well as the credibility of the source and the competence of the information provider.

    o **Sufficiency**: Evaluate whether there is enough robust and high-quality evidence to substantiate the audit's conclusions and recommendations effectively.

    o **Objectivity**: Auditors must remain objective throughout the evaluation process, ensuring conclusions are based on evidence, not biases or assumptions.

- **Documentation of evidence**: Thorough documentation is essential for maintaining transparency, supporting accountability, and facilitating future audits. This includes:

    o Detailed records of the sources of evidence.

    o Documentation of the methods used for gathering and evaluating evidence.

    o Insights and observations gathered throughout the audit process.

    o Comprehensive records help reinforce the audit's findings and ensure they can withstand external scrutiny and verification.

Finally, all evidence and evaluation steps must be meticulously documented to maintain transparency, support accountability, and facilitate future audits. Detailed records of evidence sources, methods, and insights ensure the audit's findings are verifiable and can withstand external scrutiny, reinforcing the credibility and integrity of the audit process.

Audit methodology

The internal audit process is structured into four critical phases: Planning, fieldwork, reporting, and follow-up, each playing a vital role in assessing an organization's operations and ensuring that risks are effectively managed and controls are working properly. These phases are interconnected, with each one building upon the findings and results of the previous phase, contributing to the overall success and impact of the audit process.

The following figure shows the phases of the audit:

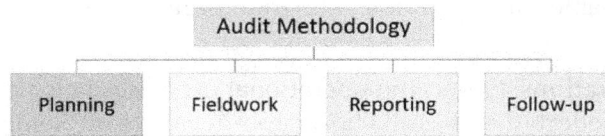

Figure 13.4: *Audit phases*

Here is the breakdown of critical audit phases:

- **Planning**: The planning phase sets the foundation for the audit, focusing on defining the audit's scope, objectives, and areas of risk. It begins with gathering relevant information and conducting a risk assessment to ensure that the audit focuses on critical areas that align with the organization's priorities. This phase involves setting clear objectives, creating a detailed audit plan, and allocating resources effectively. A well-executed planning phase ensures that the audit is efficient and focused, increasing the chances of identifying significant risks and areas of improvement. However, it requires substantial time and effort to gather necessary data and consult with stakeholders.

- **Fieldwork**: The fieldwork phase is where auditors gather evidence and test the effectiveness of controls. This phase involves conducting tests, reviewing documents, and performing interviews to understand how operations are carried out and assess compliance with policies. It allows auditors to identify operational inefficiencies, control failures, and areas of non-compliance. This phase can be labour-intensive and disruptive, requiring detailed analysis and technical expertise to ensure accurate findings. The evidence gathered in this phase forms the foundation of the audit report, enhancing the credibility of the audit's conclusions.

- **Reporting**: The reporting phase is where auditors compile their findings into a structured report, highlighting key issues, risks, and control weaknesses. The report includes actionable recommendations for improvement based on the evidence gathered during the fieldwork phase. This phase is critical for ensuring that the audit's insights are communicated effectively to management and stakeholders, facilitating informed decision-making. A well-crafted report enhances transparency and accountability, although challenges such as resistance to critical findings or complexity in communicating technical issues may arise.

- **Follow-up**: The follow-up phase ensures that corrective actions recommended in the audit report are implemented and effective. This phase involves tracking the progress of action plans developed by management to address the audit's findings. It is essential to confirm that the audit's value is realized and to promote continuous improvement. Regular monitoring and reporting on the progress of corrective actions help sustain improvements, but challenges such as delays in implementation or resistance to change may affect its effectiveness.

Vulnerability scanning

Vulnerability scanning is a proactive security assessment process designed to identify weaknesses and vulnerabilities within software applications, networks, or systems. This process helps organizations to detect potential security gaps before they can be exploited by malicious actors. Vulnerability testing, whether conducted manually, through automated tools, or ideally a combination of both, demands personnel with a strong security background and the highest level of trustworthiness. Most vulnerability scanners are specialized software tools that automatically perform these assessments, scanning and evaluating various elements such as devices, systems, code, configurations, and network dependencies. They also assess operating systems, user accounts and permissions, services, and open ports to ensure that all aspects of a network or system are secure.

These scanners work by systematically probing a network for known vulnerabilities and misconfigurations, providing detailed reports about potential security risks. By identifying areas of concern, vulnerability scanners help IT teams prioritize and address security flaws, reducing the likelihood of breaches. While they are powerful tools, it's important to remember that vulnerability scanners are not foolproof and may generate false positives or miss more complex vulnerabilities, which is why human expertise is often necessary to interpret the results effectively.

Goals of vulnerability scan

The goals of a vulnerability assessment are multifaceted and aim to provide a clear, honest evaluation of an environment's security. The goals of the assessment are:

- Evaluate the true security posture of an environment, ensuring vulnerabilities are accurately identified without exaggerating the risks (avoiding false positives).

- Identify as many vulnerabilities as possible, providing honest evaluations and prioritizations based on their potential impact.

- Test how systems react to various circumstances and attacks, learning not just about known vulnerabilities (e.g., outdated software, weak user credentials) but also how unique aspects of the environment may be exploited (e.g., SQL injection, buffer overflows, or social engineering vulnerabilities).

- Explain testing ramifications before deciding on the scope, as certain tests may disrupt vulnerable systems, potentially taking them offline, or negatively affecting production systems due to the load generated by the tests.

Vulnerability scanning process

Vulnerability scanning is a continuous process aimed at identifying and addressing security weaknesses to keep organizations ahead of emerging threats. The following figure shows the vulnerability scanning process:

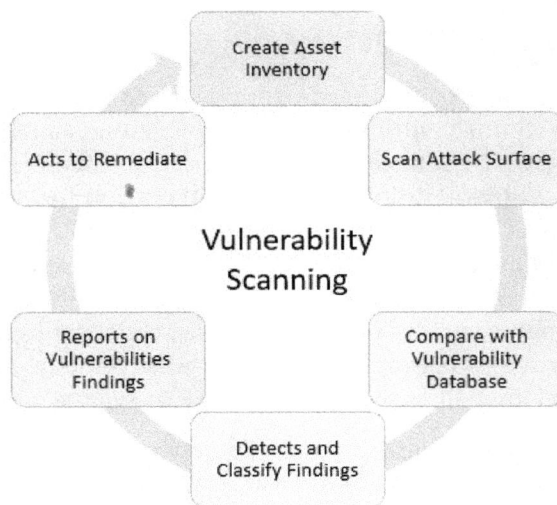

Figure 13.5: Vulnerability scanning process

Here is a step-by-step breakdown of how vulnerability scanning works:

1. **Creates an asset inventory**: The vulnerability scanner first identifies all systems connected to the network, compiling an inventory of devices. This includes details about each device's operating system, software, open ports, and user accounts.

2. **Scans the attack surface**: The scanner then examines the network, hardware, software, and systems to assess potential risk exposures and possible attack vectors that could be exploited by malicious actors.

3. **Compares with vulnerability databases**: The scanner cross-references the systems against vulnerability databases, such as **Common Vulnerabilities and Exposures (CVEs)**, to identify known flaws and potential entry points to sensitive data on the attack surface.

4. **Detects and classifies**: The tool detects vulnerabilities and classifies them based on severity, highlighting system weaknesses that could be exploited by attackers to gain unauthorized access or disrupt operations.

5. **Reports**: After completing the scan, the vulnerability scanner generates detailed reports, outlining the vulnerabilities discovered and providing recommendations on how to mitigate them. This helps organizations prioritize their remediation efforts.

6. **Acts to remediate**: Based on the findings in the vulnerability scan reports, organizations can take action to address the identified vulnerabilities. This could include applying patches, updating software, reconfiguring systems, or implementing additional security measures to reduce risk.

Types of vulnerability scanning

Vulnerability scans can be broadly categorized into two types: Authenticated and unauthenticated scans. The following figure represents two types of vulnerability scanning:

Figure 13.6: Vulnerability scanning types

Here is a detailed breakdown of each scan:

- **Authenticated scans**: Authenticated scans require valid account credentials or access rights to the target system. These scans are typically run with the same level of access that an authorized user would have, allowing the scanner to gather more detailed information from the system.

  - **Deeper insight**: Since authenticated scans have privileged access to the system, they can detect vulnerabilities that may not be visible to unauthenticated scans. For example, they can identify weaknesses that require internal access, such as configuration issues, missing patches, or weak user permissions.

  - **Identify hidden vulnerabilities**: These scans can uncover misconfigurations, missing security updates, or vulnerabilities in software components that might not be exposed externally but can still be exploited internally.

  - **Comprehensive scanning**: Authenticated scans provide a more thorough and accurate assessment of system security, as they can probe the internal system settings, installed software, and configurations, offering a better understanding of potential risks.

- **Unauthenticated scans**: Unauthenticated scans are performed externally and do not require any specific login credentials or access rights to the target system. These scans focus on identifying vulnerabilities that are visible from the outside, such as those that could be exploited by external attackers with no internal knowledge or access.

  - **External perspective**: Unauthenticated scans focus on assessing the attack surface exposed to the internet or external networks. They can identify issues like open ports, outdated software versions, and common misconfigurations that may make the system vulnerable to remote attacks.

  - **Limited scope**: Since these scans do not have privileged access, they cannot detect vulnerabilities that require deeper system-level insights, such as missing patches or configuration weaknesses within the system. They are restricted to visible external vulnerabilities and lack visibility into internal system flaws.

o **Focus on publicly accessible vulnerabilities**: These scans are useful for assessing what an attacker could discover about the system from the outside, helping organizations understand how their network is exposed to potential external threats.

Common vulnerabilities

Vulnerabilities identified through vulnerability scanning can vary depending on the scanning tool used and the specific configuration of the scanning process. Each tool has its strengths and focuses, but typically, vulnerability scans help detect a wide range of weaknesses in a system or network. Here is a more detailed look at some of the vulnerabilities that can be detected:

- **Misconfigured systems**: Scanners can identify systems that have misconfigured settings, such as default or weak configurations, which may be vulnerable to exploitation. Attackers often target these weaknesses because they are easy to discover and can lead to unauthorized access or system compromise.

- **Outdated software**: Scanners detect software versions that are outdated and known to have vulnerabilities. These vulnerabilities should be addressed by updating the software with the latest patches and security fixes, preventing attackers from exploiting unpatched weaknesses.

- **Weak passwords**: Many vulnerabilities scanning tools check for weak or easily guessable passwords. Attackers commonly exploit weak passwords through brute force or dictionary attacks to gain unauthorized access to accounts or systems. Identifying these weak points is essential to maintaining strong access controls.

- **Missing patches**: Scanning tools check for missing patches that may leave systems open to known exploits. Vulnerabilities in unpatched systems are often well-documented, and attackers specifically target them. Regular patch management is critical to keeping systems secure.

- **Open ports and services**: Scanners can identify open ports and exposed services that may present potential entry points for attackers. Unnecessary open ports increase the attack surface and can give attackers avenues to exploit, especially if those services are not properly secured.

- **Insecure configurations**: Some systems may be configured in ways that expose sensitive data or allow unauthorized access. Insecure configurations may include improperly set permissions or weak access controls, which can lead to data breaches or privilege escalation attacks.

- **Default credentials**: Devices or systems using default usernames and passwords are particularly vulnerable. Many devices, especially those that are networked, come with default credentials set by the manufacturer. Attackers can easily exploit these if not changed during setup.

- **Insecure network protocols**: Scanners can detect systems that use outdated or insecure network protocols, such as old versions of **Secure Sockets Layer/Transport Layer Security** (**SSL/TLS**). These protocols may have known vulnerabilities that attackers can exploit to intercept or manipulate data during transmission, leading to security breaches.

Penetration testing

Penetration testing is a proactive security assessment that simulates real-world attacks on a network or system, typically initiated by the organization's owner or senior management. The primary objective is to test and, if possible, bypass the security controls in place to assess an organization's resilience against cyberattacks. By using a variety of procedures and specialized tools, penetration tests help uncover vulnerabilities that could be exploited by malicious actors. This process allows organizations to measure the effectiveness of their security infrastructure, ensuring that they are not just relying on vendors' claims but on a practical evaluation of how their security measures hold up under attack.

A penetration test mimics the **tactics**, **techniques, and procedures** (**TTPs**) of actual attackers, recognizing that cybercriminals can be highly creative and resourceful in their methods. As a result, penetration testing should align with the latest hacking techniques while maintaining strong foundational testing practices. This approach ensures that an organization's defenses are not just theoretically sound but also practical and capable of withstanding sophisticated attacks. By continually evolving to incorporate new attack vectors, penetration testing helps organizations stay ahead of emerging threats and reinforces the robustness of their security posture.

Penetration testing steps

Penetration testing is a methodical process that involves simulating attacks on a network or system to identify security weaknesses. The process is typically divided into five key phases: Reconnaissance, scanning, vulnerability assessment, exploitation, and reporting. Each of these phases plays a critical role in determining the effectiveness of a system's security defense:

Figure 13.7: *Penetration testing steps*

Let us take a closer look at each phase:

- **Reconnaissance (Information gathering)**: Reconnaissance is the initial phase of penetration testing and involves gathering as much information as possible about the target system or network. This phase is crucial because attackers typically rely on publicly available data to identify potential targets and vulnerabilities. In penetration testing, reconnaissance is divided into two types: passive and active:

  o **Passive reconnaissance**: In this approach, testers gather information without directly interacting with the target system. They might use public databases, domain registrations, social media, or Whois lookups to collect details about the target's infrastructure, employees, or systems.

  o **Active reconnaissance**: This type involves directly interacting with the target system, such as pinging a network, scanning open ports, or querying publicly accessible servers. While this can provide more specific information, it may also alert the target to potential security testing.

- **Scanning**: Once reconnaissance is complete, the next step is scanning, where penetration testers attempt to map the target system and find weaknesses that could be exploited. This phase typically involves scanning the system's ports, services, and applications. Tools like Nmap, Nessus, or OpenVAS are commonly used for scanning:

  o **Network scanning**: This involves scanning a network to identify active devices, open ports, and the types of services running on those ports. It helps to map out the system's attack surface.

  o **Vulnerability scanning**: This focuses on identifying known vulnerabilities by cross-referencing the system's configurations with vulnerability databases (e.g., CVEs. Scanning can help detect outdated software, misconfigurations, and other exploitable weaknesses.

- **Vulnerability assessment**: The vulnerability assessment phase involves analyzing the information gathered from scanning to identify and prioritize potential vulnerabilities. This step is essential for understanding the risk that each vulnerability presents to the organization. During this phase, penetration testers assess the severity of each vulnerability by considering factors such as:

  o The potential impact on the organization if the vulnerability were exploited.

  o The ease with which the vulnerability could be exploited by an attacker.

  o Whether the vulnerability is part of a chain of weaknesses that could lead to a more significant attack.

Penetration testers typically use vulnerability assessment tools to check for things like outdated software, missing patches, weak passwords, improper configurations, and other weaknesses that could be exploited.

- **Exploitation**: Exploitation is the phase where penetration testers attempt to take advantage of the identified vulnerabilities to gain unauthorized access to the system. This phase mimics the techniques that real-world attackers would use to infiltrate a system:

  o **Exploiting vulnerabilities**: Using tools or manual methods, the tester actively attempts to exploit the vulnerabilities found during the scanning and assessment phases. This could involve techniques like SQL injection, exploiting buffer overflows, privilege escalation, or social engineering tactics.

  o **Post-exploitation**: If the tester successfully gains access, they may further exploit the system to gain deeper access, escalate privileges, or compromise more critical parts of the system (such as databases or administrative accounts).

- **Reporting**: The final phase of penetration testing is reporting. Once the testing and exploitation phases are complete, the findings are documented in a detailed report. This report provides the following:

  o **Overview of testing**: A summary of the testing process, including the methods used, the scope of the test, and the specific systems or applications tested.

  o **Detailed vulnerabilities**: A comprehensive list of vulnerabilities discovered during the test, along with their severity and potential impact. This also includes evidence from the test, such as screenshots, logs, and other data that demonstrate how the vulnerabilities were exploited.

  o **Recommendations for remediation**: Clear, actionable advice on how to fix the identified vulnerabilities. This can include patching software, changing configurations, implementing stronger access controls, or improving security practices.

Penetration testing approach

Penetration testing can vary greatly depending on the scope of the project, the intended outcomes, and the level of information provided to the tester. Different types of penetration testing techniques are used based on the specific goals of the assessment. Following are three common types of penetration testing as shown in figure:

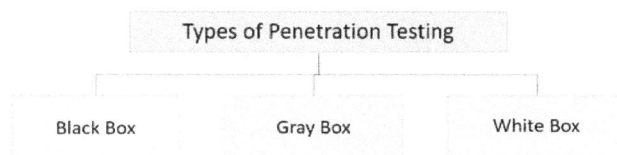

Figure 13.8: Penetration testing approach

Here is the detail of each with its unique approach and characteristics:

- **Black box testing**: Black box testing, also known as **external penetration testing**, is characterized by the tester having little to no prior knowledge about the internal systems, network infrastructure, or security controls in place within the target organization. This type of test aims to simulate an external cyberattack where the attacker has no insider information and must discover vulnerabilities without any context about the organization's setup.

  In black box testing, the ethical hacker begins their attack from outside the organization's network, treating the target like a real-world external threat. They start by attempting to gain unauthorized access from the internet, using publicly available information (such as domain names or IP addresses) and tools to identify vulnerabilities like open ports, misconfigurations, or weak authentication. Since the tester has no inside knowledge, this approach can often be more time-consuming as they must work to gather information from scratch. However, it provides a realistic simulation of how an external attacker might approach the network.

- **White box testing**: White box testing, also known as **internal penetration testing**, is where the tester is given full access to the organization's network architecture and security systems before starting the test. This can include network diagrams, source code, configurations, and detailed information about the systems in place. White box tests provide a comprehensive evaluation of a system's security because the tester has full visibility into the organization's infrastructure.

  This type of test allows the tester to explore vulnerabilities from the perspective of someone who already has access to the network, mimicking an insider threat or a situation where an attacker has gained some level of privileged access. White box testing is one of the most thorough testing methods since it helps identify weaknesses in internal systems, applications, and security configurations that might not be visible during external testing. However, despite being thorough white box testing is often faster than black box testing because the tester does not need to gather external information. That said, for large organizations with complex infrastructures, a full white box test could take months to complete.

- **Gray box testing**: Gray box testing combines elements of both black box and white box testing. In this approach, the tester is provided with partial knowledge about the organization's systems. This could include limited access to certain parts of the network or a brief understanding of how the system is structured but without full insider access.

  Gray box testing is commonly used to assess specific areas of an organization, such as public-facing applications with private server backends. The tester uses their partial knowledge to focus on particular attack surfaces, such as exposed services or entry points that could be exploited to gain further access into the network. Gray box testing strikes a balance between the time-consuming nature of black box testing and the speed of white box testing. It typically takes longer than white box testing due to the limited information available, but it is generally faster than a black box test because the tester has some initial understanding of the network.

There are various ways the pen testers can perform the security assessment to identify and fix vulnerabilities, which are mentioned as follows:

- **SQL injections**: Pen testers try to get a webpage or application to disclose sensitive data by entering malicious code into input fields.

- **Cross-site scripting**: Pen testers try planting malicious code in a company's website.

- **Denial of service attacks**: Pen testers try to take servers, apps, and other network resources offline by flooding them with traffic.

- **Social engineering**: Pen testers use phishing, baiting, pretexting, or other tactics to trick employees into compromising network security.

- **Brute force attacks**: Pen testers try to break into a system by running scripts that generate and test potential passwords until one works.

- **Man-in-the-middle attacks**: Pen testers intercept traffic between two devices or users to steal sensitive information or plant malware.

Conclusion

In this chapter, we explored various types of compliance checklists, providing a framework for identifying compliance gaps and ensuring adherence to security and regulatory standards. We also dived into the steps involved in security control assessment, enabling a deeper understanding of the security posture and how to evaluate the effectiveness of existing controls.

Additionally, the chapter highlighted key audit methodologies and evidence gathering techniques, such as document reviews, interviews, and direct observations, to ensure that audit findings are accurate and reliable. We also examined the concepts of vulnerability scanning, including common vulnerabilities that need to be addressed, and the penetration testing approach to simulate potential cyberattacks. As we go to the next chapter, our focus will shift to audit reporting and the analysis of risk findings, further enhancing our ability to mitigate threats and improve security practices within an organization.

Key terms

- NIST SP 800-53 provides a comprehensive set of security and privacy controls to secure Federal Information Systems and help organizations manage risks.

- NIST SP 800-61 offers a structured approach to computer security incident handling and response.

- NIST SP 800-171 provides specific guidance for protecting CUI in non-federal systems and organizations.

- NIST SP 800-34 focuses on the process of contingency planning for information systems, which is essential for ensuring the continuity of operations in the event of a disruption.

- NIST SP 800-30 provides a framework for conducting information security risk assessments, which is crucial for identifying, evaluating, and mitigating risks to information systems.

- The **National Vulnerability Database** (**NVD**), CVE, and other public websites contain guidance covering physical and logical security controls for IT servers, routers, and other high-value network devices.

- Vulnerability scanning is the process of identifying security weaknesses and flaws in systems and software running on them.

- Active scanning involves sending direct probes and requests to systems or devices to identify vulnerabilities. It provides detailed, in-depth information about exposed services, open ports, and potential misconfigurations.

- Passive scanning monitors network traffic without directly interacting with the systems. It identifies vulnerabilities based on observed data flows, detecting outdated software or insecure communication channels.

- An audit methodology is a systematic approach or framework used to conduct audits. It involves a series of steps and guidelines that help auditors in planning, performing, and reporting on an audit.

- Consistency ensures a consistent approach in different audits, helping in meeting audit objectives effectively.

- The CAAT method of testing is often used to analyze large volumes of data or a sample of compiled data.

Join our book's Discord space

Join the book's Discord Workspace for Latest updates, Offers, Tech happenings around the world, New Release and Sessions with the Authors:

https://discord.bpbonline.com

CHAPTER 14

Developing Report and Risk Response

Introduction

This chapter provides a detailed overview of how to prepare a comprehensive **security assessment report** (**SAR**), covering essential standards and components of audit findings. It emphasizes the importance of structuring the report to include a thorough analysis of the organization's security posture. Additionally, the chapter outlines the framework for creating a risk report that effectively captures and communicates potential risks and vulnerabilities.

The chapter also delves into the development of a risk treatment strategy, offering guidance on selecting appropriate risk mitigation options. A key focus is placed on risk prioritization, including the use of a risk matrix, to help organizations evaluate and rank risks based on their likelihood and impact. This chapter also outlines the necessary steps to prioritize risks and determine the most effective approach to address them. This helps organizations determine which risks require immediate attention and which can be addressed later, ultimately guiding the decision-making process for effective risk management.

Structure

The chapter covers the following main topics:

- Security assessment report

- Audit findings
- Risk report structure
- Risk treatment options
- Risk prioritization

Objectives

By the end of this chapter, you will have a clear understanding of how to prepare a SAR. You will learn how to identify and document risk findings, as well as the process of creating an audit report that highlights key vulnerabilities. This chapter will also introduce you to the essential components of a risk report structure, ensuring you can effectively communicate the security posture of an organization.

Furthermore, this chapter will guide you on how to plan and select appropriate risk treatment options, aligning them with the organization's risk management process. You will gain insight into using a risk prioritization matrix to assess and rank risks based on their potential impact and likelihood. The chapter will also provide strategies for managing risks effectively, helping you prioritize and mitigate threats in a structured manner, ensuring the organization's resources are used efficiently in addressing the most critical risks first.

Security assessment report

A SAR is a crucial document that outlines the findings from security assessments, highlighting any vulnerabilities, weaknesses, or deficiencies identified in the system or infrastructure. The SAR provides detailed insights into the effectiveness of existing security measures, offering clear recommendations for addressing and mitigating any issues. This report serves as an essential tool for decision-makers, helping them understand the risks and prioritize actions for improving security.

These security assessments and the subsequent generation of SARs are typically conducted both at the initial deployment phase of control systems and during periodic checkpoints throughout their operational lifecycle. Regular security assessments ensure that any emerging vulnerabilities are detected and addressed promptly, maintaining the system's integrity over time. The SAR provides a formal record of these evaluations, supporting continuous improvement in security posture and compliance with regulatory requirements.

Key components of security assessment report

A SAR is a comprehensive document designed to evaluate an information system's security posture by identifying vulnerabilities, assessing risks, and providing recommendations to enhance security. Most organizations utilize structured templates to ensure clarity and consistency across SARs. These templates typically follow a defined format, which includes several key components to ensure the report is thorough, actionable, and easy for stakeholders to understand. The following figure shows the key components of SAR:

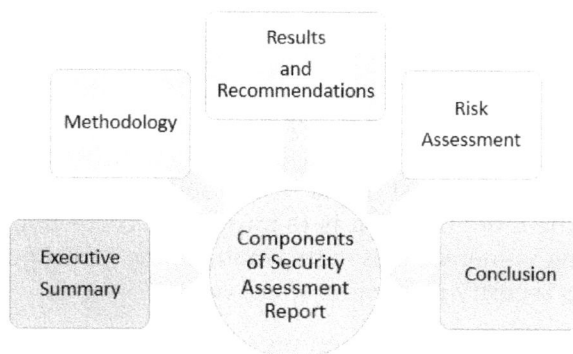

Figure 14.1: Components of SAR

Here is the breakdown of its key components:

- **Executive summary**: The summary section provides a high level overview of the security assessment. It includes the purpose of the assessment, the scope of the evaluation, and a brief description of the key findings. This section serves as an executive summary, allowing decision-makers, such as senior management or stakeholders, to quickly understand the overall security posture without diving into the technical details. It summarizes the security strengths and weaknesses identified during the assessment and gives stakeholders a snapshot of the current risk landscape.

- **Methodology**: The methodology section explains the approach and techniques used to conduct the security assessment. It outlines the steps the organization has already taken to identify and assess vulnerabilities in its systems, processes, and operations. This section is critical for ensuring transparency and reproducibility in the assessment process. It typically includes methodologies such as vulnerability scanning, penetration testing, and interviews with key personnel to gather insights into the information system's security practices. These techniques ensure a comprehensive understanding of the security risks and provide a framework for evaluating the effectiveness of existing controls.

- **Results and recommendations**: The results and recommendations section form the core of the SAR, detailing the vulnerabilities and risks discovered during the assessment. For each identified vulnerability, the report outlines actionable recommendations to mitigate the risks. These recommendations may include technical fixes (such as patching software vulnerabilities or upgrading hardware), updates to policies (such as improving access control protocols or employee training), or the implementation of additional security measures (such as adopting

multifactor authentication (**MFA**) or enhancing encryption practices). This section is typically the most in-depth part of the report, as it not only identifies issues but also provides recommendations for addressing them and improving the organization's security posture.

- **Risk assessment**: The risk assessment section evaluates the potential impact of each identified vulnerability. It assigns a risk level—low, medium, or high based on factors like the likelihood of exploitation and the potential damage if the vulnerability is exploited. This risk categorization helps prioritize remediation efforts, ensuring that the most critical vulnerabilities are addressed first. The higher the risk level, the more urgent it is to implement corrective actions. By assessing and categorizing vulnerabilities in this manner, the report guides the organization in managing its security risks more effectively.

- **Conclusion**: The conclusion section provides a summary of the assessment's key findings, reinforcing the most significant vulnerabilities and risks identified. It reiterates the critical recommendations for improvement and outlines the next steps for remediation. The conclusion also offers suggestions for ongoing security enhancements and monitoring to address evolving threats. For organizations that plan to conduct future security assessments, this section may also highlight areas that will need to be revisited or updated in subsequent SARs. It serves as a final guide for stakeholders on how to proceed with improving security measures, ensuring a continuous commitment to securing the organization's assets.

Standards for security assessment report

Different industries adhere to distinct standards for SARs to meet their regulatory requirements, and these standards often vary in terms of the inclusions and formats they mandate. The most widely recognized frameworks that guide these reports include NIST SP 800-115. The framework provide guidance to create SARs that enable organizations to effectively assess and manage cybersecurity-related risks. These standards will not only facilitate reviewing the present security controls but also make sure that compliance is properly maintained with the regulations applicable to the organization concerning information security and privacy risks.

NIST SP 800-115: NIST SP 800-115 provides a comprehensive guide to perform information security assessments. This document provides methodologies for assessing the security of information systems through various types of testing, including penetration testing, vulnerability scanning, and security audits. NIST SP 800-115 is widely used by *U.S. federal agencies* and private sector organizations, especially those subject to FISMA compliance.

Key components of SAR under NIST SP 800-115 are:

- **Assessment objectives**: Clear definitions of the assessment's goals, including the scope of testing and what the assessment is trying to accomplish, such as vulnerability identification or validation of controls. The methodology should provide detailed descriptions of the testing approaches utilized, which could include automated scanning, manual penetration testing, or other techniques utilized in conducting the assessment.

- **Findings**: Document the vulnerabilities or weaknesses found during the assessment, rank by risk level—high, medium, and low and prioritize by potential impact.

- **Risk analysis**: In-depth risk analysis based on the identified vulnerabilities, including the likelihood of exploitation and the potential impact on the organization.

- **Remediation recommendations**: Actions that could be performed to mitigate or resolve the identified security issues. This may include configuration changes, software patches, or process improvements.

- **Testing summary**: A summary of the results of testing and a conclusion on the overall security posture of the organization.

In addition to that, ISO/IEC 27001 is an international standard for setting up, implementing, maintaining, and continually improving an ISMS. It provides an overall framework that enables organizations to review the adequacy of their information security controls and thus maintain the desired level of information security. ISO/IEC 27001 basically deals with risk management for information assets, identification of threats, determination of the probability of risks, and implementing controls required to manage the risks. This approach allows for a holistic view concerning information security and its continuous improvement.

The scope of the SAR based on ISO/IEC 27001 involves the scope of an ISMS, including systems, processes, and information assets representing boundaries. It assesses the effectiveness of security controls already implemented, including technical measures on encryption and access control, organizational policies, and procedures. The SAR also focuses on risk identification to guarantee confidentiality, integrity, and availability of information. It underlines the non-conformities and gives recommendations for improvement, mentioning that only continuous improvement will ensure ISMS is effective over time.

Prepare SAR

Preparing a SAR is a critical step in documenting the results of a security assessment and communicating the findings to relevant stakeholders. The process of preparing a SAR typically follows a structured six-step methodology, which helps ensure that all aspects of the assessment are thoroughly covered and that the final report is both comprehensive and actionable. The following figure shows the key steps in preparing SAR:

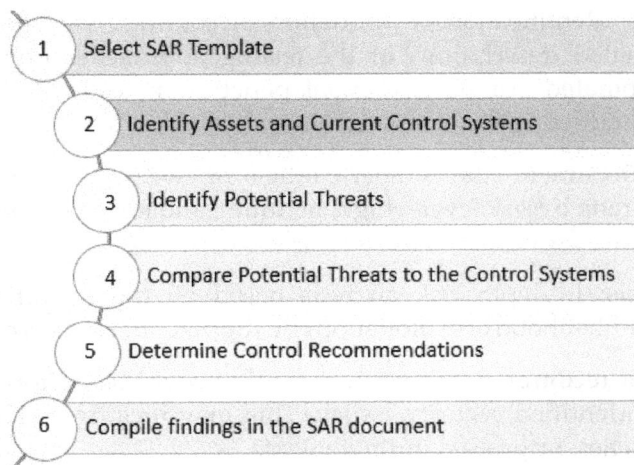

Figure 14.2: Steps to prepare SAR

Following is a detailed breakdown of each of the six steps involved in preparing a SAR:

- **Select a SAR template**: The first step in preparing a SAR is to select or create a SAR template. Many organizations will have a pre-established template for SARs which can help streamline the process of generating the report. If the organization does not have an existing template, finding one or creating one is essential to improving the efficiency of both the report generation and the security assessment process itself. The SAR template typically includes predefined sections that help structure the report, such as executive summary, scope of assessment, methodology, findings, and recommendations. Using the template throughout the assessment process can also help ensure that the report is filled in with relevant information as it becomes available, thus preventing delays at the end of the assessment.

- **Identify assets and current control systems**: The second step involves identifying the assets within the organization that need protection and understanding the current control systems in place. In this context, assets refer to any information systems, data, applications, networks, and infrastructure that your organization relies on for its operations. The goal is to document the key assets that must be secured and understand how they are currently being protected.

  This step involves gathering detailed information about the existing security measures, such as firewalls, access controls, encryption methods, **intrusion detection systems (IDS)**, and other technologies that safeguard your assets. This provides a baseline for the security posture of the organization, which will be used as a point of reference when identifying potential vulnerabilities and evaluating whether current controls are sufficient.

- **Identify potential threats to these assets**: Once you have a clear understanding of the assets and the controls in place, the next step is to identify potential threats that could target these assets. A threat is any possible danger that could exploit a vulnerability in your system, leading to a negative impact on the organization's security or operations. Threats could come from various sources, including cybercriminals, insider threats, natural disasters, hardware failures, or even human error.

This step requires a broad assessment of the possible risks to your assets, typically conducted independently from the current security controls in place. Threat identification is often performed using threat modelling techniques, such as risk assessments or brainstorming exercises with key stakeholders, to understand potential attackers, attack vectors, and the likelihood of specific threats occurring.

- **Compare potential threats to the control systems in place**: After identifying the threats, the next step is to compare these potential threats to the existing control systems that are already in place. The purpose of this comparison is to evaluate how well the current controls mitigate or protect against the identified threats.

  During this step, the security team should assess whether the existing controls are sufficient to counter the identified risks or if there are gaps. Any threats that are not fully mitigated by the current security systems represent vulnerabilities in the organization's defenses. These vulnerabilities may include technical weaknesses, gaps in security procedures, insufficient monitoring, or outdated software. It is also important to evaluate the severity of each vulnerability and its likelihood of being exploited. Many organizations use risk matrices to rank vulnerabilities based on these factors, which helps prioritize which vulnerabilities to address first.

- **Determine control recommendations**: Once vulnerabilities have been identified, the next step is to analyze them and develop control recommendations to mitigate or eliminate the risks associated with each vulnerability. This analysis involves a detailed review of potential control options, such as new technical solutions, enhanced security policies, employee training, or process improvements.

  Control recommendations should be specific, actionable, and tailored to the organization's needs, infrastructure, and resources. The recommendations may involve implementing new technologies, upgrading existing systems, strengthening access controls, or modifying internal processes. The goal is to identify the most effective and feasible security controls to address the identified vulnerabilities, reducing risk to an acceptable level while aligning with organizational priorities and budgets.

- **Compile findings in the SAR document**: The final step in preparing the SAR is to compile all the findings into the SAR document itself. This includes documenting all of the steps, findings, and recommendations from the previous stages into a structured report. The SAR should be clear, concise, and easy to understand, with detailed sections that allow stakeholders to easily digest the information.

Audit findings

An audit report is a formal document issued by an auditor that provides a detailed account of the audit process, findings, assessments, and conclusions. This report is vital for management, stakeholders, and regulatory bodies as it conveys the auditor's evaluation of the organization's information security, operations, or compliance with laws and regulations. The report typically includes the following key components as shown in the figure:

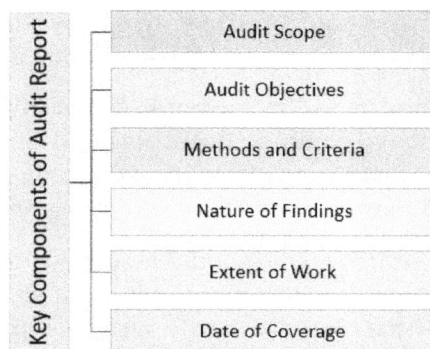

Figure 14.3: Components of audit findings

Here is the detail of the key components:

- **Audit scope**: The scope of an information security audit is defined as the explicit security controls, systems, processes, and policies to be reviewed, limitations, and exclusions in conducting the audit process. Key scopes for an information security audit may include the following:

  o The specific security control practices, operations, or business processes that were subject to examination.

  o The system's information security, data privacy, policies and procedures that were reviewed.

  o Any limitations or exclusions (for example, if certain records were inaccessible, or if parts of the operations were outside the scope).

- **Audit objectives**: The objectives of an information security audit refer to what the auditor seeks to achieve from the audit engagement on the organization's security controls. These set the course that the audit work will take in ensuring that information systems are sufficiently protected against risks. Key objectives for an information security audit may include the following:

  o Evaluating the effectiveness of security controls

  o Assessing compliance with security standards and regulations

- o Providing independent assurance on information security posture

- **Methods and criteria used**: This section explains the methodologies, tools, and criteria the auditor used to perform the audit. It provides transparency regarding the approach taken and how the audit standards were applied. The criteria often include the following:

    - o **Audit standards**: The common audit standards followed are *Generally Accepted Auditing Standards* (*GAAS*) or *International Auditing Standards* (*ISA*).

    - o **Sampling techniques**: The sampling techniques used by the auditor can be statistical or judgmental sampling to test the data.

    - o **Audit tools**: The software or tools used to analyze organization's security posture or operational processes. These tools may include vulnerability scanners, log analysis software, configuration management tools, and other security auditing applications.

- **Nature of findings**: This section outlines the key findings or results discovered during the audit process. It includes the following:

    - o Any discrepancies or weaknesses related to implementation and management of security controls or operations.

    - o Issues related to internal controls, such as lack of segregation of duties, or failures to adhere to policies and procedures.

    - o Instances of non-compliance with laws, regulations, or industry standards.

- **Extent of work performed**: This section describes the depth and breadth of the auditor's work. It communicates how much of the organization's operations or security controls were reviewed. Key points include:

    - o The amount of data tested or reviewed (for example, security logs, network traffic, or a sampling of sensitive data transmissions).

    - o Specific departments, accounts, or systems examined in detail.

    - o Any significant issues that required further investigation or in-depth analysis.

- **Applicable dates of coverage**: The dates of coverage indicate the period during which the audit was conducted and the period the audit covers. The auditor specifies the timeframe of the operations reviewed (usually aligning with the fiscal year or reporting period) and may also include the audit period itself:

    - o **Audit period**: The date range during which the auditor conducted their work.

    - o **Coverage period**: The security measures or operational period that was under review (e.g., fiscal year 2023, Q1 2024).

Risk response plan based on audit findings

Audit results are invaluable in the development of a risk response plan, as they provide a detailed assessment of an organization's compliance, security posture, and operational effectiveness. By identifying potential vulnerabilities, inefficiencies, or areas of non-compliance, audit results enable organizations to develop targeted strategies to mitigate risks. The following figure shows the key components of audit findings to develop risk response plan:

Figure 14.4: Risk response plan from audit findings

Here is how audit results will contribute toward developing a risk response plan:

- **Risk and gap identification**: Audit findings are what a system, process, or control does not meet expectations or the level set by regulatory requirements. In other words, such findings show some vulnerabilities that might lead to risks: a data breach, financial mismanagement, or operational discontinuation.

  Example: If an audit identifies a weakness in password management, it shows there is a risk of unauthorized access, which needs to be covered in the risk response plan.

- **Assessing the level of risks**: Auditors usually assess the seriousness of the findings they identify. This will assist in the prioritization of risks based on their impact. Such an assessment will make it easier to devote organizational resources to the most critical risks with the assurance that the risk response plan covers high-impact threats.

  Example: If an audit reveals that the backup process does not cover all business functions but the likelihood of data loss is very low, then the risk response plan may prioritize the improvement of backup protocols after more critical issues such as cybersecurity threats have been addressed.

- **Evidence for decision-makers**: Audit findings provide strong evidence on which decisions may be based in the risk response plan. Objective data based on the non-compliance findings, system vulnerabilities, or process inefficiencies of an audit ensure that decisions are based on fact rather than assumption.

  Example: If an audit has shown a trend of frequent system downtimes, meaning the system needs improvement in redundancy.

- **Formulation of corrective action**: Corrective action is identified to address issues highlighted by the audit, which helps in minimizing risks. These then become the main substance of a risk response plan, where these identified weaknesses would be dealt with through particular actions like upgrading systems, reviewing policies, or personnel training.

  Example: If the audit finds out that the servers are not patched, then the risk response plan might include an immediate upgrade to the latest version.

- **Control effectiveness evaluation**: The audit findings examine the effectiveness of the internal controls in place. In case some controls are not effective or do not exist at all, an audit provides grounds for enhancing those controls or instating new controls to mitigate associated risks.

  Example: If an audit finds that the logical access controls to systems are inconsistent, then the risk response plan will include authentication mechanisms using MFA.

- **Compliance with requirements**: The audit results ensure that the organization complies with regulatory requirements and industry standards. If the audit finds non-compliance, the risk response plan includes a rectification of such a situation to avoid penalties, fines, or reputational damage.

  Example: If an audit finds that data protections are not met, then a risk response plan will involve the implementation of privacy controls like encryption.

- **Improvement of risk monitoring and reporting**: Most auditing recommendations include improvements on monitoring and reporting processes. These recommendations could help further refine the risk response plan to incorporate continuous monitoring so that the rise of new risks will be detected to reinforce general risk management practices.

  Example: An audit may recommend the automation of system monitoring to identify security breaches. The risk response plan would then detail how such monitoring tools would be integrated into the organization's infrastructure.

Risk report structure

A detailed risk report structure is a formal document that presents an in-depth analysis of identified risks, their assessment, mitigation strategies, and ongoing monitoring. It should be comprehensive, organized, and tailored to the audience's needs, whether for project management, organizational leadership, or compliance purposes. A risk report structure may vary depending on its intended purpose, audience, and the types of risks being evaluated. The following figure shows the report structure components:

| Executive Summary | Risk Profile | Risk Capacity |

| Risk Tolerance | Key Risk Indicator | Risk Management |

| Conclusion | Appendices |

Figure 14.5: Audit report structure

Following is a breakdown of a comprehensive risk report structure, with each section explained in detail:

- **Executive summary**: The executive summary provides a concise overview of the key risks faced by the organization, highlighting the most critical threats and offering a summary of the report's key findings. It includes the following key elements:

  o **Key risks**: List of the top risks identified, such as information security, operational, or safety-related.

  o **Summary of risk impact**: A snapshot of how each risk might affect the organization.

  o **Priority areas**: The most urgent risks and actions that need to be taken.

- **Risk profile**: The risk profile section quantifies and visualizes the risks facing the organization, offering a clear understanding of the relative significance of each identified risk based on its likelihood and potential impact. The risk profile contains the following key elements:

  o **Risk identification**: A description of each risk.

  o **Likelihood and impact ratings**: Likelihood (probability of occurrence) and impact (severity of the consequences) are usually rated on a scale (e.g., low, medium, high).

  o **Risk rating**: Combined score based on a risk matrix, typically calculated by multiplying likelihood by impact (e.g., *low = 1, medium = 2, high = 3*).

  o **Risk prioritization**: Ranking of risks according to their total score, helping to prioritize mitigation efforts.

- **Risk capacity**: The risk capacity defines the maximum level of security and privacy risk the organization can absorb without facing catastrophic consequences. The risk capacity highlights the following contents:

    o **Definition**: A statement of the organization's capacity to withstand security breaches, data loss, and privacy violations before risking business continuity.

- **Contractual obligations**: For security and privacy risks, this might include potential financial, operational, and reputational damage the organization is able to take up due to breaches or data mishandling.

- **Risk tolerance**: The risk tolerance section represents the amount of risk an organization is willing to take on, and is generally lower than its risk capacity. It outlines the boundaries of acceptable risk:

    o **Tolerance levels**: Categorized as conservative, moderate, or aggressive depending on how much risk the company is prepared to accept.

    o **Risk appetite**: The general level of risk the organization is willing to pursue or accept to achieve its objectives.

    o **Specific thresholds**: These are well-defined limits of acceptable risks associated with specific information security events. It can refer to the quantitative measures in terms of the incident percentage rate related to data breach or maximum downtime of critical systems.

- **Key risk indicators (KRIs)**: The KRIs are measurable metrics that signal the potential onset of a risk. KRIs act as early warning systems, enabling the organization to monitor trends and take preventive actions before risks escalate. It contains the following key elements:

    o **Identification of KRIs**: Specific metrics tied to each key risk. These could be internal (e.g., number of incidents, operational downtime) or external (e.g., market volatility, regulatory changes).

    o **Thresholds and alerts**: Defines what value or trend in the KRI would trigger a response or intervention.

- **Effective risk management**: It describes the strategies and measures the organization will take to reduce, transfer, or accept risks. This section highlights both proactive and reactive risk management approaches and contains the following key elements:

    o **Mitigation strategies**: Specific actions designed to reduce or eliminate the risks (e.g., enhanced cybersecurity measures).

    o **Risk transfer**: Using insurance and outsourcing to transfer the risk to third-parties.

- o **Risk avoidance**: Actions taken to avoid risky activities altogether (e.g., abandoning a particular investment or business activity).

- o **Risk acceptance**: Recognizing certain risks as tolerable and not requiring any action unless they breach the organization's tolerance threshold.

- o **Monitoring and reporting**: Regular review of risk management actions and their effectiveness in reducing exposure.

- **Conclusion**: The conclusion summarizes the overall risk environment and outlines any immediate or long-term actions needed. It contains the following.

- o **Summary of key risks**: Recap of the most critical risks identified in the report.

- o **Action plan**: An outline of the next steps for mitigating and managing identified risks.

- o **Final recommendations**: Concrete recommendations for senior management to consider in managing the overall risk profile.

- **Appendices**: The appendices are optional, but provides additional context, detailed information, or supporting data that strengthens the risk report, like:

- o **Risk registers**: A detailed log of all identified risks with risk assessments and mitigation strategies.

- o **Detailed risk matrices**: Expanded versions of the risk profile matrix showing all identified risks.

- o **Graphs and charts**: Visual aids such as risk heatmaps, trend graphs for KRIs, or operational risk models.

Risk treatment options

Risk treatment options are strategies implemented to manage and mitigate identified risks, ensuring that the organization minimizes potential negative impacts. There is no single approach to manage all the risks in an organization and each risk should be reviewed individually to determine the most appropriate treatment strategy. These options typically include risk avoidance, risk reduction, risk transfer, and risk acceptance. The choice of treatment depends on the nature of the risk, its potential consequences, and the organization's risk tolerance, with the aim of balancing risk exposure and resources effectively. The following figure shows the various options of risk treatment:

Figure 14.6: Risk treatment options

Following is the breakdown of each risk treatment strategy in detail, based on the factors that need to be considered when choosing an approach:

- **Risk avoidance**: Risk avoidance involves changing plans or processes to completely eliminate the risk or avoid engaging in an activity that introduces the risk. This strategy is usually chosen when the potential consequences of the risk are deemed too severe and it is not worth pursuing the activity or process at all. Risk avoidance is applied when the cost or impact of the risk is too high to mitigate, or when the organization's objectives are better met by not pursuing a specific opportunity or action. The key considerations are:

  o **Impact assessment**: Evaluate if the threat is so significant that avoiding the risk altogether is the most prudent decision.

  o **Alternatives**: Find alternative processes, products, or services that pose less risk.

  Example: Suppose an organization is carrying the launch of a new product, but a risk assessment identifies the risks of production, market acceptance, and potential financial losses as extremely high. If the cost of mitigating these risks is too high or impossible to control, the company may choose to cancel the launch and avoid the risk altogether by not introducing the product line.

- **Risk reduction**: Risk reduction involves taking steps to reduce the likelihood or the impact of the risk to an acceptable level. The focus here is on making the situation safer without entirely eliminating the risk. Risk reduction is applied when a risk cannot be avoided but can be minimized. This strategy is commonly used when the organization wants to retain some level of risk but still controls its potential outcomes. The key considerations are:

  o **Cost-effectiveness**: The benefits of reducing the risk should outweigh the costs of implementing risk reduction measures.

  o **Residual risk**: Even after reducing risks, there will always be some remaining threat which needs to be monitored and managed.

  Example: Suppose an organization is installing fire suppression systems. The organization in a manufacturing facility may face the risk of fire due to highly flammable materials. The organization could implement fire suppression systems, improve employee training on safety measures, and perform regular equipment checks. These actions help reduce the likelihood of a fire occurring and limit the severity of any potential fire.

- **Risk transfer**: Risk transfer involves shifting part or all of the financial and operational burden of a risk to a third-party. While this does not eliminate the risk, it mitigates the financial or operational impact on the organization. Risk transfer is typically used when the company wants to share or offload the financial consequences of a risk, especially if the cost of managing the risk internally is too high or the organization lacks the capacity to absorb the risk. The key considerations are:

  o **Understanding the risk transfer**: It is crucial that both parties (e.g., the organization and the insurer or contractor) fully understand the risk and its consequences.

  o **Costs**: The cost of transferring risk (e.g., insurance premiums) must be justified by the reduction in exposure or risk impact.

  Example: Suppose an organization purchases insurance to protect against potential loss from natural disasters, equipment failure, or accidents. By doing so, the organization transfers the financial risk to the insurance company.

  Types of risk transfer:

  o **Insurance**: The organization purchases insurance to transfer the financial burden of certain risks, such as data breaches, cyberattacks, or equipment failure.

  o **Outsourcing**: Organization might outsource particular security functions or operations to some third-party vendors. For example, if a company outsources an external firm to handle its cloud security or data management, then the associated operational risk transfers to the vendor, who takes up the responsibility for managing risks associated with those services.

  o **Contractual obligations**: Organization may outsource risks contractually through an agreement which places liability and responsibility on a third-party. Examples include but are not limited to contracts with service providers requiring a force majeure or liability clause to state who should be responsible in cases of a specific type of security incident or breach.

- **Risk retention**: Risk retention means accepting the risk as is because the costs of mitigating or transferring the risk are higher than the potential impact. In this case, the organization decides to deal with the risk internally. Risk retention is used when the probability or impact of a risk is low or the cost of treatment outweighs the benefits. It is typically chosen after a thorough cost-benefit analysis shows that the risk is manageable. The key considerations are:

- o **Cost-benefit analysis**: The decision to retain risk should be based on whether the potential loss is low and whether it is economically unfeasible to mitigate.

- o **Monitoring**: Even when retaining a risk, it is critical to continuously monitor the situation and implement internal controls to ensure that the risk does not escalate.

Example: Suppose an organization might retain the risk of minor damages to equipment, deciding that the cost of purchasing additional insurance or taking extra precautionary measures is too high for the low likelihood of the risk occurring.

Residual risk

Residual risk is the remaining risk that is left behind after the implementation of mitigation strategies for identified risks. It also represents the risk which can still prevail even after implementing controls or safeguarding. There are continuous changes in the risk environment, and some risks simply cannot be eliminated, resulting in residual risk. Management of the residual risk requires relentless assessment and observation toitp this within an aclebility level.

Identifying residual risks that are still present after initial mitigation is the first step in effective documentation and prioritization of residual risks. The determination of the potential impact and likelihood should be followed in order to establish the severity of the risk. Assessed risks are to be documented in the risk register, including details on the description of the risk, its impact, likelihood, existing controls, and the remaining risk level.

Then, prioritization needs to be done based on the size of the risks, focusing on those with the highest impact and likelihood that demand immediate attention. Corrective actions will have to be defined in order to reduce them, and responsibilities for their implementation will also be assigned. Realistic timelines and resources should be allocated to ensure timely resolution.

Finally, regular monitoring is required in order to keep track of corrective actions that were taken, to update the documentation of risk, and to have the residual risks managed effectively. Periodic reviews and reassessments help in adjusting mitigation strategies and maintaining effective risk management.

Risk prioritization

Risk prioritization is the process of assessing and ranking potential risks based on their likelihood of occurrence and the impact they could have on the organization. By evaluating risks in this way, organizations can identify which threats need immediate attention and which can be addressed later. For example, an earthquake might pose as high-impact to a business, but if the likelihood is low in a region with no history of seismic activity, it might be deprioritized. Similarly, if an organization's critical asset is its data centers, the risk of a cyberattack, which is both likely and severe in its potential consequences, would be given top priority.

The main goal of risk prioritization is to create a clear rank order of risks from most to least critical, ensuring that the most pressing threats are mitigated first. This process helps businesses allocate resources effectively, focusing efforts on risks that align with the company's mission and objectives. By prioritizing based on likelihood and impact, organizations can maximize the effectiveness of their resources, ensuring that they are addressing the risks that could have the most significant effect on their operations and long-term success.

Level of risk

Risks can affect different levels of the organization and are generally best thought to be addressed at each of those levels. There are board-level risks, management risks, risks to specific organizational units, and risks specific to projects:

- **Tolerable risk**: Tolerable risks are the insignificant risks that have a very low probability of causing harm. These risks are generally accepted without mitigation because they have minimal or no impact on the organization.

- **Low risk**: Low risks are minor risks with a negligible chance of causing significant negative consequences. These risks are monitored but typically do not require immediate action due to their minimal impact.

- **Medium risk**: Medium risks are moderate risks that do not pose a serious threat but could cause significant harm if not addressed. These risks should be actively monitored and mitigated, as they have the potential to disrupt operations or projects.

- **High risk**: High risks are critical risks that could seriously affect a project's success or the overall operation of the organization. Immediate attention and action are required to mitigate or manage these risks to prevent substantial negative outcomes.

- **Intolerable risk**: Intolerable risks are catastrophic risks that could cause severe damage, such as major system failures, large financial losses, or operational shutdowns. These risks require immediate termination of processes, systems, or projects to prevent disastrous consequences. Immediate and decisive action is necessary to avoid organizational collapse.

Risk prioritization matrix

A risk prioritization matrix (also known as an **impact matrix** or **probability matrix**) is a valuable tool for evaluating and prioritizing potential risks based on their likelihood and impact. It provides a visual representation of risks by plotting them on a grid, with one axis representing the probability (or likelihood) of a risk occurring and the other representing the impact (or severity) of the risk if it were to occur. This matrix allows organizations to quickly assess and prioritize risks, helping to identify which ones need immediate attention and which can be monitored or deferred. By categorizing risks as high, medium, or low, the matrix helps focus resources on mitigating the most critical risks, those with both a high likelihood and high-impact, while less critical risks can be addressed later or with fewer resources, as shown in the following figure:

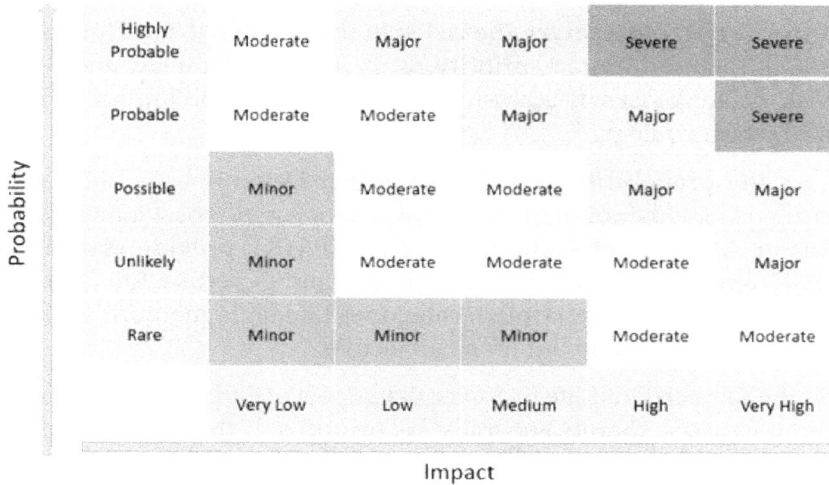

Probability \ Impact	Very Low	Low	Medium	High	Very High
Highly Probable	Moderate	Major	Major	Severe	Severe
Probable	Moderate	Moderate	Major	Major	Severe
Possible	Minor	Moderate	Moderate	Major	Major
Unlikely	Minor	Moderate	Moderate	Moderate	Major
Rare	Minor	Minor	Minor	Moderate	Moderate

Figure 14.7: Risk matrix

A risk matrix is structured by plotting risks based on two key factors: Probability (likelihood) and impact (severity). The matrix helps to categorize risks, with the y-axis representing likelihood and the x-axis representing impact. Risks located in the upper-right corner of the matrix represent high-probability, high-impact risks, which require immediate attention and remediation, as they pose the most significant threat to the organization. On the other hand, risks that fall in the lower-left corner are those that are both unlikely and have negligible impact, meaning they are low-priority and may not require significant intervention. This visual tool enables organizations to quickly assess which risks need to be mitigated first based on their potential consequences, ensuring resources are allocated to the most pressing threats.

Prioritizing risk

Managing risk prioritization involves systematically identifying, assessing, and ranking risks based on their likelihood and potential impact on the organization. By using tools, such as risk registers and risk matrices, organizations can categorize risks from high to low priority, ensuring that the most critical risks are addressed first. This process requires evaluating both the probability of a risk occurring and the severity of its consequences, allowing for efficient resource allocation. Once risks are prioritized, an appropriate response strategy is developed, focusing on high-priority risks while considering factors such as available resources, organizational goals, and potential trade-offs. Continuous monitoring and adjusting strategies over time are essential to effectively manage risks as they evolve. Here are the steps to prioritize risks:

1. **Identify the risks**: Begin by identifying risks at various organizational levels, from board to project levels. Document all identified risks in a risk register for further analysis.

2. **Use a risk register to analyze the risks**: In the risk register, include a description, likelihood, financial impact, priority rank, response strategy, and ownership for each risk. Analyze risks by assessing their probability and impact to determine the best mitigation strategy.

3. **Measure the probability of risks occurring**: Determine the likelihood of risks occurring using either quantitative or qualitative methods. Quantitative methods, like **Factor Analysis of Information Risk (FAIR)**, provide statistical data and financial values but require significant data and expertise. Qualitative methods, on the other hand, use descriptive categories like high, medium, and low, making them easier to implement but more subjective.

4. **Assess the impact**: Evaluate the potential impact of each risk on your organization. High-impact risks should generally be prioritized, though resource constraints might affect the order of remediation.

5. **Select a strategy**: Choose a risk prioritization strategy based on available resources, budget, and the severity of risks. Understand the risk threshold, deciding which risks can be accepted and which need to be mitigated.

6. **Prioritize risks**: Using the selected strategy, rank risks based on severity and likelihood. Visual tools like risk matrices can help present the risks clearly, making it easier to determine which requires immediate attention.

7. **Determine and execute the risk response**: Develop an action plan to address and mitigate the prioritized risks. Focus on high-priority risks first, ensuring a structured approach to remediation.

8. **Identify and respond to changes over time**: Monitor risks continually, as their likelihood and impact can change over time. Adjust your strategies and responses accordingly to ensure ongoing risk management.

Conclusion

In this chapter, we explored the essential steps for preparing a SAR, covering the importance of audit findings and the key components of a risk report structure. We also discussed various risk treatment options, providing organizations with guidance on selecting the most suitable strategies to address identified risks. These treatment options are crucial in ensuring that risks are mitigated effectively based on the organization's risk management approach.

Additionally, the chapter emphasized the process of risk prioritization, introducing the risk matrix as a tool for assessing risks based on their probability and impact. This helps organizations rank and address risks efficiently. As we move into the next chapter, we will shift our focus to third-party assessments, **service level agreements** (**SLAs**), and contracts, examining how these factors influence an organization's overall security and risk management strategy.

Key terms

- A risk assessment is the process of identifying potential risks and the effects they could have on the company's operations.

- A control assessment provides insight into control performance and focuses specifically on evaluating the effectiveness of existing security controls.

- Attribute sampling is a sampling technique used to study the characteristics of a population to determine how many samples possess a specific characteristic.

- Audit charter is a written document that defines the mission and goals of the audit program as well as roles and responsibilities.

- Audit logging is a feature in an application, operating system, or database management system where events are recorded in a separate log.

- Audit methodology is a set of audit procedures that is used to accomplish a set of audit objectives.

- Audit procedures are the step-by-step instructions and checklists required to perform specific audit activities.

- Compliance audit is an audit to determine the level and degree of compliance to a law, regulation, standard, contract provision, or internal control.

- A risk report is a comprehensive document that outlines the identified risks facing an organization, their potential impacts, and the strategies proposed to manage or mitigate these risks.

- Risk prioritization is the process of analyzing risks and deciding which ones should be addressed first.

- Risk severity refers to how much damage a risk could cause to the organization.

- Risk manageability is about how easily the organization can handle a risk if it happens and its potential impact.

- Risk sensitivity is a tool that measures how changes in risk affect the overall risk level and helps adjust the mitigation plan.

- Risk attitude is the way an organization or individual views and reacts to uncertainty and risk.

Join our book's Discord space

Join the book's Discord Workspace for Latest updates, Offers, Tech happenings around the world, New Release and Sessions with the Authors:

https://discord.bpbonline.com

CHAPTER 15

Introduction to System Compliance

Introduction

This chapter offers a comprehensive overview of the compliance documentation framework, aimed at streamlining compliance efforts and ensuring the proper documentation of all activities. It emphasizes the importance of having a structured approach to maintain accurate records, which helps organizations track and demonstrate compliance with legal and regulatory requirements. The chapter also highlights the significance of third-party assessments in mitigating risks and managing them effectively.

In addition, the chapter covers the vendor management process, detailing the vendor lifecycle from selection to performance monitoring. This section ensures that organizations can effectively manage vendor relationships while maintaining compliance and mitigating potential risks. Furthermore, the chapter discusses the development and implementation of contingency plans to ensure the continuity of critical services during emergencies or disruptions.

Structure

The chapter covers the following main topics:

- Compliance document
- Third-party assessment

- Vendor management
- Contracts and service level agreement
- Contingency plan

Objectives

By the end of this chapter, you will have a thorough understanding of compliance documentation and its critical role in ensuring organizational adherence to legal and regulatory requirements. You will learn the process of conducting third-party assessments, as well as how to identify and evaluate various risk factors associated with external partnerships. This knowledge will empower you to effectively manage risks and maintain compliance throughout your operations.

Additionally, this chapter will guide you through the vendor management process, offering a detailed look at the end-to-end vendor lifecycle—from selection to performance monitoring. You will also gain valuable insight into the **contingency planning (CP)** process, which is essential for maintaining business continuity during unexpected disruptions. With this knowledge, you will be better equipped to ensure operational stability and mitigate risks that could impact critical business functions.

Compliance documentation

Compliance documentation is a critical component of an organization's efforts to maintain adherence to industry regulations, legal standards, and internal policies. It includes a wide array of records, policies, procedures, and training materials that collectively demonstrate compliance. This structured collection is vital during regulatory audits and inspections, as it provides evidence of the organization's commitment to regulatory requirements. Well-maintained compliance documentation ensures transparency, traceability, and accountability, enabling organizations to demonstrate that they are operating within the bounds of the law and internal policies.

Moreover, effective management of compliance documentation helps minimize legal risks, as it provides a clear trail of adherence to relevant regulations. It supports ongoing monitoring and enables organizations to adapt quickly to evolving regulatory requirements. In this way, compliance documentation is not only about meeting current standards but also about being agile in response to future changes. It forms the backbone of any comprehensive **governance, risk, and compliance (GRC)** framework, ensuring that businesses can navigate complex legal environments while mitigating potential risks and maintaining operational integrity.

Compliance documentation framework

The compliance documentation framework is essential for ensuring that an organization adheres to the relevant legal, regulatory, and industry standards. This framework helps to streamline compliance efforts and ensures proper documentation of all processes, procedures, and policies in place. The organizations often choose a single framework or regulations such as *International Organization for Standardization (ISO) 27001*, *System and Organization Controls 2 (SOC 2)* , *General Data Protection Regulation (GDPR)*, *Payment Card Industry Data Security Standard (PCI DSS)*, or the *Health Insurance Portability and Accountability Act (HIPPA)*, depending on their specific needs. For example, an organization may choose ISO 27001 standard for managing information security, SOC 2 framework for accessing security control effectiveness, GDPR regulation for protecting EU PII data, PCI DSS standards for protecting credit card data, and HIPAA law for governing and protecting US healthcare data. Alternatively, they may implement multiple frameworks or regulations simultaneously, especially when they operate in different industries or need to meet various compliance requirements.

The compliance documentation should be comprehensive and well-structured, covering various aspects, such as policies, procedures, data protection, and incident response. While compliance documentation varies across industries and regulatory environments, the following are some common examples and categories as shown in the following figure:

Policies and Procedures	Evidence of Compliance	Training Records
Audit Reports	Risk Assessments	Incident Reports
Maintenance Records	Meeting Minutes	Correspondence with Regulatory Bodies
Inspection Records	Licenses and Permits	

Figure 15.1: Compliance documentation categories

Here is the detail of various categories of compliance documentation:

- **Policies and procedures**: These are written guidelines that describe how compliance is achieved and maintained within the organization. They often cover the following:

    o **Data privacy and protection**: This section describes how personal or sensitive data is handled, stored, and protected.

- o **Risk management**: This section defines processes for identifying, assessing, and mitigating risks within the organization.

- o **Anti-fraud and security protocols**: This section describes procedures for preventing fraud, protecting against cyber threats, and ensuring the security of organizational assets.

- o **Employee conduct and workplace policies**: This section includes anti-harassment, anti-discrimination, and workplace safety protocols.

- **Evidence of compliance**: Evidence of compliance helps to validate that the security protocols, privacy measures, and operational procedures are being properly implemented. This can include:

  - o **Screenshots**: Screenshots capture the security configurations, such as firewalls, access control lists, and system settings, which demonstrate that protective measures are in place.

  - o **Text files or code snippets**: This section documents the settings or code changes that reflect compliance efforts, such as encryption settings, data masking, or secure development practices.

  - o **Logs**: This section captures the access logs, audit trails, or system logs that show ongoing compliance actions, such as user activity or system monitoring.

- **Training records**: These are records that show all employees have received required training on compliance-related issues. Training may cover the following:

  - o **Workplace safety**: This section ensures that employees are aware of safety protocols in environments where physical hazards exist.

  - o **Sexual harassment and workplace conduct**: This section documents the organization's policies on harassment and discrimination.

  - o **Data security and privacy**: This section ensures employees are trained on the importance of safeguarding customer data, adhering to laws like GDPR, and understanding the risks of data breaches.

- **Audit reports**: Audit reports (both internal and external) provide a third-party evaluation of an organization's compliance status. The organizations may undergo audit or assessments to generate the report and all reports may not be called as audit reports.

  - o **SOC 2**: SOC 2 provides an audit report that evaluates security, availability, processing integrity, confidentiality, and privacy controls.

  - o **ISO 27001**: ISO 27001 is a standard for which organizations are audited to assess an organization's ISMS.

o **HIPAA**: HIPAA involves compliance assessments to ensure healthcare data protection.

o **GDPR**: GDPR assessment report verifies compliance with European data protection regulations.

- **Risk assessments**: Documents that identify potential compliance risks and outline measures taken to mitigate them, like:

    o **Vulnerability assessments**: This section identifies weaknesses in IT systems that could lead to security breaches.

    o **Compliance gap analysis**: This section identifies areas where the organization might not fully meet regulatory requirements.

    o **Risk mitigation plans**: This section details the actions taken to address and reduce identified risks.

- **Incident reports**: Documentation of any compliance failures or security breaches, includes the following:

    o **Incident details**: This section describes what happened, when, and how the breach or compliance failure occurred.

    o **Remediation actions**: This section outlines how the incident was addressed and mitigated, including any corrective actions taken.

    o **Prevention measures**: This section details the steps taken to prevent similar incidents from occurring in the future.

- **Maintenance records**: These are documents that ensure equipment and machinery are maintained in compliance with relevant safety and operational standards. Examples include:

    o **Safety inspections**: This section captures the records of safety checks for machinery, ensuring compliance with occupational health and safety regulations.

    o **Certification of equipment**: This section provides documentation that equipment meets regulatory standards for safety and functionality.

- **Meeting minutes**: Records of meetings where compliance-related decisions were discussed include the following:

    o **Compliance strategy**: This section outlines how the organization plans to address upcoming compliance challenges or regulatory changes.

    o **Audit findings**: This section captures decisions made regarding audit recommendations and the steps to address them.

- o   **Regulatory updates**: This section covers discussions on new regulations or changes to existing laws that impact the organization.

- **Correspondence with regulatory bodies**: Official communications with regulatory authorities include the following:

  - o   **Submissions**: Submissions are the documents submitted to regulators, such as annual reports, compliance certifications, or incident notifications.

  - o   **Responses**: Responses are the official replies from regulatory bodies regarding the organization's compliance status or inquiries.

  - o   **Penalties or notices**: Penalties are the correspondence regarding any fines or actions taken by regulatory authorities.

- **Inspection records**: Documentation from inspections, whether conducted internally or by regulatory bodies, that show compliance with various standards, such as:

  - o   **Health and safety inspections**: This inspection covers the records of compliance with workplace safety regulations.

  - o   **Environmental inspections**: This inspection ensures that the organization is meeting environmental standards, such as waste disposal or emissions controls.

- **Licenses and permits**: Copies of required licenses and permits that authorize the organization to operate legally or perform specific activities, such as:

  - o   **Business licenses**: Business licenses are required for the legal operation of a business.

  - o   **Environmental permits**: Environmental permits are required for activities involving waste disposal or emissions.

  - o   **Special permits**: These are applicable for specific industries, like healthcare or construction, where certain activities require formal approval.

Importance of compliance documentation

Compliance documentation is crucial for businesses to meet industry regulations, pass audits, and achieve certifications. It ensures that everyone is aligned on policies, processes, and changes. The following figure shows some of the benefits of compliance documentation:

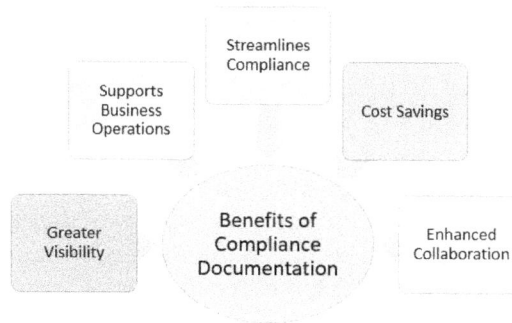

Figure 15.2: Benefits of compliance documentation

Here are a few key benefits of maintaining compliance documentation:

- **Greater visibility**: Compliance documentation helps provide a clear view of your organization's data, enabling you to identify weaknesses and prioritize risks. This allows you to make better-informed decisions and respond more effectively to potential threats.

- **Supports business operations**: Well-documented processes reduce downtime by ensuring employees understand their roles and responsibilities when dealing with security risks. This keeps critical operations running smoothly.

- **Streamlines compliance**: When employees are trained and aware of compliance policies, they are better equipped to handle sensitive data. This strengthens the organization's security posture and ensures ongoing compliance.

- **Cost savings**: Using compliance management tools helps streamline documentation and makes audits easier, preventing costly fines or penalties for non-compliance or security breaches.

- **Enhanced collaboration**: Documentation fosters collaboration across departments like IT, legal, compliance, and human resources. By coordinating efforts, teams can share critical information and work together to improve the documentation process, leading to better business outcomes.

Third-party assessment

In today's interconnected business environment, organizations increasingly rely on third-party service providers to help deliver their products and services. Rather than managing every aspect of their operations in-house, many businesses outsource functions such as cloud services, data storage, and infrastructure management to specialized providers. This approach is often more cost-effective, as it eliminates the need to invest in the infrastructure and resources required to perform these tasks internally. For example, a business may choose to use a cloud service provider to handle its data storage needs rather than setting up its data centers.

However, while outsourcing functions to third-parties can help mitigate certain risks, it is important to understand that the organization still retains ultimate accountability and responsibility. Transferring risk to third-parties, such as outsourcing accounting functions to an external firm, can reduce the organization's exposure to errors or inefficiencies. However, the organization remains legally and financially responsible for the outcomes. For instance, if a cloud service provider suffers a data breach that compromises sensitive information, the organization that contracted with the provider is still accountable to its stakeholders, regulators, and customers. Therefore, while outsourcing can be a valuable risk treatment strategy, it does not absolve organizations from the responsibility that comes with managing outsourced functions.

Third-party risk factors

Legal risks associated with third-party providers are often rooted in trust, dependencies, and an organization's reliance on the provider's services. One of the primary concerns is ensuring that the provider maintains appropriate security measures for data stored within their systems. In addition to trust, organizations must also consider the compatibility of third-party systems with their own infrastructure, safeguarding sensitive data and addressing potential legal liabilities. While an organization can transfer certain risks to a third-party provider, it often retains legal responsibility for the overall outcome. Third-party providers also bear some legal responsibility, as they are contractually bound to deliver services that meet specific legal and performance standards.

To manage these legal risks effectively, **service level agreements (SLAs)** play a crucial role. SLAs clearly outline the level of service, performance expectations, and security requirements that the third-party provider must uphold. To mitigate potential risks further, organizations may require third-party providers to undergo security assessments, including responding to security questionnaires, audits, penetration testing, and other evaluations. These measures ensure that third-parties meet essential cybersecurity standards and reduce risks before the organization enters into a contractual relationship with them.

When outsourcing services to third-party providers, it is essential to evaluate the overall risk to the organization. A thorough risk assessment should be conducted to understand the risks associated with outsourcing various services, such as cloud services (SaaS, IaaS, PaaS), managed security, or even administrative services like call centres. One of the main risks comes from the provider's access to sensitive data whether it is stored in their systems, transmitted through applications, or shared directly with them. Each identified risk should be carefully analysed, and appropriate remediation strategies should be implemented to minimize these risks. The goal is to reduce these risks to an acceptable level, comparable to what would be expected if the organization handled the service internally. This ensures that outsourcing does not introduce new vulnerabilities and that sensitive information remains secure while maintaining compliance with security standards.

Third-party service providers may gain access to an organization's information in different ways, depending on the services they offer. This access can include the following:

- **Physical access to hardcopy business records**: Providers may handle or store physical documents containing sensitive information.

- **Physical access to information systems**: Providers may need direct access to the organization's IT infrastructure or facilities.

- **Physical access to storage media**: Providers may interact with storage devices, such as hard drives, solid-state drives, backup tapes, or optical drives.

- **Logical access to information systems or sensitive data**: Providers may have remote access to systems, databases, or source code that contain valuable or confidential data.

Each of these access points presents a potential risk and should be carefully assessed and managed to ensure the security and confidentiality of the organization's information. When a third-party service provider has access to an organization's information, several risks can arise. These include:

- **Theft of business records**: Unauthorized access or theft of sensitive data by third-party providers or their employees.

- **Exposure of business records to unauthorized parties**: Inadequate security measures could result in sensitive information being exposed to unauthorized individuals.

- **Alteration of business records**: Providers with access to data may inadvertently or maliciously alter business records, impacting their integrity.

- **Damage to information systems**: Both accidental and deliberate damage to hardware, software, or data by third-party providers can disrupt business operations.

- **Failure to perform services in a timely manner**: Delays in service delivery could affect the organization's ability to meet its objectives or customer expectations.

- **Failure to perform services accurately**: Errors or inaccuracies in the services provided can lead to business disruptions or compliance issues.

- **Failure to perform services professionally**: Unprofessional conduct, such as poor service quality or lack of adherence to agreed-upon standards, could negatively affect the organization's reputation and operations.

Identifying and mitigating these risks is essential to ensure that third-party service providers do not compromise the organization's security and operational integrity.

Counter measures to third-party access

To mitigate the risks associated with third-party access, organizations should implement countermeasures and compensating controls that maintain an acceptable level of security. Some of these measures are shown in the following figure:

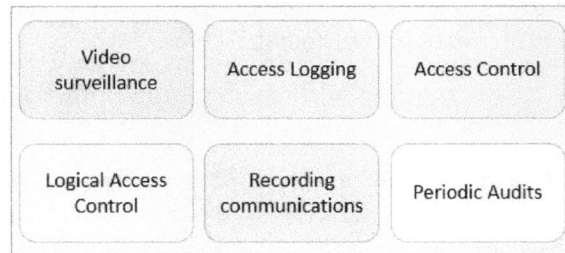

Figure 15.3: Countermeasures for third-party access

Here are the details of the countermeasures:

- **Video surveillance**: Video surveillance involves monitoring physical access to facilities where sensitive data or business records are stored, ensuring that only authorized personnel can enter restricted areas. It helps deter unauthorized access and ensures that any potential security incidents are recorded for later review.

- **Access logging**: Access logging is the process of recording and tracking all interactions with sensitive data or business records. This includes details such as who accessed the data, when it was accessed, and what actions were taken. By maintaining detailed logs, organizations can trace back any unauthorized or suspicious access and identify the responsible individuals.

- **Access controls**: Access controls involve restricting access to sensitive data and business records based on the principle of least privilege, ensuring that third-party providers only have access to the minimum amount of data required to perform their services. This could be implemented through **role-based access control (RBAC)** or other mechanisms that specify which data or systems can be accessed by specific individuals or groups.

- **Logical access controls**: Logical access controls refer to mechanisms that restrict access to specific data fields or systems based on predefined rules, such as user roles or data classification levels. This ensures that third-party providers can only access the specific information necessary for their work, preventing unauthorized access to sensitive data.

- **Recording communications**: Recording communications refers to monitoring and logging voice or data communication sessions between the organization and its third-party providers. This can include phone calls, video conferences, emails, and other forms of communication that may contain sensitive information.

- **Periodic audits**: Periodic audits are conducted regularly to assess whether third-party providers are adhering to security policies, contractual obligations, and compliance requirements. These audits evaluate the provider's security practices, controls, and overall performance to ensure they align with the organization's security standards.

Third-party risk categories

A third-party risk assessment helps organizations evaluate potential risks posed by external vendors across various categories. These categories include following:

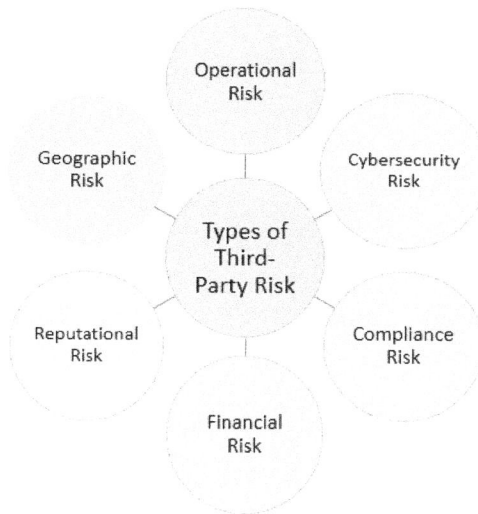

Figure 15.4: Types of third-party risk

Let us look at the detail of third-party risks:

- **Operational risk**: This assesses how much a third-party vendor might impact the availability and continuity of the organization's operations, including any disruptions that could arise from the vendor's performance.

- **Cybersecurity risk**: This category focuses on the potential threats to the security and integrity of sensitive data, especially if the vendor has access to or manages critical information.

- **Compliance risk**: This involves evaluating the vendor's ability to meet regulatory standards and requirements, ensuring that their practices align with relevant laws and industry regulations.

- **Financial risk**: This includes risks that could lead to financial consequences, such as operational failures or data breaches. Financial risks are often measured through processes like cyber risk quantification to estimate potential impacts.

- **Reputational risk**: This assesses how the vendor's actions or failures could harm the organization's reputation, including issues like leadership decisions or security breaches.

- **Geographic risk**: This considers the risks associated with the vendor's location, particularly the location of their data servers, which could involve legal or regulatory implications based on geography.

Seven step third-party risk assessment process

The third-party risk assessment process involves several key steps to ensure that an organization effectively identifies, evaluates, and manages risks associated with its external vendors. The following figure shows the complete process:

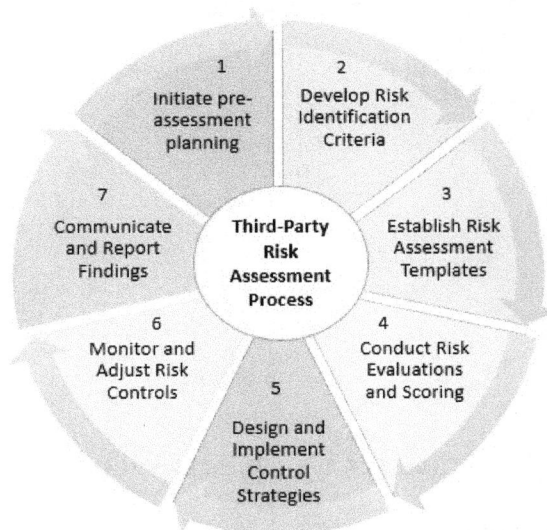

Figure 15.5: Third-party risk assessment process

Here is the breakdown of the third-party risk assessment process:

- **Initiate pre-assessment planning**: The first step is setting up a foundational plan for the risk assessment, ensuring that the organization is well-prepared to evaluate the potential risks within its third-party ecosystem. This phase helps establish a comprehensive risk management strategy and identifies the key areas to focus on in later steps.

- **Develop risk identification criteria**: Next, the organization must establish specific criteria for identifying potential risks. These criteria should be tailored to the organization's unique needs and should consider both internal data and external industry benchmarks. This ensures that the risk identification process is both thorough and relevant.

- **Establish risk assessment templates**: Once the risk criteria are in place, the organization should develop customized risk assessment templates for each third-party vendor. This step allows for a more precise and effective evaluation of each vendor's specific risks, improving the accuracy of the overall assessment process.

- **Conduct risk evaluations and scoring**: With the templates in place, the organization can begin evaluating vendor responses, scoring their risks, and validating the accuracy of the information provided. This step helps identify and prioritize potential vulnerabilities in the vendor relationship.

- **Design and implement control strategies**: After evaluating the risks, organizations must design and implement strategies to mitigate these risks. These control strategies are critical in minimizing the impact that risks could have on the organization's operations and business continuity.

- **Monitor and adjust risk controls**: Risk management does not stop with implementation. Ongoing monitoring of the control strategies is necessary to ensure that any changes in the risk landscape are promptly identified and addressed. Adjustments are made to keep the Risk Management Framework effective over time.

- **Communicate and report findings**: Finally, the results of the risk assessments should be communicated to both internal and external stakeholders. Clear and actionable reporting helps ensure transparency and enables the relevant parties to take the necessary steps to manage and mitigate risks effectively.

By following this structured process, organizations can better manage third-party risks and maintain business resilience.

Conducting a third-party risk management

Conducting a **third-party risk management** (TPRM) process involves a few significant steps to assess, manage, and mitigate third-party vendor or service provider risks. The following is the step-by-step process of conducting a TPRM, as shown in the following figure:

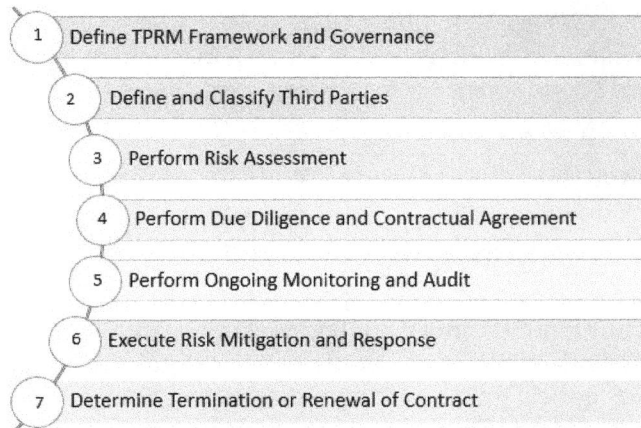

Figure 15.6: *Steps to conduct TPRM*

Here is the breakdown of conducting TPRM with examples:

- **Define TPRM framework and governance**: To establish a TPRM framework and governance, there must be a cross-functional team that oversees TPRM activity and has members from legal, IT security, procurement, and compliance. There must be clearly defined risk management policies that are developed and communicated to offer guidance on how third-party vendors are assessed and managed. In addition, the TPRM framework must be aligned with relevant federal regulations such as the *Federal Acquisition Regulation (FAR), National Institute of Standards and Technology (NIST) SP 800-53*, and *Federal Information Security Management Act (FISMA)* to ensure compliance.

- **Define and classify third-parties**: To identify and classify third-parties, start by making a list of all external vendors providing services, such as cloud providers, IT contractors, and consultants. Then, classify each vendor as to how they can impact the organization if compromised. For example, an organization processing sensitive health data for a federal agency might be classified as high risk due to the importance of it to the agency's mission.

- **Perform risk assessment**: A risk evaluation involves the risk assessment of every third-party taking into factors, like data sensitivity, security controls, regulatory obligations (e.g., FISMA, HIPAA), and financial stability. It also involves the evaluation of threats and weaknesses through audits or security evaluations like *SOC 2* or *Federal Risk and Authorization Management Program (FedRAMP)*. As an example, an organization might undergo a risk assessment to evaluate its cybersecurity controls such as data encryption and compliance with federal security protocols like FedRAMP.

- **Perform due diligence and contractual agreement**: Due diligence involves properly investigating a vendor's security policy, background, and audit reports to ascertain if they are appropriate. The contract should have clear security and compliance terms, such as notice of security violations, protection of data, and adherence to federal laws like FISMA and NIST SP 800-53. As an example, the contract may include data encryption, access control, breach notice timelines, and a requirement for independent annual audit to maintain FedRAMP authorization.

- **Perform ongoing monitoring and audit**: Ongoing monitoring involves the ongoing monitoring of the third-party vendor for any security or compliance violations, such as reviewing audit reports, performing security testing, and scanning for breaches. An example is that a federal agency receives quarterly security and compliance reports from an organization, reporting audit results, vulnerabilities, and remediation plans. When the provider is not compliant or has a breach, the agency employs defined procedures to respond and lock down risks.

- **Execute risk mitigation and response**: Risk response and mitigation is choosing the appropriate approach from the risk analysis, i.e., accepting, mitigating, transferring, or avoiding the risk. If a risk is identified, a mitigation plan is developed that can include improving the security controls of the vendor or vendor change in case the risks are too high. For example, if the cloud service provider has a top-level security risk, the federal agency can work with the vendor to implement stronger controls like **multifactor authentication** (**MFA**) or put the vendor on a corrective action plan with deadlines for rectification.

- **Determine termination or renewal of contract**: In a contract's finality or as part of scheduled checks, performance by the third-party vendor is assessed to ascertain whether they have satisfied compliance, security, and performance standards. Based on the review, a decision is made whether to renew or terminate the contract. For example, if an organization is not meeting the security needs, the federal agency may decide to terminate the contract and look for another provider.

Vendor management

Vendor management involves overseeing third-party suppliers that provide goods and services essential to a business's operations. This process includes tasks like selecting vendors, managing costs, handling budgets, processing invoices, and negotiating contracts. Effective vendor management ensures that businesses receive high-quality goods and services at competitive prices, ultimately supporting their operational efficiency and financial goals.

Each business has its own set of vendor needs based on the industry it operates in. For example, an IT company relies on vendors for equipment like laptops and cloud hosting services, while a bakery's vendors might supply ingredients like flour or rent machinery for production. Managing these vendors requires careful coordination and input from various stakeholders as it is a multifaceted process that directly impacts a business's day-to-day operations and long-term success.

Vendor lifecycle

Vendor lifecycle management is a comprehensive process that ensures effective collaboration with third-party suppliers from the beginning to the end of the partnership. It involves several key stages:

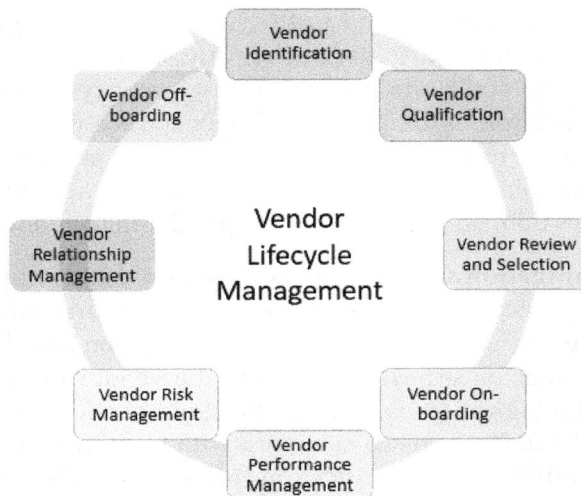

Figure 15.7: Vendor lifecycle management

Here is the breakdown of vendor lifecycle management:

- **Vendor identification and contact** is the first step in the vendor lifecycle, where an organization identifies potential vendors that can meet its specific business needs. During this phase, the company conducts research to find suppliers offering the required goods or services. Once potential vendors are identified, initial contact is made to assess their capabilities, gather information on their offerings, and determine if they can meet the organization's requirements.

- **Vendor qualification** is the stage where vendors are thoroughly assessed to ensure they meet the organization's required standards. This involves evaluating factors, such as their financial stability, reputation, operational capabilities, and compliance with industry regulations. Additionally, risk mitigation strategies are developed to identify and address potential risks, such as operational disruptions, cybersecurity threats, or financial instability, ensuring that the vendor can effectively manage any challenges.

- **Vendor review and selection** is the process where, after qualifying vendors, they are evaluated based on specific criteria such as pricing, quality of goods or services, reliability, and overall alignment with the organization's needs. This step involves comparing vendor proposals and performance to determine which one offers the best value and fits the business objectives.

- **Vendor onboarding** is the process of formally integrating a vendor into the organization by establishing clear terms for the partnership. This includes setting up contracts, defining SLAs that outline performance expectations, and ensuring alignment on goals, deliverables, and timelines. During this stage, both parties clarify responsibilities, establish communication protocols, and ensure that all necessary resources and systems are in place.

- **Vendor performance management** involves the continuous monitoring and evaluation of a vendor's performance to ensure they meet the agreed-upon standards. This includes tracking **key performance indicators** (**KPIs**) such as quality, timeliness, and service levels to assess whether the vendor is delivering as expected. Regular performance reviews help identify any areas of improvement, ensure the vendor remains accountable, and allow for timely adjustments to address any issues.

- **Vendor risk management** involves the continuous assessment and mitigation of potential risks associated with a vendor, including financial, operational, and cybersecurity risks. By regularly evaluating these risks, businesses can identify vulnerabilities that could disrupt operations and take proactive measures to minimize the impact. Effective risk management ensures that vendors remain reliable and compliant, reducing the likelihood of service disruptions, data breaches, or financial losses.

- **Vendor relationship management** focuses on developing and nurturing strong, collaborative partnerships with vendors to ensure mutual success. By maintaining open communication, providing regular feedback, and addressing any issues promptly, businesses can strengthen vendor relationships, ensuring that both parties meet expectations and objectives. This ongoing engagement fosters trust, improves problem-solving, and creates a foundation for long-term cooperation.

- **Vendor offboarding** is the final stage in the vendor lifecycle, occurring when a vendor is no longer needed or their contract concludes. This process ensures a smooth and orderly transition by handling the return of company assets, fulfilling any remaining contractual obligations, and ensuring that all relevant documentation is properly archived for future reference.

Contracts and service level agreement

Legal agreements play a critical role in defining the overall business relationship between an organization and its service providers. These agreements outline the scope of work, expectations, service levels, quality standards, and compensation terms, ensuring that all parties understand their roles and responsibilities. They also include provisions for remedies and penalties, in case the service provider fails to meet the agreed-upon expectations or service levels, protecting the organization from potential risks. The agreements should be comprehensive, addressing all aspects of the relationship to ensure clarity and minimize misunderstandings.

Appropriate levels of management must be involved in the approval process of these contracts to ensure that all relevant stakeholders have input and that the terms align with the organization's strategic goals and risk tolerance. By securing approval from key decision-makers, organizations can ensure that the contracts adequately address operational, legal, and financial concerns. This thorough approach to contract management helps safeguard the organization's interests and fosters a mutually beneficial relationship with service providers.

A SLA is a formal contract between a service provider and its customers that clearly outlines the services to be provided and establishes the service standards the provider is required to meet. The SLA specifies the expected level of performance, including response times, service availability, and quality metrics, ensuring that both parties have a clear understanding of their responsibilities. It also includes provisions for remedies or penalties if the provider fails to meet these standards, thereby protecting the customer's interests and promoting accountability on the part of the service provider.

Key components of a service level agreement

A SLA typically includes several key components to ensure clear expectations and accountability between the service provider and the customer. Some of these components are shown in the following figure:

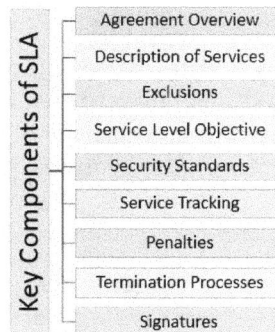

Figure 15.8: Components of SLA

Here are the common elements that can be included in a SLA in more detail:

- **Agreement overview**: This section serves as the foundation of the SLA, outlining the start and end dates of the agreement and specifying the parties involved (such as the service provider and the customer). It provides a high level summary of the services to be delivered, setting the stage for the more detailed terms that follow.

- **Description of services**: This part provides a detailed breakdown of all services covered by the SLA. It specifies the exact services offered, including turnaround times, delivery methods, and the technologies or applications used. Maintenance schedules, service hours, locations, and any dependencies are also described, ensuring both parties clearly understand the service scope.

- **Exclusions**: It is crucial to clearly define what is not included in the SLA to avoid misunderstandings. This section lists specific services, activities, or situations that are excluded from the agreement, which can help set realistic expectations and reduce potential conflicts.

- **Service level objective (SLO)**: The SLO defines measurable performance metrics agreed-upon by both parties. These can include response times, resolution times, system uptime, or other quantifiable targets. The SLO serves as the benchmark for evaluating the service provider's performance, and these metrics are typically supported by data and historical performance standards.

- **Security standards**: This section outlines the security measures the service provider will implement to protect the customer's data and information. It may include details about encryption, access control, monitoring systems, and compliance with industry standards. Additionally, this section often includes **non-disclosure agreements** (**NDAs**) or anti-poaching clauses to protect the confidentiality and proprietary interests of both parties.

- **Service tracking and reporting agreement**: This section specifies how the service provider's performance will be tracked and reported. It includes KPIs that will be monitored, how they will be measured, and the reporting frequency. It ensures that both parties agree on the mechanisms for tracking performance, such as before and after benchmarks when switching service providers.

- **Penalties**: This section defines the consequences if either party fails to meet the agreed-upon terms of the SLA. Penalties may be financial (such as discounts or compensation) or operational (such as extra service hours). This clause ensures accountability by stipulating the consequences of non-compliance or underperformance.

- **Termination processes**: The termination section outlines the conditions under which the SLA can be ended, either by expiration or termination for cause (e.g., failure to meet performance metrics). It also defines the required notice period for either party to terminate the agreement and the procedure for concluding the agreement, ensuring a smooth exit process.

- **Signatures**: To formalize the agreement, this section includes the signatures of authorized representatives from both parties. By signing, both parties confirm their understanding and acceptance of all terms outlined in the SLA. This ensures that both the service provider and the customer are legally bound to adhere to the agreed-upon terms throughout the SLA's duration.

Examples of service level agreement

In this example of an SLA between an IT service provider and a client, the agreement includes several key components:

- **Uptime guarantee**: The service provider ensures a minimum of 99.9% uptime, meaning the IT system will be operational and accessible for at least 99.9% of the agreed service period, usually calculated on a monthly basis.

- **Response time**: The SLA specifies response times for different service incidents, with critical issues (Priority 1) requiring a response within 30 minutes, while lower-priority issues are allowed longer response times.

- **Resolution time**: The agreement outlines the time frames for resolving service incidents, with Priority 1 issues to be resolved within 4 hours and Priority 2 issues within 8 hours.

- **Support availability**: The SLA ensures 24/7 technical support through various channels such as phone, email, and live chat. It also includes escalation procedures for unresolved issues.

- **Penalties**: The SLA specifies penalties for non-compliance, such as service credits for each hour of downtime exceeding the agreed-upon uptime guarantee.

Contingency plan

A contingency plan is a proactive strategy that ensures an organization can maintain business continuity during unexpected disruptions or emergencies. It outlines specific actions to take in response to unforeseen events, minimizing the impact on operations and reducing downtime. The plan focuses on preserving essential functions, protecting critical assets, and enabling a swift recovery to normal operations. By anticipating potential risks and preparing for them in advance, organizations can respond efficiently, ensuring minimal interruption to their services and protecting their reputation.

The plan typically includes risk assessments, defines critical business functions, and outlines clear response procedures for various emergencies, such as natural disasters, cybersecurity breaches, or supply chain disruptions. It also includes resource management strategies, a communication plan for stakeholders, and recovery strategies to restore normal operations as quickly as possible. Regular testing and updates to the plan ensure that it remains relevant and effective in addressing emerging threats, while training employees ensures they are prepared to act swiftly when needed.

NIST SP 800-53 specifies 9 CP security controls for information systems, not all of which apply to every system. The FIPS 199 security categorization is applied to identify the controls needed according to the system's security objectives. For example, low-impact systems need no alternate sites, while moderate-impact systems need backups. Environmental controls for the physical location and hardware of the system are also of paramount importance. NIST SP 800-53 also allows organizations to use compensating security controls, which provide equivalent protection if the baseline control is not feasible, with sufficient justification and risk acceptance.

Contingency planning process

NIST SP 800-34 provides a structured approach to CP, focusing on safeguarding Federal Information Systems against various threats such as natural disasters, cyberattacks, and technical failures. The framework emphasizes the critical need for preparedness, response, and recovery to ensure the continued availability, integrity, and confidentiality of essential information and services. By systematically addressing potential disruptions, NIST SP 800-34 aims to ensure that organizations can maintain their operations and quickly recover in the event of an incident, minimizing impact and ensuring resilience in the face of unforeseen challenges.

The CP process in NIST SP 800-34 includes several essential steps aimed at preparing an organization to respond effectively to disruptions, ensuring continuity of critical services and operations. The following figure shows the CP process:

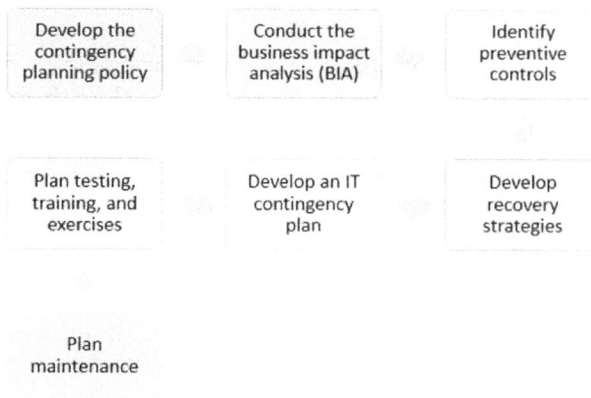

Develop the contingency planning policy	Conduct the business impact analysis (BIA)	Identify preventive controls
Plan testing, training, and exercises	Develop an IT contingency plan	Develop recovery strategies
Plan maintenance		

Figure 15.9: Contingency plan

Here is the detail of CP process:

- **Developing the CP policy statement**: This step sets the foundation for the entire CP program by clearly defining its scope, goals, and objectives. It helps establish the commitment of the organization to business continuity and guides the development of further plans.

- **Conducting the business impact analysis (BIA)**: The BIA identifies the organization's critical functions, resources, and processes and assesses the potential impact of disruptions on these operations. The analysis helps prioritize recovery efforts and resources, ensuring that the most critical functions are restored first.

- **Identifying preventive controls**: This involves implementing measures to prevent disruptions or reduce their frequency. Preventive controls might include system redundancies, cybersecurity measures, or physical security protocols designed to mitigate potential risks before they occur.

- **Developing contingency strategies**: Contingency strategies outline detailed recovery and restoration procedures for systems, applications, and services. These strategies ensure that when disruptions occur, there are predefined methods to quickly recover and return to normal operations.

- **Developing an information system contingency plan (ISCP)**: The ISCP is a comprehensive document that outlines roles, responsibilities, procedures, and resources required for response and recovery during a disruption. It details how to manage and restore information systems effectively, ensuring continuity of critical services.

- **Ensuring plan test, training, and exercise (TT&E)**: Regular TT&E are vital to ensure that the contingency plan remains effective. These activities help identify gaps or weaknesses in the plan, allowing for adjustments before an actual emergency occurs. It also ensures that key personnel are familiar with their roles during a crisis.

- **Maintaining the contingency plan**: A contingency plan is not static; it must be continuously reviewed and updated to stay aligned with changing technologies, organizational needs, and emerging threats. Regular maintenance ensures that the plan evolves and remains relevant, ensuring preparedness for any unforeseen disruption.

Disaster recovery plan

A **disaster recovery plan** (DRP) is an important part of the overall business continuity and operational resilience strategy of an organization. It addresses the recovery of IT infrastructure, applications, and systems in the event of a disaster or catastrophic disruption that prevents access to the primary facility or infrastructure. The plan is designed to accommodate such occurrences like natural disasters, fire, floods, cyberattacks, or equipment failures for reducing downtime, and data loss with uninterrupted operation of critical business processes. The DRP ensures that organizations can quickly switch to alternate sites, restore data and recover critical services with minimum impact.

The DRP typically involves a list of recovery objectives, such as **recovery time objectives (RTO)** and **recovery point objectives (RPO)**, which define the recovery window in which systems have to be recovered and the level of tolerable data loss. It involves setting up backup facilities, redundant infrastructure, and alternative recovery sites such as hot or warm, to cold sites—to facilitate operation. Regular testing, maintenance, and updating are crucial to keep the DRP in a working condition and ensure the plan is compatible with evolving business needs and technology innovations.

Steps to conduct DRP

Creating a DRP is a systematic way to support organization in recovering IT systems, applications, and infrastructure quickly in the event of a disaster or major disruption. The following figure is a step-by-step procedure for creating a DRP:

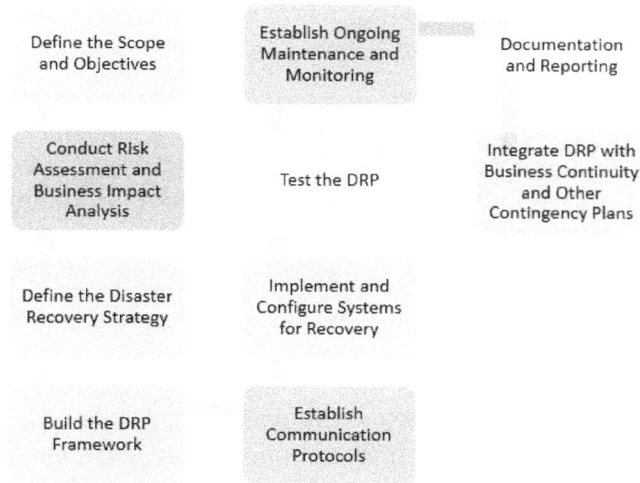

Figure 15.10: Steps to conduct DRP

Here is the description of each step in creating DRP:

1. **Define scope and objective**: Step one is to determine what needs to be supported by the DRP. This includes listing the critical systems, applications, data, and processes essential to business that require recovery. It also includes setting clear recovery objectives: the RTO, which defines how long a system can be down before it will have a severe impact, and the RPO, which defines how much data can be lost without affecting business processes.

2. **Conduct risk assessment and BIA**: Step two is to conduct a risk assessment for possible risk, such as cyberattack, natural disaster and establishing their impact on IT infrastructure. BIA deals with identifying critical systems and information that allow the business to operate, evaluating the impact of disruptions to finance, operations, and reputation, and prioritizing the systems by value to ensure business continuity.

3. **Define DRP strategy**: Step three is the creation of the DRP. It includes choosing an alternate site for systems in the event of a disaster, e.g., a hot site (fully equipped), a warm site (partially equipped), or a cold site (minimal setup). It also involves regular data backup and creating policies for data retention. For system recovery, virtualization can be used for faster recovery, data replication for keeping systems up to date at alternate sites, and redundancy for backup components like servers and power supplies.

4. **Build DRP framework**: Step four is the formulation of the DRP structure. This includes the creation of documentation that outlines the purpose, systems covered, roles, and recovery procedures for switching to alternate sites, restoring data, and reconfiguring systems. It also includes a communication plan for updating all

stakeholders and creating roles such as the disaster recovery manager, technical recovery teams, incident response team, and the business continuity team.

5. **Establish communication protocols**: Step five constitutes creating communication procedures. For communications internal to the company, create a procedure to notify employees and teams about the disaster and the DRP. Create emergency contact lists and escalation procedures. For external communications, inform vendors, suppliers, and customers about delays or interruptions and provide all interested parties with periodic updates on the status of recovery.

6. **Implement system recovery:** Step six is to set up recovery systems. This includes installing data, server, and application backup systems and hardware or virtual environments with duplicate settings for use during failure. Cloud-based solutions like **disaster recovery as a service (DRaaS)** and **backup as a service (BaaS)** can also be used. Network settings such as **Domain Name System (DNS)** and **Internet Protocol (IP)** addresses are also cloned at the redundant locations.

7. **Test DRP**: Step seven involves testing the DRP. First, conduct tabletop exercises to accustom the team to the plan. Then conduct full-scale tests by simulating an actual disaster to recover data and systems, conducting failover tests, and restoring backed-up data. After testing, review the outcome, determine any problem, and enhance the plan to capture any steps missed or delayed.

8. **Establish ongoing monitoring**: Step eight is the maintenance and management of the DRP. Ensure the plan remains current by reflecting IT infrastructure, business processes, and technology changes. Regularly test and drill to ensure recovery processes are effective and update team training when needed. Periodically review DRP performance, address shortcomings, and stay informed about new threats or business changes to keep the plan effective.

9. **Document and reporting**: Step nine deals with documentation and reporting. Keep all DRP documents current, accessible, and at multiple locations such as on-site, cloud, or off-site. Maintain records of tests, updates, and reviews to meet legal or industry requirements, i.e., HIPAA or GDPR.

10. **Integrate DRP with BIA and others**: Step ten is integrating the DRP with other plans. Make sure the DRP supports the **business continuity plan (BCP)** in order to restore IT-dependent business processes quickly. Also, align the DRP with the **continuity of operations plan (COOP)** for sustaining essential functions during a crisis.

Conclusion

In this chapter, we examined the compliance documentation framework and highlighted its importance in maintaining legal and regulatory adherence within an organization. We also discussed the process of third-party risk assessment, emphasizing how it helps manage and mitigate potential risks associated with external partnerships. Understanding these processes is key to ensuring that risks are identified and controlled effectively.

Furthermore, the chapter covered the vendor management process, focusing on the entire vendor lifecycle from selection to ongoing monitoring. We also explored the concept of CP, which is crucial for organizations to prevent and manage disruptions that could affect operations. As we transition to the next chapter, we will shift our attention to risk acceptance criteria and the system test plan, further deepening our understanding of effective risk management strategies.

Key terms

- Compliance documentation is a collection of reports that track and demonstrate how effectively a compliance program is being implemented across the organization.

- Contracts and agreements define the terms, obligations, and responsibilities of all parties involved, ensuring compliance with legal and regulatory requirements throughout business relationships.

- Licenses and permits are official documents that confirm an organization has fulfilled the regulatory requirements needed to legally operate in its industry.

- A SLA is a formal contract between a service provider and a customer that outlines the expected performance, quality standards, and responsibilities of both parties.

- Customer SLAs are the contract between a service provider and an external customer, often called an external service agreement, outlining the services provided and the performance expectations.

- Internal SLAs are used within an organization. These agreements establish service standards between departments or teams to ensure inter-departmental goals are met.

- Multilevel SLAs are applied when multiple service providers or end users are involved. These SLAs divide the agreement into levels, offering different service tiers based on customer needs or price ranges.

- SLAs contain detailed and quantifiable metrics used to measure the service provider's performance. Common metrics include:

  o **Availability/uptime**: Percentage of time the service is operational.

  o **Response time**: Time taken to respond to service incidents or requests.

  o **Resolution time**: Time taken to resolve service incidents or fulfil requests.

  o **Throughput**: Rate at which service operations are completed.

  o **Error rate**: Frequency of errors or failures in the service.

- A third-party risk assessment (also known as **supplier risk assessment**) quantifies the risks associated with third-party vendors and suppliers that provide products or services to your organization.

- A vendor contract is a legal agreement that requires both an organization and its vendor to fulfill certain responsibilities or tasks.

- While the contents of a vendor contract will not be found within an SLA, contents that are found in an SLA may be found within a vendor contract if a separate SLA is not present.

- DRP is a detailed plan that outlines how an organization can quickly recover and resume its operations after an unexpected event or disruption.

- DRaaS is a cloud-based service that helps businesses recover their IT systems, data, and applications in case of a disaster. A COOP is a set of procedures that outlines how an organization will continue its essential functions within 12 hours and up to 30 days after a disaster, before returning to normal operations.

- BIA is the process of identifying and evaluating the potential effects of disruptions to business operations.

Join our book's Discord space

Join the book's Discord Workspace for Latest updates, Offers, Tech happenings around the world, New Release and Sessions with the Authors:

https://discord.bpbonline.com

CHAPTER 16

Determining System Risk Posture

Introduction

This chapter covers a thorough understanding of risk acceptance criteria that helps organizations determine the acceptable level of risk. This chapter covers the risk profile that provides an overview of potential threats to identify, assess, and prioritize risks effectively. This chapter also outlines the critical components of the **system test plan** (**STP**) that highlight the significance of documenting the test results to meet security requirements.

In addition, the chapter also explains how to prioritize the risk, which helps organizations to focus on critical issues. This chapter also addresses the concept of risk ownership that details the responsibilities of personnel accountable for managing and mitigating risks. Lastly, the chapter goes into the verification and validation processes, which ensures that systems meet security requirements and are operational.

Structure

The chapter covers the following main topics:

- Risk acceptance criteria
- Risk profile
- System test plan

- Documenting test results
- Risk ranking
- Risk ownership
- Verification and validation

Objectives

By the end of this chapter, you will have a clear understanding of risk acceptance criteria and how to apply them to determine the acceptable risk levels within an organization. You will also learn how to create an STP document, including all the factors that will determine the risk profile. Additionally, the chapter will guide you through documenting test results to ensure thorough tracking and evaluation of security measures.

Furthermore, this chapter will provide insights into the roles and responsibilities in managing and prioritizing risks. You will gain thorough knowledge on assigning risk ownership and making informed decisions based on the risk ranking. The chapter will also explore the critical processes of verification and validation that will guide you if systems meet security requirements.

Risk acceptance criteria

Risk acceptance is integral to the risk management process. Risk acceptance is a type of risk response taken by organizations when the identified risk is within the organizational risk tolerance. It occurs when an organization decides that the cost of mitigating a risk outweighs the benefit, provided the risk remains within the organization's risk appetite and tolerance. Risk acceptance criteria should support the organization's business objectives. This alignment ensures that accepted risks do not hinder the organization's ability to achieve its goals and that resources are allocated efficiently. *International Organization for Standardization (ISO) 27001* and *National Institute of Standards and Technology (NIST)* standards influence the approach to risk acceptance by offering guidelines on how to identify, evaluate, and decide on risks in the context of an organization's overall information security posture.

There are two critical concepts generally discussed with respect to risk acceptance, which are tolerability and acceptability. Let us look at them in detail:

- **Tolerability**: Tolerability means the organization is willing to accept a level of risk for the benefits it brings provided the risk is actively managed. In other words, the organization acknowledges the risk but considers it manageable if controls are in place. Although the risk is not ignored or considered insignificant, the organization will not take strong risk reduction actions unless necessary. It is about regularly reviewing the risk and adding more controls as needed to keep it within bounds.

- **Acceptability**: Acceptability means the organization is prepared to accept the risk as is without any mitigation. The organization accepts the risks and understands and acknowledges the potential consequences. It is when the impact of the risk is deemed to be low or the organization's risk appetite allows for it.

Selection of risk criteria

Risk acceptance is a subjective decision, even though the risk levels can be assessed by using quantitative tools. Risk ranking is aligned to established frameworks like NIST SP 800-30 and ISO 31000 that helps to assess and prioritize risk-based on standardized likelihood vs impact metrics. NIST SP 800-30 emphasizes the systematic process for assessment of risk involving both the potential likelihood of the event and its impact on the organization. Similarly, ISO 31000 provides a structured method for evaluating risk, considering the probability of occurrence and the consequence effect in case the risk materializes. The decision about what constitutes an acceptable level of risk involves a combination of factual analysis, societal values, and the goals of the organization involved. As mentioned, this decision is influenced by several factors, including the benefits gained from accepting the risk, the regulatory environment, and how the risk compares to other accepted risks.

Criteria for acceptability

The acceptability of risk is usually determined using established frameworks or criteria based on the type of risk involved and its potential impact. These criteria are typically not just a single number but may use a graded or tiered approach that considers varying levels of risk and their corresponding actions. One such framework divides risks into three regions, as shown in the following figure:

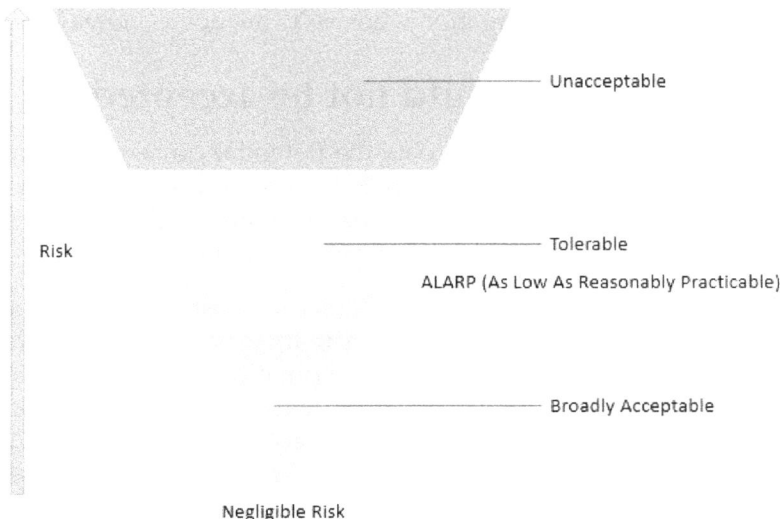

Figure 16.1: Risk acceptance map

Here are the details of each type of risk:

- **Unacceptable risks**: These risks are too high to be accepted and are only allowed in exceptional circumstances. They pose a high threat that can cause major harm to people, the environment, or the organization. These need to be addressed to reduce the likelihood and impact of the risk by significant changes to operations, designs, or processes. Unacceptable risks cannot be accepted without any risk treatment in place to get them down to a more manageable level. The risk treatment includes risk avoidance, risk transfer, risk mitigation along with risk acceptance.

- **Acceptable risks**: The **as low as reasonably practicable (ALARP)** principle applies here. While these risks are acceptable, efforts should still be made to reduce them as much as possible within practical constraints of cost, time, and feasibility. The ALARP principle says you should minimize risk as much as possible unless the effort, cost or resources to reduce the risk further is more than the benefit. This gives flexibility in decision-making by allowing risk reduction to continue up to the point where the cost or effort for further mitigation no longer justifies the benefit.

- **Broadly acceptable risks**: Risks in this region are considered so low that no further reduction is required. These are risks with minimal consequence and very low probability of occurrence. Since the impact is minimal these risks do not require ongoing analysis, mitigation or additional safety measures. They are part of the normal operational environment and their acceptance does not hinder organizational goals or objectives. One of the benefits of this system is that it allows for a clear distinction between acceptable and unacceptable risks. It prevents unnecessary burden on activities that pose low risks and clarifies which risks require significant changes. It also gives decision-makers a flexible approach to consider benefits and mitigation when risks are not too low or too high.

Situation where risk should not be accepted

It is essential for an organization to evaluate the potential consequences of risk and the ability to manage it effectively when there is a decision to accept risk. There are certain situations where risks should not be accepted because they could have a severe negative impact on the organization. These situations may include the following:

- **High-impact risks**: High-impact risks are very serious for an organization and can cause major damage or disruption if they happen. These risks can harm business operations and the company's reputation. The organization should not ignore these risks and take a proactive approach to manage. To reduce these risks, organizations can implement security measures, buy insurance, and prepare disaster recovery plans. For example, a data breach is a high-impact risk where sensitive data could be exposed, leading to financial losses, legal penalties, and damage to the company's reputation.

- **Regulatory and compliance risks**: Risks that could result in non-compliance with laws, regulations, or industry standards should never be accepted, as they can result in significant legal, financial, and reputational penalties. Non-compliance risks may lead to fines, legal action, suspension of operations, or loss of licenses. For example: Let us take an example of an organization that handles patient's data. If the organization fails to comply with industry regulations, like *Health Insurance Portability and Accountability Act* (*HIPAA*), they may face fines and legal action for mishandling patient data.

- **Reputational risks**: Risks that happen when a company's actions can damage its public image and trust. The impact of reputational risk is usually immediate; it can also be severe and long-lasting. Reputational risk is important to understand because a company's reputation can correlate with its overall success. When a negative event affects a company's public perception, customers may be less likely to choose it over its competitors. For example, let us take an example of an organization that collects user's data for the type of service they provide. If the organization is violating user privacy by misusing data, it can face negative reactions from both customers and regulators.

- **Strategic misalignment**: Every organization has strategic objectives and long-term goals. In some instances where the risk does not align with an organization's strategic direction then, it can influence business growth. Misaligned risks could waste resources on wrong initiatives and weaken the organization's competitive position. For example: Let us consider a startup organization focusing on developing innovative software solutions. If this organization does not align to long-term vision and focus on the area that is not related to software could lead to misaligned risk.

- **Unmanageable risks**: These risks occur when an organization cannot manage or mitigate risk to an acceptable level. These risks are often unpredictable or may arise from external factors like natural disasters that are beyond the organization's control. For example: Let us take an example of an organization that does not have mature security posture. If the organization keeps customer data or sensitive data with basic protections, they may face potential data breaches or fines. This is an example of unmanageable risk as the organization does not have adequate security solutions.

Establishing criteria for risk acceptance

Establishing clear and well-defined criteria for risk acceptance is critical for any organization, particularly in the critical domains like cybersecurity, where the balance between risk and reward must be carefully managed. This process ensures that risk acceptance is a thoughtful decision based on strategic thinking, business objectives, and the organization's broader goals. The following figure shows the criteria for risk acceptance:

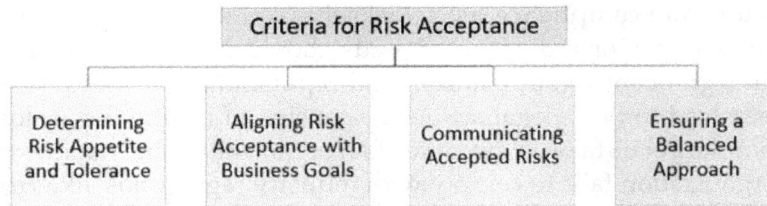

Figure 16.2: *Risk acceptance criteria*

Here is the breakdown of risk acceptance criteria:

- **Determining risk appetite and tolerance**: Risk appetite and risk tolerance are key concepts in risk management, each is distinct with regard to its scope and application. Understanding both risk appetite and risk tolerance enables organizations to make informed decisions about which risks are acceptable and how many variations they can withstand without compromising their strategic objectives. Here is the brief of risk appetite and risk tolerance:

    o **Risk appetite**: Risk appetite is the level of risk an organization is willing to accept without taking any actions to reduce risk. Risk appetite is usually an organization's strategic vision and is defined by senior management.

    o **Risk tolerance**: Risk tolerance is the amount of acceptable deviation from an organization's risk appetite. You can think of an organization's risk tolerance for a specific initiative as its willingness to accept the risk that remains after all relevant controls are put in place. Risk appetite is about taking risk, and risk tolerance is about controlling risk.

- **Aligning risk acceptance with business goals**: Risk acceptance criteria should be aligned with the organization's business goals and long-term strategy. This alignment ensures that accepted risks do not undermine the organization's objectives but support its mission and vision. Resource effectiveness and strategic decision-making helps to align risk acceptance with business goals as explained:

    o **Resource efficiency optimization**: Optimizing resource efficiency is a key element of effective risk management. Organizations should align business strategy with their risk acceptance decisions to ensure that resources are used efficiently. This approach helps organization to direct its resources effectively, preventing unnecessary expenditure on risks outside of its strategic focus.

    o **Strategic decision-making**: Strategic decision-making involves taking the right decision to align with an organization's long-term goals and vision. This requires the evaluation of the risk and determining the necessary action required by organization. The strategic decision help leaders decide on the mitigation plan by carefully assessing potential risks and their impact.

- **Communicating accepted risks**: There are various ways to communicate the accepted risks, some of which are as follows:

  o **Effective communication**: Clear communication with all stakeholders is crucial once risk acceptance criteria have been established in an organization. Clear communication ensures that all stakeholders, including employees and external partners, understand the rationale behind the decision and take necessary actions.

  o **Documentation**: Organizations should document the rationale behind risk acceptance decisions. This includes details like reason for accepting risk, potential impact, and alignment with business strategy.

  o **Contingency planning**: Contingency planning involves preparing detailed plans for how to respond if a risk exceeds its acceptable threshold. Organizations can quickly address the impact of the risk by having clear communication and contingency planning.

- **Ensuring a balanced approach**: One of the primary components of risk acceptance criteria planning is to take a progressive strategy, like:

  o **Balancing innovation and security**: One of the major problems in risk acceptance is finding the right balance between innovation and robust security controls. An example would be an organization deciding to accept some cybersecurity risks to roll out new technologies. However, this should never be at the risk of compromising critical systems or sensitive information.

  o **Continuous monitoring and adaptation**: Organizations should focus on continuous monitoring exercises in order to review their appetite, tolerance and acceptance towards risk. Like other business decisions, risk acceptance should not be a once-in-a-lifetime decision. Rather, it is a continuous process that changes as the business environment evolves. For example, an organization may have no competitors, but if such arise, it will definitely change the risk profile.

Risk profile

A risk profile is a detailed ongoing analysis to depict an organization's understanding and response to the different risks that it can withstand. Risk profiles must be updated continuously to stay up to date with new risks, evolving business environments, and changing operational priorities. The new risks can emerge from technology advancements, regulatory updates, or unforeseen events. It provides insight into the potential threats and is considered a decision-making tool. This process assists organizations in focusing on risks that are more critical and likely to occur, and therefore helps to remove some of the subjectivity from the decision-making process. In this manner, a risk profile assists in identifying the threat exposure of an organization, which in turn can be used to allocate resources towards addressing the most significant risks effectively.

A risk profile is different for every organization because it is determined by several aspects like an organization's risk tolerance, the asset protection strategies implemented and the organization's risk management policies. This self-explanatory risk profile explains the organization's level of risk it can take after the decided plans for mitigating factors have been used. Identifying the gap between an organization's risk profile and the risk it can afford is one of the most important parts of enterprise risk management. When drawing out a risk profile, many relevant elements have to be investigated to ensure that all possible risks are identified, quantified, and addressed efficiently. These factors are shown in the following figure:

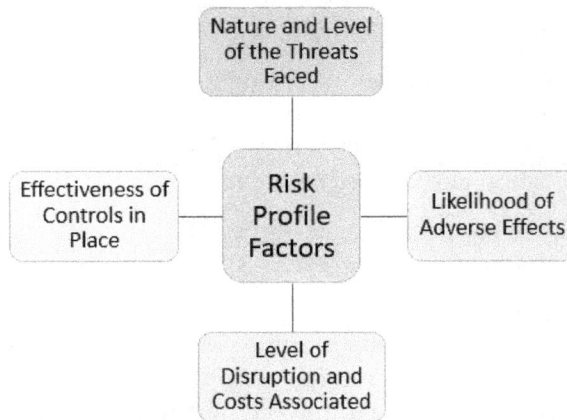

Figure 16.3: Risk profile factors

Let us look at some details of risk profile factors:

- **Nature and level of the threats faced**: The first step in developing a risk profile is identifying the types of risks an organization faces. The risk profile of an organization begins with identifying the organization's classification of risks. This includes determining whether the threat is operational, financial, strategic, technological, legal, environmental, or reputational. For instance, a company that operates in the technology sector may have a risk of cyber security threats while a manufacturing entity may give more priority to equipment breakdown or supply chain issues.

  Furthermore, the necessity of evaluating the threat level is also important, where the potential impact of each risk must be defined and the degree of severity measured. Some threats may be of low impact where minimal economic damage is incurred and some may pose serious impacts such as organization's reputational damage, legal penalties, and regulatory fines.

- **The likelihood of adverse effects occurring**: When conducting risk profiling, it is vital to assess the likelihood of each of the identified risks occurring. In this regard, one needs to analyze historical data, industry trends and authoritative sources to establish the probability of each risk. For instance, the chances of a cybersecurity breach occurring could vary with the prevailing threat environment, while the chances of a natural disaster occurring may depend on the location of the organization.

Likelihood is set and often described in terms of *likely*, *possible* or *rare* and is frequently used with the threat level and the severity to ascertain the risk level.

- **Level of disruption and costs associated with each type of risk**: Once the nature and likelihood of risk is understood, the next step is to measure the possible risk's impact or disruption if it were to happen. The impact includes direct disruption and the indirect costs of each risk as well. Regulatory fines or repairing expenses are examples of direct costs, while loss of customers, decreased employee morale, or damage to reputation, for example, are long-term impacts, which are considered indirect costs. A data breach, for instance, can have grave impacts. The organization might have to compensate legal fees, suffer loss of reputation and customer trust, and pay hefty regulatory fines. However, it is noteworthy that these costs might extend beyond the breach and impact the organization's brand image and market share. An evaluation of both direct and indirect impacts can give a clearer picture of how a risk can meddle in the operations of an organization.

- **Effectiveness of controls in place to manage risks**: A prominent element of the risk profile is understanding how effective the controls and mitigation strategies in place are. Here, it involves analysis of the current measures such as security protocols, compliance practices, and contingency measures to ascertain how they address or lower the identified risks. As an illustration, an organization may have high-level encryption protocols as a way of preventing cyberattacks or, indeed, have a strong IT disaster recovery plan in place in the event of system outages. The effectiveness of these controls can be evaluated by determining whether the risk's probability of occurrence is reduced or the damages if the risk occurs is limited. This aspect of the risk profile also deals with the evaluation of the existing controls for any shortcomings that need more mitigation.

Management of residual risk

Management of residual risk is an ongoing process that requires organizations to continuously evaluate and adjust their approach to risk management based on their objectives, risk appetite, and the effectiveness of implemented controls. Residual risk is the remaining risk after security controls have been applied, and organizations must determine how to address this residual risk consistent with their overall risk management strategy. The management of residual risk is typically handled in the manner outlined as follows:

- **Accepting residual risk**: The organization may choose to do nothing and accept the remaining risk if the residual risk is below its acceptable threshold. This could be typical of those instances when the controls put in place turn out adequate enough in reducing the risk to acceptable levels, hence having minimal potential impact within the organization's risk tolerance. This may also be accepted if the risk is unlikely to happen or when it does, its effects are manageable. Residual risk needs to be monitored continuously, re-assessed, and documented in risk registers to keep it at acceptable levels. Regular monitoring allows organizations to detect any changes in the risk environment or the effectiveness of mitigation measures and make timely adjustments if necessary.

- **Improve controls or update**: Where residual risk is not within acceptable levels, organizations can decide to either add more control or introduce new controls. It may be additional technical controls, security enhancements, or process changes that can reduce the remaining risk within an acceptable limit. For example, where a vulnerability persists after applying the initial security control, additional measures such as multi-factor authentication, enhanced encryption, or monitoring may be required to make the risk more tolerable.

- **Cost-benefit analysis of controls versus residual risk**: Sometimes, the benefit from residual risk mitigation may not be worth the cost involved. It requires organizations to balance the cost of additional controls, countermeasures, or enhancements against the possible impacts of residual risks. If the cost of mitigation is too high or the benefit from further reduction of risk is negligible, the organization may accept the risk even if it exceeds above the level of risk tolerance planned. The risk acceptance is not just based on cost-benefit analysis but also on risk appetite and risk tolerance.

Steps to address residual risk

Residual risk is a necessary element of the risk management process. Organizations often assess residual risks in the same way as original risks. Following are the steps to address the residual risk:

1. **Identify relevant governance, risk, and compliance requirements**: Organizations must understand the regulatory and compliance framework that controls the particular industry or sector in which they operate. This includes what laws, regulations, and standards to comply with, such as *General Data Protection Resolution (GDPR)*, *Health Insurance Portability and Accountability Act (HIPAA)*, or NIST. These will help to define the level of risk that can be accepted and help shape the overall risk management strategy.

2. **Evaluate strengths and weaknesses present in an organizational control framework**: This would require organizations to continually evaluate the strengths and weaknesses of their control frameworks. This includes reviewing how well

existing controls are performing and identifying any gaps that might contribute to the residual risk. Controls that have become outdated or ineffective may be either enhanced or updated to further reduce the risk exposure.

3. **Identify residual risks**: Acknowledging residual risks forms the basis of risk management. An organization needs to recognize those risks that still can affect the business after mitigation and estimate the consequences of those risks concerning the operation of their business, compliance, and security. Understanding the scope and potential consequences of residual risks helps organizations prioritize which risks require immediate attention.

4. **Identify the appetite of the organization for risk**: Risk appetite is the degree of risk an organization will accept to achieve its objectives. An organization needs to define its risk appetite to identify the level of residual risk that can be acceptable within the framework of the organization's business goals, legal obligations, and expectations of stakeholders. For example, a financial organization would have a low risk appetite toward data breach incidents compared to a non-profit, since it deals with highly sensitive financial data.

5. **Identify available options for offsetting unacceptable residual risks**: After recognizing the risks and determining the risk appetite of the organization, the next step will be to identify ways of offsetting unacceptable residual risks. It could be risk transfer, such as buying insurance; risk avoidance, for example, discontinuation of high-risk activities; or enhancing the resilience of systems and processes to cope with the risk when it arises. The organization needs to weigh the most cost-effective and practical options for mitigation or reduction of these remaining risks.

System test plan

A STP simple is an in-depth document which contains the objectives, scope, and even the strategies that will be used while sorting systems through different tests to establish whether or not requirements have been fulfilled, and the system works. In the context of NIST, the STPs are designed by the organization to suite their risk management and system security. NIST **Risk Management Framework** (**RMF**), NIST SP 800-53 security and privacy controls, and other standards are used by the organization in securing as well as testing the information system. The STP, in the context of NIST guidelines, would focus on evaluating the system's security, functionality, and performance to ensure it complies with both security requirements and operational objectives. The following figure shows the key components of STP:

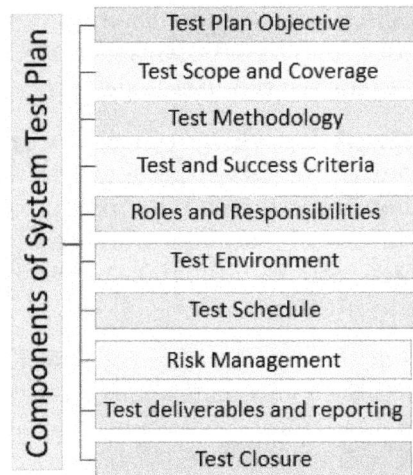

Figure 16.4: STP components

Here is a detailed explanation of the components and steps required in creating STP based on NIST practices:

- **Test plan objective**: The overarching aim of the STP is the actual verification and validation of the system's functional and non-functional requirements. This task also involves making sure that the security and privacy requirements are implemented as stated in NIST regulations, particularly within the NIST **Cybersecurity Framework (CSF)** and the RMF. Following is among the most meaningful objectives. To determine whether the system performs correctly and reliably under different operational environmental factors, like the following:

    o To ensure compliance with the applicable NIST security controls, such as the SP 800-53 publication.

    o To assess the system for vulnerabilities, weaknesses, and flaws and determine whether these have been adequately mitigated.

    o To determine the extent to which the system will be able to withstand attempts to disrupt it, and whether sufficient recovery mechanisms are in place.

- **Test scope and coverage**: Specific test scope outlines the parameters of the tests which entail the following:

    o System components include all hardware, software, network configuration, security, and user interface components of the system that will be subject to examination.

    o Functional testing is concerned with the ability of the system to carry out the requisite functions that the user demands for.

- o Performance aspects of the system considered in this category include system scalability, reliability, and security, which is why it's referred to as non-functional testing.

- o Security testing is focused on the evaluation of security mechanisms and configurations to ensure compliance to NIST security controls and other standards.

- o The purpose of interoperability testing is to make sure that the system functions properly in conjunction with other systems within a greater system.

- **Test methodology**: The test methodology specifies the approach to conduct testing, which should align with NIST's risk-based approach. The key methodologies are as follows:

  - o **Static and dynamic analysis:** Static analysis of the code and configuration helps identify vulnerabilities, dynamic analysis (e.g., penetration testing), and simulate real-world attack scenarios.

  - o **Automated and manual testing**: The automated tools are used for quick and efficient testing, while manual testing is used for more complex situations that require human judgment, like vulnerability assessments.

  - o **Security testing**: This can include the usage of specific NIST CSF test frameworks like *NIST SP 800-115 Technical Guide to Information Security Testing and Assessment*, which helps design and conduct security assessments such as vulnerability scanning, penetration testing, and risk assessments.

  - o **Performance and load testing**: This test ensures that the system can handle expected workloads and traffic volumes under stress.

- **Test criteria and success criteria**: Test criteria define the conditions under which a test will be considered successful, particularly in the context of system security and functionality. For example:

  - o **Functional success criteria**: The system should pass all functional requirements described in the specification documents, e.g., user interactions, data inputs and, outputs.

  - o **Security success criteria**: All NIST 800-53 controls applicable should be satisfied, and the system should be able to show enough protection against all known threats.

  - o **Performance success criteria**: The system shall achieve the standards set for response time, throughput, and percentage of uptime during normal and peak loads of usage.

  - o **Regulatory compliance**: The system is required to meet all applicable laws and compliance regulations, such as *Federal Information Security Modernization Act* (*FISMA*) or *GDPR*.

- **Roles and responsibilities**: The plan for the system test describes the hierarchy of individuals controlling the test activities. This may include any of the following personnel:

  o **Test manager**: The test manager is responsible for administrative management of all activities related to the testing and also for implementation of the plan.

  o **Test engineers**: Test engineers carry out and administer the tests.

  o **Security professionals**: Security professionals concentrate on the NIST security controls compliance.

  o **Developers**: The developers assist by resolving the problems or bugs that have been discovered in the course of the testing.

  o **Quality assurance (QA) team**: The QA team is responsible for ascertaining that the quality of the system in terms of features, performance, and ease of use is satisfactory.

- **Test environment**: The test environment refers to the configuration and setup in which the testing will be conducted. NIST's guidelines recommends creating a test environment that mirrors the production environment to evaluate performance, security, and interoperability effectively. The test environment must include the following:

  o **Hardware**: The servers, networking equipment, or other devices that the system will operate on.

  o **Software**: Any software or tools required for testing (e.g., load testing tools, vulnerability scanners).

  o **Network configuration**: The configuration of networks, firewalls, VPNs, and other network components required during testing.

  o **Security tools**: Tools for testing security aspects, such as encryption, access control, and user authentication.

- **Test schedule**: The detailed test schedule outlines each phase of testing that will occur. The phases are mentioned as follows:

  o **Test preparation**: Time allocated for preparing the test environment, tools, and test cases.

  o **Test execution**: Time allocated for performing the various tests (e.g., security testing, performance testing).

  o **Issue reporting and resolution**: Time for documenting any issues found, their impact, and resolution.

- **Risk management and mitigation**: The test plan should also define how risks will be managed and mitigated during the testing process. These are as follows:

  o **Risk identification**: Identify potential risks that may affect the testing process, such as resource limitations, unexpected system behavior, or incomplete test cases.

  o **Risk mitigation**: Define how these risks will be addressed, such as adjusting test schedules, enhancing the test environment, or revising test cases.

  o **Contingency plans**: Have backup plans in case critical issues arise during the testing phase (e.g., system downtime, tool failures).

- **Test deliverables and reporting**: The test deliverables specify the documentation and reports that will be generated during and after testing. These are as follows:

  o **Test cases**: Detailed steps for performing each test.

  o **Test logs**: Document the results of each test, including any issues found and their severity.

  o **Security assessment reports**: In case of security testing, a detailed analysis of vulnerabilities discovered and their severity, along with recommendations for remediation.

  o **Performance reports**: Detailed reports on how the system performed under load, its scalability, and reliability.

- **Test closure**: The test closure involves summarizing the test outcomes and determining if the system is ready for deployment. This includes the following:

  o **Final report**: A comprehensive summary of all test activities, results, and recommendations for any necessary changes.

  o **Lessons learned**: Review any lessons learned during the testing process that could help improve future testing efforts.

  o **Sign-off**: Formal sign-off from stakeholders indicating the system is ready for deployment or requires further work.

Documenting test results

Documenting test results is a critical step in the certification and accreditation process, ensuring that the security controls and other requirements of an information system are properly assessed. The goal of this documentation is to record the findings from certification testing, which includes the effectiveness and compliance of security controls as defined by security frameworks and standards. The following figure shows the key aspect of documenting test results:

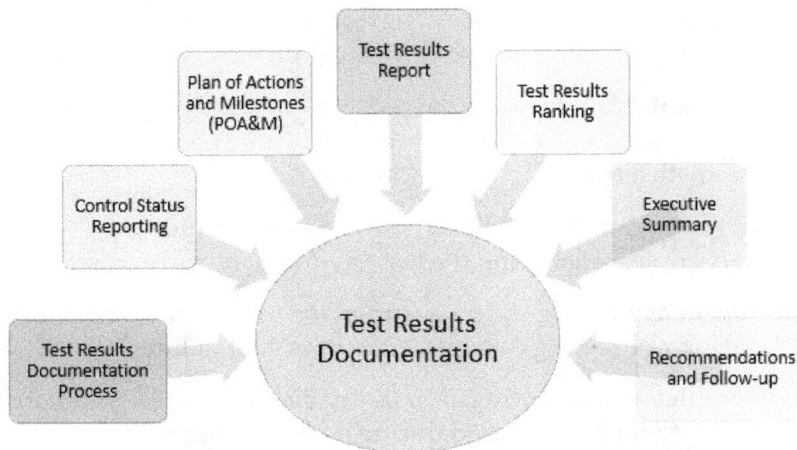

Figure 16.5: *Components of test results documentation*

Here is a breakdown of the key aspects involved in documenting test results:

- **Test results documentation process**: Once certification testing is completed, it is essential to gather and analyze the results of all control tests. The process for documenting test results should follow these steps:

  o **Test plan completion**: The results should be documented according to the test plan that was submitted and approved previously.

  o **Raw data transformation**: Immediately following the conclusion of testing, raw data collected during the testing should be transformed into documented test results while the observations are still fresh in the minds of the testing team members.

  o **Collaboration and comparison**: The test team members should work closely to compare observations and validate individual findings.

  o **Evaluation of automated testing**: The result must be evaluated if automated tools were used. This ensures that there are no false positives or duplicate findings.

- **Control status reporting**: Each control tested should be annotated as either pass or fail, and the actual findings should be recorded in detail. The following should be included in the documentation:

  o **Control status**: This identifies whether each control passed or failed based on testing results.

  o **Findings**: Findings provide detailed findings for each control tested, documenting the nature of any failures, the impact of those failures, and any mitigation recommendations.

- o **Validation process**: This process documents the sources and processes used to validate the control status, including any evidence or supporting documentation.

- **Plan of actions and milestones (POA&M)**: The POA&M is a document that identifies and tracks weaknesses in security controls. It is created or updated as part of certification testing and helps outline the steps required to correct deficiencies. The process is as follows:

  - o **Deficiency identification**: Each security control found to have a weakness must be documented, and remediation actions must be outlined. The test team may perform this step, but the system owner typically takes the responsibility for creating or updating the POA&M.

  - o **System security plan (SSP) updates**: Once deficiencies have been identified, the SSP must be updated to reflect changes in the security controls. The certifying agent may document the need for these updates as part of the POA&M.

  - o **Status of planned controls**: The POA&M should also indicate the status of planned controls, allowing the certifying official to assess the system's risk and make informed recommendations.

- **Test results report**: The test results report should provide a thorough summary of all testing activities. The report should include the following:

  - o **Personnel involved**: Document the names of the individuals who conducted the testing (testers, system owners, certifying agents) and who assisted in the testing (hosting organization personnel).

  - o **Testing locations**: Include an overview of the locations, platforms, components, and subsystems tested.

  - o **Test process summary**: Describe the overall process for conducting the tests, including methods, tools employed, and procedures followed.

  - o **Test timing**: Specify the starting and ending times of the tests. This helps establish the timeline of testing activities and can be useful for auditing purposes.

  - o **Deviations from the test plan**: Document any instances where deviations from the test plan occurred. For example, if a particular server could not be tested or if a procedure was not followed as expected, these should be clearly described.

  - o **Control applicability**: Testing may reveal certain controls that do not apply to the system, or that additional controls not initially identified may be necessary. Such deviations should be documented, and the need for additional controls should be recommended.

- **Test results ranking**: The test results should be ranked to prioritize the most significant findings. Ranking the results is critical for remediation planning and managing system security. The following should be considered:

  o **Severity ranking**: Rank weaknesses based on their severity. This is most effective when informed by a risk assessment that ties the vulnerabilities to specific threats and potential impacts on the system.

  o **Risk assessment mapping**: Map test findings to the risks identified during earlier risk assessments.

- **Executive summary**: The executive summary of the test results should provide a high level overview of the testing results. This is particularly useful for stakeholders and decision-makers required to understand the most important findings without delving into technical details.

  o **Snapshot of key findings**: Snapshot provides a summary of the most significant findings, including major security vulnerabilities or performance issues.

  o **System security benchmarking**: The benchmarking includes a comparison of the system's security relative to other similar systems or industry benchmarks.

  o **Areas of concern**: The area of concern highlights issues that require immediate attention, such as critical vulnerabilities or gaps in security controls.

- **Recommendations and follow-up**: The test results report should conclude with recommendations for improving the system's security, which are:

  o **Immediate remediation actions**: List any actions that must be taken immediately to address critical issues.

  o **Further testing**: If certain components cannot be tested or if additional controls are required, it is recommended to follow up on further testing.

  o **Ongoing monitoring**: Recommend actions for ongoing monitoring or regular security assessments to ensure the system remains secure over time.

Risk ranking

Identified risks during the assessment are typically ranked from critical risk at the top to the minor risk at the bottom. This classification is often carried out depending on various factors such as the level of impact, asset value, and likelihood. All risks are calculated during the evaluation, and a composite risk score result is always included so that the risks can be ranked accordingly. Having these kinds of risk ranking helps ensure that the most critical risks are addressed first and the organization is focusing on mitigating high-priority risk and allocating resources effectively. A more useful approach to present risk ranking with the aid of a graph is more eye-catching and appealing. One common tool of illustrating the severity of risks is the risk map, which categorizes them based on their likelihood and impact. This kind of visualization helps in providing a neatly summarized picture of the risks that exist and how they may affect the stakeholders. Furthermore, with this tool, the most severe risks can easily be spotted and dealt with as shown in figure:

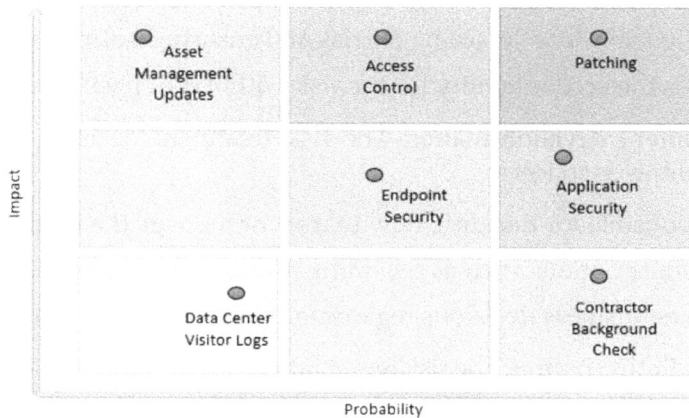

Figure 16.6: Risk map

The preceding figure demonstrates how risks are prioritized by assessing both impact and probability. For instance, it shows that data center visitor logs, which contain limited information, pose a lower risk, as mishandling them would have a minimal impact on the organization. On the other hand, application security is ranked with higher severity due to its significant potential impact and higher probability of exploitation. This prioritization helps focus resources on managing and mitigating risks that could have more severe consequences, ensuring that the most critical vulnerabilities are addressed first.

Risk ownership

Risk ownership is crucial in managing and addressing unacceptable risks within an organization. Each risk should have a designated owner, typically the department head or business unit leader responsible for the specific business process related to that risk. The business risk should not be owned by IT as they are not accountable for business risk but should be responsible for implementing risk mitigation efforts. Similarly, while the organization's cybersecurity leader (often the **chief information security officer** (**CISO**)) plays a pivotal role in facilitating risk discussions, they do not own the risks. Instead, the cybersecurity leader helps business leaders assess and decide how to address risks within their areas.

To facilitate accountability, the organization includes roles and responsibilities in the risk management program charter or other formal documentation of the company. These responsibilities are also typically captured in the risk register, a tool used to track and manage risks within the organization. In risk management, there is variety of roles which are usually assigned with each risk such as risk owner, risk treatment decision-maker, and risk remediation owner:

- **Risk owner**: Risk owners are the leaders of the department or business unit where the risk rests, and some of their responsibilities are as follows:
    - o Responsible for overseeing the risk and ensuring it is managed appropriately.
    - o Owns the accountability for the risk within the specific business process.

- **Risk treatment decision-maker**: The risk treatment decision-makers have few responsibilities as follows:
    - o Responsible for deciding how to treat or manage the identified risk.
    - o Evaluate options such as risk mitigation, transfer, acceptance, or avoidance.
    - o Makes business decisions regarding the disposition of the risk.

- **Risk remediation owner**: The risk remediation owner has a few key responsibilities, like:
    - o Handles the implementation of corrective actions or mitigation strategies selected during risk treatment.
    - o Ensures the chosen remediation measures are executed effectively and promptly.

Verification and validation

Verification ensures that security controls are properly implemented according to the design and specifications, making sure that the controls are in place as intended. Validation, on the other hand, assures that these controls are operationally effective, i.e., they function as intended in real-world scenarios to protect the organization from risks. Verification and validation are important steps that ensure the system is built correctly and meets its security, business, and mission goals when in use.

Verification

The verification process aims to provide objective evidence that a system meets its specified requirements and characteristics. In the context of a system's security engineering, it ensures that the system fulfills its security requirements and demonstrates the desired security features. This includes verifying that the system exhibits only the specified behaviors and outcomes, which requires proving the absence of unintended or unauthorized actions. The verification process also applies rigorous methods to assess whether the system meets its security goals at the required assurance level.

Security verification involves both objective evidence, such as results from testing, evaluation, and inspection, and a subjective analysis to interpret and reason about the evidence. The process also identifies and documents any anomalies, such as defects or flaws, that may impact the system's security. These anomalies are then assessed to determine whether they present vulnerabilities that affect the system's compliance with its security requirements.

Verification process

The verification process includes some high level activities:

- **Prepare for the security aspects of verification**:
  - Identify and define the security requirements and characteristics of the system.
  - Establish the criteria and methods for security verification that ensure alignment with system objectives and regulatory standards.
  - Develop a detailed security verification plan that outlines testing, inspection, and evaluation processes.
  - Select tools, techniques, and resources needed for effective security verification.
  - Assign roles and responsibilities for verification tasks.

- **Perform security-focused verification**:
  - Conduct security tests, evaluations, and inspections based on the established plan.
  - Assess whether the system meets its defined security requirements through objective evidence (e.g., testing results).
  - Identify and evaluate anomalies, such as security defects or vulnerabilities, that could impact the system's integrity or functionality.
  - Document findings and ensure proper analysis to determine the severity and implications of identified issues.

- **Manage the results of security-focused verification**:
  - Review and analyze the collected verification data to assess system compliance with security requirements.
  - Prioritize and categorize identified anomalies based on their impact on security.
  - Provide detailed reports of findings, including any vulnerabilities and the actions required to mitigate them.

o   Update the system's security documentation and ensure appropriate stakeholders are informed about the verification results.

o   Determine whether the system meets the required security assurance levels and if remediation actions are necessary.

Validation

The purpose of the validation process is to ensure that the system meets its business or mission objectives and stakeholder requirements when it is in use. It aims to demonstrate that the system, operating in its intended environment, achieves its intended purpose while safeguarding business or mission assets. This includes minimizing or containing any potential loss or consequences from asset damage or disruption. The critical aspect of validation is to ensure that the system functions as specified, maintaining trustworthiness in its behavior, interactions, and outcomes. The system must be shown to perform its intended functions without vulnerability to manipulation or interference from adversaries.

As part of security engineering, the validation process provides evidence that the system effectively achieves the established security objectives within the operational environment. This encompasses describing the fact that the system is capable of withstanding interruptions, risks, and threats that are expected to be encountered during its operation. The validation stage guarantees that the system's security features are strong enough to offer satisfactory defense and guard against breaches. By validating the system's ability to operate securely in its intended environment, organizations will have confidence that the system will fulfill its objectives while mitigating risks and vulnerabilities.

Validation process

The high level validation process consists of three main activities, which are as follows:

- **Prepare for the security aspects of validation**: This stage involves defining the security requirements and objectives of the system based on stakeholder expectations, business or mission goals, and the operational environment. It also includes planning the validation activities, identifying potential risks, and setting criteria for success. This phase ensures that all necessary resources, methods, and criteria are in place to validate the system's security.

- **Perform security-focused validation**: At this point, thorough tests and evaluations of the system must be conducted, focusing on its security capabilities to determine whether it fulfills the defined directives. This consists of conducting objective evaluations of the system's operational performance and vulnerability assessments and confirming the system's capability to control its assets and accomplish its purposes. As a result of the evaluation, one will be determined whether the system will operate as required during day-to-day activities while ensuring there are no vulnerabilities to exploit.

- **Manage results of security-focused validation**: At this stage, the findings from the security validation are recorded, studied, and prepared for future input. Any potential gaps, inconsistencies, or issues noticed during the different phases of validation are discussed, and corrective steps are taken where necessary. This step also covers updating risk assessment and confirming that the system is set to achieve the desired level of security as the organization intended. Trust is a key element in systems and decision-making, as they are closely connected. Therefore, the findings must be communicated to system stakeholders to ensure confidence in the system's security measures.

Conclusion

In this chapter, we examined the process of selecting risk acceptance criteria and managing a risk profile. We provided guidance on creating an STP and outlined the critical steps for documenting test results. These steps are crucial for ensuring that the security controls are evaluated thoroughly and efficiently.

Additionally, the chapter highlighted the significance of risk ranking and risk ownership that helps prioritize risks and assign clear responsibilities for their management. We also explored the verification and validation processes, which are crucial for assessing and measuring the system's security posture. As we progress into the next chapter, our focus will shift to training records and system configuration guides, further supporting effective risk management and security practices.

Key terms

- Risk acceptance means that the organization must accept any remaining or residual risk after all other risk response options have been implemented.

- Risk profile is a collection of detailed data on identified IT risks, typically applied to a specific system or groups of systems.

- Risk ranking is the process of prioritizing risks by placing them into a sequence, typically with the highest or most critical risks appearing at the top.

- Risk ownership refers to the process of assigning responsibility and accountability for a particular risk to an individual or group within an organization.

- Risk scenario refers to a specific, identified possibility of a risk event occurring, and it includes the following:

    o Threat actor is the entity or individual that poses a risk to the organization (e.g., hacker, competitor, natural disaster).

    o Threat is the potential event or action that could exploit a vulnerability (e.g., cyberattack, fraud, system failure).

- o Vulnerability is a weakness or gap in a system, process, or security that a threat can exploit.

- o An asset is a valuable resource or asset that is at risk (e.g., data, intellectual property, reputation).

- Risk sharing (or risk transference) involves offsetting part of a risk by transferring it to a third party.

- System testing means testing the system as a whole. All the modules/components are integrated to verify if the system works as expected or not.

- Individual risk refers to the potential impact of a risk event on a single person, organization, or entity. It focuses on how a particular risk might affect a specific individual, business, or asset.

- Societal risk refers to the broader impact of a risk event on society. It looks at how a risk can affect a large group of people, communities, or even entire nations.

- The purpose of the verification process is to provide objective evidence that a system or system element fulfills its specified requirements and characteristics.

- The purpose of the validation process is to provide objective evidence that the system, when in use, fulfills its business or mission objectives and stakeholder requirements, achieving its intended use in its intended operational environment.

Join our book's Discord space

Join the book's Discord Workspace for Latest updates, Offers, Tech happenings around the world, New Release and Sessions with the Authors:

https://discord.bpbonline.com

CHAPTER 17
Documenting System Compliance

Introduction

This chapter provides a comprehensive overview of system authorization documentation in line with *National Institute of Standards and Technology (NIST)* guidance. It details the steps involved in preparing a **system audit report** (**SAR**), outlining the process for evaluating an information system's security posture and compliance. The chapter also highlights the importance of maintaining training records to track ongoing training activities. Additionally, it explores the key elements of stakeholder concurrence, emphasizing the importance of aligning stakeholders on security controls, risk assessment findings, and authorization decisions.

Moreover, the chapter discusses the **IT contingency plan** (**ITCP**), emphasizing its crucial role in ensuring continuity of operations in the face of potential disruptions. It details the necessary phases, such as notification, recovery, and reconstitution, to maintain operational resilience. Furthermore, the chapter outlines the **configuration management** (**CM**) process, including its significance in managing system changes while minimizing security risks. It also defines the roles and responsibilities of the personnel involved in the CM process, ensuring that changes are implemented in a controlled environment.

Structure

The chapter covers the following main topics:

- System authorization documentation
- System audit report
- Training records
- Stakeholder concurrence
- IT contingency plan
- Configuration management

Objectives

By the end of this chapter, you will have a thorough understanding of system authorization documentation, including the steps involved in creating a SAR. The chapter will guide you on maintaining training records and ensuring that personnel are properly equipped to manage security tasks. Additionally, you will learn the importance of documenting and tracking training activities to meet compliance requirements.

The chapter also introduces you to the concept of stakeholder concurrence, highlighting its role in aligning all relevant parties in the authorization process. You will gain insight into developing an ITCP, which ensures operational continuity during disruptions. Furthermore, the chapter covers the CM process, providing you with a comprehensive understanding of managing system changes and maintaining security throughout the lifecycle of an information system.

System authorization documentation

The NIST SP 800-37 **Risk Management Framework** (RMF) guides the process of information systems certification and authorization. The package for certification includes security control assessments, test results for security controls and documentation of the security posture. The authorization package goes a step further. It contains all the documents of the certification package and other documents involved in the process of authorization. These documents are designed to provide sufficient, objective, and reliable evidence of the system's security controls and their effectiveness, eliminating the need for overly detailed documentation, such as a technical architecture document or disaster recovery plan. For example, the system security plan must include a more complete description of the system environment and the recovery strategy while the certification test report must provide detailed findings related to recovery plans and security control effectiveness.

The role of the approving authority, typically a senior executive, is to make an informed decision about the system's operation based on the evidence presented in the certification package. While this individual does not need to be a security expert, the security control assessor, an expert in information technology security, prepares the documentation to ensure that the required controls have been properly implemented and are functioning as intended. The certification package should, therefore, be comprehensive yet summarized to facilitate quick understanding, focusing on security weaknesses and residual risks that require the approving authority's attention and acceptance. The documentation provides not only the security status of the system but also a historical record that supports due diligence and offers a basis for auditing and compliance reviews.

The authorization package is a collection of documents that provides a comprehensive assessment of the security posture of an information system. The key components of the authorization package are as shown in the following figure:

Figure 17.1: Components of authorization package

Here is the breakdown of key components:

- **System security plan (SSP)**: This document describes the system's security controls and how they are implemented to meet organizational requirements. It provides a comprehensive overview of the system's architecture, security posture, and compliance with applicable security standards and policies.

- **Risk assessment**: This includes an analysis of potential risks to the system, identifying vulnerabilities, threats, and impacts. A minimum-security baseline assessment is typically part of this, which helps to ensure that the system meets the necessary security requirements.

- **Certification test plan and results report (or security assessment report)**: This document details the testing methodology used to verify the effectiveness of security controls. It includes test results and provides an evaluation of the system's compliance with security standards.

- **Remediation plan (or POA&M)**: This plan outlines the actions required to address any security vulnerabilities or deficiencies discovered during the certification process. It includes timelines, responsible parties, and milestones for remediating identified risks.

- **Certification statement**: This is a formal declaration by the certifying authority asserting that the system has been evaluated and meets the required security standards. It includes an acknowledgment of any remaining risks and an endorsement of the system's authorization to operate.

NIST guidance on authorization

The sixth step in the RMF ensures organizational accountability by requiring a senior management official to assess and determine whether the security, privacy, and supply chain risks associated with a system or common controls are acceptable. The following figure shows the sixth step of NIST RMF:

Figure 17.2: NIST RMF

The **authorizing official (AO)** evaluates the potential impact of the system's operation on organizational operations, assets, individuals, other organizations, and the nation, and decides whether the identified risks are manageable or if additional actions are needed to mitigate them. The following figure shows the task associated with authorization step:

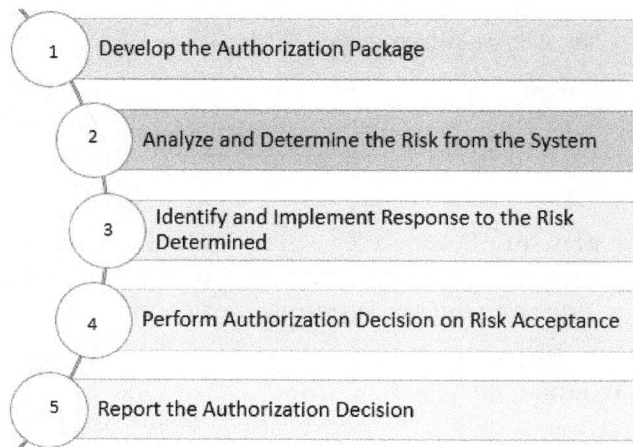

Figure 17.3: NIST authorization steps

Let us see a breakdown of authorization steps:

Task 1: **Develop the authorization package**: Authorization packages include system security plan, risk assessment, assessment reports, plan of action and milestones along with certification statement and additional information as requested by the AO. They are regularly updated for ongoing risk management and reauthorization. The senior agency official for privacy ensures systems handling **personally identifiable information** (**PII**) meet privacy requirements before the AO makes a risk acceptance decision. These packages help officials make informed, risk-based decisions, including external provider information, and can be presented in various formats for easy management and updates. Automated tools help ensure timely, efficient updates, highlighting system deficiencies and aligning with the organization's risk management goals. The following table shows the roles to develop the authorization package:

Primary responsibility	Supporting roles	SDLC phase	References
System owner; common control provider; senior agency official for privacy	System security officer; system privacy officer; senior agency information security officer; control assessor.	New: Implementation/ assessment Existing: Operations/ maintenance	NIST SP 800-18; SP 800-160 v1 (risk management process); SP 800-161

Table 17.1: *Roles to develop authorization packages*

Task 2: Analyze and determine the risk from the system: The AO, in collaboration with the senior agency information security officer and senior agency official for privacy for systems handling PII, reviews the authorization package to finalize the risk determination. This may involve further discussions to ensure a clear understanding of the risks, with input from the senior accountable official for risk management considering factors like risk tolerance, system dependencies, and mission criticality. For ongoing authorization, the process remains the same, with the AO using automated tools to assess the system's current security and privacy posture and document any new risk-related information for an informed decision. The following table shows the roles to analyze and determine the risk from the system:

Primary responsibility	Supporting roles	SDLC phase	References
AO or AO designated representative	Senior accountable official for risk management or risk executive (function); senior agency information security officer; senior agency official for privacy.	New: Implementation/ assessment Existing: Operations/ maintenance	NISTSP 800-30; SP 800-39; SP 800-137; SP 800-160 v1

Table 17.2: *Roles to analyze and determine risk*

Task 3: Identify and implement responses to the risk determined: After analyzing risks, organizations can choose to accept or mitigate them, with risk assessment results guiding the decision. For mitigation, actions are tracked in a plan of action and milestones, and controls are reassessed to ensure they meet security and privacy requirements. Assessment reports are updated with reassessment findings, while original results remain unchanged. For risk acceptance, identified deficiencies are documented and monitored. The AO reviews the assessment reports to decide if risks need to be mitigated before authorization. Risk responses are prioritized based on severity, with higher-priority risks receiving more resources, but all residual risk is acknowledged and managed within the organization's tolerance level. The following table shows the roles to identify and implement response to the risk determined:

Primary responsibility	Supporting roles	SDLC phase	References
AO or AO designated representative	Senior accountable official for risk management or risk executive (function); senior agency information security officer; senior agency official for privacy; system owner or common control provider; information owner or steward; systems security engineer; privacy engineer; system security officer; system privacy officer	New: Implementation/ assessment Existing: Operations/ maintenance	NIST SP 800-30; SP 800-39; SP 800-160 v1

Table 17.3: Roles to identify and implement risk response

Task 4: Perform authorization decision on risk acceptance: The AO is solely responsible for accepting risk and cannot delegate this duty. When making the decision, they consider factors like the potential impact on operations, assets, individuals, and the nation, balancing security and privacy with mission needs. The decision is based on the authorization package, input from other officials, and relevant details. Before finalizing, the official consults with the senior accountable official for risk management or risk executive to assess dependencies between systems. The final decision, communicated to the system owner or common control provider, includes terms for authorization, such as frequency or termination dates, and indicates whether a system or common control is authorized to operate or be used. The following table shows the roles to perform authorization decision on risk acceptance:

Primary responsibility	Supporting roles	SDLC phase	References
AO	Senior accountable official for risk management or risk executive (function); **chief information officer (CIO)**; senior agency information security officer; senior agency official for privacy; AO designated representative	New: Implementation/assessment Existing: Operations/maintenance	NIST SP 800-39; SP 800-160 v1

Table 17.4: Roles to perform authorization decision

Task 5: Report the authorization decision: AOs report their decisions on system and common control authorizations to designated organizational officials, ensuring these decisions align with the overall security and privacy risk strategy. This reporting usually happens when authorization duties are delegated below the agency head. They also report significant security or privacy vulnerabilities identified during assessments or monitoring that pose major risks. Organizations define what qualifies as significant risk for reporting, and this is reflected in their guidelines. Vulnerabilities may be reported using NIST **Cybersecurity Framework (CSF)** categories, and at the organization's discretion, authorization decisions can be tracked in the system registration process. For example, there is a category called risk assessment in identify function of CSF which has one task that describes vulnerabilities in assets are identified, validated, and recorded. The following table shows the roles to report the authorization decision:

Primary responsibility	Supporting roles	SDLC phase	References
AO or AO designated representative	System owner or common control provider; information owner or steward; system security officer; system privacy officer; senior agency information security officer; senior agency official for privacy	New: Implementation/assessment Existing: Operations/maintenance	NIST SP 800-39 ; SP 800-160 v1; NIST CSF

Table 17.5: Roles to report authorization decision

System audit report

A SAR is typically a formal evaluation of a system's compliance, performance and security with established policies, and regulations. It outlines the scope and objectives of the audit, including the system's description, audit criteria, and the methodology used. The report summarizes the findings, highlighting key risks, vulnerabilities, and areas of strength while offering recommendations for improvement. It provides detailed evidence and justifications for each conclusion, supported by logs, screenshots, and other artifacts.

The report concludes with appendices and attachments that include additional data and documentation, following organizational guidelines for formatting and ensuring accuracy and relevance throughout. The following figure shows the steps to document the SAR:

Figure 17.4: SAR

Here is the breakdown of the SAR steps:

- **Define the scope and objectives**: The first section of the audit report should define the scope and objectives clearly. This includes providing a system overview, such as the system name, description, and boundaries. The audit criteria and standards used should be stated, along with the audit methodology and tools employed during the process. Additionally, the audit period, date, and the audit team members should be identified.

- **Summarize the findings and recommendations**: This section should provide a concise summary of the audit's findings, including an overall rating or opinion on the system's security. Major risks and vulnerabilities identified during the audit should be highlighted, alongside the root causes and their potential impacts. Recommendations should be prioritized based on urgency and severity, with specific actions needed to address the risks.

- **Provide the details and evidence**: Next, the report should include the specifics of the findings, tests performed, and results obtained. This includes references to the audit criteria and standards used and any supporting evidence, such as screenshots, logs, or other documentation. The rationale for each recommendation should be explained, detailing the benefits and any potential challenges or risks involved in implementing the recommendations.

- **Include the appendices and attachments**: The final section should contain all additional supporting documents, such as the audit plan, checklist, interview notes, survey responses, or a risk matrix. Any relevant disclaimers, confidentiality statements, and acknowledgments should also be included here.

- **Follow the formatting and style guidelines**: To maintain consistency and professionalism, the audit report should adhere to organizational formatting and style guidelines. This includes standardizing the layout, font, color scheme, logo, header, footer, page numbers, table of contents, and glossary. Clear, concise, and consistent language should be used throughout, ensuring that grammar, spelling, and punctuation are correct.

- **Review and validate the report**: Before finalizing the audit report, it should undergo a thorough review to ensure its accuracy, completeness, and relevance. This involves checking all facts, figures, and sources, validating the alignment between the findings and the audit objectives, and ensuring the report's structure is clear and logical. Feedback from the audit team and stakeholders should be solicited, and revisions should be made to address any errors, gaps, or opportunities for improvement.

Training records

Training records are documented records that track the training activities and qualifications of individuals within an organization. These records typically include details, such as the name of the employee, the training program or course attended, the date of completion, the objectives of the training, and the assessment results or certifications earned. Training records help organizations ensure that their employees have received the necessary skills and knowledge to perform their job duties effectively and comply with industry regulations. They are also valuable for audits, performance reviews, and identifying skill gaps within the workforce.

NIST guidelines on training records

Training records, according to NIST, are a critical component in ensuring that individuals within an organization possess the necessary skills and knowledge to perform their duties effectively, especially in areas related to information security and privacy. NIST emphasizes that training is a key part of an organization's CSF, as it helps employees understand the risks they may face and how to mitigate them. Proper documentation of training records is necessary for organizations to demonstrate compliance with regulations and security standards. The following figure shows some guidelines for training records:

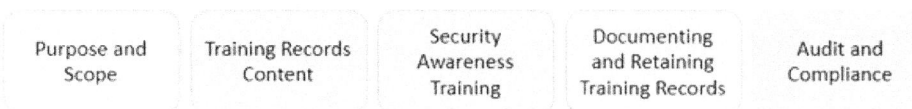

| Purpose and Scope | Training Records Content | Security Awareness Training | Documenting and Retaining Training Records | Audit and Compliance |

Figure 17.5: NIST training records guidance

Here is the breakdown of training records guidelines:

- **Purpose and scope**:
    - o NIST's CSF and information security frameworks such as NIST SP 800-53, emphasize on continuous, role-based training for employees. These frameworks recommend that organizations provide security training to their employees, contractors, and third-party vendors according to their particular job roles and responsibilities. The training records document the completion of such programs and track progress to ensure that the organization's security posture remains robust, minimizing human errors or insider threats.

- **Content of training records**:
    - o **Employee information**: The name, position, and role of the employee being trained.

    - o **Training program details**: A description of the training course or program, including the topic (e.g., data protection, incident response, phishing prevention), objectives, and the scope of the training.

    - o **Completion dates**: The start and end date of the training session, along with the duration.

    - o **Assessment results**: Information on how the training was evaluated (e.g., exams, quizzes, practical tests), including test scores or certifications issued after successful completion.

    - o **Trainer details**: Information on the instructor or organization providing the training, ensuring the legitimacy of the program.

    - o **Compliance status**: Any specific compliance requirements fulfilled by the training (e.g., HIPAA, FISMA, or other industry-specific regulations).

- **Security awareness training**:
    - o NIST provides specific guidelines on security awareness training. This is particularly relevant for ensuring that all employees are aware of organizational policies, potential security threats, and best practices for mitigating risks.

    - o According to NIST SP 800-50, employees should be trained on their individual responsibilities for safeguarding sensitive information, detecting potential threats, and reporting security incidents promptly.

- **Documenting and retaining training records**:
  - o NIST guidelines recommend that organizations maintain comprehensive training records for a specified retention period.
  - o The records should be securely stored to prevent unauthorized access and alterations. Additionally, they should be regularly reviewed to ensure that employees continue to meet required knowledge and competency standards, particularly as new security threats emerge or regulations evolve.
  - o NIST also suggests that training records be integrated with an organization's larger security management processes, including risk assessments and security reviews.

- **Audit and compliance**:
  - o NIST emphasizes that maintaining training records helps organizations demonstrate compliance with relevant laws, regulations, and security frameworks. For example, organizations seeking certification under ISO 27001 or other security standards must be able to provide documentation showing that employees have received the appropriate level of training in areas like information security, incident handling, and privacy protection.
  - o Regular audits of training records are recommended to ensure that training programs remain effective and align with organizational goals.

Stakeholder concurrence

Stakeholder concurrence refers to the agreement and approval of key stakeholders within an organization regarding various aspects of the system's security and risk management activities. This includes the evaluation of security controls, risk assessments, and the overall security posture of an information system.

Stakeholder concurrence is an essential step during the authorization process, as it ensures that all relevant parties, such as system owners, security officers, risk management executives, and other responsible individuals, are aligned on the decisions being made, particularly regarding the security authorization and risk acceptance. These stakeholders provide their input, review findings, and ensure that risk decisions align with the organization's risk tolerance and business objectives.

Key elements of stakeholder concurrence in the NIST context typically include the following, as shown in the following figure:

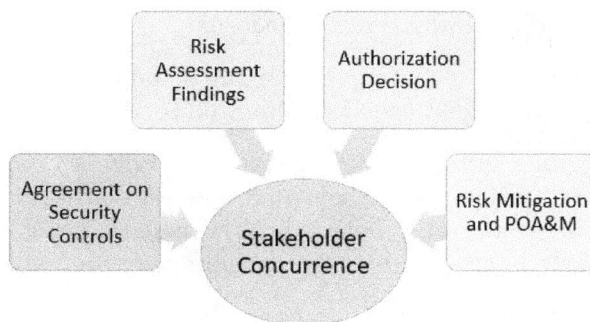

Figure 17.6: Stakeholder concurrence

Here is a detailed breakdown of the key elements of stakeholder concurrence:

- **Agreement on security controls**: Stakeholders must reach a consensus that the system's security controls are appropriate, effective, and compliant with organizational policies, as well as NIST standards. This ensures the security framework addresses all necessary vulnerabilities and protects the system appropriately.

- **Risk assessment findings**: Stakeholders are responsible for reviewing the results of the risk assessment to confirm that any identified risks are properly understood and mitigated. This step ensures that potential threats and vulnerabilities have been assessed comprehensively and that the necessary precautions are in place to address them.

- **Authorization decision**: The AO, with input from key stakeholders, must make a final decision on the authorization of the system. The AO, after considering all available evidence, concurs with the decision to approve or deny the system's operation based on the associated risks and their potential impact on the organization.

- **Risk mitigation and POA&M**: Stakeholders must agree on the POA&M, which outlines the corrective actions and timelines for addressing any remaining risks or vulnerabilities. This alignment ensures that risk mitigation efforts are systematically prioritized and executed according to the organization's risk management strategy.

IT contingency plan

An ITCP is a critical document designed to ensure the continuity of operations in the event of a disruption to information systems, whether due to cyber incidents, hardware failures, natural disasters, or other emergencies. The ITCP provides a framework for the recovery of systems and data and outlines the roles and responsibilities of the recovery team. To be effective, the plan must be comprehensive, detailed, and structured to provide clear guidance to team members at all levels. The ITCP is typically divided into five main components:

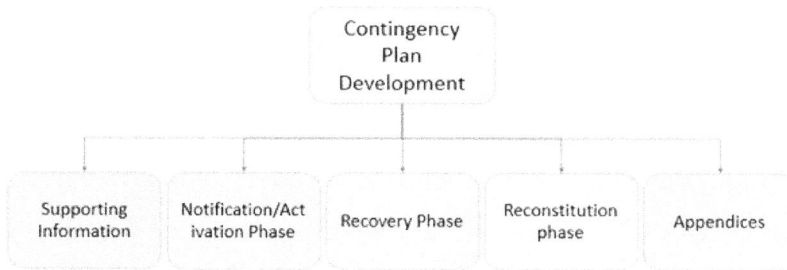

Figure 17.7: ITCP

Here is the breakdown of contingency plan development:

- **Supporting information**: This section includes all the background information required for the effective execution of the contingency plan. It is designed to provide context and ensure all stakeholders have a clear understanding of the system, resources, and dependencies that must be restored. Some of the key elements are as follows:

    o **System overview**: A detailed description of the IT system(s) covered by the contingency plan, including infrastructure, applications, and critical services.

    o **Impact assessment**: Information about the system's importance to the organization's operations and the potential impact of system unavailability.

    o **Resource inventory**: A list of necessary resources for recovery, including hardware, software, personnel, and third-party services.

    o **Dependencies**: Details about interdependencies with other systems or external services that may be critical for recovery.

    o **Recovery time objectives (RTO) and recovery point objectives (RPO)**: Specifications of the maximum allowable downtime and data loss for the system.

- **Notification/activation phase**: The notification/activation phase defines how the recovery process is initiated. It provides the steps and procedures for alerting the appropriate personnel and activating the contingency plan. Some of the key elements are as follows:

    o **Incident detection**: Defines how an incident or disruption is detected, including monitoring systems and reporting channels. It should describe how users and the IT department report potential incidents that may require the activation of the contingency plan.

    o **Notification process**: Clear steps for notifying the recovery team, management, and other stakeholders. This may include communication channels (e.g., phone, email, emergency systems).

    o **Activation criteria**: Specific thresholds or conditions that trigger the activation of the plan, such as system failure, data breach, or disaster events.

    o **Roles and responsibilities**: Assignment of roles for the recovery team, specifying who is responsible for each aspect of notification and activation.

- **Recovery phase**: The recovery phase is where actions are taken to restore normal operations as quickly as possible. This section provides detailed procedures for recovering systems and restoring critical services. Some of the key elements are as follows:

    o **Initial response**: The first steps is recovering from disruption, such as confirming the scope of the impact, conducting damage assessments, and determining what systems need to be prioritized for recovery.

    o **Recovery procedures**: Step-by-step instructions for restoring systems, databases, and applications. These procedures should be clearly defined based on the type of incident (e.g., cyberattack, system failure).

    o **Data restoration**: Procedures for recovering data from backups, ensuring that the most recent version of the data is restored while minimizing data loss.

    o **System rebuilding**: Instructions for re-establishing systems that were completely damaged, including configurations, software installation, and network setups.

    o **Communications**: Details about how information is communicated during the recovery process, including updates to management, stakeholders, and affected users.

- **Reconstitution phase**: The Reconstitution phase is the process of returning to normal operations after recovery has been achieved. This phase ensures that all systems, operations, and business functions are fully restored. Some of the key elements are as follows:

    o **System validation**: Once systems are back online, validation procedures must be performed to ensure they are operating correctly and securely. This may include integrity checks, performance monitoring, and security scans.

    o **Operational testing**: Testing to ensure all systems and processes are functioning as expected. This could involve simulating business operations to verify the completeness of recovery.

- o **Restoration of full operations**: Bringing systems back to their regular capacity, including restoring user access, re-enabling applications, and finalizing any manual workarounds implemented during the recovery.

- o **Post-recovery review**: A formal review of the recovery process to evaluate its effectiveness. This can include lessons learned, identification of any issues that arose during recovery, and recommendations for improving future plans.

- **Appendices**: Appendices provide additional detailed information, templates, tools, and resources that support the implementation of the ITCP. Some of the key elements are as follows:

  - o **Contact lists**: Up-to-date contact information for all key personnel involved in the recovery process, including IT staff, management, vendors, and external partners.

  - o **Escalation procedures**: Detailed escalation paths for escalating issues or incidents that cannot be resolved within the recovery team or initial response efforts.

  - o **Checklists**: Actionable checklists to guide recovery teams through the procedures in each phase. This ensures that no critical steps are overlooked during the process.

  - o **System configuration and architecture diagrams**: Visual aids and technical diagrams that describe system architecture, networks, and data flows, which are essential for recovery and troubleshooting.

  - o **Backup and restore protocols**: Specific guidelines for accessing and restoring backup media or cloud-based recovery solutions.

  - o **Incident logs**: Templates for recording incident-related information, including timelines of actions taken, decisions made, and communications issued during the contingency event.

Configuration management

CM is essential for maintaining the integrity, confidentiality, and availability of information systems by managing and controlling changes made to systems and networks. The primary goal of CM is to provide structured process and prevent unauthorized or untested changes that could negatively impact system security. By providing a controlled environment for system modifications—whether through installations, deletions, or updates—CM helps organizations ensure that changes are tested and evaluated before implementation, minimizing the risk of compromising system security or performance.

The CM process is not only crucial for maintaining the security posture of an information system but also for preventing inefficiencies and resource wastage. Implementing a robust CM system requires careful planning, training, and scheduling to accommodate the potential costs and complexity of managing configurations. However, the benefits of CM far outweigh the costs by eliminating confusion, reducing security risks, and avoiding unnecessary expenditures. By adhering to CM best practices, organizations can reduce the likelihood of costly problems arising from untracked or unassessed system changes.

According to NIST SP 800-64, CM is critical for establishing a baseline of hardware, software, and firmware components and for ensuring accurate tracking of any changes made to these components over time. NIST SP 800-53 further reinforces the importance of CM by recommending specific security controls for managing system configurations based on the system's security categorization. These controls are designed to ensure that any system modifications are properly documented, assessed for security risks, and approved before being implemented. Effective CM practices play a key role in securing information systems and maintaining compliance with federal standards and regulations.

Roles and responsibilities

Effective CM requires clearly defined roles and responsibilities across an organization to ensure the integrity, security, and proper implementation of system changes. These roles help coordinate the CM process, ensuring that changes are systematically controlled, tested, and approved before being implemented. The following are the key roles typically involved in CM:

- **CIO**: The CIO is responsible for establishing policies related to CM across the organization. They ensure the organization's CM practices align with strategic goals and regulatory requirements at the highest level.

- **System owner**: The system owner holds the ultimate authority over CM for the system. They develop functional requirements for the system and ensure those requirements are properly implemented and met. They are accountable for ensuring that all changes to the system are consistent with the organization's objectives and policies.

- **Information systems security officer (ISSO)**: The ISSO is responsible for addressing security concerns within the CM program. They offer security expertise and provide decision-making support to the **configuration control review board (CCRB)**, ensuring that security vulnerabilities are managed during the CM process.

- **CCRB**: The CCRB is responsible for reviewing and resolving change requests that may require additional resources or impact related systems. They ensure that proposed changes will not have an adverse effect on the system or its related components and evaluate the impact of changes on other resources.

- **CM manager**: The CM manager oversees the day-to-day management of the CM process. They document and implement the CM plan, establish baselines, evaluate controls, and manage change requests. Their responsibilities include conducting impact analyses, approving or rejecting changes, notifying stakeholders about changes, and maintaining an audit trail for all changes.

- **System users**: System users are responsible for identifying and reporting weaknesses or new requirements that arise in the current system versions. Their feedback is crucial for identifying improvements and ensuring that the system meets its operational needs.

- **Developers**: Developers work closely with the CM manager to identify, resolve, and implement changes. They ensure that controls are integrated into the system development process and that any changes made do not negatively impact the system's functionality or security.

Configuration management process

The CM process follows a structured sequence of steps to ensure changes to information systems are effectively controlled, tested, and implemented with minimal impact on the system's security and performance. Following are the detailed steps involved in this process, as shown in the following figure:

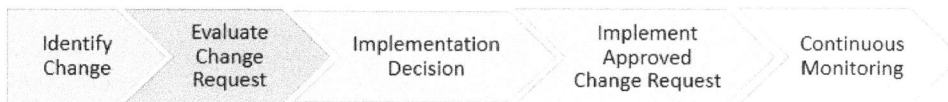

Figure 17.8: IT CM process

Here is the breakdown of each step:

1. **Identify change**: The first step of the CM process begins when a need for change is identified. This change can arise from various sources such as system users, system owners, audit findings, or other internal reviews. The need for change may involve updates to a database, the addition of new software features, or applying security patches to an operating system. Once the change is recognized, a formal change request should be submitted to the appropriate decision-making body to assess the change further.

2. **Evaluate change request**: Once the change request is submitted, it must be evaluated to assess the potential impacts on the system and its interrelated components. An impact analysis is conducted to determine the following:

   a. Whether the change is technically feasible and aligned with system constraints.

   b. Whether the change will improve the system's performance or security.

   c. The potential effect of the change on system security and whether the security components are impacted.

    d.   The costs associated with implementing the change, including potential resource and time requirements. The evaluation helps ensure that the change is viable and that it will not introduce new issues, particularly concerning system security or performance.

3. **Implementation decision**: Following the evaluation, a decision is made regarding whether the change should be implemented. Three possible decisions can be made:

    a.   **Approve**: The change is authorized, and the process of implementation can begin after proper authorization documentation is obtained.

    b.   **Deny**: The change is immediately rejected due to concerns about its impact or other factors, regardless of the information provided.

    c.   **Defer**: The decision is postponed for further analysis or testing. More information may be needed to ensure the change is appropriate.

4. **Implement approved change request**: Once a change is approved, it is transitioned from the test environment to the live production environment. This step involves careful handling, especially when updating production systems. To ensure the integrity of the process, personnel who develop the change should be separate from those who implement it in the production environment. This separation reduces the risk of unauthorized changes being introduced.

5. **Continuous monitoring**: After implementing the change, continuous system monitoring is essential to ensure the system operates as expected and that the change does not negatively impact system performance or security. Continuous monitoring includes configuration verification tests, which compare the current system configuration against the approved baseline to ensure no unauthorized changes have been made. Additionally, regular system audits are conducted to confirm that the system remains compliant with its original security and performance requirements. These ongoing checks ensure that the system is operating in its intended state, and any issues are promptly addressed.

These five steps form a comprehensive approach to managing system changes, emphasizing the need for careful planning, testing, and ongoing monitoring to maintain a secure and efficient system.

Conclusion

In this chapter, we thoroughly explored system authorization documentation, emphasizing its significance in ensuring the security and compliance of information systems. We highlighted the importance of creating a SAR and maintaining comprehensive training records to ensure that personnel are equipped with the necessary knowledge to manage security responsibilities effectively. The chapter also provided insight into the key elements of stakeholder concurrence, ensuring alignment among relevant parties in the authorization process.

Additionally, the chapter underscored the critical role of an ITCP in maintaining operations during disruptions, as well as the importance of CM in controlling system changes while minimizing security risks. With a clear understanding of these concepts, we now transition to the next chapter, where we will learn about change management and acceptance testing, focusing on the processes that ensure systems remain secure and functional through ongoing changes.

Key terms

- An audit report usually includes a cover letter, introduction, summary, audit description, list of systems examined, interviewees, evidence, explanation of sampling techniques, findings, and recommendations.

- Authorization in the context of risk management refers to the formal process of evaluating the risks associated with an information system, identifying potential vulnerabilities, and determining whether the system can be authorized to operate based on the level of risk.

- The authorization package provides relevant information regarding the security posture of the system, including effectiveness of the security controls protecting it.

- An AO is an individual with the authority to formally assume responsibility for the operation of an information system, ensuring that its risks are at an acceptable level for the organization.

- SAR is a document that summarizes the findings of a security audit conducted on an information system, network, or organization.

- Training records serve as a tool for tracking the effectiveness of training programs, identifying areas where additional training may be needed, and helping organizations plan future training initiatives.

- Stakeholder concurrence helps to ensure a collaborative and comprehensive decision-making process, aligning security, risk management, and operational needs for the effective management of the information system's lifecycle.

- The contingency plan strategy and procedures should be designed specifically around the results of the **business impact analysis (BIA)**.

- CM is a systematic process used to identify, control, track, and manage changes to the configuration of an information system or network.

- **Software CM (SCM)** is the task of tracking and controlling changes in the software through the use of authentication, revision control, the establishment of baselines, and auditing.

Join our book's Discord space

Join the book's Discord Workspace for Latest updates, Offers, Tech happenings around the world, New Release and Sessions with the Authors:

https://discord.bpbonline.com

CHAPTER 18

Introduction to Compliance Maintenance

Introduction

This chapter provides an overview of system and asset monitoring, which ensures that the organization's systems are functioning securely and effectively. This chapter outlines the importance of acceptance testing that helps evaluate if the system meets the required specifications and stakeholders' expectations. Additionally, the chapter highlights the change management process to minimize disruptions and properly manage changes within the organization. The chapter also covers the auditing change management process that helps organizations comply with policies and ensure the changes are implemented correctly.

Furthermore, this chapter describes the documentation associated with change management, including change logs and change reports to track all modifications and their outcomes. It provides a detailed explanation of the incident response process, outlining how to manage incidents effectively and respond. Finally, the chapter discusses the need for a continuous monitoring strategy, which helps organizations to detect issues and maintain the effectiveness of security control.

Structure

The chapter covers the following main topics:

- System and asset monitoring
- Acceptance testing
- Change management
- Change management logs
- Change report
- Incident response
- Continuous monitoring strategy
- Performance impact

Objectives

By the end of this chapter, you will gain a solid understanding of the key aspects of system and asset monitoring, which are essential for maintaining the health and security of organizational systems. The chapter will guide you through the various types of acceptance testing, helping you understand how the systems meet the required standards before going live. Additionally, you will learn about the change management process, including how to properly document and create change reports to track and manage modifications within the organization.

The chapter also introduces the incident response process, providing insights into how to effectively manage security incidents when they occur. It covers the *National Institute of Standards and Technology (NIST)* response framework, which offers a structured approach to incident handling. Furthermore, you will develop knowledge of continuous monitoring strategies, which are crucial for ensuring ongoing system performance and detecting potential issues before they impact operations.

System and asset monitoring

System and asset monitoring is crucial for cybersecurity and IT management in all organizations. This typically involves continuous tracking of the organization's system to ensure the effectiveness of security posture and system performance. System and asset monitoring go beyond tracking activities and involve actively monitoring and responding to potential threats in real-time. This requires the integration of threat intelligence to stay up-to-date on emerging threats, continuously identifying vulnerabilities, and using automated response tools to eliminate threats in a timely manner. The system comprises hardware, software, networks, and databases that need to be monitored and protected from threats.

The NIST framework, especially the NIST 800-53 and NIST 800-37 guidelines, emphasizes the importance of continuous monitoring. It focuses on detecting suspicious activities and mitigating risks in real-time, ensuring that systems and networks remain secure and operational:

- **NIST 800-53 (Security and privacy controls for Federal Information Systems and organizations)**: This publication provides guidelines for implementing security controls, including monitoring and asset management. It details the requirement of continuous monitoring to assess the effectiveness of security controls and detect signs of compromise.

- **NIST 800-37 (Risk Management Framework to Federal Information Systems)**: This document emphasizes risk assessment, system monitoring, and ongoing risk management to safeguard Federal Information Systems. It also focuses on risk categorization, security control selection, implementation, assessment, authorization, and continuous monitoring. The continuous monitoring is considered an essential part of maintaining an acceptable risk level.

Key aspects of system and asset monitoring

There are various aspects of system and asset monitoring essential to detect any potential threats. By monitoring in real-time, organizations can quickly respond to potential threats and mitigate risks before they impact the system. The following figure shows the key aspects of system and asset monitoring:

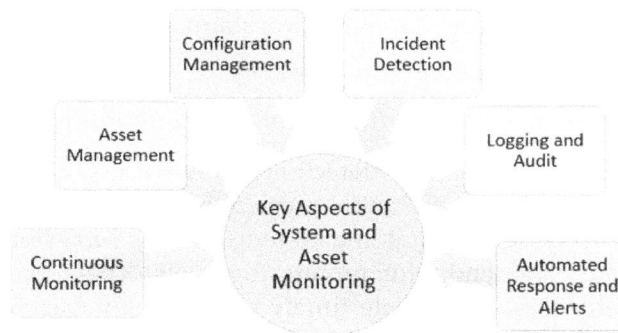

Figure 18.1: Key aspects of system and asset monitoring

Here is the breakdown of key elements of system and asset monitoring:

- **Continuous monitoring**: Continuous monitoring helps organizations detect vulnerabilities and unauthorized activities across the systems. This includes monitoring user activity, network logs, device access, and data flows to detect potential breaches. Continuous monitoring ensures that cybersecurity incidents are identified and managed before they cause significant damage. The key actions are as follows:

- o Perform regular scans for vulnerabilities and misconfigurations.

- o Monitor unusual activity, such as unauthorized logins or access patterns.

- o Trigger alerts if suspicious activity is detected by using tools like **security information and event management** (**SIEM**) systems.

- **Asset management**: Asset management is an integral part of monitoring as it involves understanding the current state and location of all assets within the organization. The effective asset management allows the organization to track and manage IT assets effectively. Asset management goes beyond tracking the location of assets and involves a comprehensive approach with asset risk categorization, data sensitivity analysis, and lifecycle management. Besides managing the complete lifecycle of assets, from acquisition to retirement, it also ensures that security threats are addressed at every stage. The key actions are as follows:

  - o Maintain a complete inventory of all hardware and software components.

  - o Track the lifecycle of each asset (e.g., from acquisition to retirement).

  - o Identify the critical assets that require regular monitoring.

- **Configuration management**: Configuration management is a key part of monitoring. The NIST framework recommends implementing baseline configurations and enforcing security controls to reduce vulnerabilities. Organizations should regularly monitor system configurations to ensure that configurations remain secure and compliant. The key actions are as follows:

  - o Establish and enforce configuration standards.

  - o Periodic review of configurations.

  - o Monitor deviations from the baseline configurations.

- **Incident detection**: The incident detection involves a mechanism to detect incidents in real-time by identifying potential security breaches, anomalies, or threats. The detection is mostly done by automated tools such as **intrusion detection systems** (**IDS**), firewalls, and endpoint monitoring tools. The organization can detect suspicious behaviors and initiate timely responses by tracking system logs and activity. The key actions are as follows:

  - o Monitor network and system traffic for malicious activity.

  - o Analyze system logs and identify anomalies.

- **Logging and audit trails**: Monitoring also requires the maintenance of detailed logs and audit trails to track activities, system changes, and access patterns. According to NIST guidelines, logs should be captured and stored securely for further analysis, both for incident detection and post-incident forensic analysis. Logs also help organizations to comply with security audit requirements and provide evidence for accountability. The key actions are as follows:

- Ensure all critical systems and assets generate logs for security events.

- Centralize logs in a secure environment for analysis.

- Retain logs for an appropriate period based on legal, regulatory, and organizational requirements.

- **Automated responses and alerts**: Automated responses and alerts are also an important part of monitoring. The systems can generate alerts to notify security teams and take predefined actions to mitigate risks, such as blocking malicious traffic or isolating compromised systems. The key actions are as follows:

  - Configure automated incident response protocols based on the type of alerts and anomalies.

  - Implement automatic containment or remediation measures.

Acceptance testing

Acceptance testing is the final stage of system/software testing, designed to evaluate whether a system meets its business and user requirements before being released to production. It ensures that software is reliable and aligns with the expectations of stakeholders. The primary purpose of acceptance testing is to validate if the software meets user expectations and complies with the project's functional and non-functional requirements. This phase helps to identify and resolve any defects or issues, improving the overall quality and reliability of the system.

By involving end users or client representatives in the testing process, acceptance testing verifies usability, functionality, and user satisfaction, ensuring that the system is user-friendly and effective. Furthermore, acceptance testing mitigates potential risks by uncovering issues early, allowing for timely resolution before the system goes live. It also ensures that the software complies with legal, regulatory, and industry-specific standards, helping organizations avoid legal challenges or penalties.

Types of acceptance testing

Acceptance testing is of several types, each with a specific focus to ensure that the system/software meets different requirements and expectations before its final release. They are as follows:

- **User acceptance testing (UAT)**: UAT is usually performed by end users or client representatives. UAT validates whether the system fulfils their business needs and expectations. It simulates real-world scenarios to ensure the software is ready for production deployment.

- **Alpha testing**: This test is conducted by the internal development team. This type of testing occurs before the software is released to a selected group of users. The goal is to identify and resolve critical issues early in the development process.

- **Beta testing**: This phase involves releasing the software to a limited group of external users. Feedback from these users helps to uncover additional issues and gather insights to improve the software before a wider release.

- **Operational testing**: This test focuses on validating the system's operational capabilities, including backup and recovery procedures, system monitoring, and maintenance.

- **Performance testing**: A performance test assesses the software's performance, ensuring it meets predefined criteria such as response time, scalability, and stability under various load conditions.

- **Security testing**: This test focuses on evaluating the security features of the software, ensuring it is protected from vulnerabilities and potential threats.

Tasks for acceptance testing

There are various tasks associated with acceptance testing. Following are some of the key tasks as shown in the following figure:

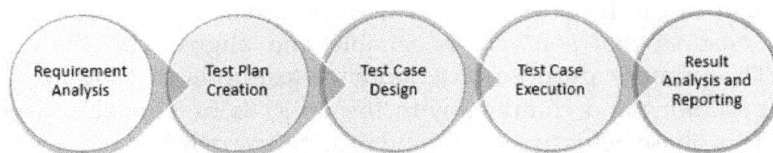

Figure 18.2: Key tasks for acceptance testing

Here is the breakdown of tasks related to acceptance testing:

- **Requirement analysis**: The goal is to understand the business objectives, user needs, and acceptance criteria. This involves collaborating with stakeholders (e.g., business analysts, developers, end users) to gather relevant requirements. This step sets the scope, focusing on key functionalities to be validated.

- **Test plan creation**: The test plan outlines the acceptance testing approach. It details the testing scope, objectives, required resources (testers, tools, environments), schedule, and acceptance criteria. The plan acts as a roadmap, ensuring all critical areas are covered and includes risk management strategies.

- **Test case design**: The test case validates the software against the acceptance criteria. Test cases should be detailed, specifying test steps, input data, expected outcomes, and any preconditions. It should cover a wide range of scenarios, including positive, negative, edge cases, and user-specific conditions.

- **Test case execution**: Test cases are executed in a controlled environment, following the outlined steps. Testers compare expected results with actual outcomes to identify discrepancies. Any failures or issues should be logged with detailed information for developers to address.

- **Result analysis and reporting**: Test results are analyzed to verify if the software meets the acceptance criteria. This identifies critical defects or issues that impact functionality or user experience.

Change management

Change management is a structured process that ensures all proposed changes to an environment are formally submitted, evaluated, and authorized before implementation. This process is designed to maintain control and oversee modifications, ensuring that they align with organizational goals and comply with established standards. The primary objective of change management is to minimize the potential risks associated with changes, such as system failures, security breaches, or disruptions to business operations.

In addition to risk mitigation, change management plays a crucial role in reducing unscheduled downtime. By carefully planning and managing changes, organizations can avoid unexpected issues that could impact system performance or service availability. This systematic approach enables IT teams to implement updates, upgrades, and other changes with minimal disruption, ensuring smooth transitions and maintaining the integrity of the IT environment. The components of the change control process are essential for managing changes to system configurations in a structured and controlled manner, as shown in the following figure:

Figure 18.3: *Key components of change management*

Here is the breakdown of the key components of the change management process:

- **Change management plan**: This is a comprehensive document that outlines the approach and processes for managing changes to the system configuration.

It defines roles and responsibilities accountable for managing and approving changes. The plan also details the change management procedures, such as how changes should be requested, reviewed, implemented, and documented. It establishes documentation requirements to ensure that every change is thoroughly recorded for future reference, audit, and compliance.

- **Change control board (CCB)**: The CCB is a group of individuals responsible for reviewing, approving, or rejecting proposed changes to the system configuration. The board typically includes representatives from various departments or stakeholders, such as IT, security, operations, and business units. Their role is to assess the impact, feasibility, and risks associated with proposed changes and determine whether they align with business objectives and regulatory requirements.

- **Change request process**: This component involves the formal process of requesting and documenting changes to the system configuration. The change request should provide detailed information, including the reason for the change, desired outcomes, potential risks, and a plan for implementing the change. The request process ensures that changes are well analyzed and documented before any action is taken, allowing for proper review and approval.

- **Change evaluation and approval**: Once a change request is submitted, it undergoes an evaluation process to determine its impact on the system configuration. This evaluation involves assessing the potential risks and benefits of the change, checking for conflicts with existing configurations, and ensuring that the change aligns with business objectives.

- **Testing and validation**: It is crucial to test and validate the changes in a controlled environment before making any configuration changes live. This component includes preparing test plans, creating test environments, and executing validation procedures to verify that the proposed changes will not negatively affect system stability, security, or functionality. Testing ensures that the changes achieve the desired results without introducing unintended consequences.

- **Documentation and reporting**: Documentation plays a crucial role in the change control process, as it allows for accurate tracking and auditing of all configuration changes. This component includes maintaining detailed records of each change, including the rationale behind the decision, the approval process, the test results, and any issues encountered during implementation. Regular reporting ensures that stakeholders are kept informed about the status of changes, ongoing compliance with policies, and emerging risks or issues related to the system configuration.

Types of change

There are three main types of change management, namely standard changes, normal changes, and emergency changes, as shown in the following figure:

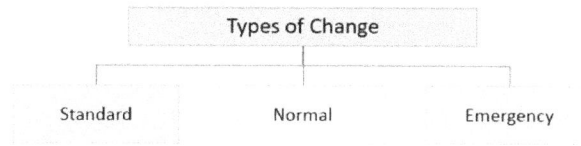

Figure 18.4: Types of change

Here is the detail of the types of changes:

- **Standard changes**: These changes are low-risk, frequently repeated changes that follow a pre-approved process. These changes are well-documented and do not require additional approval each time since they have been already assessed and approved. Due to their repetitive nature, many standard changes can be automated, which helps teams to focus on other tasks. Examples of standard changes include adding memory or storage in the system, regular updates to operating system etc.

- **Normal changes**: These changes are non-emergency changes that do not have a pre-approved process. They may vary in risk level depending on the complexity. Some changes require a detailed risk assessment and approval from a change advisory board, while others are approved more quickly by designated authorities. Examples include upgrading to a new content management system, migrating to a new data center, etc.

- **Emergency changes**: These changes are needed immediately due to unexpected errors or threats. These changes are urgent and must be handled quickly to restore service or secure systems. Emergency changes should follow a documented, risk-based approval process to ensure that potential risks are assessed and mitigated before implementation. This process ensures that changes made as a result of emergency circumstances are analyzed for their impact on system security and compliance. Examples of emergency changes include implementing a security patch, addressing a server outage, or responding to a major incident.

Key steps of the change management process

There are five key steps in the change management process that ensure changes are implemented in a structured and controlled manner, minimizing risks and maximizing the benefits for the organization. The five steps are:

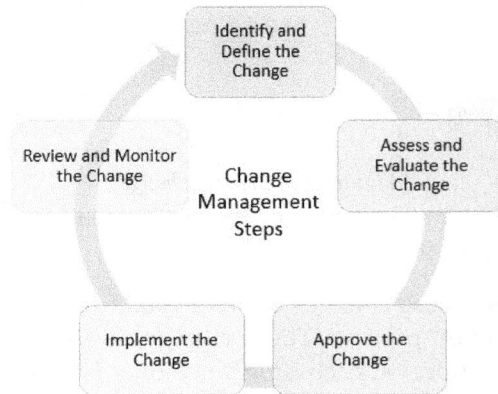

Figure 18.5: Steps to implement change management

Here is the breakdown of detailed steps to implement the change management process:

- **Identify and define the change**: The first step in the change management process is to identify the requirement for change. This involves recognizing problems or opportunities that require adjustments in systems, processes, or practices. Once the requirement is established, the change must be thoroughly defined, including the specific objectives, scope, and impact. A detailed change request is created, outlining the reason for the change, the expected outcomes, the stakeholders involved, and any potential risks associated with the change.

- **Assess and evaluate the change**: After the change is identified and defined, the next step is a comprehensive assessment to evaluate its feasibility and implications. This involves analyzing the potential risks and benefits the change may bring to the organization. The assessment also includes understanding how the change will affect existing systems, processes, and resources. It is essential to review the change against the organization's policies, business objectives, and any potential conflicts with other projects or ongoing operations.

- **Approve the change**: Once the change has been assessed and its potential impact understood, it is presented to relevant stakeholders for approval. Usually, a CCB or similar decision-making body is involved in this process. The CCB consists of representatives from various departments, including IT, management, and relevant business units, who review the change proposal in detail. The approval process ensures that all stakeholders are aligned on the necessity and feasibility of the change.

- **Implement the change**: Once the change is approved, the implementation phase begins. This involves executing the change according to the predefined plan, using the agreed-upon methods and instructions. The implementation is typically carried out by the designated team or individuals responsible for making the change. It is crucial to follow the procedures exactly as laid out in the plan to minimize errors and disruptions. Communication with all affected stakeholders is essential during this phase to keep them informed of the change's progress and to ensure smooth execution.

- **Review and monitor the change**: After the change has been implemented, it is important to monitor and review its effectiveness. This includes assessing whether the change has achieved its intended outcomes and if any unforeseen issues have emerged. A series of tests or performance evaluations is often conducted to verify the success of the change. If the change does not meet the desired objectives or creates new problems, corrective actions must be taken, which may include rolling back the change. Feedback from stakeholders is also crucial in this phase to understand the impact of the change and identify areas for improvement in future change management processes.

Auditing change management

The change management audit process assesses whether the organization effectively controls and manages changes to its environment. The IS auditor should focus on the following areas:

- **Existence and adherence to change management policy**: The auditor should verify whether a formal change management policy and process are implemented and if they are being followed consistently in practice. This includes checking for documented procedures and ensuring they align with industry best practices.

- **Adequate records of the change management process**: The auditor should examine whether sufficient records exist to show how thoroughly the change management process is being followed. This includes reviewing documentation for each change, such as requests, approvals, and outcomes, to ensure compliance with the established process.

- **Emergency changes and frequency**: A high number of emergency changes may indicate a lack of adequate planning or testing, leading to unplanned alterations. The auditor should assess whether emergency changes are being made frequently and, if so, investigate whether they are a result of inadequate preparation or insufficient testing of changes in a controlled environment.

- **Implementation procedures and test results**: The auditor must confirm that proposed changes are well-documented with clear implementation procedures, back-out procedures (in case the change needs to be reversed), and results from testing conducted in a controlled environment. This ensures that changes are carefully planned and validated before implementation.

- **Minutes of change management meetings**: The auditor should check whether proper meeting minutes are kept during change management meetings. This documentation should reflect the discussions, decisions, approvals, and any issues that arise during the meetings, ensuring transparency and accountability in the process.

- **Adequate review of emergency changes**: Finally, the auditor should verify whether emergency changes are reviewed adequately. The emergency changes should be subject to appropriate scrutiny to assess their impact, ensuring they meet organizational policies and minimize risks.

Change management logs

A change management log is a vital tool for tracking and managing changes within a project or organization, providing a clear and organized method for documenting all changes throughout their lifecycle. By maintaining this log, team members can ensure that changes are evaluated, approved, implemented, and closed in an organized manner. The key elements of the change management log are shown in the following figure:

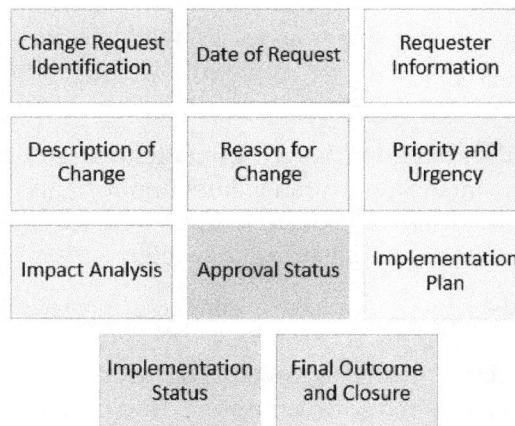

Figure 18.6: Elements of change management log

Here is a detailed breakdown of the key elements of a change management log and their importance:

- **Change request identification**: The purpose of assigning a unique identifier to each change request is to provide a clear and organized way to track and reference changes throughout their lifecycle. This identifier plays a crucial role in ensuring that each change is monitored individually, which helps to prevent confusion and ensures that records can be easily retrieved when needed. By assigning a unique ID, organizations can maintain a structured approach to manage changes, making it simpler to review and audit changes over time.

- **Date of request**: The purpose of recording the change request date is to establish a clear timeline for the change request process. This data helps track the progress of the request, ensuring that each change is addressed in a timely manner. The importance of this timestamp lies in its ability to highlight any delays or ensure prompt handling of requests, which is crucial for maintaining efficient workflows and meeting deadlines.

- **Requestor information**: The purpose of including details about the individual or team requesting the change is to provide clear identification of the requester, including their name, role, contact information, and department. This information is crucial for establishing a point of contact for any follow-up communication regarding the change request. The requester information ensures accountability, as the requester can be held responsible for providing additional information or clarifications if needed.

- **Description of the change**: The purpose of including a clear and concise description of the proposed change is to outline what is being changed, why the change is necessary, and what the desired outcome is. This description ensures that all stakeholders understand the scope of the change, the problem it aims to address, or the opportunity it seeks to capitalize on. The importance of description is that it provides clarity and context, helping everyone involved to align on the objectives, expectations, and reasons for the change.

- **Reason for the change**: The purpose of this section is to detail the rationale behind the change request, explaining why the change is needed, whether it is to resolve a problem or enhance a system or process. This information is crucial because it helps decision-makers to understand the context and urgency of the change, providing the necessary justification for the request. By clarifying the reasons for the change, it ensures that all stakeholders are aligned on the objectives and the importance of addressing the change.

- **Priority and urgency**: The purpose of this section is to assess the urgency and priority of the change compared to other requests, often categorizing it as low, medium, or high priority. This assessment is important because it helps to prioritize changes, ensuring that critical or time-sensitive changes are addressed first. By assigning a priority level, it enables effective resource allocation and ensures that the most important changes are given the attention they need in a timely manner, preventing delays or potential issues from escalating.

- **Impact analysis**: The purpose of this section is to evaluate the potential impact of the proposed change on different aspects such as project scope, schedule, cost, resources, stakeholders, and ongoing activities. This evaluation is important because it provides valuable insight into the possible risks, challenges, and benefits associated with the change. By understanding these impacts, stakeholders can make informed decisions about whether the change should proceed.

- **Approval status**: The purpose of this section is to indicate whether the change request has been approved, rejected, or is still under review. It includes details about the approval committee or individual responsible for the decision. This is important because it helps to track the decision-making process, ensuring that all necessary approvals are obtained before moving forward with implementing the change.

- **Implementation plan**: The purpose of this section is to provide a detailed plan for how the change will be implemented, including the necessary resources, timelines, responsible parties, and specific actions to be taken if the change is approved. This is important because it ensures that everyone involved is aware of their roles and responsibilities, and there is a clear, actionable roadmap for carrying out the change. A well-defined implementation plan ensures that tasks are completed on time and allows for smooth coordination among all stakeholders.

- **Implementation status**: The purpose of this section is to provide ongoing updates on the progress of the change implementation, including completed milestones, any challenges encountered, and adjustments made. This is important because it offers a transparent view of how the change is progressing, allowing stakeholders to track its development and identify potential issues or delays early on. With this information, necessary corrections can be made promptly, ensuring that the change is implemented efficiently and successfully.

- **Final outcome and closure**: The purpose of this section is to document the completed change, including a post-implementation review that assesses the effectiveness of the change and identifies any lessons learned. This is important because it helps to evaluate whether the change met its objectives and was implemented effectively. The post-implementation review provides valuable insights into the success of the change and highlights areas for improvement.

Change report

A change management report is a document that summarizes the process, progress, and results of changes implemented within an organization. It covers both the strategic planning and the practical steps taken to manage the change, while evaluating how effective the changes were. The report typically includes details about the change objectives, planning, execution, impact, stakeholder feedback, and lessons learned, as shown in the following figure:

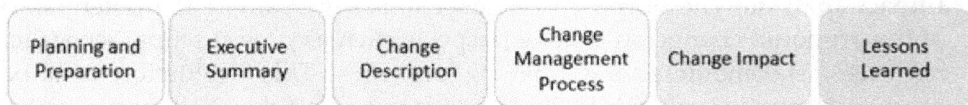

Figure 18.7: *Key elements of the change report*

Here is a breakdown of the components of the change report:

- **Planning and preparation**: In the planning and preparation phase, the steps for the change are outlined, which include analyzing key stakeholders, developing communication plans, and conducting risk assessments. This ensures that all affected parties are identified, informed, and supported throughout the process. A timeline is also provided, highlighting the key milestones of the change management process, from initial planning through to implementation, helping to track progress and ensure that the change is delivered on time.

- **Executive summary**: The executive summary provides an overview of the change, that summarizes the key aspects of the change process, including objectives, outcomes, and any significant findings. This section is mainly for senior management to quickly understand the importance and results of the change.

- **Change description**: This section provides a detailed description of the change itself, including what was changed, why the change was necessary, and how it aligns with the organization's goals. It includes technical details of the change and any specific actions or updates that were made.

- **Change management process**: This section outlines the steps taken during the change process, from the submission of the **Request for Change** (**RFC**) to the approval, planning, implementation, testing, and validation phases. It provides transparency and clarity on how the change was managed and monitored.

- **Change impact**: The change impact section assesses how the change influenced the organization, systems, users, and processes. It highlights both positive outcomes, like enhanced performance or security, as well as challenges, such as disruptions or delays. Performance metrics are used to measure success, focusing on improvements in efficiency, employee satisfaction, financial performance, and customer service.

- **Lessons learned**: This section focuses on the lessons learned from the change process, covering what went well and areas for improvement. It offers suggestions for future changes and adjustments to the change management process to improve efficiency and effectiveness.

Incident response

Incident response is a critical aspect of an organization's security posture, ensuring that it can quickly and effectively address security incidents. A security incident refers to any event where sensitive data or systems are at risk of being compromised, whether through unauthorized access, exposure, theft, or damage. An **incident response plan** (**IRP**) serves as a formalized guide that outlines how the organization should respond when such an event occurs, detailing roles, responsibilities, and actions to mitigate the impact of the incident. The plan is designed to enable rapid identification, containment, eradication, and recovery from incidents, thereby minimizing potential damage and preventing further escalation.

An effective IRP should cover a wide range of potential security incidents, including data breaches, system intrusions, malware attacks, and information theft. The plan should also outline the procedures for communication, both internally and with external parties, such as regulatory bodies or customers, during and after an incident. Additionally, the plan should include mechanisms for documenting the incident for later analysis, reporting, and improving future response efforts. Regular testing and updating of the IRP are essential to ensure it remains relevant in the face of evolving threats and to maintain the organization's readiness to respond to security incidents effectively.

NIST incident response framework

The NIST incident response process is a continuous, cyclical activity that focuses on improving an organization's ability to protect itself from cybersecurity threats. These guidelines provide a common framework to ensure consistent and reliable responses to security threats. NIST's incident handling guide is technology-neutral, meaning it can be applied to any type of information system, regardless of the hardware, software, or protocols used. It is also compatible with the NIST **Cybersecurity Framework (CSF)**, making it versatile for various organizations and systems.

The NIST incident response cycle consists of four main parts, namely:

- Preparation
- Detection and analysis
- Containment, eradication, and recovery
- Post-incident activity

These stages are designed to help organizations respond effectively to cybersecurity incidents, ensuring the protection of systems, data, and operations. The following figure shows the four stages of incident response:

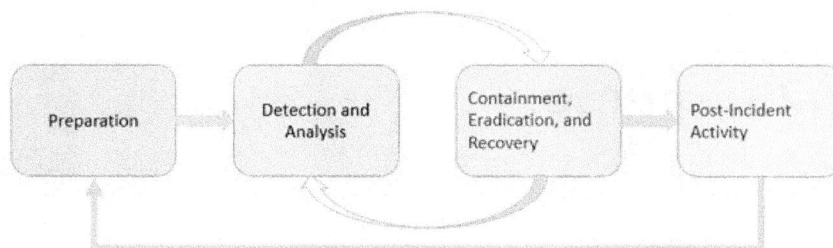

Figure 18.8: Incident response framework

Here is the breakdown of the incident response framework:

- **Preparation**: This phase focuses on establishing a robust incident response capability before an incident occurs. It includes creating an incident response policy, preparing a response team, and equipping them with the necessary tools, such as forensic software, monitoring tools, and communication systems. Preparation also involves securing IT systems by performing risk assessments, applying security measures like anti-virus software, and security awareness.

- **Detection and analysis**: Once a potential incident is detected, the goal is to confirm if it is indeed a security incident. In this phase, the response team identifies the type of threat and gathers information using monitoring systems, such as IDS and SIEM tools. The team looks for precursors (signs that a threat may occur) and indicators (signs of an ongoing or completed attack). This stage also involves documenting and prioritizing incidents based on their severity and potential impact on the business.

- **Containment, eradication, and recovery**: This is the critical phase where immediate action is taken to stop the spread of the incident and minimize its impact. The response team isolates the affected systems to prevent further damage, with containment strategies tailored to the type of threat. Once contained, the team works to eradicate the cause of the incident, such as removing malware or disabling compromised accounts. After the threat is neutralized, the recovery process begins, which involves restoring systems, applying security patches, and verifying that no further threats remain. Recovery may include restoring data from backups, rebuilding systems, and strengthening defenses to prevent future attacks.

- **Post-incident activity**: After the incident is resolved, the post-incident phase focuses on evaluating the response and learning from the experience. This phase includes conducting a lesson learned meeting, where the team reviews the incident's handling process, analyzes what worked and what did not, and identifies improvements for future responses. A detailed report is created documenting the incident, including detection, containment, and recovery actions, as well as any damage caused. This phase also involves updating security protocols, improving monitoring systems, and providing additional training to staff.

Continuous monitoring strategy

A continuous monitoring strategy is essential for ensuring that the security controls of an information system remain effective throughout its lifecycle and changes or developments in the system's environment are promptly assessed for security impacts. This strategy, as described by NIST (particularly in NIST 800-53 and NIST 800-137), outlines the practices and methodologies for monitoring and maintaining security controls continuously, thus enabling organizations to manage risks and compliance effectively.

The primary goal of a continuous monitoring strategy is to track and evaluate the effectiveness of the security controls employed over time, ensuring that they perform as intended in mitigating risks and protecting information systems. This includes the following:

- **Monitoring effectiveness**: Continuously assess the effectiveness of security controls to understand how they protect the system and manage risks.

- **Security posture over time**: Assess how the system's security posture evolves over time, especially in response to external threats, vulnerabilities, and internal changes.

- **Impact of changes**: Evaluate the security impact of any proposed or actual changes made to the system or its environment of operation, including software upgrades, hardware changes, or network modifications.

Key components of the monitoring strategy

The strategy should include several critical components that contribute to a comprehensive and effective monitoring approach:

- **Automated tools for near-real-time risk management**: Automated tools play a vital role in supporting near-real-time monitoring of the system's security state. They enable quicker detection of threats and vulnerabilities and control effectiveness. These tools can provide immediate alerts about potential security breaches, misconfigurations, or deviations from security policies.

- **Monitoring inherited controls and configuration management**: It is important to monitor inherited controls from third-party services or external environments. These controls need to be checked regularly based on the level of trust in the third-party provider and their security measures. Configuration management is crucial for maintaining the integrity of the system, and monitoring helps ensure configurations remain secure and comply with security policies.

- **Security impact analysis for changes**: Any changes to the system or its operational environment, whether planned or unplanned, must undergo a security impact analysis to determine potential effects on the system's security posture. This analysis should assess the risks introduced by the change, and appropriate measures should be taken to mitigate any identified risks.

- **Control assessment and reporting**: The strategy must include a framework for assessing the performance of selected security controls regularly. This includes audit trails, logging, and regular assessments to ensure controls are functioning as intended. Reporting mechanisms are required to keep management and other stakeholders informed of the security status, incidents, and necessary improvements.

Defining what to monitor and how

The strategy should outline which security controls to monitor, how often monitoring should occur, and how the controls will be assessed:

- **Criteria for selecting controls to monitor**: The criticality of the system plays a key role in determining which controls to monitor, as more critical systems handling sensitive data require more frequent and thorough monitoring. Similarly, controls that are prone to change or address high-risk areas, such as access control or encryption, should be prioritized for continuous monitoring due to their volatility. Additionally, controls identified in the POA&M as improvement or remediation should also be closely monitored to ensure timely resolution and mitigate potential risks.

- **Frequency of monitoring**: The frequency of monitoring varies based on several factors. The criticality of the system plays a significant role, with more critical systems requiring continuous or real-time monitoring to ensure their security and functionality. Volatility is another factor, as controls that are frequently changing or are related to high-risk areas may need more frequent monitoring to detect and address potential issues promptly. Additionally, for controls inherited from third-party service providers, the frequency of monitoring depends on the provider's trustworthiness and past performance history.

Performance impact

A successful performance measurement program for information security is built on several key factors that ensure its effectiveness and alignment with organizational goals. These factors help organizations assess and improve the performance of their security measures while making data-driven decisions. The key elements are shown in the following figure:

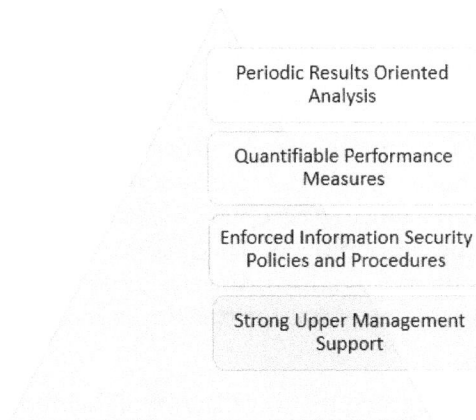

Periodic Results Oriented Analysis

Quantifiable Performance Measures

Enforced Information Security Policies and Procedures

Strong Upper Management Support

Figure 18.9: Performance impact elements

Here is the breakdown of key elements of performance impact:

- **Strong upper management support**: Upper management's commitment is essential for the success of an information security program. Leadership must actively support and advocate for information security, ensuring the program is protected from organizational pressures and budget constraints. Without this support, the program may face difficulties in securing the necessary resources and priority within the organization.

- **Enforced information security policies and procedures**: Well-defined and enforced information security policies and procedures serve as the foundation of a successful performance measurement program. These policies outline the roles, responsibilities, and management structure for information security, ensuring that everyone understands their obligations. They also provide the framework for measuring progress, tracking compliance, and the availability of data required for measurement activities.

- **Quantifiable performance measures**: For performance data to be useful, it must be based on clear, measurable information security goals and objectives. These measures should be quantifiable, easily obtainable, feasible to implement, and repeatable. The data collected should help track performance trends over time and inform decision-making, particularly in determining where to allocate resources or adjust strategies to strengthen the security program.

- **Periodic results-oriented analysis**: Regular analysis of performance measurement data is crucial for identifying areas for improvement and ensuring the continued effectiveness of the security program. This analysis should focus on lessons learned, adjustments to current security controls, and the implementation of new measures to meet evolving security needs. Stakeholders must be committed to accurately collecting and analyzing data that is meaningful, enabling the program to adapt and enhance its overall effectiveness over time.

Conclusion

In this chapter, we gained a comprehensive understanding of the key aspects of system and asset monitoring, emphasizing its vital role in maintaining operational efficiency and security. We explored the importance of acceptance testing to ensure that systems meet the required standards before being deployed. The chapter also provided valuable insights into the change management process, including the creation of change logs and change management reports, which are essential for tracking and auditing modifications within the organization.

Additionally, the chapter highlighted the significance of incident response and continuous monitoring strategies to detect and address issues proactively. With these foundational concepts, we now transition to the next chapter, where we will explore compliance measurement and performance monitoring, focusing on how organizations can measure adherence to standards and evaluate the effectiveness of their systems over time.

Key terms

- The change management is the process of managing change through a lifecycle process that consists of request, review, approve, implement, and verify.

- The change management process should be formalized and include a documented process, procedures, forms, and recordkeeping.

- IT change management is a standardized end-to-end process that enables changes, including application, infrastructure, and configuration changes, to be deployed to a production IT environment in a controlled and consistently repeatable manner.

- Preparation is the key to effective incident response. By establishing an incident response capability and developing a comprehensive plan, organizations can be better equipped to handle security incidents and minimize their impact.

- Effective IRPs enable organizations to identify, contain, and remediate security incidents quickly and efficiently, minimizing the overall impact on business operations.

- Acceptance testing is defined as the formal testing conducted to determine whether a software system satisfies its acceptance criteria and to enable the customer to determine whether to accept the system.

- Manual acceptance testing involves human testers executing test cases without using automation tools. This approach is often used for smaller projects or scenarios where automation must be more practical and cost-effective.

Join our book's Discord space

Join the book's Discord Workspace for Latest updates, Offers, Tech happenings around the world, New Release and Sessions with the Authors:

https://discord.bpbonline.com

CHAPTER 19
Monitoring Compliance

Introduction

This chapter provides an overview of the compliance measurement process that helps organizations to follow established standards. The chapter elaborates on key compliance standards, such as *International Organization for Standardization (ISO) 27005*, and *ISO 31000* which highlights risk management, and overall organizational governance. The chapter also provides detailed information on **configuration items** (**CIs**) to monitor and manage compliance across various organizational systems and processes.

Moreover, the chapter explains the privacy **Risk Management Framework** (**RMF**) aligned with the *National Institute of Standards and Technology* (*NIST*), which enables organizations to address and reduce privacy risks while safeguarding sensitive data. Additionally, the chapter outlines performance monitoring that helps organizations evaluate performance and ensure continuous improvement. The chapter provides strategies to assess performance and ensure that organizations can effectively monitor and optimize their operations. Furthermore, this chapter provides a good understanding of **Cybersecurity Framework** (**CSF**) and organization profiles.

Structure

The chapter covers the following main topics:

- Compliance measurement
- Compliance standards
- Configuration item
- System maintenance
- Privacy Framework
- Performance monitoring
- NIST Cybersecurity Framework

Objectives

By the end of this chapter, you will be able to explain how to measure compliance and define the **key performance indicators (KPIs)** for its measurement. Various compliance standards such as ISO 27005, ISO 9001, and ISO 31000 related to risk management and quality assurance will be covered in this chapter. The chapter will also explain why managing compliance standards is important for the mitigation of risk and the regulation of the organization.

Additionally, you will gain a good knowledge of the NIST Privacy Framework that provides a comprehensive understanding of the management of privacy risks and protection of personal information. You will also learn the fundamentals of CIs, which enable organizations to define and control their security configurations. Furthermore, you will be able to acquire skills in performance monitoring and the ways to implement performance measures to support continuous improvement. Lastly, you will delve into the CSF to improve the organization's cybersecurity posture.

Compliance measurement

In essence, compliance measurement involves assessing the system or operations of an organization to ensure it complies with their policies, relevant laws, regulations, and standards. Compliance metrics and KPIs are crucial tools for organizations to verify their adherence to compliance standards and business strategy. These metrics collect data from multiple sources that enable an organization to evaluate how well the organization is meeting the regulations and internal main control requirements.

Organizations can identify gaps and address potential risks by consistently monitoring the identified KPIs. This proactive approach prevents organizations from potential legal and financial penalties as well as promotes a culture of accountability, transparency, and trust. These goals enable an organization to prosper in the trust-sensitive on economic environment to achieve long-term success and maintain integrity in highly regulated business landscape.

In addition to that, compliance metrics aids in providing a more comprehensive benchmark for assessment of performance of compliance programs. It has also additional importance to the IT and compliance teams in measuring controls effectiveness. This data-driven approach allows organizations to make informed decisions and maintain a continuous cycle of improvement.

Compliance measurement KPI

Compliance measurement is an essential component of effective governance that enables organizations to monitor ongoing operations to ensure they adhere to applicable laws, regulations, standards, and internal policies. The organization can track and assess various aspects of compliance through compliance KPIs. The following figure shows some of the KPIs:

Figure 19.1: Key KPIs of compliance measurement

Here is the breakdown of compliance measurement KPIs:

- **Regulatory compliance rate**: Regulatory compliance measures how well the organization adheres to applicable laws, regulations, and industry standards. This metric provides organizations with snapshots of legal standing by comparing the total number of regulatory requirements and the organization's actual compliance rate. Regular assessments of the regulatory landscape ensure that the organization stays aligned with evolving regulations by preventing legal penalties, fines, or damage to reputation.

- **Policy adherence**: Internal policies and procedures are key to an organization's compliance framework. This KPI tracks how well employees or departments follow these policies, ensuring smooth and consistent operations. A high adherence rate indicates that the employees are following the organization's guidelines, which minimizes error and regulatory issues. Regular reviews of organizational policies ensure that they stay relevant and effective by adapting to changes in regulations and internal goals.

- **Incident reporting and response time**: This KPI emphasizes the organization's capability to report and respond to compliance incidents. The response time plays a crucial role in reducing the impact of compliance breaches and regulatory violations. This KPI evaluates how quickly incidents are identified, reported, and addressed to quickly mitigate potential risks. An effective incident response process maintains stakeholder trust and demonstrates proactive risk management.

- **Audit findings and remediation time**: Compliance audits evaluate the organization's compliance with internal policies and external regulations. This KPI measures the time taken to identify, address, and remediate issues or non-compliance findings from audits. Tracking audit findings and their resolution times indicates how effectively the organization is responding to identified weaknesses or gaps in compliance.

- **Third-party compliance performance**: Organizations' reliance on third-party vendors, contractors, or partners for various business functions has increased over the years. As these dependencies have grown, it has become essential for third-parties to comply with the organization's compliance and regulatory standards. This KPI monitors third-party performance, ensuring that vendors and external partners fulfill compliance requirements. The compliance performance can include contract compliance checks, due diligence assessments, and ongoing monitoring. Effective management of third-party compliance reduces the risk of reputational damage or regulatory issues that could stem from external sources.

- **Data privacy compliance**: Data privacy has become essential for most organizations, depending on the nature of their business. There are some renowned data protection and privacy laws such as *General Data Protection Regulation* (*GDPR*) and the *California Consumer Privacy Act* (*CCPA*) to help organizations in achieving compliance. This KPI assesses the organization's capability to meet data privacy regulations and monitors how well personal and sensitive data is handled, stored, and protected against unauthorized access or disclosure. Organizations must implement robust data privacy policies, procedures, and compliance mechanisms to ensure that they can gain customer trust and avoid legal consequences.

- **Compliance training effectiveness**: Compliance awareness and training is one of the most important pillars for any organization to prevent data breaches. This KPI measures how well employees can retain or recall the compliance knowledge. Organizations can gauge how effective the training is through pre and post-training evaluations, tests, or practical assessments. Organizations can refine their training modules for maximum impact and risk mitigation by understanding how training translates to hands-on compliance behaviours.

- **Compliance risk assessment results**: This KPI measures the results of compliance risk assessments, which uncover emerging risks and validate if controls are effective. The results help organization to determine and prioritize areas where compliance efforts should be focused first. Organizations can prioritize risks and allocate resources by assessing the likelihood and impact of each risk. This helps them identify where to focus their compliance efforts and concentrate resources on the areas that pose the greatest threat to their operations.

Compliance standards

Compliance standards consist of rules and regulations as well as guidelines and best practices an organization must follow to meet legal requirements and ethical standards specific to their industries. The standards aim to fulfill multiple requirements like data privacy protection and safety assurance, along with fairness promotion and fraud prevention. Business operations should follow compliance standards that cover areas such as environmental practices together with workplace safety and information security. Below are some explanations of specific standards.

ISO/IEC 27005

ISO/*International Electrotechnical Commission (IEC) 27005* establishes an essential framework for organizations to handle information security risks. Organizations can protect their information assets by following ISO/IEC 27005 guidelines to identify, assess, evaluate, treat and monitor risks. Organizations need this standard to achieve their information security goals as this standard aligns with ISO 31000.

The risk management process requires organizations to perform regular risk reassessments as well as implement risk treatments with ongoing follow-ups and maintain stakeholder communication through continuous scrutiny and review according to ISO/IEC 27005. Organizations must create detailed records of all risk management procedures and the results they generate. Organizations seeking ISO/IEC 27001 certification can use ISO/IEC 27005 to strengthen their **information security management system** (**ISMS**) while addressing security threats.

Organizations of every size in various industries can use ISO/IEC 27005 to implement complete information security practices based on risk management principles. Organizations can meet ISO/IEC 27001 requirements through ISO/IEC 27005, which helps them perform risk assessments and apply necessary security controls from Annex A to establish a full risk management system.

Risk management process

ISO 27005 is an international standard that guides how to conduct an information security risk assessment. There are six key components of risk management process, as shown in the following figure:

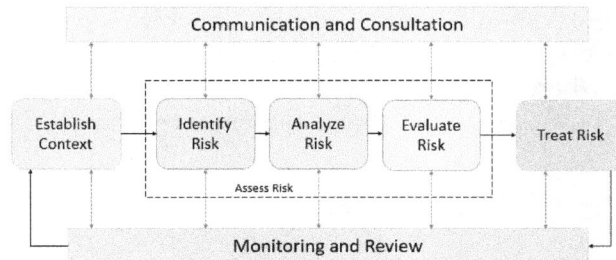

Figure 19.2: *ISO 27005 risk management process*

Here is the detail of key components of the risk management process:

- **Context establishment**: This step sets the foundation for managing risks. It defines how risks are identified, who is responsible for them, how they affect the **confidentiality, integrity, and availability (CIA)** of information, and how risk impact and likelihood are calculated.

- **Risk assessment**: This process helps identify and assess risks. It typically includes as following:

  o Compiling information assets.

  o Identifying threats and vulnerabilities for each asset.

  o Assigning impact and likelihood values based on risk criteria.

  o Evaluating each risk against predetermined levels of acceptability.

  o Prioritizing risks that need to be addressed and in which order.

- **Risk treatment**: Once risks are identified, organizations have four options to treat them as following:

  o **Avoid**: Eliminate the risk entirely.

  o **Mitigate**: Reduce the risk by applying security controls.

  o **Transfer**: Transfer the risk to a third-party (e.g., through insurance or outsourcing).

  o **Accept**: Accept the risk if it falls within acceptable criteria.

- **Risk acceptance**: Organizations set criteria for risk acceptance based on their policies, goals, objectives, and stakeholder interests. Risks that meet these criteria can be accepted without further action.

- **Risk communication and consultation**: Communication is key to effective risk management. It ensures all stakeholders understand the basis of decisions and actions. Regular exchange of information about risks helps ensure that everyone is on the same page regarding how to manage risks, both in routine operations and during emergencies.

- **Risk monitoring and review**: Risks can change over time, so they must be continuously monitored. This includes tracking the following:

    o New assets added to the risk management scope.

    o Changes to asset values based on evolving business needs.

    o New or emerging threats.

    o Information security incidents that could affect the risk landscape.

ISO 31000

The globally recognized ISO 31000 RMF, developed by the ISO, offers organizations a set of guidelines and principles to effectively manage risk. Its broad applicability is beneficial for organizations of various sizes across different industries and sectors. Unlike compliance efforts mandated by regulators, which tend to be confined to particular regions or industries, ISO 31000 has universal applicability, whether within the public or private sector, across large or small enterprises, or within non-profit entities. Its objective is to assist organizations in the more efficient identification, evaluation, and control of risks, thereby optimizing resource allocation and refining decision-making processes.

ISO 31000 defines risk management as a systematic process, emphasizing the identification, analysis, and mitigation of potential threats to an organization's capital, earnings, and operations. This standard advocates for a comprehensive approach to manage a wide array of risks, encompassing financial, operational, strategic, and compliance risks. Adopting ISO 31000 allows organizations to build a robust RMF, empowering them to proactively tackle weaknesses and boost their resilience.

ISO 31000 clauses

ISO 31000 is organized into three primary clauses, which offer a holistic approach to risk management, as illustrated in the following table:

Clause number	Clause name	Clause description
3	Principles	This clause outlines the fundamental principles for effective risk management, emphasizing inclusivity, dynamism, evidence-based decisions, and integration of risk management across the organization.
4	Framework	The framework clause focuses on establishing a supportive environment for risk management, promoting leadership, stakeholder engagement, and alignment with organizational goals.
5	Process	This clause provides a detailed process for managing risks, including steps for identifying, assessing, evaluating, treating, and monitoring risks. The process is iterative, ensuring that risk management remains adaptable and aligned with organizational objectives.

Table 19.1: ISO 31001 clauses

ISO 31000 framework

The ISO 31000 RMF comprises six essential elements, which enable organizations to handle risks in both an effective and efficient manner. These elements are structured to guarantee the incorporation of risk management into the organization's culture, procedures, and decision-making, as illustrated in the following figure:

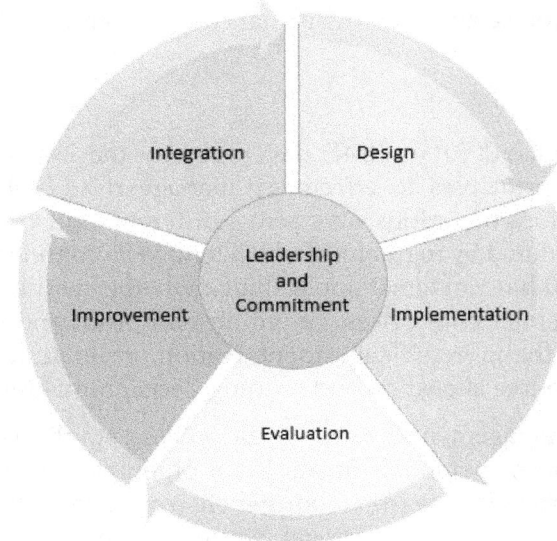

Figure 19.3: *ISO 31000 framework*

Here is the detail of each component of ISO 31000 framework:

- **Leadership**: The successful implementation and application of the ISO 31000 framework requires strong leadership. In order to foster a risk-aware culture at all levels, leaders should ensure that risk management practices are in accordance with respective cultures and strategic objectives of organization.

- **Integration**: In getting things to go well, risk management should form an integral part of all organizational processes. A delicate balance is required between risk mitigation efforts and the need for business to run smoothly, avoiding needless bottlenecks whilst still addressing key risks.

- **Design**: When it comes to design, it is all about creating a risk management strategy that aligns with the unique needs and context of the organization. This includes recognizing major risks and designing a structure of management.

- **Implementation**: Implementation is the next step which entails integrating the risk management approach into the organization's daily operations. It encompasses establishing clear goals, determining timelines, and implementing reporting systems to achieve the efficient execution of risk management initiatives.

- **Evaluation**: Evaluation is one of the key stages to conduct regular evaluations in order to gauge how efficient is RMF. Organizations are required to examine their risk management procedures and processes to identify strong elements and areas requiring enhancement.

- **Improvement**: ISO 31000 focuses on the aspect of continuous improvement. Organizations should carry out risk assessment regularly and seek chances to enhance their risk management methods, making certain that they adjust to changing risks and organizational requirements with time. This continuous process leads to better preparedness and long-term success of organizations and builds resilience as well.

ISO 31000 principles

ISO 31000 is not designed to eliminate risks but to simply help the organization identify those risks and handle them in the most appropriate ways. It enables the organization to develop a process for mitigating or reducing risks that are within acceptable levels instead of the removal of risks. A structured approach within the framework offers the facility to continuously adapt and improve in pursuit of maintaining a risk management regime that proves efficient and congruent with organizational goals.

This framework on risk management is based on eight principles of ISO 31000 that will enable organizations to conduct proper risks and effectiveness management:

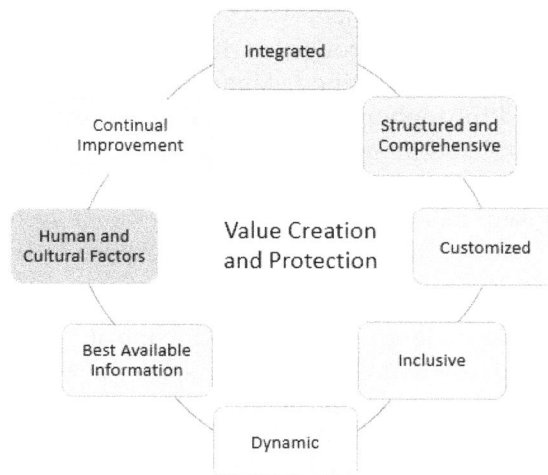

Figure 19.4: *ISO 31000 principles*

Let us look at the breakdown of core principles of ISO 31000:

- **Customized**: The RMF should be tailored to the specific context, objectives, and risk profile of an organization. It makes such a framework practical, and effective for that organization.

- **Inclusive**: It is important that the active involvement of the stakeholders is included within the process. Their views and inputs have to be taken into consideration. The risk management processes and procedures should be transparent such that they can be understood with simple terminology that is not complicated.

- **Dynamic**: Organizations are changing, and so are their risks. A continuous analysis of risk is required by the dynamics of the circumstances to cope with risk management strategies.

- **Best available information**: Decisions on the management of risk should be based on the best available information. However, organizations should also recognize the inherent uncertainty and the possibility of unforeseen risk.

- **Human and cultural factors**: Human behavioral aspects and the culture of the organization play a huge role in this. Risks related to human errors and culture should also be considered in identifying risks.

- **Continual improvement**: ISO 31000 promotes a commitment to continuous improvement, ensuring that risk management processes evolve and improve over time for greater effectiveness.

Configuration item

Within the concept of **security configuration management (SecCM)**, a CI is a uniquely identifiable part or assembly of components of a system that is subjected to **configuration management** (**CM**) and managed throughout its lifecycle as a single unit. In other words, CIs should be uniquely identified, labelled, and tracked so that appropriate management is guaranteed throughout different configuration control activities, such as configuration change control and monitoring. These could be everything from individual system components, such as servers, workstations, and routers, to a collection of related components, such as a group of servers of the same operating system or a set of network devices like routers and switches. In essence, the main purpose of defining CIs is to provide a structured way to break down a system into smaller, manageable parts.

This decomposition enables one to manage and control the configuration of each constituent part with confidence that changes or updates can be controlled and kept safe. CIs can be defined to a higher or lower level of detail depending on the requirements of the organization. In some organizations, it will be sufficient to consider all laptops within a particular organization as one CI, whereas in others it may be necessary to track each individual laptop.

Determining CI

Determining CIs is a critical part of the CM process, as it helps to define and manage the individual components that constitute a system. Following are the key components to determine CI, as shown in *Figure 19.5*:

Decompose the system	Assign unique identifiers	Assign baselines and version control	Maintain essential data elements	Control and monitor dependencies	Include non-component objects

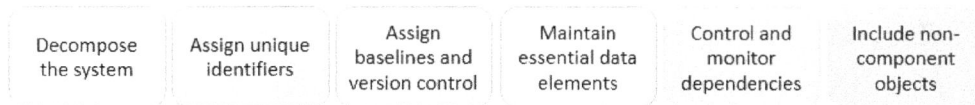

Figure 19.5: *Determine CI*

Here is the breakdown of each element:

- **Decompose the system**: The system owner determines how to break down the system into one or more CIs based on the components and elements that require CM. This decomposition could involve system components, documents, network diagrams, scripts, and custom code.

- **Assign unique identifiers**: Every CI should be given an unambiguous identifier, ensuring that it can be uniquely referenced within the CM processes. This identification ensures consistency and traceability.

- **Assign baselines and version control**: Each CI may have several approved baseline configurations as it moves through its lifecycle. This includes tracking version numbers of each and every component for consistency and management of changes all through its lifetime.

- **Maintain essential data elements**: For every CI, there should be thoroughly maintained data elements to define and describe it effectively. These elements help organizations manage and rebuild the CI when necessary. The important data elements are:

  o The system to which the CI belongs.

  o Logical and physical placement within the system.

  o Ownership and management details.

  o Inventory of system components and documentation.

  o Version numbers of both components and non-components (e.g., firmware, software).

  o Relationships and dependencies with other CIs within the system.

- **Control and monitor dependencies**: Understanding and tracking dependencies between different CIs within the system is crucial. Changes to one CI may affect others, so it is important to control these relationships to avoid configuration drift or system issues.

- **Include non-component objects**: A CI is not always just a physical or software component; it can also include non-component objects, such as documentation or configuration diagrams, that are vital for system management.

System maintenance

System maintenance ensures that the security features of the system maintenance process are well addressed. This ranges from all types of maintenance processes, whether local or remote, and all components of the system, including peripheral devices like scanners and printers. The process of maintenance itself involves recording of some important information so that the system remains safe and efficient. Thw following are the key components of system maintenance that help in tracking and managing maintenance tasks:

- **Maintenance activities record**: Records of maintenance should provide the date and time the maintenance was performed, a description of what was done, names of all persons and/or teams involved, including the name of an accompanying person, and the component or equipment removed or replaced within the system.

- **Maintenance scheduling and documentation**: Organizations should schedule, document, and review all maintenance, repair, and replacement activities according to the requirements of the manufacturer or vendor, or an organizational policy.

- **Approval and monitoring**: All the maintenance activities done either on-site or remotely must be approved and closely monitored, whether the serving of system components is done on-site or taken to another location.

- **Approval for off-site maintenance**: Any removal of system components for off-site maintenance, repair, or replacement shall be approved by the personnel or roles identified within the organization.

- **Sanitization of equipment**: All the equipment that may be taken away for maintenance, repair, or replacement should be sanitized beforehand and its associated media free from any sensitive information. The procedures for information removal, which is necessary, should clearly be specified by an organization.

- **Verification of security controls**: At the end of all the activities related to maintenance, repair, or replacement, all the security controls impacted shall be reviewed for correctness of operation.

- **Comprehensive maintenance records**: All maintenance should be recorded with relevant details like nature, personnel involved, and effect on system components. The organization should specify the information that would be necessary for effective recordkeeping to provide complete transparency and accountability.

Privacy Framework

The Privacy Framework consists of a set of guidelines that enable organizations to manage privacy risks regarding personal information. It provides the flexibility needed by businesses to tailor their privacy programs to their unique needs and particular risks. Core privacy principles underlying this framework are similar to common laws and regulations and therefore can be applied in helping an organization strengthen and maintain the best privacy practices.

Key principles of Privacy Framework

The five key principles of the NIST Privacy Framework are designed to guide organizations in managing privacy risks effectively. The following figure shows the key principles:

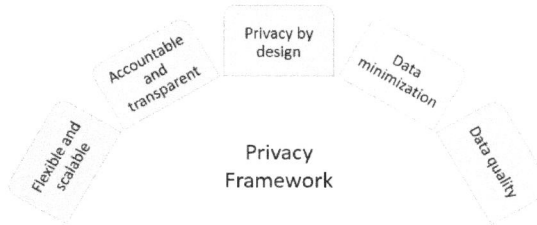

Figure 19.6: Privacy Framework

Here are the details of each principle:

- **Flexible and scalable**: Organizations should create flexible and agile privacy plans because the nature of the digital environment is fluid. Therefore, the privacy design will be in such a manner that it will grow and change with the needs of the organization, among other external factors.

- **Accountable and transparent**: An organization shall be open to its privacy practices; thus, the privacy policy shall be accessible and clear. They should review and update such privacy practices periodically in order to keep itself accountable to the stakeholders.

- **Privacy by Design**: The privacy concerns should be in-built at the very inception phase of product development or formulation of services. Being proactive helps to eliminates potential risks regarding privacy.

- **Data minimization**: Organizations should collect only the data that is necessary for a specific purpose, reducing the risk of unnecessary data exposure and enhancing privacy protection.

- **Data quality**: The data should be accurate, up-to-date, complete, and relevant to the purposes for which it is used, so that the privacy practices can be based on reliable information.

NIST Privacy Framework

The NIST Privacy Framework is a framework developed by the NIST to help organizations manage privacy risk and protect personal privacy. It is designed to be complementary to the NIST CSF but focused specifically on addressing privacy, helping organizations integrate privacy into their operations and risk management processes.

The framework mainly contains three parts: Core, profiles, and implementation tiers. These allow organizations to assess and improve their privacy practices, reduce risks related to personal data, and comply with privacy regulations. The five functions: Identify, govern, control, communicate, and protect, can be used to manage privacy risks arising from data processing. The following figure shows the core functions of the NIST Privacy Framework:

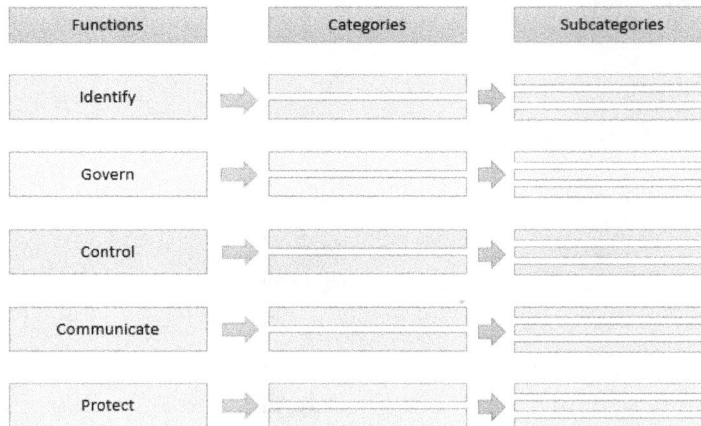

Figure 19.7: NIST core functions

Following are the details of core functions:

- **Identify**: The identify function deals with the development of an organizational knowledge to address privacy risks emanating from data processing activities. It involves documenting the types of data being processed, understanding the privacy interests of the affected individuals, making privacy risk evaluations, and prioritizing risks based on their severity.

- **Govern**: The govern function deals with establishing governance structures to manage privacy risks within the organization. It involves having clear privacy policies, adhering to relevant privacy laws (e.g., GDPR, CCPA), establishing the risk appetite of the organization, and having a governance framework with privacy officers and committees.

- **Control**: The control function is about controlling data to reduce privacy risks using controls like data classification, access controls, and data minimization. It involves ensuring that only necessary data is collected, implementing controls for data use and sharing and using privacy-enhancing technologies like encryption and anonymization to protect data.

- **Communicate**: The communicate function focuses on making sure that organizations and individuals understand data processing practices and associated privacy risks. It entails providing clear privacy notices, talking to stakeholders (e.g., employees, customers, regulators), and enabling individuals to exercise their privacy rights such as view or delete their data.

- **Protect**: The protect function involves safeguarding information to prevent privacy risks associated with cybersecurity. It involves the use of data protection measures like encryption and access controls, harmonizing privacy and cybersecurity operations, designing data breach incident response plans, and regular monitoring of systems to detect and respond to privacy intrusions.

Example of categories and sub-categories:

Let us take an example of first function identify. The function identify has various categories such as ID.IM-P: Inventory and mapping, ID.BE-P: Business environment, ID.RA-P: Risk assessment, ID.DE.P: Data processing ecosystem risk management.

Let us elaborate more on risk assessment categories. The risk assessment categories can be divided into various sub-categories as following:

- **ID.RA-P1**: Contextual factors related to the systems/products/services and the data actions are identified (e.g., individuals demographics and privacy interests or perceptions, data sensitivity and/or types, visibility of data processing to individuals and third-parties).

- **ID.RA-P2**: Data analytic inputs and outputs are identified and evaluated for bias.

- **ID.RA-P3**: Potential problematic data actions and associated problems are identified.

- **ID.RA-P4**: Problematic data actions, likelihoods, and impacts are used to determine and prioritize risk.

- **ID.RA-P5**: Risk responses are identified, prioritized, and implemented.

ISO 27701

ISO/IEC 27701:2024 is a robust standard for dealing with **personally identifiable information** (**PII**). It can be used by any organization involved in PII processing, e.g., PII controllers, joint PII controllers, PII processors, and sub-PII processors. The standard structure follows the typical high level format, with clauses 4 to 10, and includes annexes with reference controls and control objectives. ISO 27701 helps organizations comply with privacy regulations like the GDPR by guiding them on how to establish, implement, and maintain a **privacy information management system** (**PIMS**). The ISO 27701 standard provides a complete collection of privacy controls customized for use by different roles in the PII processing system:

- **Privacy controls for PII controllers**: These controls help organizations make decisions about purposes and methods of processing PII in adhering to privacy regulations as well as in protecting individuals right to privacy.

- **Privacy controls for PII processors**: These are controls for organizations processing PII as processors on behalf of controllers to safeguard data and handle it securely.

- **Security controls of PII controllers and processors**: These are targeted at the security controls to be used to protect PII from unauthorized disclosure, modification, destruction, and access.

ISO 27701 clauses

The standard's structure follows the typical high level format, with clauses 4 to 10, and includes annexes with reference controls and control objectives. ISO/IEC 27701:2024 standard consists of several key clauses 4 to 10, including reference controls and control objectives, which outline the requirements for implementing a PIMS. The following is a concise overview of the clauses:

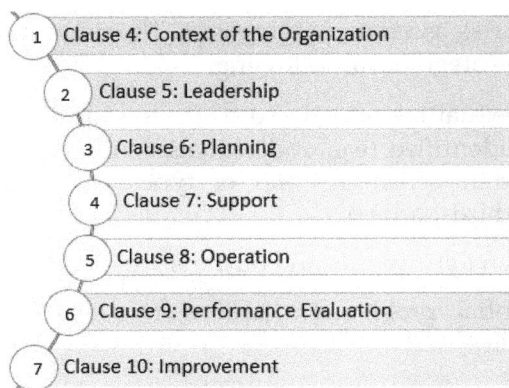

1. Clause 4: Context of the Organization
2. Clause 5: Leadership
3. Clause 6: Planning
4. Clause 7: Support
5. Clause 8: Operation
6. Clause 9: Performance Evaluation
7. Clause 10: Improvement

Figure 19.8: ISO 27701 Clauses

Here is the detail of key clauses:

Clause number	Clause name	Clause description
4	Context of the organization	Organizations must define the internal and external factors affecting their PIMS. They must also be aware of the stakeholders requirements and expectations and scope of their PIMS.
5	Leadership	The senior management must be actively involved in sponsoring and overseeing the PIMS. This includes assigning responsibilities and roles, giving adequate resources, and maintaining constant improvement.
6	Planning	There is a need for organizations to assess risks and opportunities in privacy management. This includes setting privacy objectives and planning steps to achieve them with due consideration of any legal or regulatory requirements.

Clause number	Clause name	Clause description
7	Support	The support focuses on ensuring there are adequate resources, trained staff, and good communication within the organization. It also touches on awareness and maintaining documentation.
8	Operation	Organizations must have mechanisms in place to accomplish privacy objectives and management of PII processing. This includes operational controls and risk management practices for managing PII.
9	Performance evaluation	This clause involves monitoring, measuring, and evaluating the effectiveness of the PIMS through audits, evaluations, and reviews. It guarantees that the system works as intended.
10	Improvement	Improvement addresses how organizations should handle nonconformities and undertake corrective action. It also focuses on continuous improvement to ensure that the PIMS is effective in the long-term.

Table 19.2: *ISO 27701 clauses*

GDPR core principles

GDPR is a comprehensive data protection and privacy law introduced by the EU for the protection of citizens personal data. This law provides guidelines on data collection, data processing, and data storage to ensure that an individual's rights and privacy are maintained. The GDPR applies to all organizations that are established in the EU, as well as any organization outside the EU if they process the personal data of EU citizens. The GDPR defines various core principles to handle personal information securely, as shown in the following figure:

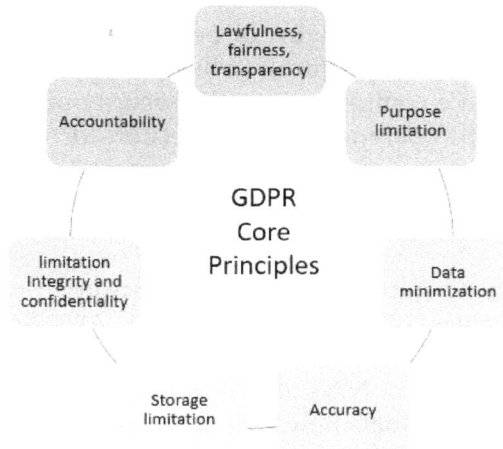

Figure 19.9: *GDPR core principles*

Let us look at the principles in detail:

- **Lawfulness, fairness, and transparency**: This principle ensures that personal data of subjects must be processed lawfully and their use of data is transparent to data subjects.

- **Purpose limitation**: This principle ensures that personal data must be collected for a specific, legitimate purpose and not further processed in a way that is incompatible with those purposes.

- **Data minimization**: This principle ensures that only the data necessary for the intended purpose is collected. It is not advisable to collect excessive or irrelevant data.

- **Accuracy**: This principle ensures that personal data should be accurate and recent. Any inaccuracies should be corrected or deleted as soon as possible.

- **Storage limitation**: This principle ensures that personal data should be kept only for the purpose for which it has been obtained. Once the purpose is over, the data must be anonymized or destroyed.

- **Integrity and confidentiality**: This principle ensures that personal data should be handled in a manner to protect it against unauthorized access, loss, or destruction. It includes maintaining confidentiality and data integrity.

- **Accountability**: This principle ensures that organizations take responsibility to comply with GDPR principles and demonstrate their compliance. This entails keeping records of data processing activities, conducting regular audits, and implementing necessary policies and procedures.

Performance monitoring

NIST SP 800-55 highlights the importance of performance measurement programs in selecting and implementing security controls, which are critical for safeguarding the CIA of information systems. These controls ensure the security of an organization's systems and assets, enabling smooth operations and protection for both the organization and individuals. Effective performance measurement programs designed by organizations can help them to measure the effectiveness of their security controls and make sure they work as intended.

In federal agencies, security control selection is a structured process defined by *Federal Information Processing Standard* (*FIPS*) *199* and *FIPS 200*. Agencies categorize their information systems based on the security objectives that are low, moderate, or high, then select controls from NIST SP 800-53. NIST SP 800-55 builds on this to develop performance measures that can be used to evaluate how well these security controls protect systems. It provides a number of supplementary measures that an agency may adapt to its specific needs in enhancing its security while constantly improving the programs.

Implementing performance measures

Information security performance measurement program means implementing a formal process in an organization to monitor, analyze, and make improvements to the real performance of its security controls. The essence is improving effectiveness continuously by using the performances metrics to identify and correct the weaknesses in the security measures. The following figure shows the steps to implement performance measures:

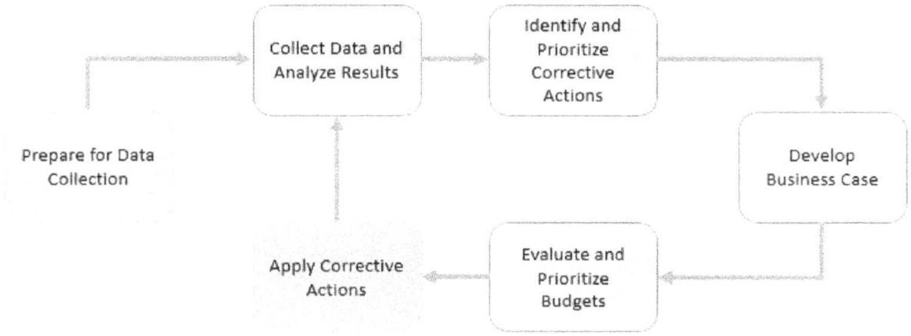

Figure 19.10: Performance measurement

The following steps outline how organizations can implement performance measures effectively:

1. **Prepare for data collection**: The first step in implementing a performance measurement program is to identify, define, develop, and select appropriate information security measures. Above all, an implementation plan needs to be developed in order to make the program successful. The plan should outline how performance will continuously be monitored through activities such as CM, security impact analyses, assessment of security controls, and status reporting.

2. **Collect data and analyze results**: The organization can start collecting data regularly once the program is running. Collected data should be aggregated, consolidated, and gap analysis performed to highlight areas of poor performance and root causes.

3. **Identify and prioritize corrective actions**: Once performance issues have been identified, the next step is to develop corrective actions. These should be prioritized based on the organization's risk mitigation goals. The best corrective actions should be selected, and a full cost-benefit analysis conducted to ascertain the feasibility and impact of each proposed solution.

4. **Develop a business case**: Industry best practices should form the basis for developing a business case necessary to justify the corrective actions; this shall be in line with federal guidelines such as *OMB Circular A-11*, the *Clinger-Cohen Act*, and the *Government Performance and Results Act (GPRA)*. The business case should encapsulate the outcome of the preceding steps, including gaps identified, corrective actions proposed, and their related benefits.

5. **Evaluate and prioritize budget requests**: Once the business case has been developed, organizations should analyze budget requests to prioritize resources for implementing corrective actions. This process would involve assigning the appropriate resources to the most critical issues. Further, funding needs to be allocated in order to address the most impactful security improvements.

6. **Apply corrective actions**: Lastly, the corrective actions should be implemented into the information security program, which may include technical, management, or operational security controls. It is very important to document and monitor the status of corrective actions to ensure the effective treatment of performance issues and improve the overall security posture of the organization.

NIST Cybersecurity Framework

The NIST CSF is a trusted source that can be used by all organizations of different sizes and business areas, including government, academia, and non-profit. The framework is designed to be flexible and adaptable to organizations at any stage of their cybersecurity maturity. The CSF applies universally; hence, public and private organizations, irrespective of sector and region, can implement this. Some sectors may also follow the CSF because of government policies and mandates, even if it is voluntary. This framework is flexible and can be tailored for every organization according to need and circumstance.

Probably one of the main strengths of the CSF is that it can complement other cybersecurity-related frameworks and standards, becoming part of a wider risk management strategy. It is customizable to the particular risks, vulnerabilities, and regulatory requirements of diverse organizations. In this respect, it becomes effective in managing cybersecurity risks across diverse environments and missions. Version 2.0 of the CSF provides high-level guidance to assist organizations in understanding and reducing cybersecurity risks while continuing to adapt to emerging threats.

Cybersecurity framework overview

The CSF core is the central part of the framework, outlining the essential cybersecurity outcomes that organizations need to achieve. It is organized into three levels of taxonomy:

- **Functions**: Functions are the broad, high-level cybersecurity activities that represent the major areas of focus in managing cybersecurity risks.

- **Categories**: Categories represent the particular cybersecurity outcome that each function supports.

- **Subcategories**: Subcategories represent more detailed, actionable outcomes that further subdivide categories into specific tasks or goals that will help in guiding implementation.

These outputs should be intelligible to all levels of stakeholders, from executives to technical staff, regardless of prior experience or background in cybersecurity. The CSF core is designed to be neutral with respect to sector, country, or technology, allowing flexibility for organizations to adapt it to their unique needs and risks. The CSF core is structured into functions, categories, and subcategories, as shown in the following figure:

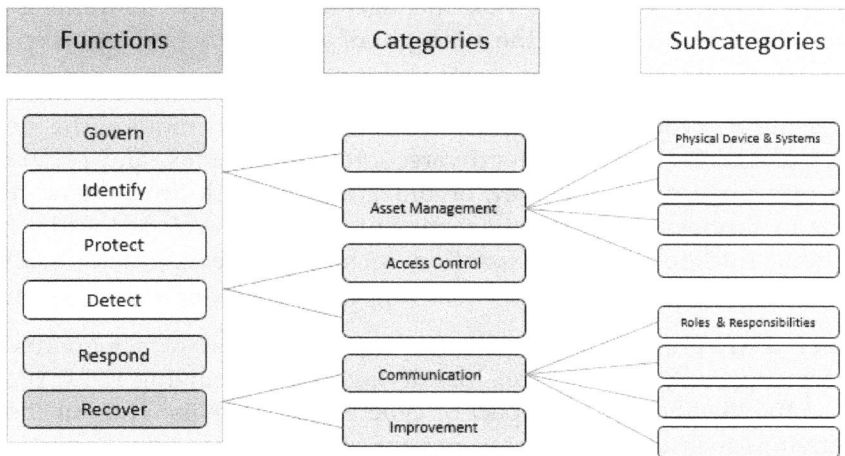

Figure 19.11: CSF framework

CSF core functions

The core functions of the NIST CSF are govern, identify, protect, detect, respond, and recover, which is vital for different controls with respect to managing and improving an organization's cybersecurity posture. These functions represent the highest level of outcomes that organizations strive for to prepare them against malicious cyber-attacks and other risks:

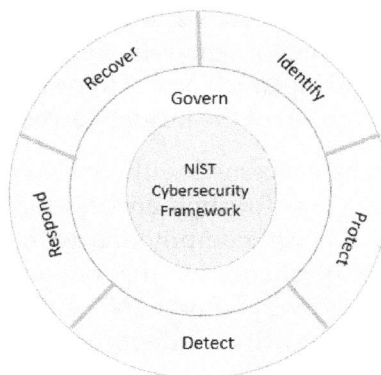

Figure 19.12: CSF core functions

Let us look at the functions in detail:

- **Govern (GV)**: Govern focuses on the organization's overall cybersecurity governance. It ensures the establishment, communication, and monitoring of the cybersecurity risk management strategy and policies. Govern provides the framework for aligning cybersecurity efforts with the organization's mission and stakeholder expectations. It provides a critical function to embed cybersecurity into the broader enterprise risk management strategy, addressing roles and responsibilities and guiding the oversight of activities regarding cybersecurity.

- **Identify (ID)**: Identify is the first core function that involves identifying the organization's cybersecurity risks and assets. It basically requires the identification of key assets, such as data, hardware, software, systems, and personnel, along with associated risks. This way, organizations can prioritize their cybersecurity efforts in support of the risk management strategy developed under the govern function. Additionally, this function includes reviewing and enhancing the policies, processes, and practices that support cybersecurity risk management.

- **Protect (PR)**: Protect focuses on the implementation of safeguards to secure the organization's assets. After identifying and prioritizing risks, protect helps reduce the likelihood and impact of cybersecurity events. This function consists of activities such as identity management, authentication, access control, training, data security, and platform security. Its objective is the protection of assets and technologies against possible attacks or adversarial actions.

- **Detect (DE): The** Detect function helps organizations to identify and analyze real-time cybersecurity threats. It allows for anomaly detection, indicators of compromise or any incidents at runtime that can mark an ongoing cyber-attack or a security breach. Early detection is a must for enabling timely responses and ensuring that the cybersecurity incident will be contained.

- **Respond (RS)**: Respond means to act upon the detection of any cybersecurity incident. The focus of this function is to manage the response to cybersecurity incidents including containment, analysis, mitigation, and reporting. It ensures that the organization can take quick action in order to minimize the damage and coordinate the communication of the incident across the relevant stakeholders.

- **Recover (RC)**: Recover is concerned with restoring operations and assets after a cybersecurity incident. This function ensures that the organization can return to normal business operations promptly and with minimal disruption. Recover supports the long-term resilience of the organization by allowing effective communication during recovery efforts and improving the recovery process to reduce the impact of cybersecurity incidents on operations.

CSF organizational profiles

Organizational profiles introduce a way for organizations to describe the as-is or to-be state of their cybersecurity posture. They are used to set an organization's objectives and priorities relative to the outcomes in the CSF core. Organizational profiles provide a starting point for the organization to understand its current cybersecurity maturity posture and the desired future posture, thereby giving a roadmap to improvement. This profile can thus be used to make informed organizational decisions on setting priorities for cybersecurity action while communicating effectively.

Each organizational profile contains one or both of the following components:

- **Current profile**: The current profile includes the core outcomes that the organization is currently achieving or attempting to achieve. It provides a snapshot of the organization's existing cybersecurity posture, helping to characterize how well each outcome is being implemented and to what extent it is being realized. The current profile offers a baseline for assessing where improvements are needed.

- **Target profile**: This represents the desired outcome of cybersecurity an organization would wish to achieve, considering its objectives of risk management. The target profile takes into consideration imminent changes in cybersecurity requirements, the adoption of new technologies, and emerging threat intelligence. It acts like a roadmap for cybersecurity improvements that assists the organization in prioritizing future actions toward the desired cybersecurity maturity level.

CSF tiers

CSF tiers help organizations assess the rigor of their cybersecurity risk management practices. Tiers provide a way to characterize an organization's cybersecurity maturity and its ability to manage risks effectively. These tiers are used in conjunction with the organization's risk profile to give context to an organization's cybersecurity strategy and governance. They also put into perspective the overall strategy that an organization adopts in managing cybersecurity risks from reactive to more proactive and integrated practices. They provide very important context for gaining insight into how an organization views cybersecurity risks and how an organization manages these risks across various stages of maturity. The tiers, thus, provide a useful way of helping to illustrate the progression from informal, reactive measures to structured, proactive approaches, as shown in the following figure:

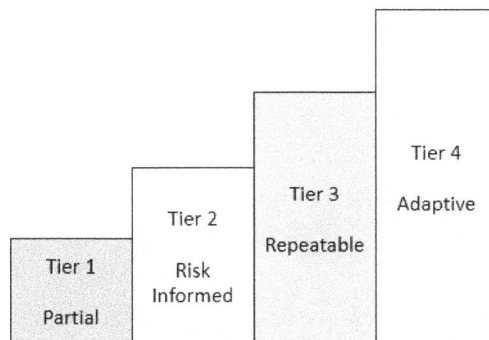

Figure 19.13: CSF tiers

The tiers are categorized as follows:

- **Tier 1—partial**: The cybersecurity practices in an organization at this stage are informal and reactive. There is little coordination, little or no formalized structure, and responses to cybersecurity risks tend to be ad-hoc.

- **Tier 2—risk informed**: At this stage, an organization's cybersecurity practices are more organized but still fundamentally informed by a risk assessment to make decisions. There is an increased understanding of cybersecurity risks; however, processes may not be fully integrated or consistently applied.

- **Tier 3—repeatable**: At this stage, the organization is starting to show more consistency and repeatability relative to cybersecurity. Risk management processes are in place, a product of repetitive application guided by formulated guidelines. Emphasis is laid on enhancing resilience through structured processes.

- **Tier 4—adaptive**: This is the state of complete maturity where cybersecurity practices are agile, iteratively improved, and highly adaptive. Although organizations may face emerging risks, they proactively enhance their security by using real-time threat intelligence.

Conclusion

In this chapter, we emphasized the significance of compliance measurement and explored some important compliance standards on risk management, such as ISO 27005 and ISO 31000. Such standards help an organization mitigate risks properly and stay aligned with the regulatory requirements. The chapter also provided an overview of CIs, explaining how they form a basis for compliance and also facilitate system management in an efficient way.

Additionally, the chapter also introduced the NIST Privacy Framework, focusing on how this provides a structure to manage privacy risks and protect personal data. We then covered some performance measurement concepts, which are helpful in understanding organizational performance, evaluation, and optimization. As we transition to the next chapter, the discussion will cover security testing and system maintenance, giving further detail on how these practices contribute to maintaining secure and reliable systems.

Key terms

- Compliance monitoring is the process that ensures organizations meet the policies and procedures to identify compliance risk issues in their day-to-day operations and functions.

- Compliance measurement refers to the process of assessing whether an organization, system, or individual adheres to relevant laws, regulations, standards, or internal policies.

- Assessing compliance is essential for maintaining organizational integrity in several key ways:

    o **Prevent legal issues**: Regular assessments help avoid legal penalties and sanctions.

    o **Enhance trust**: Ensures stakeholders feel confident in the organization's integrity.

    o **Identify risks**: Helps spot and reduce potential compliance risks.

    o **Improve efficiency**: Streamlines operations by ensuring procedures align with relevant standards.

- A compliance policy is a key part of cybersecurity. It outlines the standards and rules organizations must follow to create risk-based controls that protect the CIA of data.

- ISO 27005 is an international standard that provides methods and best practices for creating an ISMS. It helps protect your organization from cyber threats and prevents the loss or corruption of sensitive data.

- ISO 19011 is a critical standard for any organization looking to implement an audit program or manage external audits. It establishes a common framework for audits, ensuring they are conducted consistently and effectively.

- ISO/IEC 27701 is an international standard that provides a framework for PIMS.

- The GDPR is a law that protects the personal data of EU citizens and applies to any organization that processes or stores their data, regardless of where the organization is located.

- A CI is a specific component of a system, such as hardware, software, firmware, or documentation, that is managed and controlled through configuration processes.

- Performance measurements are valuable tools that produce useful, timely information about the security of information systems for the decision-makers of organizations.

- Performance measures are especially useful for federal managers who must meet regulatory, financial, and organizational requirements for their information security practices.

Join our book's Discord space

Join the book's Discord Workspace for Latest updates, Offers, Tech happenings around the world, New Release and Sessions with the Authors:

https://discord.bpbonline.com

CHAPTER 20

Optimizing Risk and Compliance

Introduction

This chapter offers a detailed overview of continuous monitoring, covering essential roles and responsibilities involved in maintaining system security. It highlights the importance of system decommissioning, ensuring the secure retirement of systems that are no longer in use. The chapter also emphasizes the need for ongoing system maintenance and assessments to ensure that security controls remain effective over time. Additionally, it discusses the significance of configuration scanning to identify vulnerabilities and ensure compliance with security standards.

Furthermore, the chapter explores various security testing techniques to validate and assess vulnerabilities in systems and networks. It also examines risk impact assessments to evaluate potential consequences and prioritize risk management efforts. The chapter concludes with an overview of third-party contract management, stressing the importance of managing agreements with external vendors to mitigate risks and ensure compliance with security requirements.

Structure

The chapter covers the following main topics:

- Continuous monitoring
- System decommissioning

- Ongoing system maintenance
- Configuration scanning
- Ongoing assessments
- Security testing
- Risk impact
- Third-party contract management

Objectives

By the end of this chapter, you will have a clear understanding of continuous monitoring, including its key components and how it ensures the effectiveness of security controls over time. You will gain valuable insights into the system decommissioning process, which ensures the secure removal of outdated systems. The chapter also highlights the importance of ongoing system maintenance and regular assessments to ensure systems remain secure and compliant.

Additionally, you will be introduced to configuration scanning and security testing, both critical in identifying vulnerabilities and strengthening system defenses. The chapter will also help you understand risk impact analysis, aiding in the evaluation of potential threats. Lastly, you will learn about third-party contract management, which plays a crucial role in mitigating risks and maintaining security standards in external partnerships.

Continuous monitoring

After accreditation, the system owner must track and complete corrective actions, ensuring periodic updates are provided to the approving authority. If additional resources are needed, the system owner should brief the approving authority to address any resource issues. Once corrective actions are completed, they must be documented and reported to the approving authority to confirm that residual risks have been addressed. Though accreditation is based on specific conditions at a given time, the system's security posture must continue to be managed, including regular self-assessments, automated vulnerability detection, and timely incident reporting and resolution.

Changes in the system's environment must be assessed for their impact on security controls, and systems should be evaluated to determine if re-accreditation is necessary. The approving authority must be informed of new threats, evolving risks, changes in data sensitivity, and any operational changes to decide whether recertification is required. Additionally, when multiple systems are consolidated, they may need to be reaccredited as a new, redesigned system.

Key roles in continuous monitoring

Continuous monitoring is essential for identifying emerging risks, reducing the impact of security incidents, and ensuring the overall security and integrity of information systems. There are some key roles that play an important role, as shown in the following figure:

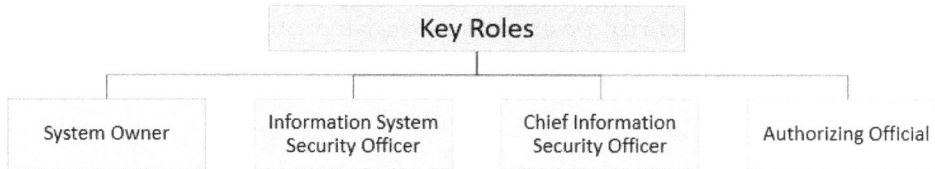

Figure 20.1: *Key roles in continuous monitoring*

Here are the responsibilities for each role:

- **System owner**:
  - Responsible for operating the system and ensuring standard configuration management procedures are followed.
  - Implements controls for continuous monitoring of system security.
  - Review monitoring results to identify any negative impacts on the effectiveness of security controls.

- **Information system security officer (ISSO)**:
  - Collaborates closely with the system owner to monitor the security posture of the system.
  - Reports any discrepancies or issues to the system owner immediately.

- **Chief information security officer (CISO)**:
  - Provides oversight of the system owner's activities.
  - Performs trend analyses to identify potential security problems that could affect multiple systems.
  - Reports organization-wide security risks to **authorizing officials** (**AOs**) and system owners.

- **AO**:
  - Reviews security reports of the system.
  - Decides whether to continue authorizing the operation of the system based on its security posture.

NIST guidance on continuous monitoring

The seventh and final step in the **Risk Management Framework** (**RMF**) emphasizes the continuous monitoring of system security controls to ensure their ongoing effectiveness. This includes documenting any changes made to the system, conducting security impact analyses to evaluate the potential effects of those changes, and regularly providing status updates on the system's security posture to designated officials. The following figure shows the seventh step of the NIST RMF:

Figure 20.2: NIST RMF steps

NIST SP 800-37 offers detailed guidance on this continuous monitoring phase, outlining the need to track the performance of security controls, assess their effectiveness, and ensure that the system maintains its security throughout its lifecycle. The following figure shows the steps of continuous monitoring:

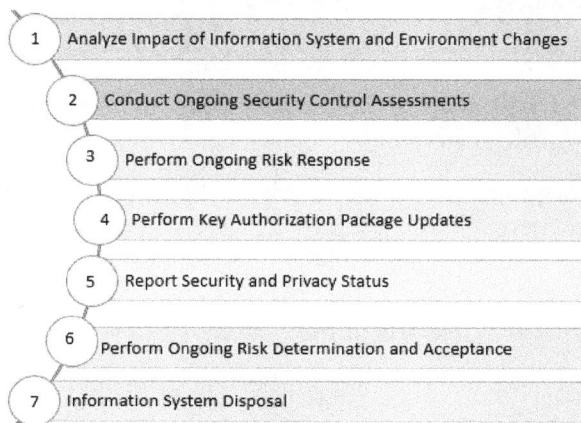

Figure 20.3: Continuous monitoring steps

Here is the breakdown of continuous monitoring steps:

- **Task 1: Analyze the impact of the information system and environment changes**: Systems and environments are constantly changing due to updates in technology, machine elements, human factors, and physical or environmental conditions. These changes can include hardware or software upgrades, staff turnover, or adjustments in physical security. External changes can be particularly difficult to detect, making it crucial for organizations to adopt a structured approach to manage, control, and document these changes. Configuration management and control processes are essential for maintaining security and privacy, ensuring that changes are in line with authorization terms.

  Changes within organizations, such as hardware installations, configuration adjustments, or unapproved patches, can significantly affect security and privacy. Unauthorized changes may result from intentional attacks or unintentional mistakes by authorized personnel. To prevent and address these issues, organizations must monitor for unauthorized changes, investigate their causes, and take appropriate actions. If an unauthorized change stems from an attack, actions like incident response, adjustments to security tools, and stronger controls may be required. If the cause is a failure to adhere to management processes, remedial training might be necessary. The following table shows the roles to analyze impact of information system and environment changes:

Primary responsibility	Supporting roles	System development lifecycle (SDLC) phase	References
System owner or common control provider; senior agency information security officer; senior agency official for privacy	Senior accountable official for risk management or risk executive (function); AO or AO designated representative; information owner or steward; system security officer; system privacy officer	New: Operations/ maintenance Existing: Operations/ maintenance	NIST SP 800-30; SP 800-128; SP 800-137

Table 20.1: *Roles to analyze system and environment changes*

- **Task 2: Conduct ongoing security control assessments**: After the initial authorization of a system or common control, organizations continuously assess the effectiveness of their controls as part of their ongoing monitoring activities. The frequency of these assessments is determined by the organization's monitoring strategy and may be supplemented by specific system level strategies. Continuous monitoring also ensures that the organization adheres to the terms set by the AO. The results of these assessments are analyzed and reported to senior leaders to ensure ongoing control effectiveness.

To meet the annual security assessment requirement under *Federal Information Security Modernization Act (FISMA)*, organizations can reuse assessment results from previous evaluations, such as those during authorization, reauthorization, or continuous monitoring. These results must be current, relevant, and independently obtained. For example: An organization stores PII data and has completed an assessment during the first year and the results can be reused next year if there were no major changes or new vulnerabilities and an assessment was done by third-party. Reusing assessment results is an efficient way to maintain a cost-effective security program while ensuring the necessary evidence for evaluating system security. Automation further supports control assessments, increasing their frequency, volume, and coverage. The following table shows the roles to conduct ongoing security control assessments:

Primary responsibility	Supporting roles	SDLC phase	References
Control assessor	AO or AO designated representative; system owner or common control provider; information owner or steward; system security officer; system privacy officer; senior agency information security officer; senior agency official for privacy	New: Operations/ maintenance Existing: Operations/ maintenance	NIST SP 800-53A; SP 800-137; SP 800-160 v1

Table 20.2: Roles to conduct ongoing security assessments

• **Task 3: Perform ongoing risk response**: Assessment information from continuous monitoring is shared with the system owner and common control provider through updated reports or automated security tools. The AO decides on the appropriate risk response based on the assessment findings, either accepting or approving responses proposed by the system owner or common control provider. If the response is accepted, the findings are documented and monitored for changes in risk. If mitigation is required, the actions are tracked in the plans of action and milestones.

If requested, control assessors or automated tools may provide recommendations for remediation actions. Organizational and system level risk assessments help guide risk response decisions. When controls are modified or added to address risks, assessors reassess them to ensure they are correctly implemented and meet the security and privacy requirements of the system. The following table shows the roles to perform ongoing risk response:

Primary responsibility	Supporting roles	SDLC phase	References
AO; system owner; common control provider	Senior accountable official for risk management or risk executive (function); senior agency official for privacy; AO designated representative; information owner or steward; system security officer; system privacy officer; systems security engineer; privacy engineer; security architect; privacy architect.	New: Operations/ maintenance Existing: Operations/ maintenance	NIST SP 800-30; SP 800-53; SP 800-53A; SP 800-137; SP 800-160 v1; NIST CSF

Table 20.3: Roles to perform ongoing risk response

- **Task 4: Perform key authorization package updates**: To manage risk in near-real-time, organizations continually update security and privacy plans, assessment reports, and plans of action. These updates reflect changes in controls due to risk mitigation efforts, additional assessment activities, and progress on outstanding items. Plans are also revised to address new risks identified through control effectiveness monitoring, keeping the system owner and common control provider aware of the security and privacy posture. These ongoing updates support real-time risk management and the continuous authorization process.

  The frequency of updates is determined by the system owner, common control provider, and AOs, based on federal and organizational policies. Automated tools and security program management practices ensure that senior leaders can access up-to-date information on the system's security and privacy status. This timely access supports continuous monitoring and ongoing authorization, facilitating effective risk management for the organization. Additionally, configuration management ensures that information for oversight, management, and auditing is not altered or lost, maintaining transparency, accountability, and traceability in security and privacy activities. The following table shows the roles to perform key authorization package updates:

Primary responsibility	Supporting roles	SDLC phase	References
System owner; common control provider	Information owner or steward; system security officer; system privacy officer; senior agency official for privacy; senior agency information security officer.	New: Operations/ maintenance Existing: Operations/ maintenance	NIST SP 800-30; SP 800-53A

Table 20.4: Roles to perform key updates

- **Task 5: Report security and privacy status**: Monitoring results are documented and reported to the AO and other key organizational officials regularly, following the organization's continuous monitoring strategy. These officials may include roles like the **chief information officer** (**CIO**), senior security officers, and risk management leaders. Security and privacy posture reports can be event-driven, time-driven, or a combination, and they provide information on the effectiveness of implemented controls, ongoing monitoring activities, and any discovered risks. The reports also detail how these risks are being addressed by system owners or common control providers.

The frequency and format of these reports are determined by the organization, following federal and organizational policies. Reports are made at appropriate intervals to convey key security and privacy information without causing unnecessary burden. They summarize updates to security plans, assessments, and action plans since the last report. Automated reporting tools help improve the timeliness and effectiveness of these reports. The reports are handled according to policy and can be used to meet FISMA reporting requirements. Overall, the goal is to maintain ongoing, cost-effective communication about the security and privacy posture of systems. The following table shows the roles to report security and privacy status:

Primary responsibility	Supporting roles	SDLC phase	References
System owner; common control provider; senior agency information security officer; senior agency official for privacy	System security officer; system privacy officer	New: Operations/ maintenance Existing: Operations/ maintenance	NIST SP 800-53A; SP 800-137; NIST CSF

Table 20.5: Roles to report security and privacy status

- **Task 6: Perform ongoing risk determination and acceptance**: To support ongoing authorization, organizations implement continuous monitoring at both the organization and system levels to assess control s regularly. The results of this monitoring help AOs make near-real-time, risk-based decisions by reviewing the system's security and privacy posture. The AO evaluates whether the current risk is acceptable and provides guidance to the system owner or common control provider. Depending on the findings, the official may determine that the risk is acceptable for continued operation or decide to deny authorization or take other corrective actions.

Changes in risk are reflected in security and privacy posture reports, which help determine how evolving conditions impact organizational and individual risks. By continuously assessing and accepting risks, AOs can maintain the system and control authorizations over time. Reauthorization is done based on federal or organizational policies. Automated tools like dashboards and metrics play a key role in managing and displaying risk information, helping decision-makers at all levels understand and respond to security and privacy risks efficiently.

The following table shows the roles to perform ongoing risk determination and acceptance:

Primary responsibility	Supporting roles	SDLC phase	References
AO	Senior accountable official for risk management or risk executive (function); CIO; senior agency information security officer; senior agency official for privacy; AO designated representative	New: Operations/ maintenance Existing: Operations/ maintenance	NIST SP 800-30; SP 800-39; SP 800-55; SP 800-160 v1

Table 20.6: Roles to perform risk determination and acceptance

- **Task 7: Information system disposal**: When a system is taken out of operation, organizations must take several risk management steps to ensure proper disposal. This includes implementing controls for tasks like media sanitization, configuration management, and ensuring the authenticity of components. Tracking systems and inventory records are updated to reflect the system's removal. Security and privacy posture reports are adjusted to show the current status of the system, and users and application owners are notified. Any control inheritance relationships are reviewed for potential impact.

The same procedures apply when specific elements of a system are removed. Organizations update their inventory systems to reflect these changes, and system owners and security personnel ensure compliance with applicable laws, regulations, and standards during the disposal process. This ensures that all disposed systems are properly managed and in line with federal requirements. The following table shows the roles to perform information system disposal:

Primary responsibility	Supporting roles	SDLC phase	References
System owner	AO or AO designated representative; information owner or steward; system security officer; system privacy officer; senior accountable official for risk management or risk executive (function); senior agency information security officer; senior agency official for privacy	New: Not applicable Existing: Disposal	NIST SP 800-30; SP 800-88

Table 20.7: Roles to perform system disposal

System decommissioning

Information disposition and sanitization decisions are critical throughout the information SDLC, starting with the system's initial development phase. During this phase, the system requirements should specify hardware, software, interconnections, and data flow, which help the system owner identify the types of media used within the system. Some storage devices offer enhanced sanitization commands, which can simplify and improve the effectiveness of media sanitization. However, for emerging media types, effective sanitization procedures may not be fully defined, and in such cases, the destruction of the media may be the only viable option, preventing reuse by other organizations.

Determining the types of media used to create, capture, or transfer information should be part of the system requirements phase. This analysis, which balances business needs with risks to confidentiality, helps ensure the media used conforms to FIPS 200 standards. While media sanitization and information disposition activities are most critical during the system's disposal phase, throughout the system's life, various media containing sensitive data will be transferred outside the organization's control. This transfer may occur for maintenance, upgrades, or configuration changes, requiring ongoing attention to secure handling and sanitization of the data involved.

Types of sanitizations

Sanitization is the process of making data on a storage device impossible to recover, no matter how much effort someone puts into trying to get it back. The level of difficulty in retrieving the data can range from basic attempts, like simple hacking methods, to advanced techniques that require specialized tools and knowledge. The goal of sanitization is to ensure that unauthorized people cannot access or recover the data, no matter what tools or skills they have. Here are the three categories of media sanitization, as defined by NIST SP 800-88:

- **Clear:**
  - Applies logical techniques to sanitize data in all user-addressable storage locations.
  - Protects against simple, non-invasive data recovery methods.
  - Typically, it involves overwriting data with new values or using a reset option to restore the device to its factory state.
  - Used when a device can be reused after sanitization.

- **Purge:**
  - Uses more advanced physical or logical techniques to make data recovery infeasible.
  - Protects against data recovery using state-of-the-art laboratory techniques.
  - Often involves techniques that make it difficult to recover data using advanced recovery methods.

- **Destroy:**
  - Makes data recovery infeasible by using state-of-the-art laboratory techniques.

- o   Results in the complete destruction of the media, making it impossible to reuse for data storage.
- o   Ensures that no data remains recoverable, even by sophisticated means.

Key roles in system decommissioning

The roles and responsibilities in system decommissioning are vital due to the involvement of information types in media disks and data sensitivity. Following are the key roles in decommissioning based on the information provided:

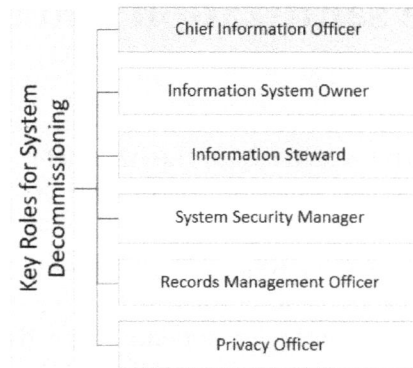

Figure 20.4: Key roles in system decommissioning

Here is the breakdown of responsibilities:

- **CIO**: The CIO is responsible for developing and enforcing information security policies, including those related to information disposition and media sanitization. As the information custodian, the CIO ensures that the organization's sanitization practices comply with established guidelines and are consistently applied during decommissioning.

- **Information system owner**: The system owner is responsible for ensuring that contracts or maintenance agreements are in place to protect the confidentiality of system media and information. They ensure that the system's data is sanitized in accordance with its security categorization before decommissioning.

- **Information owner/steward**: This role involves overseeing media maintenance and ensuring that service providers follow appropriate sanitization practices. The information owner is also responsible for understanding the sensitivity of the data and ensuring users are aware of its confidentiality requirements.

- **System security manager/officer**: Often called the ISSO, this person manages the day-to-day security of a system. They coordinate and implement security measures for a particular system and ensure that all security requirements are met during the decommissioning process.

- **Records management officer**: This officer advises the system or data owner on the legal and regulatory retention requirements for records. Their role ensures that necessary records are not destroyed during the sanitization of media, and that proper retention is followed according to policy.

- **Privacy officer**: Responsible for addressing privacy concerns, the privacy officer advises on issues related to the disposition of private or sensitive information, ensuring that any privacy-related data is properly handled and sanitized in compliance with relevant laws and organizational policies.

Factors to decide sanitization and disposal decisions

The decision to sanitize and dispose of media should be based on the confidentiality of the information it contains. The sensitivity of the data determines the level of protection required during sanitization. For example, highly sensitive or classified information demands stricter methods to ensure the data is unrecoverable.

Once the level of sanitization is set, the type of media, such as hard drives, optical disks, or flash drives, determines the specific technique to use. Methods like overwriting, degaussing, or physical destruction may be employed depending on the media type to ensure the data is securely erased. In addition to confidentiality, factors like cost-effectiveness also play a role in the decision-making process. For instance, using expensive methods for cheaper media may not be justified, and simply destroying the media might be more cost-effective in some cases. Organizations may also increase the level of sanitization if the risk assessment supports the need for it. Following are the factors involved in the decommissioning decision-making process:

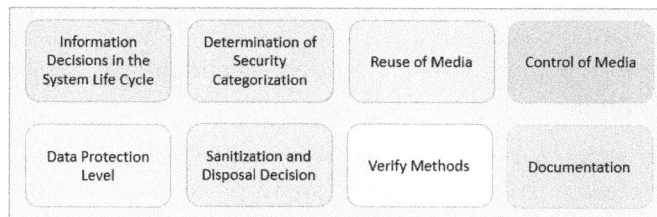

| Information Decisions in the System Life Cycle | Determination of Security Categorization | Reuse of Media | Control of Media |
| Data Protection Level | Sanitization and Disposal Decision | Verify Methods | Documentation |

Figure 20.5: Factors affecting system decommissioning

Here is the breakdown of the decommissioning decision-making process:

- **Information decisions in the system lifecycle**: Throughout the lifecycle of the system, decisions related to the management of information need to be made. These decisions include data storage, access control, and, ultimately, the proper disposal or sanitization of data when the system is decommissioned.

- **Determination of security categorization**: Before decommissioning a system, it is essential to assess the security classification of the system and its data. This categorization determines the level of protection and sanitization methods required. High-security systems may require more robust sanitization and destruction techniques.

- **Reuse of media**: If any media (such as hard drives, tapes, or other storage devices) is intended for reuse, it is crucial to assess the risk involved in repurposing the media. This involves considering whether the media can be securely wiped, whether it can be used in another system without compromising data security, and if the sanitization techniques are sufficient.

- **Control of media**: Proper control over the physical and logical access to media is essential during decommissioning. This step ensures that only authorized personnel handle the media and that it is adequately tracked during the disposal or sanitization process.

- **Data protection level**: The level of protection required for the data should be assessed, considering the sensitivity and confidentiality requirements. This will dictate the sanitization methods used (clear, purge, or destroy) to ensure that no data can be recovered from the media.

- **Sanitization and disposal decision**: Based on the security categorization and data protection requirements, decisions should be made regarding how the media will be sanitized or destroyed. This may include wiping data using software methods, physically destroying the media, or applying other techniques like degaussing.

- **Verify methods**: After applying the chosen sanitization or destruction methods, it is essential to verify that the data has been effectively removed and that the media is no longer usable. Verification ensures that no sensitive information remains recoverable.

- **Documentation**: Finally, the entire decommissioning process, including the sanitization and disposal methods, must be thoroughly documented. This documentation serves as evidence for audits, regulatory compliance, and risk management purposes. It should include records of what data was removed, how it was sanitized, and any verification or disposal activities carried out.

Ongoing system maintenance

Ongoing maintenance of the **system security plan** (SSP) is essential to ensure that it remains accurate and up-to-date throughout the lifecycle of an information system. Regularly reviewing the SSP helps ensure it reflects any changes in the system's status, design, or functionality. This review is critical for system recertification and reaccreditation activities. At a minimum, the SSP should be reviewed and updated annually. During this review, several key changes should be considered as following:

- **Change in the information system owner**: If there is a change in ownership or responsibility, the new owner must ensure that security controls remain adequate.

- **Change in the information security representative**: Updates should be made if there is a new designated security representative overseeing the system.

- **Major changes in system architecture**: Significant architectural modifications may introduce new risks or vulnerabilities that need to be addressed in the SSP.

- **Change in system status**: Any shift in operational status, such as a transition to a different environment or modification of system functionalities, should be incorporated.

- **Additions or deletions of system interconnections**: New interconnections or the removal of existing ones could alter the security landscape of the system.

- **Changes in system scope**: Expanding or narrowing the system's scope could affect security requirements and need to be documented.

- **Change in the AO**: If the individual responsible for system authorization changes, it may require a reassessment of risks and security measures.

Regular updates to the SSP ensure that security measures continue to reflect the system's current state, helping protect sensitive information and maintain the system's accreditation. This process aligns with requirements set by the *Office of Management and Budget* (*OMB*) and the FISMA, ensuring that systems remain secure and compliant over time. Reauthorization should occur before significant changes, or at least every three years, to maintain the validity of the system's security posture.

Develop and implement an ISCM strategy

The process for developing and implementing an **information security continuous monitoring** (**ISCM**) strategy and program is crucial for maintaining robust security controls and ensuring timely, risk-based decision-making across an organization. The strategy helps organizations continuously assess, monitor, and report on the security status of their information systems. Here is how to develop and implement an ISCM program, as shown in the following figure:

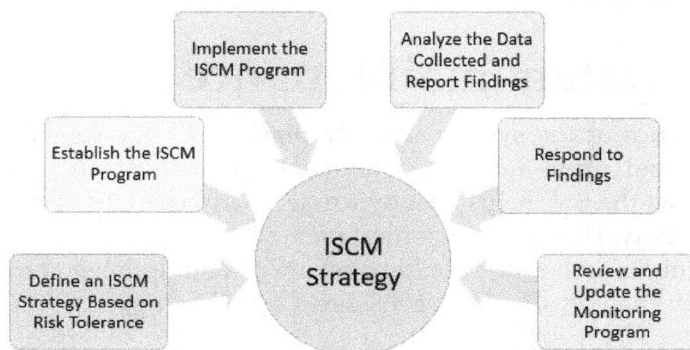

Figure 20.6: *ISCM strategy*

Here is the breakdown of the ISCM strategy:

- **Define an ISCM strategy based on risk tolerance**:

  o Establish clear goals for visibility into organizational assets, awareness of vulnerabilities, and understanding of potential mission or business impacts.

  o Ensure that the strategy incorporates up-to-date threat intelligence and prioritizes security based on the organization's risk tolerance and specific needs.

  o Align the ISCM strategy with the overall RMF to ensure effective risk-based decision-making across the organization.

- **Establish the ISCM program**:

  o Determine key metrics and establish monitoring frequencies to assess the status of security controls.

  o Define the frequency of conducting security control assessments and ensure continuous alignment with business objectives.

  o Design the technical architecture for the ISCM program, including tools, systems, and platforms needed to support data collection, analysis, and reporting.

- **Implement the ISCM program**:

  o Collect security-related information required to monitor metrics, conduct assessments, and generate security status reports.

  o Automate data collection, analysis, and reporting where feasible to improve efficiency and reduce manual effort.

  o Use appropriate tools and technologies to gather real-time data, such as intrusion detection systems, vulnerability scanners, and **security information and event management** (**SIEM**) systems.

- **Analyze the data collected and report findings**:

  o Continuously analyze the collected data to assess the effectiveness of security controls and identify potential weaknesses or vulnerabilities.

  o Create detailed reports on security status, highlighting significant issues and trends.

  o When necessary, gather additional information to clarify findings or supplement existing data to ensure a complete and accurate understanding of the security posture.

- **Respond to findings**:
  - o Determine the appropriate response to identified vulnerabilities or security risks, such as:
    - ▪ **Mitigating activities**: Implement technical, management, and operational measures to reduce or eliminate identified risks.
    - ▪ **Acceptance**: Accept certain risks if they fall within the organization's risk tolerance.
    - ▪ **Transference/sharing**: Share risks with external parties (e.g., outsourcing, third-party risk sharing).
    - ▪ **Avoidance/rejection**: Avoid activities that introduce unacceptable risk or reject systems/processes that pose too great a threat.
  - o Ensure timely and appropriate responses to mitigate or resolve vulnerabilities, making informed decisions based on risk assessments.
- **Review and update the monitoring program**:
  - o Regularly review the ISCM program's performance and effectiveness.
  - o Adjust the ISCM strategy as necessary to improve asset visibility, increase awareness of vulnerabilities, and enhance organizational resilience.
  - o Evolve measurement capabilities to adapt to changes in the organization's infrastructure, emerging threats, or new regulations.

Configuration scanning

Configuration scanning is a process used to assess and verify the security settings of information systems, networks, and devices to ensure compliance with established security standards. Automated tools are typically used to examine system configurations, such as software settings, hardware setups, and network configurations. These tools help detect vulnerabilities, misconfigurations, or deviations from security policies, aiming to identify potential risks and fix them to improve the system's security.

These tools compare system configurations against predefined benchmarks, such as CIS Benchmarks or NIST SP 800-53, generating reports that highlight areas of non-compliance or weaknesses. Regular configuration scanning is crucial for maintaining secure configurations, especially as systems are updated or changed. It helps organizations identify and address vulnerabilities before they can be exploited, reducing the risk of security breaches or system failures.

Configuration management tools also play a key role in automating the process of configuring, monitoring, and restoring system settings. They enhance efficiency, reliability, and cost-effectiveness, offering significant improvements over manual configuration management methods. These tools ensure compliance with security standards and help maintain system integrity by verifying that systems align with secure baseline configurations, preventing deviations that could compromise security.

Monitoring and security metrics

Ongoing monitoring and configuration scanning ensure systems remain in compliance with security policies and help mitigate risks of security breaches. Following are the key monitoring and security metrics:

- **Visibility into the security posture**:
  - Continuous monitoring tools provide real-time insight into the overall security status of systems and networks.
  - By tracking compliance with predefined security metrics, these tools give administrators a clear view of how systems are performing in terms of security.

- **Tracking security metrics**:
  - Key metrics include system configurations, patch management, threat detection, user activity, and adherence to security policies.
  - These metrics allow organizations to stay updated on the effectiveness of security controls and identify areas that need attention or improvement.

- **Identifying weaknesses and risks**:
  - The tools help in spotting vulnerabilities, misconfigurations, or deviations from established security protocols.
  - Continuous monitoring can detect potential security incidents, such as unauthorized access attempts, policy violations, or failed system updates.

- **Proactive risk management**:
  - With ongoing tracking, organizations can act quickly when deviations or failures in security controls are detected, reducing response time to threats.
  - This proactive approach helps minimize the risk of data breaches and improves the overall security resilience of systems.

- **Compliance and reporting**:
  - Continuous monitoring tools support compliance by ensuring that systems remain aligned with regulatory requirements and security standards.
  - These tools often generate reports, helping organizations document their security posture and compliance for audits and other assessments.

Ongoing assessments

After the initial system or control authorization, organizations must continuously evaluate the effectiveness of their security controls as part of their ongoing monitoring activities. This helps ensure that security measures remain effective over time and that they still comply with the requirements set by the AO. The frequency of these assessments is based on the organization's monitoring strategy and can be adjusted at the system level to align with specific needs.

The assessments are usually conducted by independent evaluators to ensure objectivity, which is crucial for unbiased results. These assessments can also be reused for future assessments or reauthorizations, helping organizations save time and resources. For example, results from previous evaluations or audits can fulfil annual security assessment requirements as long as they remain current and relevant. There are various ways to determine if the assessment results are current and relevant. This includes if there are changes in the system/environment or regulations, if there are emerging threats or vulnerabilities, if the risk profile is up-to-date, and if there are any incidents reported. Automating some of these processes can further increase the efficiency and effectiveness of control assessments, helping organizations maintain a secure and compliant system.

Ongoing risk response

During continuous monitoring, assessors gather and provide assessment information to the system owner and common control provider, usually through updated reports or automated tools. The AO reviews these findings and determines the appropriate response to the identified risks. The system owner and control provider then implement the decided risk response.

If the response is accepted, the findings are documented, and the risks are continuously monitored for changes. If the response is mitigation, specific actions are outlined in **plans of action and milestones** (**POA&Ms**), with progress tracked. In some cases, the AO may ask control assessors for remediation recommendations, which, along with insights from automated tools, guide the remediation process. If controls are modified or added, they are reassessed to ensure proper implementation and effectiveness in reducing security and privacy risks.

Security testing

Security testing is a crucial process in determining how effectively an entity, such as a system, network, or procedure, meets specific security objectives. It is one of the key assessment methods, along with examination and interviewing, used to evaluate the effectiveness of security controls. During security testing, assessment objects (system, network, security controls or other components) are subjected to controlled conditions to compare their actual behavior with expected outcomes. This helps identify vulnerabilities, weaknesses, and non-compliance with security requirements. The results of the testing process are used to support ongoing evaluations of security control effectiveness and to guide improvements in security posture.

Security testing is an essential part of compliance with regulations like the FISMA, as well as other industry standards. It serves to validate and assess technical vulnerabilities, offering a way to confirm that systems are properly secured and that all necessary security measures are in place. While security testing does not replace the implementation of security controls, it plays a vital role in ensuring that these controls are functioning as intended and in identifying areas that need further attention or improvement.

Testing viewpoints

From a testing viewpoint, security tests can be performed from various perspectives to evaluate the system's resilience against different threats. One important distinction is between external and internal viewpoints. An external viewpoint simulates attacks from outside the organization, typically by an outsider with no prior knowledge of the system. This helps assess the effectiveness of perimeter defenses, like firewalls, intrusion detection systems, and access control mechanisms. In contrast, an internal viewpoint simulates attacks from within the organization, such as by a malicious insider or an attacker who has already bypassed external defenses.

Another key consideration in testing viewpoints is the previous knowledge that assessors have of the target system or environment. Testing can be conducted with limited knowledge (often called **black-box testing**), where assessors have no insight into the system's architecture or operation, mimicking a real-world attack scenario. Alternatively, grey-box or white-box testing may be performed, where assessors have varying degrees of knowledge, such as access to system documentation or the source code. These differing knowledge levels allow for more targeted testing approaches, with black-box tests simulating a real attacker and white-box tests providing deeper insights into vulnerabilities by reviewing system design and configurations.

Technical assessment techniques

There are numerous technical security testing and examination techniques available to assess the security posture of systems and networks. These techniques can be categorized into the following three main groups:

- **Review techniques**: These are primarily manual examination methods used to evaluate systems, applications, networks, policies, and procedures for vulnerabilities. They include reviewing documentation, logs, rulesets, and system configurations, performing network sniffing, and checking file integrity. These techniques are focused on discovering weaknesses through careful inspection of existing materials and systems.

- **Target identification and analysis techniques**: These techniques, often automated, are used to identify systems, ports, services, and potential vulnerabilities. Methods like network discovery, network port and service identification, vulnerability scanning, wireless scanning, and application security examination fall under this category. These techniques are generally automated, allowing for efficient scanning and identification of vulnerabilities across large systems.

- **Target vulnerability validation techniques**: Once vulnerabilities are identified, these techniques are used to validate their existence. They include password cracking, penetration testing, social engineering, and application security testing. These methods, which may involve both manual efforts and automated tools, are crucial for confirming vulnerabilities and testing the effectiveness of security measures in real-world scenarios.

Risk impact

Risk impact assessment involves evaluating the potential effects of identified risks on a project's key objectives, including cost, schedule, technical performance, and other relevant factors, such as political or economic impacts. The assessment aims to gauge both the likelihood of risk events occurring and their potential severity. This often involves subjective probability techniques when direct evaluation is not feasible. Furthermore, the assessment should account for risk dependencies and interdependencies, as well as the timing of the potential impact, whether it is short-term, mid-term, or long-term.

Steps to create a risk impact matrix

Creating an effective risk impact matrix involves four key steps to ensure a thorough and actionable risk management process. The four steps are shown in the following figure:

Identify Risks	Analyze Risks	Assess Risk Impact	Prioritize Risks

Figure 20.7: Steps to create the risk impact matrix

Here is the breakdown of each step:

- **Identify risks**: The first step is gathering a comprehensive list of potential risks. You can involve team members from various departments to get diverse perspectives and consider risks from different categories such as financial, operational, and strategic. Use techniques like SWOT analysis, historical data review, and expert interviews to identify risks. These risks should be documented in a risk register for reference and further analysis.

- **Analyze risks**: Risk analysis helps assess the likelihood and impact of each identified risk. Quantitative methods, like assigning numerical probabilities and estimating financial impacts, can be used, especially in complex scenarios. Qualitative analysis relies on descriptive scales to categorize risks as Very Low, Low, Medium, High, or Very High.

- **Assess risk impact**: After analyzing the risks, it is important to assess their potential consequences. Create a standardized impact scale (e.g., 1-5 or 1-10) and define criteria for each level of impact—such as financial loss, operational disruption, reputational damage, or legal compliance issues. For example, a data breach might have a medium probability but a high impact due to significant financial and reputational consequences.

- **Prioritize risks**: With the risk impact matrix, you can prioritize risks based on their probability and impact scores. High-priority risks are typically in the top-right quadrant of the matrix. Develop mitigation strategies for these risks, such as avoiding, transferring, mitigating, or accepting them. Allocate resources effectively based on risk priorities. Regularly review and update the matrix to accommodate new information or changing circumstances.

Third-party contract management

Third-party contract management involves overseeing agreements between an organization and external entities like suppliers, vendors, contractors, or service providers. These external parties play a crucial role in an organization's operations; hence, managing the entire contract lifecycle is essential to ensure compliance, mitigate risks, and enhance performance. This includes drafting and negotiating contracts, conducting due diligence, and monitoring the performance of these third-parties.

The key elements of a third-party contract include the rights, duties, and benefits of the third-party, as well as the conditions under which they are involved. Understanding these elements helps clarify the roles and responsibilities of all parties involved, ensuring that the third-party's participation is clearly defined. By doing so, the contract becomes a comprehensive framework for managing relationships and expectations between the original parties and the third entity. Effective contract management ensures both parties meet their obligations and comply with legal and regulatory standards. By addressing any issues that arise, organizations can reduce risks and legal liabilities.

Managing third-party contracts

Managing third-party contracts is crucial for mitigating risks such as financial, legal, operational, and reputational hazards. Effective contract management ensures clarity, compliance, and accountability, helping to avoid penalties, disputes, or business disruptions caused by vendor failures or violations. A structured approach to managing contracts can significantly reduce these risks and maintain smooth business operations as shown in the following figure:

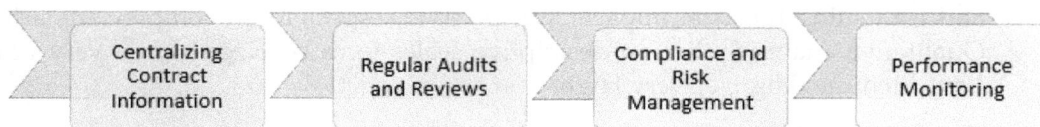

Figure 20.8: Third-party contracts management

Here is the breakdown of the approach to managing third-party contract:

- **Centralizing contract information**: Centralizing contract data in a single repository improves control and access. Using tools, businesses can track contracts, maintain version control, and ensure that stakeholders are always working with the most current information. This centralization also allows for tighter access control, limiting sensitive contract details to authorized personnel and reducing the risk of unauthorized changes.

- **Regular audits and reviews**: Ongoing audits and reviews are vital to maintaining compliance and improving contract performance. These reviews track deliverables, ensure adherence to **service-level agreements** (**SLAs**), and identify risks early. Performance evaluations and legal compliance audits should be conducted regularly to spot issues and make adjustments.

- **Compliance and risk management**: Managing third-party risks is essential to avoid financial and legal penalties. Contracts should comply with relevant industry regulations, such as GDPR or HIPAA, especially when working with international vendors. Conducting thorough risk assessments, including evaluating the vendor's financial stability and reputation, is critical.

- **Performance monitoring**: Monitoring vendor performance ensures they meet contractual commitments. Setting measurable KPIs and SLAs from the start helps track performance in areas such as quality, timeliness, and customer satisfaction. Tools performance dashboards provide insights to monitor vendor performance and identify issues early.

Conclusion

In this chapter, we thoroughly discussed continuous monitoring and its key role in maintaining the effectiveness of security controls. We highlighted the importance of the system decommissioning process and provided insight into the significance of ongoing system maintenance and assessments to ensure continued security. Additionally, we explored configuration scanning and security testing, emphasizing their role in identifying and mitigating vulnerabilities.

We also covered risk impact analysis, helping to understand potential threats and their consequences, and third-party contract management, which is crucial for managing external risks and ensuring compliance. As we transition to the next chapter, we will now dive into practice questions that will help reinforce and test your understanding of the concepts covered.

Key terms

- A risk impact matrix, also known as a risk assessment matrix, is a powerful tool that combines the probability and impact scores of each identified risk and ranks them in terms of priority for management.

- Active security testing involves direct interaction with a target system or network to assess its security. This testing typically includes sending packets, requests, or commands to the target to evaluate how the system responds to potential threats or vulnerabilities.

- Covert testing involves testing a system or network without the knowledge of the organization's IT staff, but with approval from upper management.

- Overt testing is security testing conducted with the full knowledge and consent of the organization's IT staff.

- Information security testing is the process of verifying that security controls for information systems and networks are properly implemented, based on the organization's security requirements.

- A SSP is a formal document that outlines the security requirements for an information system and details the security controls implemented or planned to meet those requirements.

- Continuous monitoring of security controls, supported by automated tools, enables near-real-time risk management and marks a significant shift from traditional security authorization methods.

- Acceptance testing is conducted after system testing and just before product deployment. It takes place in the final stages of the software development lifecycle to ensure the system meets the required specifications and is ready for release.

- UAT, also known as application testing, is the final stage in the software development or change request lifecycle. It occurs before the system goes live, ensuring that the software meets the needs and expectations of the end users.

- Security impact analysis is conducted by an organizational official to assess how changes to an information system have impacted its security state.

- Third-party risks can greatly affect an organization, especially when it comes to security. These risks can lead to data breaches, compromising sensitive information and potentially violating privacy laws.

Join our book's Discord space

Join the book's Discord Workspace for Latest updates, Offers, Tech happenings around the world, New Release and Sessions with the Authors:

https://discord.bpbonline.com

CHAPTER 21
Practice Tests

Practice test 1 questions

1. What Risk Management Framework role is primarily responsible for tasks 1, 2, and 3 in assessing security controls?

    a. Security control assessor

    b. Security assessment report

    c. Security control assessment

    d. Assess security controls

2. Which organizational official is responsible for identifying assessment methodologies and metrics to ensure that privacy controls are meeting the organization's privacy requirements?

    a. Security control assessor

    b. Authorizing official

    c. Senior Agency Official for Privacy

    d. Information system owner

3. **The National Institutes of Standards and Technology guidance classifies security controls as?**

    a. System-specific, common and hybrid

    b. Production, development, and test

    c. People, process, and technology

    d. Technical, administrative, and program

4. **Testing must include an assessment of the _____ as described in the system security plan, as recorded in the risk assessment, and reflected in the accreditation boundary; all should be the same.**

    a. System boundary

    b. Authorization boundary

    c. Network boundary

    d. All of the above

5. **An organization's decision on acceptable degrees of residual risks should be based on what? Choose one.**

    a. System-level risk appetite

    b. Organizational risk picture

    c. Organizational risk tolerance

    d. Tier 3 risk tolerance

6. **Which of the following statements is true about residual risks?**

    a. It is a weakness or lack of safeguard that can be exploited by a threat.

    b. It can be considered as an indicator of threats coupled with vulnerability.

    c. It is the probabilistic risk after implementing all security measures.

    d. It is the probabilistic risk before implementing all security measures.

7. **Who is primarily responsible for the development of system-specific procedures?**

    a. The system owner

    b. Information system security officer

    c. The system architect

    d. The system administrator

8. **Which NIST SP describes various sensitivity rankings for federal systems; Guide for Developing Security Plans for Federal Info Systems?**

    a. NIST SP 800-18

    b. NIST SP 800-15

    c. NIST SP 800-19

    d. NIST SP 800-20

9. **XYZ hardware is located in a single computer room, and access to the room is permitted only to the few system users who have the required privileges. To access the computer room, which is restricted by door locks, proximity cards, and personal identification pins are required. Relative to the hardware in the computer room, the door lock and the PIN are examples of what type of security control?**

    a. Managerial

    b. Technical

    c. System-specific

    d. Common

10. **Which NIST SP 800 series document is concerned with continuous monitoring for Federal Information Systems and organizations?**

    a. SP 800-26

    b. SP 800-64

    c. SP 800-137

    d. SP 800-144

11. **The final security assessment report should contain findings from the security control assessment and which of the ensuing?**

    a. Determination of residual risk

    b. Security control assessment plan

    c. System security plan and concept of operations

    d. Recommendations for control remediations

12. **James works as an IT systems personnel in XYZ Inc. He performs the following tasks:**

    a. Runs regular backups and routine tests of the validity of the backup data.

    b. Performs data restoration from the backups whenever required.

    c. Maintains the retained records in accordance with the established information classification policy.

What is the role played by James in the organization?

    a. Manager

    b. Owner

    c. Custodian

    d. User

13. **What type of testing is a physical review or examination of control, such as review of the security setting or software version number?**

    a. Inspection

    b. Demonstration

    c. Examination

    d. Organization

14. **The change control board team at XYZ Tech has determined the security impact of proposed changes to an application, what would be the team's next action?**

    a. Update the system security plan, security assessment report, and plan of action and milestones based on the results of the change control board's security impact analysis.

    b. Assess a selected subset of the security controls employed within and inherited by the application in accordance with the organization-defined monitoring strategy.

    c. Prepare the security assessment report documenting the issues, findings, and recommendations from the security control assessment.

    d. Prepare the plan of action and milestones based on the findings and recommendations of the security assessment report excluding any remediation actions taken.

15. **Which publication that has the minimum-security requirements for Federal Information and Information Systems?**

    a. FIPS 199

    b. FIPS 200

    c. FIPS 299

    d. FIPS 300

16. **Which security category guards against the improper modification or destruction of information and includes ensuring information non-repudiation and authenticity?**

    a. Confidentiality

    b. Availability

    c. Integrity

    d. Authenticity

17. When making a determination regarding the adequacy of the implementation of inherited controls for their respective systems, an information system owner can refer to the authorization package prepared by which of the following?

    a. Information owner/steward

    b. Information system security engineer

    c. Information systems security officer

    d. Common control provider

18. **Which Risk Management Framework role establishes risk management roles and responsibilities and provides advice and relevant information to authorized officials concerning the risk management strategy to guide authorization decision-making?**

    a. Risk executive

    b. System owner

    c. Common control provider

    d. Information system security engineer

19. **When carrying out ongoing risk response, the effectiveness of new, modified, enhanced, or added controls must be?**

    a. Verified

    b. Reassessed

    c. Examined

    d. Tested

20. **Which of the following is an official authorization decision that is focused on specific controls implemented in a defined environment of operation to support one or more systems residing within the environment?**

    a. Authority to test

    b. Facility authorization

    c. Type authorization

    d. Joint authorization

21. **FIPS 200 provides how many minimum-security requirements for federal information and information systems?**

    a. 5

    b. 17

    c. 21

    d. 10

482 ■ Ultimate Guide to CGRC Certification

22. **The test plan should evaluate plans that support the information system; such as incident response, disaster recovery, and _____ plan to ensure they are up to date and meet the protection needs of the system.**

    a. Contingency plan

    b. Security plan

    c. Assessment plan

    d. Remediation plan

23. **Anything that can exploit a vulnerability, intentionally or accidentally, and obtain, damage, or destroy an asset best describes?**

    a. Risk

    b. Impact

    c. Vulnerability

    d. Threat

24. **Prepare, categorize, select, and implement are steps or phases of the Risk Management Framework that can be described as?**

    a. The certification phase of the system authorization plan.

    b. The pre-certification phase of the system authorization plan.

    c. The authorization phase of the system authorization plan.

    d. The post-authorization phase of the system authorization plan.

25. **Which role has the primary responsibility to conduct ongoing assessments after an initial system authorization?**

    a. Authorizing official

    b. Common control provider

    c. Security control assessor

    d. Information system owner

26. **At which point in the Risk Management Framework process is a system analyzed for changes that impact the security and privacy posture of the system?**

    a. Implement

    b. Assess

    c. Select

    d. Monitor

27. **In the case of a complex information system, where a leveraged authorization that involves two agencies will be conducted, what is the minimum number of system boundaries/accreditation boundaries that can exist?**

    a. Only one.

    b. Only two, because there are two agencies.

    c. At least two.

    d. A leveraged authorization cannot be conducted with more than one agency involved.

28. **What should the system owner use to prioritize mitigation actions when developing the plan of action and milestones?**

    a. Budget constraints

    b. Risk assessment results

    c. Continuous monitoring strategy

    d. Recommendations of the information owners

29. **During the security impact analysis, vulnerabilities were uncovered in the information system. Which of the following documents should address the outstanding items?**

    a. Plan of action and milestones

    b. System security plan

    c. System discrepancy plan

    d. System deficiency plan

30. **Why are subsystems within complex systems not treated as independent entities, whereas the subsystems may exist as complete systems?**

    a. Because subsystems cannot be authorized separately.

    b. Because subsystems are typically interdependent and interconnected.

    c. Because the system owner for the complex system is responsible for all the systems.

    d. Subsystems can be treated as independent entities.

31. **Assessment methods have a set of associated attributes that help define the level of effort for the assessment. Which of the following is the right pair of attributes?**

    a. Depth and coverage

    b. Coverage and scope

    c.   Breadth and coverage

    d.   Rigor and level of detail

32. **All components of an information system to be authorized for operation by an authorizing official and excludes separately authorized systems to which the information system is connected best defines?**

    a.   Authorization boundary

    b.   System boundary

    c.   Network boundary

    d.   Accreditation boundary

33. **A measure of the degree to which an organization depends on the information or information system for the success of a mission or of a business function best defines which of the following?**

    a.   Criticality

    b.   Sensitivity

    c.   Assurance

    d.   Confidentiality

34. **What are the five keys to a successful risk management program?**

    a.   **Option 1:**

        i.   Senior management's commitment

        ii.   Full support and participation IT team

        iii.   Competence of the risk assessment team

        iv.   User community awareness and cooperation

        v.   An ongoing evaluation and assessment of the IT-relate mission risks

    b.   **Option 2:**

        i.   Competence of the risk assessment team

        ii.   User community awareness and cooperation

        iii.   An ongoing evaluation and assessment of the IT-relate mission risks

        iv.   Junior management's commitment

        v.   Full support and participation IT team

    c.   **Option 3:**

        i.   Senior management's commitment

        ii.   Full support and participation IT team

        iii.   Competence of the risk assessment team

      iv.   An ongoing evaluation and assessment of the HR-relate mission risks

      v.   User community awareness and cooperation

   d. **Option 4**:

      i.   Full support and participation IT team

      ii.   Competence of the risk assessment team

      iii.   User community awareness and cooperation

      iv.   Senior management's commitment

      v.   An ongoing evaluation and assessment of the IT-relate mission safe

35. **Applying the first three steps in the Risk Management Framework to legacy systems can be viewed in what way to determine if the necessarily assessment report and sufficient security controls have been appropriately selected and allocated?**

   a. Sequential

   b. Level of effort

   c. Gap analysis

   d. Common control

36. **System authorization programs are marked by frequent failure due to, among other things, poor planning, poor systems inventory, failure to fix responsibility at the system-level, and?**

   a. Inability to work with remote teams.

   b. Lack of a program management office.

   c. Insufficient system rights.

   d. Lack of management support.

37. **When an authorization to operate is issued, which of the following roles authoritatively accepts residual risk on behalf of the organization?**

   a. Information owner

   b. Chief information security officer

   c. Authorizing official

   d. Authorizing official or the authorizing official's designated representative

38. **Information developed from Federal Information Processing Standard 19 may be used as an input to which authorization package document?**

   a. Security assessment report

   b. System security plan

    c. plan of action and milestone

    d. Authorization decision document

39. **Which of the following in an assessment plan that protects the security control assessment team from liability should the security control assessment result in unforeseen damage?**

    a. Non-invasive testing

    b. Manual testing

    c. Vulnerability scans

    d. Rules of engagement

40. **A written plan for recovering one or more information systems at an alternate facility in response to a major hardware or software failure or destruction of facilities. Which of the following supports this?**

    a. Disaster recovery plan

    b. Common Vulnerability Scoring System

    c. Continuity of operations plan

    d. Common Vulnerability and Exposures

41. **In which of the Risk Management Framework phases (task 3) is the conduct remediation actions based on the results of ongoing monitoring activities, assessment of risk, and outstanding items in the plan of action and milestone and milestones?**

    a. Risk Management Framework step 7, monitor

    b. Risk Management Framework step 6, authorize

    c. Risk Management Framework step 4, implement

    d. Risk Management Framework step 5, authorize

42. **A security control accessor was completed two years ago, but the surrounding environment had a major change. What, if anything, should the assessment team do with the previous results?**

    a. Assess only the controls that have changed.

    b. Determine changes and impacts.

    c. Reuse the results on the old assessment.

    d. Assess all controls for the system.

43. You need to create an overall policy for your organization that describes how your users can properly make use of company communications services, such as web browsing, e-mail, and File Transfer Protocol (FTP) services. Which of the following policies do you implement?

   a. Acceptable use policy

   b. Due care

   c. Privacy policy

   d. Service level agreement

44. You are developing metrics for senior management regarding control effectiveness and the risk posture of the organization. You need to create a metric that shows managers how potential risk has been reduced due to implementing several new controls over the past six months. You want to aggregate this measurement into one indicator. Which of the following would be the most effective indicator to show this reduction?

   a. Key performance indicator

   b. Key risk indicator

   c. Key management indicator

   d. Key control indicator

45. When determining the applicability of a specific security control, the security professional should utilize which type of guidance?

   a. Categorization guidance

   b. Selection guidance

   c. Scoping guidance

   d. Remediation guidance

46. The implementation of the assessment and the authorization process is an example of what type of risk response?

   a. Transfer

   b. Remediate

   c. Share

   d. Mitigate

47. A chronological record of system activities, including records of system accesses and operations performed in a given period best defines?

   a. Adequate security

   b. Resilience

    c. Assurance

    d. Audit log

48. **Which role has the supporting responsibility to coordinate changes to the system, assess the security impact and update the system security plan?**

    a. Information system security officer

    b. Information system owner

    c. Common control provider

    d. Senior agency information security officer

49. **A risk manager wants to better understand the factors in particular business processes that could lead to an incident. What activity should the risk manager perform?**

    a. Risk analysis

    b. Threat modelling

    c. Vulnerability analysis

    d. Root cause analysis

50. **If an organization shares financial and personal details of a client to other companies without prior consent of the individuals that organization is violating what following internet law?**

    a. Security law

    b. Copyright law

    c. Privacy law

    d. Trademark law

Practice test 1 answers

1. a
2. c
3. a
4. a
5. c
6. c
7. a
8. a
9. d

10. c
11. d
12. c
13. a
14. a
15. b
16. c
17. d
18. a
19. b
20. b
21. b
22. a
23. d
24. b
25. c
26. d
27. a
28. b
29. a
30. b
31. a
32. a
33. a
34. a
35. c
36. d
37. c
38. b
39. d
40. a
41. a
42. d

43. a

44. b

45. c

46. d

47. d

48. a

49. a

50. c

Practice test 2 questions

1. **An initial remediation action was taken by the information system owner based on findings from the security assessment report. What is the next appropriate step based on the Risk Management Framework ?**

    a. Information system owner documents the remedial action in the security plan.

    b. Include the remediation action taken by information system owner as an addendum to the security assessment report.

    c. Information system security officer documents the remediation action and informs the Information system owner.

    d. Remedial action taken is sent for review to the Information system security officer.

2. **Which of the following software development lifecycle phase maps to Risk Management Framework step 3 (select controls), task 6, plan review and approval?**

    a. Development/acquisition

    b. Operation/maintenance

    c. Mission/business process

    d. Criticality/sensitivity

3. **Which of the following NIST publications is the guide for security and privacy control assessments in Federal Information Systems and organizations?**

    a. NIST SP 800-53

    b. NIST SP 800-53A

    c. NIST SP 800-30

    d. NIST SP 800-39

4. **The assessed potential impact resulting from a compromise of the confidentiality, integrity, or availability of an information type is expressed as a value of low, moderate, or high?**

    a. Impact value

    b. Potential impact

    c. Impact result

    d. None

5. **A risk manager is performing risk analysis on a specific risk to better understand the risk and to identify potential remedies. Various aspects of the initial risk and its potential remedies are scored on a scale of 1–10. What type of risk analysis is being performed?**

    a. Qualitative risk analysis

    b. Quantitative risk analysis

    c. Semiquantitative risk analysis

    d. Factor Analysis of Information Risk

6. **What type of analysis is conducted before finalizing the security assessment report when using agile, iterative development?**

    a. Regression analysis

    b. Interim assessment

    c. Incremental assessment

    d. Executive assessment

7. **What key information does the authorizing official use to assist in determining the risk of an information system?**

    a. Security authorization package

    b. Plan of action and milestones

    c. Security plan

    d. Interconnection security agreement

8. **Which of the following potential inputs to the authorization package is not considered a living document?**

    a. Supporting assessment documents

    b. plan of action and milestones

    c. Security and privacy assessment reports

    d. Security and privacy plan

9. **What key information is used by the authorizing official to assist with the risk determination of an information system?**

    a. Security authorization package

    b. Plan of action and milestone

    c. Security plan

    d. Interconnection security assessment

10. **A key part of the risk-based decision process is the recognition that regardless of the risk response, there remains some risks known as?**

    a. Risk analysis

    b. Risk mitigation

    c. Residual risk

    d. Risk tolerance level

11. **What should the system owner use to prioritize mitigation efforts when creating the plan of action and milestone?**

    a. Budget constraints

    b. Risk assessment results

    c. Continuous monitoring strategy

    d. Recommendations of the information owners

12. **When attempting to categorize a system which two Risk Management Framework starting point inputs should be accounted for and are critical input to categorization?**

    a. Architectural descriptions and organizational inputs.

    b. Federal laws and organizational policies.

    c. Federal laws and Office of Management and Budget policies.

    d. Federal Information Security Management Act and the Privacy Act.

13. **Which organizational official is responsible for identifying assessment methodologies and metrics to ensure that privacy controls are meeting the organization's privacy requirements?**

    a. Security control accessor

    b. Authorizing official

    c. Senior Agency Official for Privacy

    d. Information security owner

14. **The initial security plan for a new application has been approved. What is the next activity in the Risk Management Framework ?**

    a. Develop a strategy for the continuous monitoring of security control effectiveness.

    b. Assess a selected subset of the security controls inherited by the information system.

    c. Develop a new strategy for the continuous monitoring of security control effectiveness.

    d. Assemble the security authorization package.

15. **A security officer is implementing a new system with their existing organization IT environment. What objectives are considered when determining possible impact to risk?**

    a. Low, moderate, and high

    b. Authentication, authorization, and accountability

    c. Common, hybrid, and system-specific

    d. Integrity, confidentiality, and availability

16. **Which of the following are phases of the National Institute of Standards and Technology Risk Management Framework ?**

    a. Categorize, select, implement, authorize

    b. Assess, certify, accredit, manage

    c. Prepare, execute, authorize, monitor

    d. Assess, mitigate, authorize, monitor

17. **Which of the following is the primary risk factor when integrating new or emerging technologies into an existing IT infrastructure?**

    a. Security mechanisms

    b. Data format

    c. Vendor supportability

    d. Interoperability

18. **You are preparing to start the qualitative risk analysis process for your project. You will be relying on some organizational process assets to influence the process. Which one of the following is not a probable reason for relying on organizational process assets as an input for qualitative risk analysis?**

    a. Information on prior, similar projects

    b. Review of vendor contracts to examine risks in past projects

    c.   Risk databases that may be available from industry sources

    d.   Studies of similar projects by risk specialists

19. **The documentation of a predefined set of procedures or instructions to identify, respond to, and mitigate the effects of malicious cyberattacks on an organization's information system(s). Which of the following support this?**

    a.   Incident response plan

    b.   Contingency plan

    c.   Operations plan

    d.   Disaster recovery plan

20. **The use of automation to manage changes to the information system or its environment of operation facilitates which of the following?**

    a.   Security impact analysis

    b.   Plan of actions and milestones

    c.   Remediation plans

    d.   Security control assessments

21. **The amount of time mission/business processes can be disrupted without causing significant harm to the organization's mission?**

    a.   Maximum tolerable downtime

    b.   Recovery time objective

    c.   System of records notice

    d.   Disaster recovery plan

22. **Basic testing is a testing methodology that assumes no prior knowledge of the internal structure or implementation details of the assessment object. This type of testing is also referred to as?**

    a.   Gray-box testing

    b.   White-box testing

    c.   Black-box testing

    d.   Penetration testing

23. **Which authorization approach considers time elapsed since the authorization results were produced, the environment of operation, the criticality/sensitivity of the information, and the risk tolerance of the other organization?**

    a.   Leveraged

    b.   Single

    c. Joint

    d. Site specific

24. **Which NIST SP describes various sensitivity rankings for federal systems; Guide for Developing Security Plans for Federal Info Systems?**

    a. NIST SP 800-18

    b. NIST SP 800-15

    c. NIST SP 800-19

    d. NIST SP 800-20

25. **The security controls for an information system that focus on the management of risk and the management of information system security are known as?**

    a. Operational controls

    b. Technical controls

    c. Management controls

    d. Logical controls

26. **The Risk Management Framework Step and task where the system security plan is initially approved by the authorizing official or authorizing official designated representative is?**

    a. Risk Management Framework step 3, task 4

    b. Risk Management Framework step 3, task 2

    c. Risk Management Framework step 2, task 3

    d. Risk Management Framework step 2, task 1

27. **Who is responsible for securing an information system, managing all security aspects of the system, and assembling the security accreditation package while serving as the point of contact for the security control assessor?**

    a. Information system owner

    b. Information system security officer

    c. Common control provider

    d. Information system security engineer

28. **What are the management, operational, and technical controls (i.e., safeguards or countermeasures) prescribed for an information system to protect the confidentiality, integrity, and availability of the system and its information?**

    a. Security controls

    b. Configuration controls

    c. Hybrid controls

    d. System-specific control

29. **What is the first system development lifecycle phase which maps to the Risk Management Framework steps (categorization)?**

    a. Initiation

    b. Categorization

    c. Implementation

    d. Disposition

30. **This process is used to assess whether the security controls in the information system remain effective over time, considering the inevitable changes in both the system itself and the environment in which it operates between authorization decisions. Which of the following supports?**

    a. Continuous monitoring

    b. Configuration management

    c. Vulnerability assessment

    d. Certification and accreditation

31. **How frequently must key authorization package documents be updated to achieve near-real-time risk management?**

    a. Every three years

    b. Quarterly

    c. Annually

    d. On an ongoing basis

32. **Which Risk Management Framework role can be appointed at the discretion of the approving/authorization authority?**

    a. Disaster recovery

    b. System development lifecycle

    c. Risk Management Framework

    d. Plans of actions and milestones

33. **The documentation of a predetermined set of instructions or procedures that describe how business processes will be restored after a significant disruption has occurred?**

    a. Business recovery/disruption plan

    b. Common Vulnerability and Exposures

    c.   Business impact analysis

    d.   Business continuity plan

34. **When should the information system owner document the information system and authorization boundary description in the security plan?**

    a.   After security controls are implemented.

    b.   While assembling the authorization package.

    c.   After security categorization.

    d.   When reviewing the security control assessment plan.

35. **Which of the following best defines the purpose of security assessment?**

    a.   To determine if the remaining known vulnerability poses an acceptable level of risk.

    b.   To determine the extent to which the security controls are implemented correctly and operating as intended.

    c.   To perform oversight and monitor the security controls in the information system.

    d.   To perform initial risk, estimate and security categorization of the information system.

36. **Which of the following is not an authorization decision identified in the Risk Management Framework ?**

    a.   Authorization to operate

    b.   Denial of authorization to operate

    c.   Common control authorization

    d.   All of the above

37. **What type of testing involves evaluating through operation, movement, or adjustment under specific conditions to assess the success of a control?**

    a.   Demonstration

    b.   Inspection

    c.   Examination

    d.   Organization

38. **Which of the following is primarily used to confirm that information system is achieving their defined security goals and objectives?**

    a.   System plan

    b.   Requirements traceability matrix

c. Risk assessment

d. Security control assessor

39. **The authorization boundary of a system undergoing assessment comprises of?**

    a. The information system elements to be authorized for operation.

    b. Any elements or systems specified by the Chief Information Owner.

    c. Any components found within the given Internet Protocol range.

    d. The information system elements to be authorized for operation, as well as interconnected systems.

40. **Who is primarily responsible for the withdrawal and decommissioning of an information system?**

    a. Security architect

    b. Senior information system security officer

    c. Information system security engineer

    d. Information system owner

41. **What is the name of the formal document that provides an overview of security requirements for the information system and describes the security controls in place or planned for meeting those requirements?**

    a. Security authorization package

    b. Plan of action and milestone System

    c. Security and privacy plan

    d. Security assessment report

42. **What are the security controls (i.e., safeguards or countermeasures) for an information system that primarily are implemented and executed by people (as opposed to systems)?**

    a. Operational controls

    b. Common control

    c. Visual controls

    d. Embedded controls

43. Your company is expanding internationally, and one of its key overseas business partners requires the adoption of international security standards. After reviewing various standards, you find that your internally developed controls may be mapped to a new standard. Which of the following control standards would be most suitable for collaborating with international partners?

    a.　NIST SP 800-53

    b.　CIS Controls

    c.　ISO/IEC 27001/27002

    d.　HIPAA controls

44. Tailoring refers to the process by which a security control baseline is modified based on all but one of the following?

    a.　The security categorization of the information system.

    b.　The application of scoping guidance.

    c.　The specification of compensating controls.

    d.　The specification of organization-defined parameters in controls via explicit assignment and selection statements.

45. A group of any records under the control of any agency from which information is retrieved by the name of the individual or by some identifying number, symbol, or other identifying particular assigned to the individual defines which of the following?

    a.　System of record

    b.　System interconnection

    c.　System of records notice

    d.　System inventory process

46. Which of the following is a security policy implemented by an organization due to compliance, regulation, or other legal requirements?

    a.　Advisory policy

    b.　Informative policy

    c.　System Security policy

    d.　Regulatory policy

47. According to NIST SP 800-53A, the extent to which controls are implemented correctly, operating as intended, and producing the desired outcome with respect to meeting the security requirements of the system defines which of the following terms?

   a. Control effectiveness

   b. Adequate security

   c. Assurance

   d. Information security

48. **What is the first task in security controls assessment; where the assessment plan is developed, reviewed, and approved to assess the controls?**

   a. Assessment preparation

   b. Assessment plan

   c. Assessment security

   d. Assessment controls

49. **Which plan documents objectives for the security control assessment and details how to conduct such an assessment and records assessment procedures (security plan, assessment plan, plan of action and milestone)?**

   a. Assessment plan

   b. Security plan

   c. Plan of action and milestone

   d. Contingency plan

50. **The overall length of time an information system's components can be in the recovery phase before negatively impacting the organization's mission or mission/business functions?**

   a. Recovery time objective

   b. System of records notice

   c. Maximum tolerable downtime

   d. Disaster recovery plan

Practice test 2 answers

1. b
2. a
3. b
4. a
5. a
6. c
7. a

8. a

9. a

10. c

11. b

12. a

13. c

14. c

15. d

16. a

17. d

18. b

19. a

20. c

21. a

22. c

23. a

24. a

25. c

26. a

27. b

28. a

29. a

30. a

31. d

32. a

33. d

34. c

35. b

36. d

37. a

38. a

39. a

40. d

41. c

42. a

43. c

44. a

45. a

46. d

47. a

48. a

49. a

50. a

Join our book's Discord space

Join the book's Discord Workspace for Latest updates, Offers, Tech happenings around the world, New Release and Sessions with the Authors:

https://discord.bpbonline.com

Index

www.ingramcontent.com/pod-product-compliance
Lightning Source LLC
Chambersburg PA
CBHW061738210326
41599CB00034B/6716